For Mary —
Who is very:

YOUNG AT HEART!

AGING GRACEFULLY WITH ATTITUDE

ANNE SNOWDEN CROSMAN

Anne Snowden Crosman
July 2004

Hara Publishing Group, Inc.
P.O. Box 41
514 N. Sterling Ave.
Veedersburg, IN 47987
1-866-828-8935

10 9 8 7 6 5 4 3

Printed in the United States of America

LCCN 2003105947
ISBN 1-887542-02-7

Cover Design: Laura Zugzda
Proofreader: Vicki McCown
Interior Layout: Stephanie Martindale

"Young at Heart"

Fairy tales can come true,
It can happen to you,
If you're young at heart.
For it's hard, you will find
To be narrow of mind,
If you're young at heart.

You can go to extremes
With impossible schemes
You can laugh when your dreams
Fall apart at the seams

And life gets more exciting with each passing day
And love is either in your heart or on the way.

Don't you know that it's worth
Every treasure on earth
To be young at heart?
For as rich as you are,
It's much better by far
To be young at heart.

And if you should survive to 105,
Look at all you'll derive out of being alive.
And here is the best part
You have a head start
If you are among the very young at heart.

Words by Carolyn Leigh
Music by Johnny Richards

DEDICATION

To my parents,
Ruth Aileen Burkholder and Irwin Barker Crosman,
and to their ancestors.

CONTENTS

ACKNOWLEDGMENTS

I thank everyone who encouraged and helped me with this book. Most especially, I thank my old people, who gave so generously of their time and wisdom.

INTRODUCTION

I got the idea from my parents.

They were getting old, aging gracefully.

What was their secret?

I remembered the song "Young At Heart," recorded by Frank Sinatra. It was about positive attitude and open-mindedness. Money wasn't important—only a state of mind.

Both my parents worked, took care of their health, contributed to their community, and loved heartily. Age didn't change their activities.

Their secret was not to dwell on aging.

They learned it from their parents. My grandparents worked hard under terrible conditions, survived and succeeded through sheer will. They just kept going, always with grace.

I looked around me. Some of my friends were old. I asked them and they confirmed that age was just a number. Their stories of drive and persistence were inspiring, often fascinating. They were no-nonsense people, without an ounce of narcissism.

At the opposite end of the spectrum were my friends in their fifties. Hit by their first major illnesses, divorces, job firings, spiritual crises, and deaths of parents, they were starting to face their mortality.

They were frightened, worried, and did not have tools for successful aging.

I decided to write a book.

I had no lack of material. At the time, millions of Americans 65 years and older were living happy and productive lives. That number has grown every year. Medical science is helping old people live longer and stay healthier. We see it all around us. Sixty-five is no longer considered old.

I interviewed hundreds of old people, mostly in their seventies, eighties, and nineties.

All of them agree that three things keep them young: staying in shape with good diet and exercise, continuing to work professionally or voluntarily, and cultivating love and friendship.

I was impressed with how warmly they welcomed me and how openly they spoke. Linus Pauling, Nobel prize winner and Vitamin C advocate, says he started to wear his trademark beret because he was losing his hair and his head was cold. He cheerfully admits to wearing flannel nightcaps made by his wife.

Benjamin Spock, the baby doctor, says he dearly loves his wife, but detests the macrobiotic diet she forces him to follow. "I can't even have a glass of red wine," he wails. He acknowledges that he hasn't been sick since he started the diet.

Elisabeth Kübler-Ross, psychiatrist and author of *On Death and Dying*, admits to being starved for company. She entertains me and my photographer at her Virginia farm, feeds us lunch and dinner, gives us a tour of the property, and invites us to return in the spring when her new lambs are expected.

Ruth Stafford Peale, widow of the Reverend Norman Vincent Peale and a spiritual leader herself, patiently poses a second time for photos, after my first series does not turn out well. I know that she is tired and pressed for time, but she smiles and encourages me as I click away.

All the old people say it's hard work to stay on top of the aging process. Art Linkletter, television entertainer and seniors' advocate, puts it most succinctly: "You have to work harder to maintain the status quo." When Edmund Campbell, a well-known civil rights lawyer, jokingly threatens to list his illnesses, his wife Elizabeth, founder and vice president of WETA, a public broadcast station in Washington, D.C., sharply cuts him off, "I don't want to hear them!" They both laugh.

Many people I interview think little about aging and talk about it even less. They belong to a generation that was raised to work hard, minimize their problems, and smile, not complain.

Some say it's a mystery how they lasted so long. They're genuinely baffled. Often I'm the first person with whom they've discussed it.

A few make a career out of successful aging. Linkletter lectures and writes books on the subject.

My old people say they have to work diligently to keep their health, courage, dignity, optimism, creativity, determination, and agility of mind. Ethel Keohane, a master bridge player, says she allows herself to think only of what she CAN do, not what she can't. "I keep repeating, 'I can do this, I can do this,'" she says.

The old people emphasize the importance of discipline, tenacity, faith, and desire to accomplish. Some developed these qualities on their own. Others believe they inherited them from a family member. A handful has no idea where they came from. And a couple of people are impatient that I even asked.

Those who are fortunate enough to have happy families say they are their greatest joy. Steve Allen, pianist, entertainer, and author, says his most fun is getting down on the floor and playing with his grandchildren. Almost all the people believe in God and think that their faith helps them stay solid.

My old people are poetic. No matter how educated, each person speaks lyrically about growing old. Some are funnier than others. None is sad about the inevitability of dying. They have made peace with it and say that when the time comes, they want to go quickly.

Some worry that the younger generation of Americans is soft, spoiled, and unhappy. To them, they offer advice. They also speak to fellow elders who might be depressed.

I find the wisdom of old people easy to accept. They have credentials. They speak from the heart, often humorously. They are the parents or grandparents whom some of us never knew or did not appreciate until they were gone.

When they speak, you realize that old age is not to be feared, as long as you're armed with strength of body and mind, love of work, and kindness to others.

You see that aging is easier to accept if you don't waste time worrying and even laugh at the prospect.

And you understand that old age brings more joys than you ever imagined. The art of loving grows deeper, the act of learning becomes more precious, and the rewards of work multiply. Appreciation and gratitude for the blessings of life flow more easily.

In each chapter, I have backgrounded one person or couple enough to make his philosophy understandable. I have not written biographies. *Young at Heart* is a book about spirit and belief. Its theme is brightness and hope. It contains the best of our elders' wisdom.

It also contains their energy.

A while ago Ethel Keohane called me. "When's your book going to be published?" she barked. "I want to buy a copy." I told her that my mother had just died and I was still numb.

"But you must finish the book," she insisted. "Your mother would've wanted it."

And so she would have. It's done!

"Get interested in something other than yourself. Tutor
children in a poor neighborhood, cook something
for the woman downstairs, go to school, learn something:
Polish history, anything!"

STEVE ALLEN

> Born: December 26, 1921,
>   New York, NY
> Profession: Pianist, composer,
>   author, comedian
> Home: Los Angeles, CA

Steve Allen stays young by playing. Playing music, playing around, and playing with his grandchildren.

"Such laughs! Such love! Such fun! Such delight," he exclaims, grinning. "My favorite role is grandpa, my FAVORITE thing of all the things I've ever done in life."

He has 14 grandchildren, scattered across the country, and he savors every moment with them. "I wish we all lived in one big cave with bear rugs on the floor! Only two of my grandchildren live nearby, just a few blocks from us. We play on the floor, do jokes, horse around at the piano. We dance. I become like them.

"I am so addicted to having time in their presence that if I go two or three days without it, I have to have a Bradley-Bobby fix," he says. "I HAVE to go over there and visit them. It just lifts me. I smile. I even smile thinking of them." Bradley, eight, and Bobby, six, are the sons of his youngest son Bill and wife Marie.

"I also try to mature them up a little bit, but not too fast," he adds quickly. "I work on their vocabularies. One of my greatest kicks is to teach Bradley or Bobby some very adult phrase and then whisper, 'Say that to your father.' Bradley will walk over to his father and say, 'Dad, I'm very impressed with your PROWESS.'" He chuckles. "And, of course, Bill laughs, because I did it to him when he was five years old."

Admittedly Steve is crazy about children. "I LOVE children. I cannot resist smiling at children in airports or doctors' offices. It's not that I've decided it's nicer to smile at children," he explains. "It's just the same kind of smile that advertisers count on when they put a darling baby or a puppy or a kitten into an ad for soap or toothbrushes. I smile my face off when I see any little child."

He sits at a huge oak desk, covered with neat piles of books and papers, in his suburban Los Angeles office. Standing 6 feet 3 inches and weighing 210 pounds, he looks fit and tanned. He is impeccably dressed in crisp shirt, blazer, and slacks. For our photo session, he wears facial and hand make-up. He offers orange juice to me and my assistant, takes a glass for himself, then sits quietly, attentive to each question.

Are you a child at heart? I ask.

"Oh, yes, I've always been aware of the child in me," he answers quickly, carefully articulating each word. "I think it has something to do with the poetry I create, with the music I create, and certainly with the humor I create. Because humor, especially the best of it, is very childish. It can be wise, philosophically valuable, or helpful to the world. But childishness is one of the marvelous things about humor.

"My oldest son Dr. Steve, who is a physician, lectures on stress and humor, and he makes that very point. He tries to get his group to relax, to open up, to bring out the silliness, the childishness that is in all of us."

Silliness is evident in Steve's work as creator and first host of television's *The Tonight Show*. His jokes, ad-libs, pranks, and skits established him as one of the great comedic talents of his day. The greeting "Hi Ho, Steverino!" became a household word. His cackle, a high-pitched laugh delivered when he utterly lost it, became a trademark.

"Some people become very serious, once they become the lieutenant governor or something," he says. "They deny the child in them. They shouldn't! First of all, it's there. And second, it's good to let it out. If you're making a presidential address, you don't want to stick your thumbs in your ears and waggle your tongue. There are times when things are appropriate and times when they're not. But that side of us should NEVER be denied or inhibited."

As a child growing up in Chicago, Steve felt younger than his contemporaries. "When I was about 15, my school chum Richard Kiley and I discussed it. I said to him, 'How old do you feel? I'm 15, but I don't feel it. I feel about 13.' He understood. 'I guess I do, too,' he said.

"When you're seven or eight," says Steve, "you begin to form an image about what it's like to be 15 or 20 or 96. When you're ten, a 15-year old seems very mature and even getting along in years. But when I got to be 15, I didn't feel like the way I thought it was, when I was ten."

"Dick and I run into each other every two or three years, usually by accident, and we continue to bring up this question. When we were both about 30, I reported that I felt about 25." He grins. "When we were both about 50, I reported that I felt 40. Now that I'm 70, I feel about—oh, 58, I guess." He smiles.

Do you think about aging? I ask.

"The idea of being old just never occurs to me, any more than it would occur to me to become a Tibetan monk," he answers. "There are literally unlimited or infinite possibilities for any one of us, since we cannot predict the future."

He recalls writing an article for *Cue* magazine about Marilyn Monroe turning 30. "At the time, it seemed she was really getting up there in age." He wags his head in disbelief. "We see things from our own perspective, of course. In the article, I made the point that, all things being equal, she would actually be more attractive at 30 than at 20 or 25, because she would be wiser, she would be more experienced, she would know more, and therefore would be generally improved."

He's certain that he's improved with age. "My own experience shows that I am better now, at age 70, than I was at 40, 50 or 60," he says, without hesitation. "That is absolutely clear as regards playing jazz piano. My technical facility is much superior presently and seems to be improving all the time."

Steve has written more than 6,000 songs. The *Guinness Book of Records* lists him as the most prolific composer in history. His songs include "This Could Be the Start of Something Big," "South Street Rampart Parade," and "Pretend You Don't See Her." He performs them at numerous club gigs, college concerts, and charity events, and enjoys playing them on the piano at home.

With age, his wit has also grown sharper. "I've always done a lot of ad-libbing in my nightclub and concert work," he explains. "Generally I just answer questions that the audience submits to me backstage, just before I go on. I'm much quicker-minded in that way now than I was in years past.

"As regards my writing ability, writing poems, short stories, novels, things of that sort, there, too, has been improvement. Not as sharp as the jazz piano work, but demonstrable and recognizable. I write a great deal faster than I used to."

He carries a tape recorder and dictates ideas, poems, songs, book chapters, and anything else that comes to mind. Later his secretary transcribes it. He's written 40 books on subjects ranging from comedy and mystery to the Bible and American education.

"My book *Dumbth* deals with the sad fact that we have the dumbest American young people we've ever had." He frowns. "I'm ENERGIZED by an anger, so I wrote this book. Our young people are ignorant about things that were a matter of common knowledge 30 and 40 years ago, even among the generally poorly-informed. Much of the book material is anecdotal, based on my own experience. It's depressing. I don't see any immediate likelihood that it will change." His voice is somber.

Television is another target of his anger. "TV has almost totally failed to live up to its responsibilities," he says fiercely. "I don't see the slightest prospect that it ever can, short of an actual revolution and dictatorial control, which none of us wants. If you had that, you could turn the American education system around and create a much better-informed race of people in ten years."

Steve succeeded in raising the level of television with *Meeting of Minds*, an award-winning series on the Public Broadcasting Service. He wrote and hosted the shows, which are conversations of historical characters played by actors dressed in period costumes. One program brought together Theodore Roosevelt, Thomas Aquinas, Thomas Paine, and Cleopatra, played by Steve's wife, actress Jayne Meadows.

"That was wonderfully educational," he recalls. "It still has its ripples. It's been published as a four-volume set of books and there's an audio version of all 24 shows.

"The main problem with TV today is human nature," he continues. "It's susceptible to distraction, to temptation, to degradation. Everyone knows that if you had only two TV channels, one with the best presentation of *Hamlet* with the world's

greatest actors, and the other with pretty women engaged in mud
wrestling and a talk show on which most of the casual banter is
filthy, vulgar, and in the poorest possible taste—everyone knows
which channel the American people would watch. Maybe 3 percent would watch Shakespeare, and 97 percent would be
destroying themselves.

"I call it junk food for the mind," he growls.

"People, even those in the TV industry, don't perceive the
harmful effects of TV on us for 30, 40, 50 years of exposure to
the most mindless or even actively destructive material. There
are two kinds of bad news. One is the stuff that is morally or
ethically neutral. The other is the messages that are actively
negative, where virtue is a subject for jokes and evil makes you
the star of the movie. I don't think many people who are introduced to that sort of film at age 47 would be much harmed by it.
But when people are introduced to it at the age of five and get a
lot of it over the next 20 years, they are terribly harmed by it."

Steve's range of interests unfolds during the interview.
When asked his profession, he refers to an alphabetical list
included in his thick press package. It starts with A. A is for
author and actor. He starred and played clarinet in the movie
The Benny Goodman Story. B is for book reviewer and biogra-
pher, C for comedian, composer, clarinetist, and columnist.

For each letter, he lists a job he loves and does well. P is for
pianist, playwright, poet, and philosopher. S is for scholar,
songwriter and singer. He recently played the lead in *The Mikado*
on Broadway. T is for teacher, trumpet player, and television pro-
ducer. X is for xylophonist, Y for youth leader, and Z for zany.

"Yes, I have a great zest for life," he admits, grinning. "Yet,
I take no credit for it. I don't even know if it would make any
sense to advise others to have a similar zest. It might be like
advising them to be taller or have brown eyes or blonde hair or
another nice thing. I'm not sure how much we can change ourselves by our acts of will. I believe we can—I'm not a deter-
minist—but I'm very unsure as regards the extent to which we
can. Our fates are much more limited. Not many people want
to hear that," he observes.

"For some people, life can be very limited and dull. But I
think the universe is DAZZLING." Gesticulating, he straightens

in his chair. "The universe cannot be boring. My God, we don't even know about it yet! I can get excited just thinking about what the word 'light year' means. I really can get quite animated contemplating the wonders of the spatial universe. We live in the most incredible universe and on the most bizarre planet." His eyes shine behind dark-rimmed spectacles.

Enthusiasm is normal for Steve. "I was always an 'Isn't-the-grass-pretty?' type of person," he says. "I've spent my whole life smelling the roses. I've always loved nature and flowers. In fact, I sometimes don't understand. I'll be with someone else and say something very simple like, 'My God, look at that ocean!' Or 'Isn't that an incredible rainbow?' In many cases, they don't seem to be interested. I'm not putting them down," he says quickly. "They can't decide to be interested in something if they're not interested in it. But I've always been interested in flowers and breezes and trees and water.

"I've liked everybody. I'm a people-liker. I LOVE people." His mother, a comedian, may have had something to do with that. "She was a very funny comedian," he recalls affectionately. "Milton Berle was kind enough to refer to her as the funniest woman in Vaudeville, and I believe she was. She was very witty and truly funny." His father died before Steve was two years old.

A bout with colon cancer when he was in his early sixties made life more precious to him. "I'd already suspected I had cancer, because of some symptoms," he explains. "At the moment it seemed very important. I didn't simply dismiss it and go have lunch or go to a ball game. But I don't remember being bowled over by the possibility. Finally, my hypothesis was confirmed. That moment was a little shaky, not as dramatic as one might expect, but depressing, annoying, and inconvenient. Nevertheless, I survived the moment." He takes a sip of orange juice and leans back in his chair.

"It was after the surgery that, thank goodness, was successful," he goes on quietly. "I thought that was the end of it. The next day I got a call from the doctor. 'Now we'll start the radiation therapy,' he said. For some reason or other, I felt as if the rug had been pulled out from under me. I thought, 'Oh, I thought I was okay now!' That shook me. I remember feeling that emotion for about 43 seconds. Then I went on about my business." Today he is cancer-free.

Steve has recorded public service announcements about colon cancer. It doesn't stop there. "There well may not be a single charitable activity in the country on whose behalf I have not done a film, television tape, or audio recording," he says. "I don't think I deserve any special credit for that. I think any-body who is requested ought to do that."

He carefully watches his health, getting regular medical checkups, taking asthma medicine, and eating fruits and veg-etables, which he naturally likes. "From time to time, Jayne and I get religion, so to speak," he chuckles, "and do the full Pritikin diet. We both exercise. A little exercise every day is absolutely necessary to keep you from falling apart altogether."

He began to exercise when he was 40, and still does what he calls standard exercises—running in place, running up and down stairs, and doing knee bends, both in and out of a swimming pool. "The thing is to do them almost every day, or ideally a little bit every day. I've even written a book, which I have not yet arranged to have published, called *The Lazy Man's Exercise Book*."

Do you believe in plastic surgery to look younger? I ask.

"It's the smartest thing in the world for those who present themselves physically," he replies promptly. "That's basically what an actor does for a living. If you can get another 12 years in the movies by simply having your jowls tightened or your eyelids tidied up a little bit, do it! I had some fat removed under my chin, surgically removed, probably 15 years ago. Many more men in the theatrical professions have had such treatment than the public knows."

He doesn't smoke, says he detests the smell. "I think ciga-rette smoke stinks like other people think garbage stinks," he says, wrinkling his nose and grimacing. Steve was an early activist for smoke-free airplanes and airports, and co-wrote *The Passionate Nonsmoker's Bill of Rights* with Bill Adler, Jr.

Occasionally he has a glass of wine or beer. "If someone forces champagne on me at a wedding, I'll sip it," he says. "But liquor means nothing to me. I hate the taste of almost all of it. Orange and pineapple juice I love."

For a long time, he's taken a daily dose of one aspirin and 500 milligrams of vitamin C. He sleeps ten or eleven hours a night, a necessity that he thoroughly resents. "I wish I could get by on four or five hours a night," he laments. "Boy! I could have written 70 books instead of 40! Because I've got a lot more ideas than I'll live long enough to bring into reality.

"I ENJOY my sleep," he goes on. "It's not that I feel bad in bed. I zonk out right away. If somebody rubs my neck or gives me a beer, I'm asleep."

The reality of death does not frighten him, only the possibility of pain. "The idea that I will someday not exist, doesn't mean a damn to me," he says strongly. "We're all going to do that same strange thing. Jayne and I have discussed it and she knows I do not want to be kept on life support if I'm in serious physical trouble.

"Let me go!" he exhorts, leaning forward. "What's the point of staying alive another eleven days, if you're suffering or not even conscious? It's good to have documents drawn up, so there won't be any nonsense about saying, 'That man must stay alive because God says so.' God never said so." He looks annoyed.

Steve intends to keep working, which he usually does seven days a week and far more than eight hours a day. "I don't know if creative people ever retire, or if they do, it's not come to my attention," he says. "You have to retire from certain trades or professions, if they make intense physical demands, like prize fighting or football. But in the creative arts, it doesn't matter how old you are. That's encouraging." He smiles broadly.

Is sex alive after 70? I ask.

"Yeah, and sometimes I wish it were not." He laughs softly. "I thought that by the time one was 70, sex, on your list of interests, would be at the bottom. But the interest is still there, whether it's a plus or a minus factor.

"Yes, I'm a romantic. Love and the expression of it come easily to me," he says. "Love has always been important to me. If hired as an attorney, I could build a case that it's been TOO important to me. I can remember feeling that I was in love for the first time when I was about eight. I can still remember her name: Betty Lou Billton."

Steve has written many love songs, and I ask if he'd sing one of his favorites. He thinks for a moment.

"I recently wrote a song that argues for a return to gentleness and romanticism," he says. He begins to recite gently:

> Kiss me with a smile,
> Kiss me from a distance.
> Take a little while
> To wear down my resistance.
> Kiss me with your eyes,
> Time enough to touch.
> And my heart can already
> Feel so much.

He speaks with a rich rhythm, a touch of yearning.

> Promise me the moon,
> Time enough to reach it.
> We've so much to learn
> And the stars can teach it.
> Love will bring its passion
> In a little while.

He pauses.

> So for now, my darling,
> Kiss me with a smile.

Yes, he's old-fashioned, he admits. "Love is about subtleties, nuances, romanticism. It can be very simple things. You don't have to write poems or bring flowers. It's a matter of relationships. I still have that in my life, certainly as an ideal. And occasionally," he says quietly, "it is achieved."

He sits back, relaxed, smiling dreamily.

RAY GEIGER

Born: September 10, 1910,
Irvington, NJ
Profession: Editor, *Farmers'
Almanac*, businessman, social
activist
Home: Lewiston, ME

When you reach 80, you become a philosopher. I bought a $4500 tombstone in a cemetery just around the corner. The epitaph reads, "Each year is a bonus year after 80." Fifty or 60 people gathered for the unveiling. Two people gave eulogies, and then we had a big party. I gave a tombstone dissertation:

> Friends, I am delighted and really quite excited
> That you came to this unusual grave event,
> For I'd rather have you gather as I write it
> Than to have you come to see me when I'm dead.
>
> 'Twas 46 years ago to this moment
> That I was wounded on the isle of Leyte,
> And I thought my hour had come all too soon
> As I headed toward St. Pete's pearly gate.
>
> But the good Lord must have had some things for me to do
> To meet and marry Ann, have a daughter and four sons too,
> Then to bring Geiger Brothers from New Jersey up to Maine
> Where we got to know and love each one of you.
>
> Now at 80 I have reached the plateau of my life
> And each year as it comes and passes is a bonus year,
> For me to pay more attention to my sainted wife
> And still continue with my editing career.

How many extra years will the good Lord give me?
There's really no way I can tell.
But I will promise, and if I fail, forgive me,
To use each one as best I can and try to use them well.

As a Boy Scout I was told to be prepared,
And I have gone as far as I can go.
I want to enjoy the beauty of this tombstone while I'm living
For there's no enjoyment in a tombstone when you're dead.
Yes, you can't enjoy your tombstone when you're dead.

Enjoy everything, enjoy reading. Don't worry. Worry never will get you anywhere.

I just keep going. I fall quite a bit because I have Parkinson's Disease and that limits the ability to control the muscles. I put on bandages and away I go!

"I never think about whether I'm happy.   It doesn't really matter.
It's whether I'm interested.   And I'm very interested
in many things."

Lina Berle

Born: September 1, 1893,
  Brighton, MA
Profession: Lecturer, retired
  legal assistant, teacher
Home: Washington, DC

Staying young means not wasting a moment.

Every morning Lina Berle, 97, wakes up between 4 and 6 o'clock, brews two cups of extra-strong coffee, and reads *The Washington Post*. "I go through the newspaper very carefully indeed," she says in a high, intense voice, looking at me closely through big-rimmed glasses. "I don't watch television. The newspaper is quite enough."

After breakfast and washing-up, she tackles a book she's reviewing, *The Search for Modern China*, by Jonathan Spence. Lina gives regular book-review lectures at Thomas House, a seniors' apartment home in which she lives. "My real career began here, quite surprisingly, at age 90." She speaks quickly, stroking her hands. A tiny woman with blue eyes and a pouf of fluffy, white hair, she sits alertly in a rose-colored armchair that matches her home-made velvet dress with white lace collar. Scattered about her living room are stacks of papers, a magnifying glass, sewing basket, and bits of fabric.

"I was looking around at the possibility of volunteer service and not seeing anything that looked like me," she says, enunciating each word carefully. A *cum laude* graduate of Radcliffe College in 1913, with an M.A. two years later, Lina received a classic, humanist education. Today she is what some people might call an intellectual.

"I remembered one of the pilots who had been in prison in solitary confinement by the Japanese in World War II," she continues. "When he got out, he said the only thing that kept him sane was remembering all the poetry he'd ever learned in school. I thought to myself, 'I can do a talk on poetry as a survival tool.' So accordingly I did, and a lot of people came to see the talk and liked it." She smiles contentedly and adjusts her glasses.

My photographer Ann Parks Hawthorne and I are visiting Lina in her cozy, one-bedroom apartment. It's crowded with bookcases, chairs, tables, and footstools, all filled with books and magazines. She makes no apologies for the clutter. "Oh, I'm in the middle of reading all of them," she motions breezily toward one particularly large pile.

Writing book reviews takes a good deal of research, but that comes easily and joyfully to Lina. She was schooled in Greek, Latin, French, and German, and received her college degrees in English. She wrote some fiction, taught high school English, then went to work as office manager in her brothers' law firm in New York City. She also did legal research. Today she remains a voracious reader and debater of ideas.

Do you consider yourself young at heart? I ask.

She is hard-of-hearing and asks me to repeat the question. Then she straightens in her chair and looks puzzled.

"I never think one way or the other about it," she answers. "When I was growing up, the word for me was never 'young.' The word was 'mature.' Adult and mature. As I remember, it was the same way we always wanted to put up our hair." Her eyes twinkle.

I rephrase the question. I mean young at heart in that you have a passion for knowledge, a childlike wonder at things around you.

"Yes, that is perfectly true," she says immediately. "The people whom I appeal to and appeal to me are deeply alive, and alive in all kinds of ways. Most of them are connected with literature, journalism, or social work. With some, it's a sexual accommodation. In other words, you wake up something in them that they have waked up in you. Somehow or other in the vibrations, you hit the same key and go on to understanding."

She smiles and thinks for a moment. "When you ask if I'm young at heart, I'd say I'm RECEPTIVE. You should always be receptive."

Lina's articulation and candor are qualities that were carefully nurtured by her parents. Her father was a Boston Congregational clergyman whose book *The School in the Home* (1912) advised parents how to train children to love learning. Her Ohio mother spent a year working as an assistant to a medical missionary on an Indian reservation in South Dakota, before she raised her family.

"My mother took us on walks and taught me to recognize flowers," recalls Lina. "She and my father guided us, and we picked out books at the local library. There were four of us brothers and sisters, and we always read everything we could get hold of. We began early."

Her intellectual interests have grown recently to include Oriental and American Indian culture. She gestures to nearby books: *The Search for Modern China, The People Named the Chippewa*, and *Fox at the Wood's Edge*, stacked on a chair. Oriental prints hang next to Southwestern landscapes on the walls, and a small jade statue sits on a table. "If I could travel, which, of course, I can't do now, I'd like very much to visit China and the Southwest. Albuquerque, New Mexico!" Her eyes light up.

"With the American Indians, I got hold of the edges of a big subject that I'd like to learn more about," she goes on enthusiastically. "Many of the western colleges have Indian Affairs departments and there's quite a literature written by Indian students. I ought to go into all of that, be able to find out what's important.

"I want to go BEYOND. I've used up everything that was on the surface of my mind, and now I want to know a little bit more about life."

She pounces on the newspaper each morning. "I clip a lot of things that I send to my younger sister Miriam and I always read the financial stories by John Berry. He's the husband of Mary, one of my nieces. I call that my 'Economics Lesson Number One,' because I'm studying a good deal of economics that I don't have much background in. I'm bound to confess, mathematics was not my strong suit." She looks slightly pained.

"I have never read magazines very much, except *The New York Times Book Review* and *Audubon*, partly because my nephew Peter is president. I also like *Smithsonian*."

Lina has always pursued knowledge. "Reading the papers is what you DO," she exclaims. "It's keeping abreast of the world you live in. Here at Thomas House, a lot of people who could do that have very definitely and very unhappily put everything they knew in mothballs and have forgotten about it." She speaks benignly, without a trace of criticism.

"My oral book reports seem to strike a chord with some of the residents," she says. "I reviewed *The Call* by John Hersey, and there were lots of people there. Somebody yelled, 'Do it again!'" She allows herself a luxuriant laugh of pleasure. "It's the same kind of thing I'd have done if I'd been teaching school.

"You see," she continues, "I choose different writers, people I don't think my audience knows very much about. I also make a very careful point of always finishing on an upbeat level, which makes people feel comfortable about themselves or what they've heard. I want to give them something to think about and talk about. Over the years I've done about 15 book reviews.

"Periodically, somebody will say, 'When are you going to do another talk?' Not very long ago, I met somebody downstairs and I said, 'I don't know your name, I'm so-and-so.' And she said, 'Oh, you're famous! I know you.' And there you are." She folds her hands in her lap, looks satisfied, and relaxes in her chair.

When I turn to her personal life, she becomes fidgety and impatient.

Are you lonely, now that many of your contemporaries are gone? I ask.

"I can get lonely," she replies slowly. "But I don't let myself. It passes. I believe you spend the early part of life making connections and friendships, and the latter part you spend learning how to be alone." Her two nieces visit every week. Mary comes on Sunday and Beatrice on Tuesday.

Do you regret not marrying? I ask.

She doesn't flinch. "No, I found out very quickly, in college, that I wasn't likely to marry," she says easily. "There were lots of Asiatic and Middle Eastern immigrants who weren't considered suitable at the time. The only man of my own generation whom I ever met was an American-born Chinese student at Harvard.

"As I look back now, based on what I know of Chinese history and literature, I'm inclined to think that if he had been Caucasian, it would have been a very good marriage. But, of course, as far as my family was concerned, a mixed marriage was hopeless." She raises her eyebrows and purses her lips. "It would have been equally hopeless from his family's point of view. We were extremely good friends and I learned in that experience just what the relation of human beings was.

"I remember a comment of my mother: 'You seem to be a useful woman.' In her thinking, a useful woman was a thing I never had a chance to do, that is, marry and bring up children. That didn't happen to me. I know now that I was very different from my sister. She always wanted children. I knew perfectly well that I wouldn't know if I wanted children until I lived with their father for six months or more and knew what he was likely to be. That was going to be a piece of it.

"I've had close friends," she continues. "But they were always 15 to 20 years older than I. Somebody once asked my father, 'When are you going to marry your daughters?' He said airily, 'They're going to be married to the men for whom they are TRAINED.' Well, those were men of his generation, but not of mine. And I was not impressed." She speaks with resolution and a tinge of triumph.

"I'm not a virgin," she volunteers. "There have been many men in my life. With two of them, I went with them all the way, to the end of their lives. I don't think you should marry anyone without having sexual experience. That's built into me."

Are you open to new experiences? I ask.

"Yes, the experiences come, you don't look for them. You should be receptive always," she says. "I think that in living with people, your job is not to shut yourself off to them."

Lina seems to be a serious person. What makes you laugh? I ask.

"Ha!" she cries. "Very little. I don't laugh a lot, but I appreciate irony. I do have a sense of humor, but not the ordinary one." Restless, she shifts in her chair. I sense that she'd rather be discussing ideas.

What is your health regime? I ask.

"I don't have one, and I've always hated sports," she states briskly. "But as a girl, I did enjoy riding the neighbor's horse. We understood each other. I don't do any exercise now, except for some stretching in the morning. I broke my hip recently, so I use a walker. That takes a lot more time to do things. Oh, my eyes and hands get tired, especially later in the day, and my knees get stiff. But nothing more." She waves a hand absently.

"I eat less as I get older. But I eat what I like: cake, wine, meat, everything." She stops abruptly. "Would you like a piece of cake? I baked a pineapple upside-down cake. And some wine?" She looks at us anxiously.

Yes, thank you, we reply. She gets up, refusing offers to help, takes the cake out of the refrigerator, and cuts three huge pieces. She places each one on a china plate, along with a sterling silver fork. From a heavy, cut-glass decanter, she pours sweet white wine.

We carry our food and drinks back to the living room and resettle in the overstuffed chairs. She watches us closely and clearly enjoys our pleasure and requests for seconds.

"When I came to Thomas House," she goes on, "I asked the doctor about alcohol. He said the latest study showed that, in proper moderation, alcohol was a good thing for people as they grew older. So I took that to heart and usually have a glass of wine at lunch, then another drink, usually a highball with bourbon, at dinner. Once in a while, I have another one later on. And it makes a difference!" She smiles brightly.

To what do you owe your longevity? I ask.

"It's all heredity, just the family stock," she says simply. "A lot of things were done right by my parents, both of whom were extremely healthy. We were an exceptionally healthy family."

She has never smoked.

Are you flexible? I ask.

She pauses. "Our KNOWLEDGE is flexible," she replies. "It changes as our knowledge grows wider. So some of us are really flexible and others can't live, excepting in a highly structured performance. I don't know what you do with them, because the world isn't structured." She gives a short, dry laugh.

"In reading *The Search for Modern China*, I was noticing the Confucian doctrine. They don't believe in progress as a strict line, the way we do. We think we begin here and go on up there. The Confucians say there was originally some kind of a chaos, then a slow motion out of that, a cycle. And finally you get to a circle of everlasting peace. Ultimately, I suppose, it begins all over again.

"I'm perfectly convinced that today we're living in what would be called one of those cycles of utter confusion. We have all sorts of people trying all kinds of things, and not really knowing what they are doing, like the Chinese in Tiananmen Square.

A lot of them thought they believed in democracy, but they hadn't the faintest idea of what democracy was." She sounds impatient.

"The last time we went through a similar thing was the fall of the Roman Empire. The fall of the Ming Empire was such a period. The Manchu Invasion.

"As I look at modern literature, I realize we are again at the bottom of a cycle, in a definitely decadent mood. I think that everything that glorifies eccentricity or quirkiness or feistiness or gutsiness indicates something that is out of the mainstream and not getting anywhere. It's really a form of decadence. I could do with a little more of the standard Puritan virtues." She looks serious.

"I don't know any young people personally, except my two nieces," she continues. "But from my knowledge of current events, I think that young people are untrained. Most of them had a very sketchy education. If I had a chance, I'd tell them to try to get a broad, humanist, classic education. It provides you with an opportunity to figure out what life is all about.

"And READ. If you grow up in a reading household, as I did, college education doesn't add anything. Also, don't hurry things, because you probably haven't enough experience. In other words, you haven't seen enough different kinds of people. So take the time to look around you."

Do you believe in God? I ask.

"I'm a pagan all the way through," she responds heartily. "I'm also not in any sense an atheist. The thing that impresses me is that there is a set of powers OUTSIDE OURSELVES and very largely outside of our control and understanding, which deal with the problems of the world. The problems are too big for human ingenuity to solve. The problem of overpopulation, for example." She takes a quick breath, then plunges on.

"It will take a famine or flood or earthquake or explosion or eruption to take care of the world's surplus people. Do you remember Loren Eiseley's poem *Wounded Knee*? I've thought of that over and over again. He said that extinction is an art too great for man. He bungles it. It should be left to the earthquakes, to the great natural forces, because they do it without malice." She smiles calmly.

Lina lives in her world of books, ideas, and friends. There is a peace about her. She seems secure in her accomplishments, undeterred by old age. "I could go out tomorrow and not miss a thing," she says blandly.

"I know I've had practically everything that I had any business to have. In a place like this apartment, where a lot of people have really serious things the matter with them, which I haven't, to see somebody who is healthy is very much to the point. Insofar as I have any usefulness, I can give people something to think about with my talks on books."

Usefulness. That may be a key to her longevity. She closes her eyes for a moment. "I remember a story in *The Anglo-Saxon Chronicle*. It was about 800 A.D. near York, England, and the king, I think it was Edgar, was sitting with his counselors on a winter day. Some monks came to his castle and wanted permission to come in and preach.

"One counselor looked thoughtfully and said, 'Your Majesty, I've been noticing while you were sitting here at the table by a roaring fire with your friends and your food, that a sparrow flew in the window. It fluttered around and finally flew out again by the other window. From cold to cold. Man's life is a little bit like that. We know something about it while it's in the human body, but whence it came and whither it goes, we do not know. If these monks can tell us that, we ought to welcome them.'"

She sighs. "Now THAT's a man I'd dearly like to know.

"Death really doesn't bother me because I'm not afraid," she says. "I'm not anxious at all, which shows I've accepted the facts as they necessarily are."

She looks intently at me. "I know perfectly well that I've made all the contribution I can. This interview might be one of the things where I've made a contribution for you. Bless your hearts, I wish you luck. If I've got you thinking, then I've done something worthwhile."

She gets up to see us out, asking us to stay in touch, urging us to call anytime, and wanting to see a copy of my chapter on her.

I promise it all.

MALCOLM BOYD

> Born: June 18, 1923,
>   New York, NY
> Profession: Episcopal priest,
>   poet/writer-in-residence,
>   Cathedral Center of St. Paul,
>   Los Angeles, California,
>   social activist
> Home: Los Angeles, CA

I don't want to DO something. I want to BE something. And that something is myself. While I'm alive. Life is so precious and frankly, I adore it. I hope that when I die, it's at noon, so that I'm able to read the morning newspaper before. I always read the morning newspaper!

My passion is being alive. I was looking at the AIDS quilt in a huge auditorium and I saw one panel that said, "Being alive." Simply gorgeous. Life, this great gift of being alive. I know people who are wasting life. One analogy that I use is, when you let water pour into the kitchen sink, you're wasting it. The water is just pouring out. Some people let their lives do that. They just throw them away. Instead, their lives are to be treasured and healed.

Approaching 80, I find life more and more fulfilling, because perspective is possible. Patience is possible. Unconditional love is more possible. I don't run into the fray anymore. I'm able to stand back and take a look. A sense of humor is really the most valuable thing in the world. It helps us not to have to judge people so harshly. I don't look at things in blacks and whites anymore. Things are very much in the grays and earth tones.

"If I could have a wish, I'd like to wish for another 50 years.
I think that people in the next 50 years are going to
see things beyond, beyond belief."

SAMMY CAHN

Born: June 18, 1913,
  New York, NY
Profession: Songwriter,
  performer
Home: Beverly Hills, CA

He doesn't sit still. "I'm moving all the time," he says lightly, welcoming me to his home office in Beverly Hills. Dressed casually in a cotton shirt and light-blue slacks, he has a hearty handshake, a fringe of gray hair, and lively brown eyes. Every few minutes, he answers the phone, calls to his wife Tita, and searches for newspaper clippings to give me.

It's an hour and one half of noise and activity, in which he tells me his life story and wonders at the good luck and beauty of it all.

"May I sit down next to you?" he asks, alighting briefly on a green Ultrasuede couch. The room is carpeted in rich forest green, the walls covered with photos and awards. A Yamaha upright piano stands in one corner. Neatly arranged on a desk are piles of papers around an electric typewriter. It's here that Sammy writes his famous lyrics.

"I'm busier today then I've ever been in my life," he says sounding surprised. He has a pronounced New York accent and enunciates each word. "I'm 79 years old. My new vocation is composing and singing special lyrics for special occasions."

He walks over to his desk and picks up a schedule. "A week from today, I'll be in New York City on the aircraft carrier Intrepid. It's a museum now. I'll do 'The Fleet's In Medley' at the yearly ball. I'll tell the story of the evening with all my old song titles: 'Time After Time,' 'The Tender Trap,' 'High Hopes.' I'll sing 'Tonight Is the Loveliest Night of the Year.'" Sammy changes some of his original lyrics to mirror the event.

"Then I have a meeting about the Songwriters Hall of Fame Museum at 56th Street and 8th Avenue. This was Johnny Mercer's dream and I'm trying to bring it about. It's taken me 18 years to get it built. It's supposed to open at the end of this year.

"Then I'll appear at the Brooklyn Community College. They're doing a thing on Brooklyn. On June 3rd, the University of Massachusetts is giving me a Doctorate of Fine Arts in the Kennedy Library, which is very, very meaningful, because I never finished high school. For me to get a Doctorate of Fine Arts is kind of an accomplishment, especially in the Kennedy Library, because I wrote the campaign song for Jack Kennedy." He speaks quietly.

"On June 8th, I'm going to be honored by the Philadelphia Pops Orchestra. Then on June 10th, I fly to London to help them honor Sammy Davis." He puts down his schedule and returns to his seat.

"People say, 'Do you have a computer?' I say, 'I AM a computer!' They say, 'Do you know all your lyrics?' I say, 'I know all my lyrics and everyone else's lyrics and all the SPECIAL lyrics.' And if you ever watched me write a lyric at that typewriter there, it's a miracle!" His voice rises to a high note.

"I mean that in the most modest sense," he explains quickly. "I put a piece of paper in the typewriter, start at the top, left-hand corner, and—I've developed an audacity." He sits down at his typewriter and starts singing. "Call me irresponsible, call me unreliable, but I have to say loud and clear...." He tries a variety of new rhymes. "The words just come," he explains. "They're rhymed impeccably.

"People don't understand—the song's already written—I'm just taking advantage of it." He pauses. "God has radar on my typewriter." He draws out each word for dramatic effect. "He must be watching."

Sammy puts three exclamation points at the end of a song when he's finished writing it. "You know, I'm almost afraid to hit a third exclamation point," he jokes. "Because when I hit it, the phone rings!" He raises an index finger. "Someone needs a lyric. It's funny, it's absolutely funny.

"People say, 'Which comes first? The words or the music?' I say, 'The phone rings and tells me what to do.' The fax machine, another miracle, tells me what to do. I do what I'm asked to do. I let fate control me.

"My problem is, I don't turn down any requests. I do everything I'm asked to do. My wife tries to control a little of this activity." His voice grows warm. "'Why don't you say no?'

she asks." He looks at me closely. "This is where I'm a coward. I'm afraid if I say no, that'll be the end of what I'm about. So I don't say no. I DO."

Excusing himself, he jumps up and leaves the room, returning with something in his hand. "I'm going to give you a rare gift," he says. "This is a cassette tape of a one-man show that I did at the San Francisco Marines Memorial in 1991." He hands it to me and I thank him.

"I've been doing my one-man show for 19 years now. It started in 1972 at the 92nd Street Y in New York City. That audio cassette became a collector's item.

"In 1974, I did the show on Broadway to the most incredible reviews you ever read in your life. It's a two-hour show. I have a pianist and a little cast of young people who sing my songs. By the end, I'm singing and dancing like a lunatic, all over the theater.

"I've had all the ailments of my age. I'm a diabetic, I've had two major surgeries. I have a little heart condition and a little blood pressure condition, but that doesn't stop me from doing what I'm doing. My wife doesn't think I eat well, but I do what I do. I used to drink and I used to smoke, but I don't do either anymore. Now and again, I'll have a sip of light beer. Light beer on the rocks!" He smiles.

"An extraordinary thing happened to me," he goes on. "I flew to Chicago to do special lyrics for a man's birthday—that's another thing I do—I did Lee Iacocca's 65th birthday party, I did Ronald Reagan's 78th birthday. That was Saturday night.

"On Sunday night, I was in Skokie, Illinois, at the Skokie Center. I did my two-hour show with my young people. This is not ego. It's simply reporting. Every time I finish a show, they stand up and cheer. It's the only reason I do it, I must tell you." He pauses and grows serious. "But I KNOW they're going to stand up and cheer!

"On Monday, I flew to Palm Beach for a three-week run. The first night, I didn't feel good, but I just kept going. Same thing for those two weeks. My California doctor thought it was diabetic-related, so that's how he treated it.

"At the beginning of the third week, I told him, 'Look, whatever you think you're doing, it's not helping me. I only do this show for the pleasure it gives ME. The audience has pleasure along the way, but I'm having the most fun. Which the audience knows, too. But this isn't any fun for me anymore.'

"My doctor said, 'I want you in the hospital early in the morning.' So I went and stayed a week." Sammy looks resigned. "They found I had a heart problem. One of my heart valves was not working correctly. Some water was getting into my lungs. I take pills now.

"The point is, I had to cancel that last week, and I don't like that. That's not how I do business.

"I look stupid," he says, deadpan. "But I really am not. I do what I need to do and my wife's there all the time. I refuse to be old. A lot of people think I'm foolhardy. Let me give you a great line of Bob Hope. 'What'll I do if I retire?' he says. 'You'll go fishing.' He pauses. 'Fish don't APPLAUD,' says Hope. I know how he feels. I love my audience. I have an audience if I walk into an elevator. I'm a recognizable factor.

"I turned a corner one day in New York and almost knocked over this fellow. He looks at me and says, 'Oh, my God! Sammy Cahn.' He says, 'You could knock me down and step on me!' I embraced him and said, 'That's the nicest compliment I've ever been paid.' And my whole life is compliments." His tone is incredulous.

"I was in a very famous restaurant in New York and I walked by a table and a voice said, 'My hero!' I turned and it was Woody Allen. I said, 'Woody, I've earned ALL my privileges.' He said, 'Yes, you have.' I said, 'Except one. I've had all the honors that you can have except one.' He said, 'What's that?' I said, 'I want to be in a Woody Allen film.'

"He's thinking about it," laughs Sammy.

Again he excuses himself and I hear him talking with Tita. He returns and sits down next to me.

Are you flexible? I ask.

"I'm not flexible," he says quickly. "I'm FUN. I'm opinionated. I like my own way. I like to be in control. But I am FUN. Wherever I go, people smile. I don't smile, they smile!"

Does time seem to go faster as you get older?

"Oh, God! There's not enough time. I wish the days were longer. They're not long enough at all. Like today, I hope to finish the lyrics for the Intrepid show."

What age do you feel now? I ask.

"I know I'm going to be 80 years old, so I don't take the steps two and three at a time, although I'd like to. I go down the steps a little more gingerly than I used to. But that's not my fault. That's NATURE's fault. Mentally, I'm going up two and three steps at a time." He looks pleased.

Do people treat you differently now that you're older?

"Yes, I think they do," he replies. "People of grace and sensibility treat age with respect.

"I want to live to be 87 so I can celebrate 2000," he states firmly. "This past Wednesday night, at the Beverly Hills Hilton, I received the first ever Golden Word Award from ASCAP. That's the American Association of Composers, Authors, and Publishers. If you look up on the wall," he motions to one side, "you'll see I have four Oscars and an Emmy Award. But no award is quite as meaningful as the Golden Word.

"It was rather moving, because I really, really received a standing reception. It was just very emotional." His voice breaks and he clears his throat. "When I finally got them to quiet down, I said, 'Thank you. Thank you. This kind of a reception would test any man's ego. But I can handle it!'" He grins.

He shows me a note he received from Frank Sinatra, many of whose musical hits Sammy wrote. It reads, "Dear Sammy, I share your joy in being honored by ASCAP. Your unique talent has given me a glorious ride—I've been 'All the Way' and have 'High Hopes' that you will 'Come Fly With Me' to the heights of the magnificent music you have been so generous to share. You are a national treasure, Sammy. Barbara and I warmly congratulate you and send love and friendship. We raise a glass to toast you on this most special day." It's signed "Francis Albert."

Sammy has touched shoulders with many famous people. He delightedly relates a story about England's Prince Charles. "I did an evening for him many years ago. At the end of the evening, he said, 'I didn't realize you'd written so many songs.' I said, 'That was just part of them.'

"Then I said, 'It must be very difficult to be a prince.'

"He said, 'Why do you say that?'

"I said, 'Because I saw your itinerary. "Eight o'clock, prince arrives. 8:05, prince greets people. 8:10, prince sits down. 8:15, prince makes a toast." It must be very difficult to be a prince.

"He said, 'You know what's difficult? Meeting someone like you who'll speak to me the way you're doing.'

"Then he said, 'I find it very difficult to write.'

"I said, 'Oh, do you write?'

"He said, 'Well, you know, I give all these speeches and they write them for me, they give them to me. And I like to change them!'"

Sammy chuckles. "So I said, 'Yeah? Look.'" He assumes a theatrical voice. "'Good evening, ladies and gentlemen. Ladies and gentlemen, good evening.'" He laughs.

"So we have a kind of relationship. As a matter of fact, on the way out, I'll show you a personal letter from him to me. I'll show you a personal letter from Princess Margaret to me.

"I never met Princess Diana until some years later at a reception. My wife and I were in a receiving line and as they came up, Prince Charles said, 'THAT'S HIM! THAT'S HIM! He wrote every hit for Sinatra!'" Sammy's voice becomes excited. "And Diana said, 'Did you write "My Way?"'" I said, 'That's the only song I didn't write!'" He laughs.

The phone rings. "This happens all the time," he says. "Excuse me." He gets up and answers it, "Morris, Hi! I'm always in touch with you through a fella called Jim Mitchell. Did you have the eye operation? I had both eyes, and it's sensational. It's a miracle. Yeah, I had it in California. Who'd you have?" Silence. "All right. Hey, can I tell you something? My guy invented the implant." Silence, then a laugh. "We gotta figure out which guy is telling the truth.

"The point is," says Sammy, "I need a favor. Monday and Tuesday, I want you to get a couple into the Desert Inn. Just Monday and Tuesday night. I'll give you the name." He spells it out, thanks Morris, and hangs up.

"Yes, I help people," he says, returning to the couch. "If somebody asks me to do something, I do it. That's part of my upbringing. My parents were immigrants from Galicia, Poland.

They came here without any money or any knowledge of English, and they made a life.

"My mother was a rare, rare woman. She was an incredibly, incredibly forceful woman. In 1937, when I had my first major, international song hit, 'Bei Mir Bist Du Schoen,' I moved my family from the Lower East Side to a new community, Sheepshead Bay, Brooklyn.

"Their house became like the House of Lourdes," he says reverently. "People lined up outside to get advice from my mother.

"My father was shy, he was backward, without any pretense. He was a quiet, lovely man. I always went to temple with my father when I was in New York for the High Holy Days.

"There's a 'Forgive Me' prayer, where you beat your breast and say, 'Do not punish me for this.' Once my father was pounding his breast, as I was. He said, 'I don't know why I'm beating my breast, I haven't done anything wrong.' And he hadn't. I promise you, he hadn't done anything." Sammy looks down and shakes his head.

"Whatever's about me that's decent, a man doing a favor and never stopping, is my father. Everything about me that's witty or sharp, is my mother.

"I'm not a religious man in the organized sense of religion. The trouble with Christianity is I meet too few Christians. If I meet a Christian, whom I think is a Christian, he's a very rare human being to me. If I call a man a Christian, I pay him a high compliment.

"I'm Jewish because I have to be," he goes on emotionally. "If I could be anything else, I would be. I say this very candidly and I tell this to Jewish people. I'm Jewish because they won't let me be anyone else!"

Do you believe in God? I ask.

"I really do not know if there's a God," he responds slowly. "But every night before I close my eyes, I say a prayer, IN CASE." He smiles. "It's a very simple prayer, a Hebraic prayer." He recites it in Hebrew, then translates, "'I beg you God to bless me, I beg you God to honor me.'"

Sammy appreciates his traditional upbringing. He loved his parents and respected his elders. "That's just what you did when I was growing up. I have such anger when I hear the modern attitude about hating parents," he exclaims. "There's a change in American culture.

"That box! TV is crazy-making. Do you know you can't watch that box for 30 seconds without something changing and turning and twisting? It cannot be just a word written slowly and quietly. It has be flashing and turning and spinning and doing something. Now, what do you think that effect has on you? It's unnerving, it's unsettling. In a 30-second commercial, they have about 60 pictures.

"When I was a boy on the Lower East Side, there was a terrible paper called *The Evening Graphic* and it was called yellow journalism. All of television today is yellow journalism. If it bleeds, it leads," he trumpets. "If it's gore, give 'em more!" He pulls out each word slowly.

"I remember when America used to export films that had beauty, music, lovely singing, stories of families, love, morals. Now all we export is violence, violence, violence." His voice is sad. "Someone says, 'It's an escape and a release that we're getting externally.' But I say no. I challenge it. I challenge that moral."

Sammy proudly admits to being old-fashioned. He married late, then divorced, much to his dismay. "Tita is my second wife," he explains. "And she had only one ambition. She wanted to pass my first wife's longevity." He laughs. "I was married 18 years the first time. The happiest year of Tita's life was when we reached 19. Now we're at our 22nd year.

"My first wife and I got divorced. That was one of the real cruel blows of my life. It was really a cruel blow, because I got married at age 35 to a girl who was 19, and I got married to BE married. That's what I lived for.

"People said, 'What do you do for a living?' I said, 'I'm married.' They said, 'What about your songwriting?' I said, 'That's my relaxation.' So that was one of the cruel blows of my life." His voice is quiet.

"Somebody said, 'How does it feel to be hurt so badly?' I said, 'It's good for the ballads.'"

Is love more important now that you're older? I ask.

"Love is a word in songs, for me," says Sammy. "You have to LIKE somebody. Love is too demanding, it's too emotional, it's too oppressive. Liking is easier. Like my lyric in

the song 'The Second Time Around.'" He begins to sing.
"'Love's more comfortable, the second time you fall. Like a
friendly home, the second time you call.'" He looks at me
keenly. "I like love to be FRIENDLY."

Sammy's voice grows excited as he talks about his two children. "My son Steve gave me a grandson and my daughter Laurie
gave me a granddaughter. My grandchildren give me
absolute pleasure. I see them as often as I can. Heath is at Stanford
University. He called yesterday from Santa Barbara. Rachel's
going to be 12. She's a miracle. She's a very special person."

He points to his desk and a framed photo of the two of
them together. "I'm always talking to her. Rachel and I are
good friends. I knew she was special when she was three years
old. I called her and said, 'Hi, Rachel!' She said, 'Hi, Grandpa.'
I said, 'What are you doing, Rachel?' She said, 'I'm speaking
to you on the phone.'

"I knew right away I was in trouble." He grins.

"She writes poetry. You see that piece of paper on my light
over the typewriter? Take a look at what it says." I read out loud:

> Plans. P-L-A-N-S.
> The plans you make
> Will always take
> A payment from your heart.
> But if you learn
> To take a bit of sorrow,
> There's always
> A wonderful tomorrow.
>   -Rachel Cahn Leifer

He beams. "She wrote that when she was nine years old."
Do you have faith in young people? I ask.

"Oh, yes, yes," he replies quickly. "Look, we've been here
before. We've been there before. There's really nothing new.
The past is prologue and the prologue is past. If I had to choose
one word to sum it all up, it's 'paradox.' Paradox. Life is
imperfect, which makes it perfect.

"If you wake up in the morning and the birds are singing
and the sun is shining and everything is exactly as you want it,
YOU ARE A VEGETABLE. Life has to be up and down. It's

the downs that make the ups, and the ups that make the downs.
And you must be in between.

"If you believe that you and I are sitting here at this
moment, are on a ball spinning in space, which we are, then
why are you so relaxed?" He raises his eyebrows. "Paradox!
Just get up and just go with it! Don't try to decide your fate.

"And another rule I believe." His voice becomes serious.
"If you do something to hurt someone, you WILL be punished.
I believe the law of retribution is absolute."

What advice would you give young people? I ask.

"First of all, you've got to pick a goal. And you've got to
work at the goal you choose. I say if you're going to be a
songwriter, if you can be 'successful,' underline 'successful,'
there is no greater career, no more rewarding career.

"I said this at a college once and a young fellow said to me,
'What about a successful architect?' I said, 'Hey, that's mar-
velous. But who walks down the street humming a building?'"
He looks amused.

Do you have any advice to old people?

"If you're inclined to depression, become DIS-inclined,"
he says shortly. "If you wake up and you're breathing, you're a
miracle of miracles! Someone told me—and I believe it—that
a human mind is the equivalent of a computer as large as the
universe. You wake up in the morning and you HAVE one of
those things! Rare. Rare. Rare."

Are you afraid of death? I ask.

"No," he says, without hesitation. "Did you ever hear the
expression, 'I slept like the dead last night?' I think that's what
death is—the best night's sleep you ever had."

Do you believe in reincarnation?

"If this life isn't heaven...." he exclaims. "I'll give you
another one of my favorite lines. The phone rings. I pick it up
and the fella says, 'How are you?' I say, 'I answered the phone.'
He enunciates each word. "I answered the phone."

"You might make that the title of this chapter in your book,"
he adds.

"The phone's my umbilical cord. When it stops ringing,
it's over. You know the greatest invention?" His voice fills
with awe. "The cell phone. Just think of it. You're holding

metal, whatever a cellular phone is composed of. You're holding it in your hand and a voice from Paris is speaking to you. Now if you believe that, you'd better believe anything!" He looks triumphant.

"I'm going to have to quit this now," he says abruptly. "I gotta go and finish writing the medley. I'm going to my office at the Warner/Chappell Music Company."

He gives me a quick tour of his home. "It's a very rare house. I built it. It does everything a house should do." The front has no windows, and the entry hall, with black marble floor and zebra rug, opens into a spacious living room furnished in tones of ivory, with a full view of the back yard and swimming pool. In one corner is a Steinway concert grand piano. Nearby is a bar, holding a big bowl full of pretzels.

"I wish you could know the great people who've been in this house," Sammy says. "One night we had a party with Gregory Peck and Cary Grant sitting on the couch, singing along with me." He smiles, then becomes all business.

"C'mon." We walk outside past a row of aromatic jasmine bushes. "This is my car. My license plates say 'Lyrically.'" He poses for some photos, then jumps into his Chrysler New Yorker and drives off to work.

The man just keeps moving.

RESSA CLUTE

Born: March 28, 1904,
  Fowler, IN
Profession: Rancher
Home: Musselshell, MT

I was always very proud of being a good athlete. And that's helped me keep in shape all my life. When I grew up, we had all our own garden stuff and beef and pork. Just pure food. I'd lay a lot of that to my good health today. Oh, sure, I eat meat. You might say I was raised on it. I probably don't eat quite as many vegetables as I should, but I do eat some, because I know it's necessary. And I take one of those one-a-day vitamins, when I think about it.

After a person has had several small letdowns in various ways, why, you just learn to overcome it. If you work hard, are able to work hard, you have that on your mind instead of your difficulties.

I listen to the news considerable, and become peeved at times and joyous at times. But, here, I will say this. I can be so irritated at the news and I'll just step to the door and see Mother Nature—birds and maybe antelope or deer, and turkeys—and it will just change my attitude. I'm a different person then. I have a little calico cat who's there when I come home every night. I just like having something out there to greet me. It's companionship, wonderful Mother Nature.

I think you should stay as young as you can, in your mind as well as your body. I've seen men who were 50 years old, all bent over. Of course, maybe it's not their fault, but maybe it is. They're just old, completely old. I think you should think young. It does me so much good to watch kids do sports. That's why I'm so in favor of school sports, because it keeps the kids' minds alert and on something useful and good.

Sure I've had medical problems. I still have stiffness from a broken femur long time ago. They put a plate in there and I was laid up in Tucson for nine months. I just made up my mind that I was going to get well. See, that's the point when I had that saddle horn accident. The horn punctured my intestines and peritonitis set in. I was in perfect physical condition, no fat on me, and the doctors liked that. I never let it enter my head that I might not make it. When you give up, that's the last straw.

I never thought I'd live to be 88. When you're just a kid, well, you think grandma and grandpa are old, but I never figured, I still don't figure, anyone's age. They're just a certain person. With my friends, some stranger can come up to me and say, "How old is that party?" I says, "I don't know." And I don't. They're just friends to me. After kids leave high school, I lose track of their age. In high school, you know what grade they're in. Age don't mean a thing to me.

If a person can be happy, I think it's half your life. If someone's grouchy, seems like it just shows on your face and entire body and your friends, too. I like to see little kids happy and enjoying themselves playing. I really do. Before I became quite so stiff, I used to enjoy getting down on the floor and playing with them little kids.

"We've had 55 years of marriage. We know each other.
We love each other. We take care of each other."

ELIZABETH

AND

EDMUND

CAMPBELL

Born: December 4, 1902,
    Clemmons, NC
Profession: Founder and vice
    president, WETA TV,
    educator, community activist
Home: Arlington, VA

Born: March 12, 1899,
    Lexington, VA
Profession: Lawyer, civil rights
    and community activist
Home: Arlington, VA

Elizabeth and Edmund Campbell credit their long lives to a faith in God and a harmonious 55-year marriage.

"We thank God every day, MORE than once," says Elizabeth, 89. "We're in a very special period of our lives. We have our health and we have each other and we are grateful. It's not given to many people to have this."

She looks fondly at her husband and smiles. "We watch out for each other. That's the most important thing to us now." He returns the smiles and pats her hand.

"Elizabeth and I have so many of the same interests," says Ed earnestly. "We both are involved in the community, she as an educator and vice president at WETA. She goes into the office every day and directs the volunteers and raises a lot of money." He speaks with pride.

"I USED to raise a lot of money," she corrects him gently. "I don't raise a lot of it anymore, but I'm glad to have my name used. I'm continuity," she says firmly. "I think that people who give money like to feel that they're giving to something that has ROOTS and that will CONTINUE." She pronounces it "cuntinue," in a soft North Carolinian accent. "I try to be that link."

Ed, 93, speaks modestly of his work. "I still do a little counseling at my law firm Jackson & Campbell in Washington, D.C. I go in a couple of times a week, but I don't want to suggest that I'm now practicing law there. I did, however, continue to practice reasonably actively until my late eighties." He speaks in quiet, measured tones.

Elizabeth adds quickly, "Ed is still a very important part of our condominium association here. The neighbors call him and come to talk to him and ask his legal advice."

"Before that," he goes on, "we were involved in groups to improve the schools. As a lawyer, I argued a case that broke the massive resistance laws that the state of Virginia had passed to avoid desegregating schools." He pronounces it "Vuh-ginia," drawn out slowly.

"I also argued before the Supreme Court for the one-man, one-vote principle. That was my biggest win, because one-man, one-vote really went to the heart of American government."

They both enjoy civic and church work. "We'd get into one group," says Ed, "and then—you're DRAFTED." He and Elizabeth laugh together. "So many people in life tire around 30 and keep on living in their bodies until they finally SUCCUMB," he goes on. "I think life is a journey.

"I was taught that we ought to keep on learning and keep on doing and really keep on GIVING as long as we can. It's really what life is all about." He looks at her and smiles.

"But you have to have something to give," offers Elizabeth.

"Serving and giving," he agrees. "I don't say there isn't an element of pride or an element of selfishness in all of this, because I'm sure that in giving, people want to be appreciated." He cocks an eyebrow and smiles mischievously.

"My mother told me that nothing made you feel better than to make a gift of something anonymously—and have it found out by accident." He bursts into laughter and we all join in.

My photographer and I are guests at the Campbells' home, a modern townhouse in suburban Washington, D.C. They welcome us warmly and invite us downstairs to the family room, furnished in early-American calico and chintz. In one corner is Elizabeth's mother's piano, and family pictures cover the walls.

The Campbells sit side by side on separate chairs and immediately start talking about their family.

"We have four children," says Elizabeth. "Our daughter Virginia lives in Phoenix, Arizona, so we don't see her very often. But we talk on the telephone very often, LONG conversations that we both enjoy." She beams.

"Our eldest son Ed, Jr. is an Episcopal priest in Florida. We hear from them very often by telephone. Telephone is pretty wonderful," she exclaims with childlike happiness. "We have a son Ben in Richmond, he's an Episcopal priest. His twin Don lives here in Arlington. He's an accountant and works at the General Accounting Office."

The couple has eight grandchildren, five great-grandchildren, and one great-great-grandchild. They make a point of keeping in touch, and the grandchildren visit often.

Ed explains, "I think probably you want to know that the two older children were from a prior marriage. I married Esther Butterworth in 1925 and she lived only ten more years. When Elizabeth and I were married after Esther's death, Elizabeth adopted the children, so they are her children. Then she had twins at the age of 39, which is pretty rare." He looks at his wife with admiration.

She throws back her head and laughs. "Yes, it was considered old at that time, but now it is not," she says. "It was not easy, but it was worth it. It was worth it," she repeats fiercely.

"Ed's mother lived with us the last ten years of her life and the first ten years of our married life, and she was a wonderful, wonderful person. Mother made it possible for me to do many of the things that I did, without feeling that I was neglecting the family, because she wanted to be NEEDED. And she WAS needed." She looks at Ed appreciatively.

The Campbells are a contrast. Elizabeth is 5 feet 3 inches, Ed is 6 feet 2 inches. She has long silver hair, swept into a French twist. He is totally bald. "I've been bald for 40 years," he laughs shortly. "I lost my hair almost all at once, after I'd been through a political campaign and run for Congress." He smiles, referring to the D.C. political scene.

Both are dressed with casual elegance, Elizabeth in a gray-green paisley dress with lace collar and a double strand of pearls,

Ed in a beige jacket and tie. "When I'm here during the day," he says, "I generally wear corduroys and a sweater. I wear a tie simply...."

"Because I don't like the way he looks without one!" she interjects tartly. They look at each other and laugh.

"I either wear a tie or a bolo," he adds.

"Yes, he has a very good-looking bolo that he wears," she says.

"But strangely enough," he continues, "I generally take off my sweater and put on a coat for dinner. I don't know why." His eyes dance merrily and regard her with amusement.

"Well, I know why," she says firmly. "I think one of the most important things about living is to have certain standards that you meet. I don't leave this house without having the bed made and I try to keep everything in order. I try to keep a SCHED-ULE, because I really think that's terribly, terribly important."

Ed adds, "A certain amount of structure."

"Yes," she agrees. "And when the time comes that we are not directly involved in what's going on, on the outside, I still want to keep a schedule. I just feel that people who do not have a schedule lose the incentive to keep going."

Is that a secret of staying productive? I ask.

"Oh, yes," they carol.

Elizabeth founded WETA (Washington Educational Television Association) in 1961 and has worked as vice president for volunteers ever since. "We have many volunteers working for us," she explains. "I oversee them and know what they're doing. And I thank them. I've always been interested in what I think is the reason for public broadcasting, and that is EDUCATION."

She warms to her subject. "I am particularly interested in helping with our children's educational programs. Fifteen years ago I started the Children's Art Festival. Children in the metro-politan-area schools participate by painting a picture on a theme. This year we chose 'One World Through Communication.' We make a calendar with the children's artwork. I watch over that," she says, with quiet satisfaction.

Elizabeth and Edmund start the day early. She wakes up at 6 a.m. and drinks a cup of coffee. Ed has prepared her bedside coffee pot the night before. For 15 minutes she reviews her schedule, then dresses and goes outside to pick up the newspaper.

"We read *The Washington Post* every morning," she says. "I read the headlines to Ed so we know what's going on in the world." Ed has macular degeneration and can't see to read, but keeps track of news through tapes and talking books. *Newsweek* magazine is his favorite.

"You know," says Elizabeth, "there's nothing very strange to me about wanting to know what's going on in the world. The fact that we're physically well has a great deal to do with the fact that we can still be involved."

She drives to the office in nearby Arlington. He goes to his law office or stays at home to see neighbors or friends who call and drop by on condo business.

"Elizabeth puts in a hard day," he says sympathetically. "She comes home at 5 o'clock. She has a special look and I say, 'You'd like to go rest, wouldn't you?' And she says, 'Yes.' So she goes upstairs and lies down on the bed, and I go up about one minute later to say something to her, and she's sound asleep!" They both laugh delightedly. "Then she wakes up 15 or 20 minutes later and she's refreshed. She fixes us dinner and we watch the news on public television, and she goes on for ...."

"Until about 9:30," she says.

"Or 10 o'clock," he continues. "Then she says, 'I'd like to go to bed.' And she goes up and the same thing happens!" They laugh again. "She drops right off to sleep. I'm the night owl," he says. "I'll go to bed but won't fall asleep right away. I listen to books on tape, or get up and eat a dry roll, or do this or that.

"A lawyer friend once said, 'As you get older, you need less sleep, but it takes you a whole lot longer to get it.'" He looks at us with a smile. "Sleep is not one of the things I do best."

Elizabeth explains, "All my life, I have enjoyed going to bed at night, because I felt the day was over! I had no more responsibilities, nobody could ask me for anything. It was my time to sleep, and I just went to sleep. It's a wonderful, wonderful thing.

"I think about all the nice quotations about sleep. Do you know this one?" She recites,

> Oh, sleep, it is a blessed thing,
> Beloved from pole to pole.
> To Mary Queen, the praise be given,
> She sent the blessed sleep from Heaven,
> That stole into my soul.

Ed comments, "Now, I've never heard that before."

"Oh, that's from Shakespeare," laughs Elizabeth. "And I like the prayer,

> Now I lay me down to sleep,
> I pray the Lord my soul to keep.

"I taught our children the lines:

> When, with the morning light I wake,
> Help me the path of LOVE to take,
> And keep the same for thy dear sake, Amen.

"My father was a Moravian bishop," she explains. "Ed was raised a Presbyterian."

Their religious upbringing has strengthened their lives. "As people get older, they either get serenity or they get bitter," says Ed. "Don't you think that's true?" He regards us intently. "They either fight their age and say, 'Why did this have to happen to me? Being old is terrible.' Or they get serenity. And I do think both of us have serenity. It's because of our faith."

Elizabeth continues, "I believe that life goes on. I don't know how it goes on, but I believe that we will be shown what we can do, as we go along. I was thinking this morning: Do I really believe that when I die, it will not be the end? And I do," she concludes. "But I have to keep telling myself I do." She laughs easily.

Adds Ed, "I believe the spirit continues and we have come back to earth many times."

"Well, Ed believes that," says Elizabeth. "I don't like to think I come back in any special form. I like to believe that I am I, and that I come back as I am." Her voice is resolute.

Says Ed, "In any event, if you're going to live, you've got to be a part of life, because you cannot live and fight life. You cannot live and be afraid of life. You'll not only get too tired, you'll not open the channels by which you get strength."

On Sundays, they attend services at nearby St. Peter's Episcopal Church, which they helped to found in 1961. They also pray daily, as the need arises. "I think," says Elizabeth, "that as you grow older, prayer just becomes a part of living."

Ed goes on, "I don't think either of us is preachy. We're just telling you this because you asked. I HOPE I'm not preachy," he laughs. "I am not concerned about what any individual's beliefs are. They change from time to time, from year to year. Certainly mine have. It's faith in life and in God that is part of all life."

She echoes, "We don't preach it. It's a part of our life. That doesn't mean that we haven't had problems, that we haven't had sorrows, that we haven't had times when it was hard to keep on being cheerful."

Adds Ed, "I have faith in life and in the creativity of the individual. That creativity comes from something beyond the individual. I have faith that whatever the process, that goes on."

Are you afraid of death? I ask.

"No," says Elizabeth quietly. "I'm afraid of dying and suffering."

"I suppose that's true of all of us," observes Ed. "You know, I've often thought that we can talk about the strength of our faith, yet when we get really sick or have a very bad pain, THAT takes over.

"In one of the Gospels, Jesus said, 'My God, my God, why hast Thou forsaken me?' I know Teilhard de Chardin, the great French religious philosopher, had that experience when he was on his deathbed.

"Physical pain may, for the moment, blot out the expression," continues Ed. "That's the reason we're afraid of the process of dying. A person, when his hip is broken and is suffering badly—that blots out, for the moment, the expression, the eternal that is in him."

He pauses and smiles. "I don't think I believe these old bones are ever going to rise up again!" He makes a face and she laughs. "I hope not!" he adds.

Elizabeth says, "You see, we have very few aches and pains."

"Well," teases Ed, "I haven't told you about them all."

"No, I don't want you to, either," admonishes Elizabeth. "I can tell you that!" He chuckles.

How do you view death? I ask.

Both are silent. After a long pause, Ed says, "I was making a talk at the funeral of one of my law partners not too long ago, and I thought of the quotation from a poem of Longfellow: 'The grave itself is but a covered bridge, passing from light to light.' It's very interesting. I don't know what death is. I think it's only passage." His voice is light and wispy.

Says Elizabeth, "There are so many things I don't understand about the world I'm living in today. You see, I've seen all this new technology, everything that has come in my lifetime in this century. If I can't understand THIS world, why should I worry about understanding the other?" She laughs.

"I know that life goes on, that it is not wasted. And what I bring to it now is somehow going to be used in the next life. That doesn't mean I want to die, because I don't. I think particularly about WETA and our plans."

"How are they going to get along after she's gone?" cries Ed in dismay.

"Our plans for the FUTURE," she goes on. "I think, 'I won't be a part of that.' And I regret that. Our grandchildren— I'd like still to be a part of them. Our daughter Virginia called before my 89th birthday and said, 'Mother, what are you going to do for your 90th birthday?' You see, Ed had a wonderful celebration that his office gave, a big party at the Mayflower Hotel in Washington, and a stretch limousine that came for us and our granddaughters, all dressed up in their finery to ride with us. A Scottish piper to pipe us into the Mayflower. It was wonderful, and, of course, our children all came.

"So I said to Virginia, 'Darling, if my family can't plan something for my 90th birthday, I'm just not going to have one!'" She laughs. "Ed and I can always celebrate my 90th birthday together," she muses.

"Well, if I'm around, I promise you there's going to be a BIG bash," he says. She smiles and takes his hand impulsively, holding it for a few moments.

Do you still feel useful and productive? I ask.

"Oh, yes," says Elizabeth. "And being needed. Maybe we're not as needed as we think we are," she says.

"I think each of us wants to live thinking that the other needs us," says Ed.

"That's right, exactly," she says. "We're friends."

Adds Ed, "Best friends. Which I think is ...."

"Essential," she says.

"Essential," he repeats, looking at her admiringly.

"We had 42 years in our big house before we moved here," she continues. "Our children thought this was going to shorten our lives. Actually Ed and I have had more time with one another, more opportunity to do the things that just the two of us wanted to do, without thinking about what our children wanted us to do.

"Finally we realized—it was easier for Ed to do it than for me—that they're our children, but we don't own them. We can't do anything about it, we've done the best we could. We kind of released ourselves from the feeling of responsibility for them."

"It was a little hard, hard for you," offers Ed gently.

"It was hard, right," she agrees.

"I wondered if ...." he says.

"If we were going to live through it," she says shortly, and they both laugh. "The move was hard." She gives us a knowing look.

"I was so glad," he says, "because the house was getting to own US instead of us owning it. Here we pay a condo fee and other people take care of the house."

Elizabeth says, "Ed is a very important part of our association here. The people come to talk to him, ask his advice. That's important to us."

Older people have a lot to give, I say.

"We think we do," says Elizabeth brightly.

"How many people are you talking to?" asks Ed. "Forty or 50?"

A couple of hundred, I say.

He nods and looks pleased. "Don't you agree? That the essential thing is keeping alive IN THE PRESENT?"

Does that include keeping up with current events? I ask.

"Oh, yes," says Elizabeth. "We watch the evening news and I watch television over at the studio more than I do here. I read *TIME* and *The Washington Post*. I look at *National Geographic*. And *Southern Living* is a wonderful magazine, if you don't want to have any problems in the world! I keep it for that purpose, it's my relaxation." She smiles serenely.

"It's very important to stay current," says Ed. "It's so easy for an old person to say that things are not like they used to be. It's true that you are a part of existing life." He hesitates, then plunges in, "Don't you believe that today we're in a sort of a Blah Generation?"

Elizabeth explains quickly, "Today it's often hard for individuals to find where they are important and can make a CONTRIBUTION. Because there's so much choice. One of the things that worries me about young people today is the feeling of importance in the family. You see, I always knew I was important in my family. I had a place."

"Self-esteem," says Ed.

"When I was growing up, I was assigned chores. If I didn't do what I was assigned, it wouldn't get done," she says sharply. "I was important. Well, today in the families, there are no chores ...."

"I wash the dishes," chimes in Ed.

"I know, I give YOU chores," says Elizabeth cheerfully. "But in families today, the children do not have to do chores. Because somebody else does it FOR them." She looks disturbed.

"If children don't have a place, an importance, then life has no meaning," she goes on. "I think we have not given children the opportunities they ought to have. I think society has legislated against the importance of the individual."

Adds Ed, "I know some very LIVE young people. They are my friends. Was it Edna St. Vincent Millay who said, 'It is better to light a candle than to curse the darkness'? Have you heard that? There are a great, great many people who have that sense, that inquiring mind, and they want to serve. You find them all over. But they are, shall I say, struggling to some extent, in a wilderness of mediocrity today."

"That's right," agrees Elizabeth.

"Television and automobiles are their interests," observes Ed.

"We're not so much a 'doing' society as just 'receiving,'" she says.

"Think of people watching television for six or seven hours a day," he continues. "Youngsters are becoming more passive, are they not? And to the extent that they are passive, they are not community-minded. That shows itself in the political scene that we have nationally and statewide.

"We don't want to discipline ourselves, or do we?" he asks. "As a nation, we are spending ourselves, so to speak, into bankruptcy. Yet we don't want to be taxed for it. It's a difficult situation. I sound pessimistic when I say it, but we've got to FIND ourselves as a nation."

Elizabeth adds, "I see these large groups of young people protesting and that's because they don't know anything else to do. A protest is action of some kind, you see. And many of them don't even know what they're protesting."

Do you have hope that this will change? I ask.

"Oh, yes, oh, yes, oh, yes," says Ed fervently.

"Ed has more hope than I do," says Elizabeth dryly.

"If you want to go from a Biblical point of view," he says, "this is an era when the children of Israel are having such a good time that they've turned to Bacchus instead of the Lord. It may take a catastrophe to bring us around.

"We are in the early stages of a catastrophe already with the AIDS epidemic, the economy, and the overpopulation problems," he goes on. "Do you know any of Arnold Toynbee? The history of civilizations and the way they're going? I think we are near the END of this particular civilization." He speaks quietly.

Will something stronger result? I ask.

"Oh, yes," he replies. "All over the country, there are cells of very strong, dedicated people who have strength and knowledge. They are active, vigorous, brilliant cells." His voice is animated. "They're called the 'older souls,' and you're going to see the results of it."

Elizabeth continues, "Our son, the Episcopal priest, took over this monastery in Richmond about six years ago. It's become a conference center and a place where people come to pray, particularly for the city of Richmond. He feels that somehow, we've got to save the city of Richmond!" She smiles with pride.

"It's a very great resource," says Ed.

"People come there to pray for the city of Richmond and for the WORLD," she explains. "It's a very, very remarkable thing. You ask if we have hope? As Ed said, I think you have to think in terms of small places where people are meeting to keep the light alive."

"It's like the monasteries in the Middle Ages," he says.

"A little bit," she reflects. "Because the world is so big today. We are in a world and yet, we're not ready for living in a world, because in this country, we're bound by our lack of language skills. We are so really HANDICAPPED by being unable to speak more than one language. And we're not making any great effort to overcome it.

"When I feel discouraged about the world, and I do when I read the morning paper, I just have to remember that each of us has an area in which we can operate and we've got to do that." She speaks briskly.

They both are quiet, lost in thought. Ed shifts in his chair. "I occasionally get depressed at the state of the world," he ventures. "And yet, there is so much in it—"

"That is good," finishes Elizabeth.

"That is good," he nods. "And it's up to us to participate, not retreat from it. It would be easy to retreat and say, 'To hell with it.'"

"There are many, many more people today who are searching to find their way," says Elizabeth. "This is one of the things that I'm sure of. Years ago, when people were brought up in a church, we just accepted what was there. We didn't look for a special thing that was ours. I think today, many young people are looking."

We've talked a long time. I wonder if they'd like to take a break.

"What time is it?" asks Ed. "We're going to feed you some lunch. Come on up to the kitchen." It's a welcome surprise. We all stretch and climb the stairs to a sunny kitchen. Elizabeth sets out soup and sandwiches and starts the electric coffee maker. Ed says mischievously, "I don't drink coffee. It's very bad for you. It keeps you awake." Elizabeth laughs unashamedly. "It's my greatest vice."

How do you maintain good health? I ask.

"We take CALTRATE every day," says Elizabeth quickly, and they both roar with laughter.

"To keep from breaking our hips," says Ed.

"To keep from breaking our hips," she repeats, beaming. "Our son in Arlington, the one who kind of looks over us, said to me, 'Mother, are you still taking your Caltrate?'" She laughs, "And I said, 'Yes, I'm STILL taking my Caltrate.' And we eat well, in moderation. I plan the meals with all the right things in them. I've always eaten that way. I eat three meals a day; Ed eats oftener."

"I eat six little meals," he says.

"When our sons come here, Ed eats about half or maybe a third of what each one of them eats."

Adds Ed, "I do take a vitamin pill. And I take one of the beta drugs to keep my heart beating normally."

Do you drink or smoke? I ask.

"I don't smoke and I have wine occasionally at dinner," says Elizabeth.

"I used to smoke cigars," says Ed. "But that's many years ago and I do not smoke now. I find I'm better off without any drinking, so I don't drink. I exercise, I make a point of it. I walk practically every day, half to three-quarters of a mile."

"I get so much exercise just doing what I have to do at work," exclaims Elizabeth. "Going in and out and up and down, and on these steps. That's another thing that this son of ours says. 'Mother, those steps are good for you! I remember Grandma and Poppa in their big house in Winston-Salem. They had steps, and that was one of the things that was important for them, to go up and down those steps.'"

Eyes twinkling, Ed adds, "I think I ought to tell you that I have enjoyed ill health for some 90 years." Elizabeth responds with a chuckle. "I was a very sickly child and my mother didn't think I would ever really grow up. I had to wear rubber boots when my brothers did not have to." She laughs again. "I was a little boy, physically. When I went to college at the age of 15, I weighed 100 pounds and was five feet high. And I have always been sickly, haven't I?" He turns to Elizabeth. She touches his hand.

"Well, I got him out of it!" she replies amiably. "Of course, he got better as he got older."

She takes no vitamins, but an occasional Bufferin for aches and pains. "You know, my joints get a little creaky, particularly when I have to get up and down out of low chairs," she acknowledges.

"I take Bufferin every day," states Ed.

"They say Bufferin or aspirin is really good for almost anything these days," she says.

"Do you want me to give you a list of my ills?" he jokes. "My heavens, I'll be glad to." We all laugh.

"Well, I don't want to hear them!" she cries.

"I'm 93 and I've been a hypochondriac most of my life," says Ed, straight-faced. "The doctor says, 'You must've done something right or you wouldn't have been here.'" He grins.

Ed wears a hearing aid. "It's the greatest advantage of getting old, turning off the hearing aid." He smiles innocently.

You have a good sense of humor, I say.

"Oh, it's certainly important to a happy marriage," says Elizabeth quickly.

"I don't think anyone can be creative unless they have a sense of humor," says Ed. "Incidentally, I think my wife is the most creative person I ever knew." She looks surprised and pleased. "Elizabeth can think up things to give people for presents for Christmas," he goes on. "She can think up places that this old piece of furniture ought to go to. But more than that, she is creative in life, in EVERYTHING in life," he says with pride.

"Well, it makes life exciting," she responds quietly.

"You must be able to laugh at yourself," continues Ed.

"Because life is funny," she interjects. "And if you look at yourself, you can kind of be amused at yourself."

Ed tells me, "I think you hit the nail on the head when you speak of a sense of humor. It's awfully hard to be alive without a sense of humor. And not a bitter sense of humor, but a happy sense of humor."

"Well, we help each other. We have to," says Elizabeth. "I mean, if I didn't appreciate his views and he didn't appreciate mine, it wouldn't be much fun." They exchange smiles.

"I feel that I'm a much richer person because I married Ed," says Elizabeth.

Tears well up in his eyes. "Thank you," he says, in a courtly manner.

"You've heard me say that before," she chides him.

"No, I never did," he jokes. "It's the first time. It's the first time."

"He just likes for me to say it," she laughs. "And I'm GLAD to say it. It certainly is true."

Her family, she says, did not want her to marry a lawyer. At one point, she decided she never would. Then she met Ed. "I thought a lawyer was always dealing in squabbles and unhappiness, and I didn't want that," she says. "But, you see, I didn't understand what a lawyer was."

Ed explains, "I didn't think I wanted to be a lawyer, even after I graduated. The law is a good profession, not for the fights that we get into, although some of them are fun, like we're playing poker, but because of the OPPORTUNITIES that it gives you to participate in the community.

"Lawyers can do more for the community, if they will," he says eagerly. "Almost more than the members of any other profession. And they get enriched by it. I've been in two of these big Constitutional crises that I'll never forget. One of them was breaking the massive resistance to desegregation laws in Virginia in 1959. Elizabeth and I were both on the school board and trying to bring desegregation to the schools.

"I went down there to Norfolk at the special request of the business people and argued that case before a three-judge court. We really broke massive resistance, got the schools reopened. And a great neurosis lifted from the whole state of Virginia."

Elizabeth continues, "We live in a society of laws, and if you want to change society, you have to change the laws. If you're going to keep your society going, you have to keep your laws and have to interpret the laws for people who don't understand. I learned to have great respect for the law after I married Ed."

Ed asks which books I've written, and where I've traveled. He and Elizabeth listen attentively. They say they've often visited England, Europe, and the Far East. "Ed is now talking about our next cruise," says Elizabeth delightedly. "We like cruises because it's easier, we have all our things in one place, and we can go off the ship, as we want."

Ed adds, "I hope we can go on a cruise up the Amazon this spring."

"We love England," Elizabeth goes on. "We have friends there, and Ed thinks London is so wonderful. We're interested in travel because we read about it and hear about it." She pauses. "One of the things that bothers me about education today is that there are no maps in the schools. And if there are, they are so outdated.

"Television can assist here," she says. "We can put maps on television and any teacher can dial them up, to discuss with the children. Television does not take the place of the teacher, but it can assist her."

Her voice becomes passionate. "If I were going to make a real change in education today, I would insist on more memorizing. I would insist that people put something into their minds that they can bring back when they are by themselves, when they are driving, when they are working. It's important to have something in your mind that you can really call out and think about.

"The hymns of our church that I memorized," she says. "I had a junior choir for many years. I had to memorize the hymns in order to teach them to the children. So I know a great many hymns, and the words mean a great deal to me.

"I taught English for a number of years and I memorized poetry and passages. They come back to me now. I wonder what people do who are listening all the time to one of these gadgets?" She cups her ears, imitating headphones. "They never have any time to bring back some of the things they know, if they do know anything. I wonder what happens to their minds?" Her voice trails off, then grows hopeful.

"Our daughter-in-law teaches first and second grades in Richmond. She makes her classes memorize verses every week. Someday those children are going to be very grateful."

Adds Ed, "Memorizing is a great help. I am so greatly thankful for a college professor in English who made me memorize things. In college I said, 'That's crazy to come to college and have to memorize poems.' But I've been thanking him ever since."

Ed was a late bloomer, which, he says, adds to his hope for others. "I didn't really have self-esteem until I was 60. I had what they call a nervous breakdown, didn't we?" He glances at Elizabeth and she nods sympathetically. "It was when I was in my late thirties, for a couple of years. I never did have the stability that Elizabeth had until I was much older, until I began to see where I could really participate effectively in community life and not simply be a workaholic and introverted."

He holds up a forkful of dessert and asks, "What is this, honey?"

"It's cranberry bread with applesauce on top," she answers warily.

"Did you make it?" he says, with a twinkle in his eye.

She looks at him hard, sensing a joke, then laughs. "I just put it together," she says evenly. Turning to us, she explains, "Cooking is way down on my list."

The meal ends with strong coffee. We all help clean up. They ask us downstairs to continue the interview and we return to the family room. They briefly point out photos and awards, including Annenberg and AAUW (American Association of University Women) awards for Elizabeth's educational work at WETA.

She walks over to a desk and takes out two personal treasures. One is a Mother's Day card, written in poetry by their twins. The other is a Christmas card that the family sent in 1961.

"Actually, it was our dog Sno-foot who sent out the card that year," she says with a laugh. "We were all so busy because that was the year we went on the air with WETA and got our St. Peter's Church started."

She reads the card:

> The Campbells' Christmas Epilogia:
> Ben has gone away to Oxford,
> My master heads the D.C. Bar,
> Don is studying accounting,
> And my mistress roams afar.
> She's busy with the school board,
> And educational TV,
> So any verse this Christmas,
> Has GOT to come from me.
> My master and my mistress

Send you their love and say,
'May happiness and blessings
Be yours, this Christmas Day.'
Sno-foot, the Dog.

She adds, "Sno-foot got a good many cards in response."
We all laugh.

"From other dogs," quips Ed.

"From friends who had dogs," she clarifies.

I notice a small framed quotation on the wall: "Our life is
an apprenticeship to the truth that around every circle, another
can be drawn. That there is no end in nature, but every end is
a beginning."

That seems to be your philosophy, I observe.

"Absolutely," says Elizabeth. "Ed and I live life day by
day. It's the only way to live. Each day is a new day. Learn
from the past, don't let it bog you down. It's stupid to make the
same mistake over and over.

"And do what you LOVE to do," she continues. "Do what
you CAN do and do well, and feel fulfilled in. Something that
you're satisfied with after you do it."

Do you ever worry? I ask.

"Oh, no, no," says Ed, emotionally. "Worry is a very
destructive emotion. It's almost impossible not to worry about
some things, because we're human. But worry is an extremely
destructive emotion. Worry is bad, inherently bad." He shakes
his head.

"Elizabeth and I are basically optimistic," he goes on. "It
doesn't mean we know what's going to happen, and it doesn't mean
we think we'll win every election. I've been in a good many of
them, local and otherwise," he says with a smile. "But it means
you can have a sort of peace and joy, regardless of what happens."

He takes a quick breath. "I believe you should do what
you feel FULFILLED in doing. The results are out of your
hands, in a sense. And don't try to be good, necessarily. That
was a great sin on my part, trying too hard to be good. If
you're trying too hard to be good, that means you want to be
something that you're not."

Elizabeth picks up. "I think the important thing is to have a goal. If it's a goal of a day, you set your goal for the day. If it's a goal for your life, that's pretty difficult to set. But you can set a goal for a day, and then the next day is another day.

"I would like to continue to do what I'm doing as long as I feel I'm needed," she states emphatically. "And at WETA, I feel I'm needed now. I'm needed because I want to be needed, you see? And I like people. I love people. At WETA, I fill in the little cracks. One of the most wonderful things to me, and I think I've come to treasure this, is the importance of a smile."

"The smile is a universal language, isn't it?" says Ed, with feeling.

"It is," agrees Elizabeth quickly.

"And if you smile at a person and get a returning smile, somehow that's a very plus," he says. "As I've gotten older, and I use a cane most of the time, sometimes when I get ready to open a door in the office building, somebody comes ahead and opens it for me. And we smile at each other. I have learned about smiles the last few years, the way I never knew before."

Elizabeth wonders, "It's a phenomenon that I'm not sure has ever been explained. What is it? What's back of it?"

"Well, LOVE is back of it," he says quietly.

"We talk about body language and the smile is body language," she adds.

"A real smile is, for the moment, unconditional love, isn't it?" says Ed.

"It's a reaching-out," she replies.

"A mother's smile for a baby has a little possessiveness in it," he goes on. "But if you've done somebody a favor and you smile, or he smiles at you, it's unconditioned."

Is love more precious as you get older? I ask.

"I think it has been for us," says Elizabeth.

"I think love is important in ALL stages of life," says Ed. "I don't know that ...."

"Now, Ed," she says, sounding a warning, then laughs.

"You appreciate love more as you get older," he goes on, acknowledging her look. "Just think, in the heady days of your life, if you don't have love and companionship, your values are apt to be warped. You miss love more as you get older, because you have less of it. You have fewer old friends. It's rarer."

Elizabeth adds, "There has to be somebody whom you can love. This is one of the tragedies today, that people are living longer and living alone. That's one of the reasons that they have little dogs and cats and something to love, something that they feel is dependent on them.

"Our daughter Virginia said she always remembered that her father put me first. She said she resented it sometimes, but it worked out." They nod and smile.

The Campbells invite us to come again. The following spring I spend a morning alone with Ed in the family room.

Once again, he is tastefully dressed in a coat and tie. His voice and eyes are bright and he welcomes me enthusiastically. We settle into easy chairs in the family room.

You look relaxed, I say.

"Thank you," he says. "I used to be very tense, mainly about work. Too much work, too much introversion," he sighs. "That's when I began to realize the joy and importance of taking walks. You cannot get straightened out unless in the presence of something living—plants, sky! You can't get straightened out in a room. You have to be outdoors.

"This may be esoteric or seem a little strange," he says apologetically. "But I believe your level of consciousness is raised when you're outside and taking certain types of exercises. Your attitude toward life, your realization of what it's all about, is DEEPENED by being in nature or talking to people.

"You get a sense of oneness of life, the unity, let's call it the universal love that you see. You feel like you're part of something so much bigger than you are."

I notice plants and flowers outside on the patio. Do you garden? I ask.

He looks amused. "I pull a few weeds," he admits, sliding open the door. "See that?" He points to the ground. "The bricks on our patio are laid on a sand base and nothing is supposed to come between them. But every summer the little weeds come up, even though there's no room between the bricks. And I have to pull them up. They are smarter than any of us." He smiles ruefully. Their garden holds tulips, geraniums, a potted

Christmas poinsettia under a Japanese cherry tree, a pine and a willow tree.

We sit on lawn chairs in the sun and he ponders the passage of time. "As you age, the days go faster, the weeks go faster, the months go faster," he says, without sadness. "When you're a child, the years are much longer than they are at my age. It's like a butterfly that lives only a few months. For a child, one year out of four is only one-quarter of his life. For me, one year out of 90 is more compressed."

He is happy at his age. "In many ways, Elizabeth and I agree, these are among the happiest years of our lives," he says with a tinge of wonder. "Because we know, or we think we know, more about life and our relationship to all of life and the contributions we made to each other and to living.

"I'm not referring to material things that we may have accomplished," he says quickly. "I'm referring to our relationship to life in general. We've worked out problems over the years so now we can really enjoy." He savors his words. "We're best friends. We're more philosophical than we were. We can see that rewards of life come from recognition of your relationship to all of life.

"Elizabeth and I have done well together. You can so easily fall into a rut. She is an enormously creative person and we've matched and stimulated each other in that regard. I doubt I could've succeeded in life without her."

Do tolerance and patience increase with age? I ask.

"I hope I've become more tolerant," he answers. "I think I have. Some people don't. They don't mellow. Tolerance really begins before old age. People become more mellow or more constricted. They either continue to keep an open mind and grow, as I try to do and hope I do, or they begin to atrophy at the age of 30 and don't have any new ideas or new thoughts.

"I consider the greatest blessing in my older age is that I haven't lost my mind and verbal skills. It also helps to be part of this community."

Ed has lived in Arlington since the mid-1920s and has a host of friends and acquaintances. They frequently get together to talk politics, philosophy, business, and theology. "It makes me feel worthwhile," he says gently.

Do you have any regrets? I ask.

His face grows sad, his voice pained. "Oh, yes, I have a number of regrets. Some people I treated badly. For example, I had a younger brother whom I teased. I remember in early middle age, he'd married, and I was acting superior to him from time to time. We weren't in sync at all.

"Once he wrote me a long letter and exploded, told me all the things that I'd done. I wasn't smart at all. I took the letter and mailed it back to him. It was the worst thing I could POSSIBLY have done. He gave me an opportunity which I'd never get again.

"He's no longer living. The relationship didn't improve. In a relationship, the suppressed things need to come out. That had to come out. I could've opened it out. I should've done it different." He looks at me and smiles.

Age has brought another shift. "Of course, values change with age, if you're still GROWING," he says with enthusiasm. "You should get a sense of proportion, shouldn't you? The God that you worship changes as you change. Your attitudes toward ambition, money, women, children, all of them change.

"And you change, you adapt," he continues. "You can hardly say the world is a fair world, from a point of view of what happens outwardly to people. You have to take it as you find it. Happenings make it impossible for some people to develop. It isn't what happens to you that counts. It's how you take it that counts.

"I have seen people who've had accidents and become paraplegics, who become warped and bitter." His voice deepens. "I have seen others like that who expand, grow, and become beautiful people. So it's what you DO with what you get that counts."

He's learning not to fear old age and death. That's a change. "I had a very large part of my life where I was really afraid of death," he confides. "I am no longer afraid of it. You might as well get used to it, it's coming. Death is a part of life. The essential person that I am or that we are, doesn't cease to exist.

"I'm 93," he says. "I'm not supposed to be here at all. So anything that comes is all right. I'm playing on velvet now." He has a quiet, contented look on his face. "I'm living on velvet."

I remember and treasure that day with Mr. Campbell.

Later he wrote his philosophy in a book, *The Musings of a 95-Year-Old.*

Ed Campbell died in December 1995 at the age of 96. He fell while walking to his mailbox. "A blood clot formed and doctors removed it," says Elizabeth. "Physically, he couldn't quite survive the surgery.

"Ed didn't suffer," she says in a quiet, low voice, touched with sadness. "He was conscious, but he didn't know exactly what period he was in. One night late, while I was sitting by his bed, holding his hand, he said, 'Elizabeth, I'm so worried about segregation.' I said, 'Ed, you don't have to worry about segregation. We have integration. There was a case in your court and you won it, and now we have integration.'

"He was still a few minutes and then said, 'Elizabeth, are you sure?' 'Yes, Ed, I'm sure.' 'In the schools?' 'Yes,' I said. 'In the hospitals?' 'Yes,' I said. 'In THIS hospital?' 'Yes,' I said.

"I know he said that because there were two black nurses in this hospital who just adored him and they were in and out all the time. He wanted to be sure they were being treated in the same way as the white ones." Elizabeth smiles.

"They told me on a Monday they didn't think he could make it. So I said, 'Well, bring him home.' And they did. He died quietly on a Thursday. I was there and our son was there. Our rector had just walked in the door and come downstairs. So it was just one of those beautiful things.

"More than a thousand people came to church where his body lay, and I spoke to all of them. I lived my whole life that Sunday between 5 and 8 p.m. Men came up and said, 'Do you remember me?' Boys who'd played with my boys. People who hadn't seen one another for years visited with each other.

"Next day, we had a beautiful church service. Then we took Ed down to Lexington, Virginia, where he wanted to be buried. There was just room for one more in the family plot. After a very brief burial service, the president of Washington and Lee University, who lived in the Robert E. Lee house, invited us all to come over for some food and to have a rest.

"Ed would've loved it, because he and I had been there so many times and it was next door to the house where his grandfather lived, and just up from the place where he'd lived all his life.

His father was a professor at Washington and Lee, and three generations before that had been connected with the school. It was a beautiful evening and a beautiful ending. I'm so grateful."

Elizabeth Campbell, now 96, still goes to work every day at WETA. She welcomes me to her gaily decorated office at company headquarters. "It's so nice to see you again," she says, standing up from her desk and shaking my hand warmly.

I'm happy to see you still working, I say.

"Yes," she replies. "I'm fortunate in having a place that wants me and where I'm making a contribution. People who are happiest still have something to do." Her voice is as strong as ever, her face and figure the same.

Juliet Spall, her long-time executive assistant and friend, picks her up every morning at 9 o'clock and drives her home between 4 and 5 p.m. "Juliet is just wonderful," says Elizabeth. "I couldn't operate without her." Says Juliet, "She calls me her alter-ego. I feel like her daughter."

How do you feel? I ask Elizabeth.

"I live by the day and it just gets a little harder," she says quietly. "Of course, there are some aches and pains, so I still take Tylenol, but no other medicine. I wear glasses to read at my desk and my hearing is pretty good.

"I have someone spend every night with me, because I broke my hip and elbow three years ago. I don't want to fall again, and my children don't want me to be alone at night. It's a luxury to have someone help me with my shower!" She smiles. "I still have my cleaning lady and she helps me keep the house ready for guests. One of my grandchildren is coming next week."

Since a hip replacement, Elizabeth uses a cane during the day and a wheelchair to attend theater or art exhibits at night. She also carries a cell telephone. She continues to stay in touch with her children and family. Her oldest son Ed, Jr., died of lung and spine cancer in 1996, and his widow and two daughters have become even closer to Elizabeth.

"You haven't seen me since my accident," she says. "I broke my hip and elbow. My doctors said I made a quick recovery from hip replacement, but it seemed long to me!" She spent a week in the hospital and three weeks in rehabilitation at a managed-care facility.

Brimming with enthusiasm, she recounts the adventure. "I think I learned a great deal. All the time I was there, I tried to think, 'How could I make this experience a POSITIVE one?' I worked on it very hard and I found a number of wonderful things. With my elbow, I could not use my left arm for quite a long time, so I couldn't open anything or feed myself very well.

"The women in my church set up a regular system, and somebody always came over and helped me at lunch and dinner. The last week, the men said they wanted to come," she laughs. "So I had men helping me with dinner. By that time, I could do my lunch alone.

"The advantage was that I got to know people whom I'd never really known. It was a WONDERFUL experience of having them reach out and help. The first Sunday I went back to church, the minister spoke about how the church community needed to reach out and help people. So when he came to the announcements, I told the congregation, 'I'm a living example of what individuals can do.'"

She goes on earnestly. "The whole idea of people being closed in, having nobody to come to see them, is one that I've really been working on, to get better visitation for people who have no families. There are a good many people living longer and landing in places with no families to come and talk to them. Groups make an effort to bring in animals and pets every so often, but it needs to be an organized and planned thing."

Elizabeth learned lessons from the other patients. "I have a great respect for these people who are in therapy, but know they can never really be well," she says. "There was a man with only one leg. He was working hard so he could go home and operate with just one leg. There was a woman who couldn't speak. They were working with her and she was TRYING. When I left, she could tell me, 'Goodbye.'

"There was a woman who had lost the use of one arm and wanted to continue to live in her apartment. She was working to be able to do as much as she could with the one arm. These are experiences that I never could've had, if I hadn't been there." She pauses to reflect.

"I also saw some problems in that place. I've promised to write this up, to say they need better training for the young workers who come from other countries and speak very little English. It's not the lack of English that handicaps them. They just do not understand our culture.

"When I wanted to wash my hands after I went to the bathroom, the sink was in another room. The fact that I wanted to stop and wash my hands seemed very strange to this little girl from Sierra Leone. She must've been 18, 19 years old. The fact that I wanted to wash my face before I ate breakfast was strange. These are the kinds of things they ought to be taught before they're hired to work with Americans."

Elizabeth had hip and elbow surgery October 4. She informed her surgeon that on October 10 she was scheduled to make a speech for WETA. He said, "You can." She said, "I will." On the appointed night, she was driven to the Marriott Hotel in Washington, D.C., for a Board of Trade dinner. She entered the ballroom in a wheelchair and gave her speech.

"My two sons helped me," she explains. "Ben had the opening prayer. Don wheeled me up on the platform and I walked over to the rostrum and spoke for ten minutes. I told the 600 people that they ought to be supporting WETA. I told our story. And I got a standing ovation." Her voice has a touch of pride.

"It wouldn't have gone that way if I hadn't gone from the hospital in a wheelchair. I made the most of it," she says forcefully. "I turned it around. My arm was still in a cast and I couldn't walk. But I could get in a wheelchair and I could stand. It was something that needed to be done."

Elizabeth was a hit. The next morning, WETA received a check for $2,000. "Since then, we've gotten more financial support," she says. "I think it's partly due to the Board of Trade's pledge."

She continues to travel. Her first trip after surgery was to Phoenix for Thanksgiving with her daughter Virginia. "She had arranged for me to stay at a place where I'd have a special room for people who have difficulty in walking," says Elizabeth. "So I did that and had a wonderful time. My son Don flew out with me.

"Soon after that, my sister-in-law died and I made a trip down to North Carolina for the service. I was able to do that.

"You see, I have had REASONS for getting well as fast as I can," she explains. "My next goal is to go to Florida. Ed and

I always went to Florida in March to visit friends. I've got that date set up. I told my son that I'd go without him, because I can take a plane and don't have to change, and I'll be met.

"The point is, if people feel they have a goal of some kind, they will WORK to meet it. It's people who have nothing to live for, nothing to look forward to, who don't TRY. Sometimes, even when they try, they can't do it. But there is a finality that people sometimes accept, particularly in nursing homes.

"One of the things I'm interested in now is helping to get pets into nursing homes. Flowers, too. If all a patient needs is to water a flower so it doesn't die, that's something! I've always felt this way. I learned it from my mother and father."

How are you dealing with the loss of Ed? I ask.

"I try to keep life as much the same as I can," she says calmly. "By living at home, I'm surrounded by all the things that we had together. I get up at the same time, I have my coffee like I did before. I set a table for dinner like I always did. I'm alone a good many nights, so I eat in the dining room. I bring out the silver and set the little mats. Ed would want me to keep this up. He was very proper about those things.

"The worst thing is when I come home in the afternoon and he's not there. But I turn on music or a very wonderful CD player, or the FM radio. WETA-FM has come to mean more to me than it ever has before, because I like to have something playing in the house. I have a feeling that Ed is with me. At the same time, he could be with the people who've gone before. It's a wonderful thing and I don't try to analyze it. I just feel it."

She also left his voice on their telephone answering-machine message.

"There are times when I feel very sad, but most of the time, I don't," she says. "I'm so grateful that I didn't have any of my accidents while he was living, because I couldn't have taken care of him. As it was, we lived a normal life, up to the very afternoon when he fell."

You always look on the positive side of things, I say.

"Well, I WANT to," she replies. "I couldn't live any other way. It's self-preservation."

SERVANDO TRUJILLO

Born: May 6, 1926,
  Roswell, NM
Profession: Native American
  teacher, leader of sweat lodge
  ceremonies
Home: El Valle, NM

I was born Apache and took up the Sioux way. I like the Lakota way. We get our strength from helping, from giving, because when we pray, we pray for the people first, and then we give thanks. I seldom ask for anything for myself, because I've been given everything. If you pray for the people, the people give you what you need.

There's only one God for everybody, the Great Spirit. Life, as I was taught when I was young, is hard and good, hot and cold. I was taught to accept that. What we do is to think life is perfect, and when it isn't, we're doing something wrong. That's a mistake. My father told me you work and you learn every day of your life, and when you stop working, you stop learning.

I walk in prayer. I pray in the morning and offer to the relatives. We never say, "Amen." We say, "All my relatives." At breakfast I pray over food, offer it to the people, and put a little bit outside and let birds or whatever needs it, eat it.

Today we have an overabundance of materialism and not spiritualism. Life has got to come back into balance, if we're going to survive. Since the family circle has broke up, it changed everything. That's why we have so much trouble with the youth today. We'll never solve the problem until we go back to the family unit, because that's where your strength is. It's a shame that grandparents and elders go to rest homes, leaving grandchildren behind. They need the wisdom and guidance of grandparents.

I don't remember ever thinking about getting old. To kids, 30 is old. I listened to my parents. I was taught to listen. They'd tell fascinating things, stories, what life was about. You had to be quiet and listen, not like kids today who scream and holler. You can't talk and listen at the same time.

"My father was a military man and vice minister in China. He always said, 'There are always two points of view. You have one point of view. Just listen for the other point of view. Even if you don't agree, you might learn something.'"

NIEN CHENG

Born: January 28, 1915,
   Beijing, China
Profession: Author, historian,
   retired businesswoman
Home: Washington, DC

I have always been fascinated with China. In 1979, I fulfilled a dream to visit. The U.S. and the People's Republic of China had just established diplomatic relations and the Chinese government was welcoming Western visitors and their hard currencies. I joined a Swiss tour group in Geneva and flew to Beijing. There a Chinese tour guide met us and took us all over the country to beautiful cities, monuments, schools, communes, and theaters.

I felt an affinity with China and its people. I was mysteriously drawn to their spirit and creativity. I heard about the Cultural Revolution of the 1960s and Mao Tse-tung's Red Guards, who rampaged through the streets and tried to destroy all vestiges of capitalism and Western thinking. Our guide's party line was the official story, but I wanted to know more.

Later, the best seller *Life and Death in Shanghai* (1987) by Nien Cheng came to my attention. I'd read rave reviews but had no inkling of the high drama in the story. For several hours every day, I was riveted to a Chinese woman's account of life that turned from gracious living to chaos and horror.

Nien Cheng was one of many cultured, upper-class Chinese accused of treason and acts against their country. She came under suspicion because she had managed the Shanghai office of Shell Oil, an international company. Red Guards occupied her house, burned her possessions in front of her, wrecked everything else, and took her to prison. Her only daughter disappeared. Years later Nien learned that government zealots had murdered her.

For six and one half years, Nien endured solitary confinement, interrogations, and torture. She survived, by sheer strength of will and belief in herself and God. The price was high. When the government gave up and let her go, she was diminished in health, size, and amount of hair, but not in spirit. She is proud that she never buckled to her keepers' demands to admit treason.

I noticed on the book jacket that Nien lived in Washington, D.C. I was living there, too. Never expecting that she would be in the telephone directory, I looked up her name and found that she lived ten minutes from me. I was elated. I called and she answered the phone. Explaining that I had read her book and believed she was the epitome of young at heart, I asked if she would be interested in being interviewed. She agreed immediately, and on a hot, humid summer day, my photographer and I drove to her apartment for tea and talk.

It was one of the richest, most delightful interviews I've had.

Nien answered the doorbell and gave us a firm handshake. A slim, petite woman with straight spine, white skin, high cheekbones, and gleaming black eyes, she was elegantly dressed in a classic navy suit and red silk blouse. "Please come in," she said in a light Chinese accent, showing us into a pale green living room, tastefully furnished in Oriental art.

We sat on a velvet sofa and drank jasmine tea that she poured from a porcelain teapot. Poised on the edge of her armchair, flanked by tall vases of tiger lilies and black-eyed Susans, she chatted easily and asked about my book. How was it going, who else was in it, what had we learned?

At her request, I'd already sent a list of my questions, so now she answered them quickly. "What keeps me young? Routine! I keep a routine. I exercise, I read, I have a positive outlook and an interest in everything that's going on. I have this urge to acquire KNOWLEDGE." Her speech is impeccable and she enunciates every syllable. Her voice has a melodic, bell-like quality.

Nien's routine includes daily reading and writing. In order to keep up with current events here and in China, she reads a host of newspapers and magazines. She speaks to school and book groups. She invites admirers to her home and encourages intellectual discussions over tea. She corresponds with friends and family around the world, dines out, attends cultural events, and practices Tai Chi, a Chinese exercise meditation.

For several years, she researched and began writing a book on modern Chinese history. But she decided to drop the project when her arthritis got worse. She also wrote a movie script of *Life and Death in Shanghai*.

"It was routine that helped me survive imprisonment," she explains. "Today, routine keeps me productive. I don't do anything inadvertent." She looks at us pointedly. "I'm very high on principle and responsibility. I'm very good at self-control," she states simply, with no trace of boast. "I'm the last person to be sentimental. My sisters are different from me. I was the eldest sister, first-born. That is part of it." She pauses thoughtfully.

"Look at my life!" she laughs, throwing up her hands in mock dismay. "I'm completely overwhelmed with things to do. I never have enough time to do it all. And so many books and magazines to read." Her living room is pristine, but her study is full of books, magazines, and newspapers piled neatly on desk and table tops.

"I always read one novel and one nonfiction book at once," she explains. "I read *TIME*, *The New York Review of Books*, *The New Yorker*, *Smithsonian*, *National Geographic*, and Chinese newspapers and magazines. I have to be kept informed of what's going on in China, Taiwan, and Hong Kong," she says with a sense of urgency. "I read while I'm drying my hair and while I'm eating breakfast."

Every morning at 6 o'clock, she awakens, without the aid of an alarm clock, she notes proudly. Then she goes to the apartment's center courtyard and circles it seven times. "That's a total of one mile," she says. "I don't walk very fast, but when I walk, I think of a string pulling me from the top of my head." She demonstrates, *à la* ballet teacher, pulling an imaginary string above her wavy gray hair.

After walking, she does half an hour of an advanced version of Tai Chi. "I cut out the one-leg stands because I have osteoporosis and I'm afraid to fall," she says. "On cold days, I go down about 11 o'clock, when the air is warmer. I taught a neighbor and she often joins me. If I were alone in the garden, I'd murmur prayers before doing the Tai Chi.

"Exercise is important; I believe in exercise," she says firmly. "I have arthritis in my feet and back, and exercise helps. It keeps me limber."

Over toast, fruit, and coffee, she reads *The New York Times* and *The Washington Post*. She takes a megadose vitamin and calcium tablet. "I absolutely believe in vitamins," she says. "This vitamin includes zinc. It's very good for your hair. It stopped my hair from falling out. I lost half my hair while in prison." She speaks with no sadness or rancor.

In winter she adds Chinese ginseng. "That's for resistance," she explains quickly, "because I cannot have a flu shot. I have only one kidney. I lost one from tuberculosis in 1953. I drink a LOT of water!" She laughs lightly. "Since I've been here in the U.S., I've been sick only once. I don't even go to have a medical once a year. I do go once every two or three years.

"I feel good and I have a way to check whether I'm healthy or not," she continues. "I will eat big meals, go to a restaurant with friends, and right away, I can put on two pounds. If I go without or cut down a couple of days, I lose two pounds.

"If you can gain weight quickly and lose weight quickly, there's nothing wrong with you, your metabolism is good," she says firmly. "My husband just lost weight, no matter how much he ate. He died of cancer when he was 47." She pauses a moment, then resumes.

"I don't eat too much. I don't taste the food as well as I used to. I think that with age, you lose your taste buds, just like hearing or sight."

After working at her desk, she makes lunch, vegetable soup with crackers or noodles. Later she reads or takes a nap, answers phone calls, and prepares tea for guests. They arrive almost daily. "Lots of people call me," she says happily. "They're usually young fans of my books, and if they're in town, I invite them to tea."

Strangers in your home? I ask.

"Oh, yes, I allow them to drop by," she says matter-of-factly. "I never say no to anyone who telephones. That would hurt a young person. You GUIDE a young person by engaging them, not by saying no." They talk mainly about China. Many of her guests are Chinese who have recently returned from visiting the mainland. Nien has not been back since she moved to the U.S. in 1983.

In the evening, she watches the *Lehrer Report* on public television. "I don't watch network shows," she says flatly. Occasionally she has a drink before dinner. "I like sherry because I lived in England," she smiles. "They all drink sherry."

Dinner is substantial Chinese fare: stir-fried meat or fish with vegetables and boiled rice or noodles. Later she reads or joins friends for a movie or concert at the Kennedy Center, a favorite cultural spot. Occasionally she entertains a house guest. By midnight she's in bed.

"I always believe in a good night's sleep," she says. "If I'm concerned about something, the stock market, for instance, I always say, 'No, no, no! Let's not think about that.'" Her voice is animated. "'Go to bed. Have a hot bath and go to bed.' Next morning, you're much brighter."

She prays regularly. "I don't ask for anything, just guidance. I don't wait until night time. As things happen, I will say, 'Thank you.' I go to church every Sunday. I'm a Methodist, so was my husband.

"My head touches the pillow, and I always sleep like a log," she continues. "I don't worry about things I cannot control. After that great injustice," referring to her time in prison, "everything else is insignificant.

Age seems to have improved her health. "You know, I was always sick when I was young, but now I don't get sick," she says, looking pleased. "I think it was prison. I survived such terrible deprivation there: a starvation diet, cold, heat, pneumonia so many times, scars from torture. I think that made me stronger. I have better resistance.

"This summer I've been feeling quite good. You know, I'm 84 1/2!" she states proudly. "After I turned 80, I noticed a gradual decline. I'm not sick," she adds quickly. "I just feel my arthritis more, and I've adjusted my life. I used to shop once a week, but now I go two or three times a week, because I can't carry so much at once."

A porter in the apartment helps with big bottles of water. For you? I ask.

"No, for the plants," she says. "Tap water turns their leaves brown." She drinks tap water, but boils it first, another health precaution.

Nien is content to stay close to home, although she gladly accepts invitations to speak. "Two weeks ago, I drove to George Mason University in Arlington, Virginia. I answered questions for one hour from students in a modern history class. I've spoken to several high schools, libraries, and book clubs. All free!" She gestures expansively and smiles. "I don't charge anything. I do it all for pleasure, to get to know the people. At the book clubs, we all have a chat afterwards." She folds her hands gently in her lap.

After *Life and Death in Shanghai* was published, she promoted the book internationally, giving an average of 40 speeches a year. It was exciting, but hectic. "I have decided no more travel, I am too old!" She laughs heartily. "I find I was getting to know the airports much too well."

Do you miss writing? I ask.

"No," she replies. "I researched and wrote four chapters of a second book, a history of China up to the Cultural Revolution. But I was not well enough to continue." Arthritis has taken a toll on her hands. "Besides, there are plenty of young people, writers and photographers who go to China all the time. They are doing very good jobs of writing on China today. I just had two of them to tea the other day.

"You see, back in 1983, when I settled in the U.S., Americans did not know anything about China. That was a reason to write the book. Now Americans know more about China. And many are no longer interested in past Chinese history. Americans don't look at the past. They're always looking ahead." She speaks affectionately.

Nien has maintained strength of character detailed in her book. "Part of my strength during that time came from anger," she says quietly. "I was so insulted that they should accuse me of being a spy for a foreign country, against my own country. I was furious! It was the greatest insult anybody could have inflicted on me." Her voice is indignant and her eyes flash.

"You know, anger can make you fight," she sputters. "Americans won't understand this, but Chinese are very patriotic because China's history MADE them patriotic. From 1842 to the founding of the Republic, China suffered defeat and humiliation from Western powers. The educated Chinese people felt this shame keenly. They became very patriotic." Her voice is full of emotion.

Strength to survive imprisonment also came from faith in God. "I think religion and psychology are all wrapped together," she says. "I'm a Christian. I believe in God. I was in solitary confinement for six and one half years. During the entire time, I did not see a smiling face. I did not hear a friendly voice. Everybody who spoke to me was abusive, they were accusing me, they were shouting at me, they were calling me dirty names. They humiliated me in every way they could.

"When you live like that for six and one half years," she goes on, "it's very easy to lose your self-respect and self-confidence. But in my case, I closed my eyes every night and I prayed. Every night I'd tell God what went on today: the interrogations, everything! I asked for guidance and courage. I asked God to give me courage so I can face tomorrow, so I don't get depressed and not want to live on. Give me the courage to fight on and the intellect to fight effectively!" She closes her eyes and clenches a fist.

"Every day I could talk to God. I felt His love for me. I knew that what I was experiencing—the humiliation, the denunciation, the deprivation of my life—was unimportant, because I had the love of God. That love is more important and better than any human love. I didn't care if these people all hated me. I knew God knew the truth, that I was not guilty of spying for foreigners." She grows quiet.

In prison, Nien steadfastly maintained her innocence. She refused to confess to trumped-up charges against her. Finally the government released her and allowed her to leave China.

She traveled first to Canada, then in 1983 to the U.S., where she became a citizen. "I was sworn in August 16, 1988, at the Statue of Liberty," she says, smiling widely. "It was by special arrangement that I went to New York, because of the TV and radio people.

"I was very, very moved," she says slowly. "It's a very important moment of my life. I took an oath of allegiance to America and I had to pledge that I renounce my previous allegiance to wherever I came from." She pauses. "You know, nobody in America even KNOWS that oath. But I think every American teenager ought to be made to recite that oath, so that they will know that America is their country. They owe America their allegiance."

Nien feels comfortable with young people. "I always have a yearning for talking to young people, ever since my daughter died," she says. Meiping was considered an enemy of the Mao regime and was killed during the Cultural Revolution. Nien doesn't give any details.

"I love young people," she goes on enthusiastically. "They are adventurous, intelligent, and observant. They think differently than I do. They broaden my horizons. They bring something of their lives to me. I keep myself up-to-date with them. Especially," she adds, "since my older friends are dying out. I lose one or two every year.

"The young people who come to my home are all very serious-minded. These teenagers and college kids are my readers. Most of them are interested in international affairs or in China. A lot of them have been to China to teach English or to learn Chinese. They want a career in the U.S. Foreign Service, to serve in Asia."

A few ask her advice and she gives it freely. "I had a high school boy who kept calling me to ask which college to apply to. I said, 'Why don't you talk to your parents?' 'My parents always abroad,' he said. 'Oh, what about your aunts and uncles?' I said. 'I don't have any.' 'Well, what are you thinking of?' I said. 'Brown or Harvard? What about Yale?' I like Yale very, very much because a lot of their graduates learn something really solid.

"I believe girls should go to college," she says emphatically. "Boys can be all right, even without a college education. But girls must be educated to be independent."

In memory of her daughter, Nien set up the Meiping Cheng Memorial Scholarship at Slippery Rock University in Pennsylvania. "I went there to give a speech and saw how many kids were deserving," she says. "Beginning in 1989, we have given two students a scholarship every year." Applicants must be American citizens entering their junior or senior year, achieve at least a 3.5 grade point average, and demonstrate financial need.

The scholarship is Nien's way of thanking America. "I'm grateful to America because I've been given the chance of a new life," she says earnestly. "I want to do something meaningful instead of just waving the flag." In her will, she's left money to Slippery Rock and to the London School of Economics, which she and her late husband attended. She also helped finance a six-year college education of her goddaughter's son. He now works for a computer software company in California.

Nien's life is American, but she maintains an active interest in China. A film company wants to make a movie of her book and she has consented. But she felt compelled to rewrite the script. "The Hong Kong film company did not give me a script to my satisfaction," she says tersely. "The company's writers were too young. So I worked on it. It has been very tedious.

"Long ago I told my London publisher that I don't care if the whole project falls through. Just don't give in and agree on their changing ANYTHING. I'd rather not have a film if it's not accurate. It's got to be truthful or else none at all." Her voice is sharp, her expression stern.

The film company has accepted her rewrite, but not begun shooting. It wants to film on location in Shanghai, but the Chinese government won't allow it, she says. "Whenever the film company applies to the Cultural Department for permission, the communist government says, 'Not now, not now.'" She smiles knowingly.

"You see, the company wants to make the film in Chinese, for the Chinese audience, to show on the mainland. But the authorities don't want them in. The Chinese are very unforgiving. They do not forgive me for writing about my life in prison. The Chinese remember a grievance ALL their lives."

Really? I ask.

"Oh, yes," she nods quickly. "There is a Chinese saying: 'A gentleman's revenge takes more than ten years!' It is true." She smiles assuredly.

Her professional reputation is tough as nails, but with friends, she is soft and warm. Grateful for their support in her turbulent years, she stays in close touch. "I have friends whom I've known 30, 40 years, and I hang onto them," she says fiercely.

"I'm like that." They are scattered around the world, many in France and England, where they went to school together.

"And now I have e-mail!" she says gleefully. "I bought a computer six months ago, after I went to a Staples store to buy more typewriter ribbons. The salesman said that pretty soon they wouldn't be making typewriter ribbons anymore. I thought I'd better do something!" She laughs.

"So I arranged for a friend to come over on Saturdays to teach me how to use a computer. After a month or so, I had learned the basics. Now I send e-mail to my nieces and nephews and friends all over the world. It's wonderful!"

By choice, Nien lives alone. "Yes, I'm terribly independent," she admits. "I'm perfectly happy by myself. In fact, sometimes I prefer to be by myself." She believes it's because she was forced to adjust to the loss of her husband in 1957 and her daughter ten years later.

She misses them both acutely, but has never considered remarriage. "I couldn't bring myself to marry again," she says quietly. "I was 42 when my husband died and I looked about 35. I was very well-off. My daughter used to joke, 'Don't go out with that man, he's got his eyes on your money.'

"I was very lonely then," she says. "I was too young to be a widow. I got fond of one or two people, but always when it came to facing the issue, I could not marry, because it was not possible to put my husband aside. He was with me all the time. Even though I can't see him, I feel his presence, like I do my daughter. I thought, 'It's not fair to the other man.'

"I never really think about it," she continues. "I don't think, ever in my life, that I was a passionate person. Reason," she leans on the word, "is important to me. I think a sense of duty is mixed up with my love for my husband and daughter, a commitment that I married this man and it's easy for me to love him. I have tried to change, but I cannot. I am a person of habit." She sits ramrod straight in her armchair.

"Often I feel a void," she says easily. "I have something that is interesting or a big joke, or something that's happened to me that's funny. And I have nobody to talk to. It's a matter of having somebody sympathetic to share things with." She speaks calmly, without sadness.

"It's not just sex," she continues. "Sex is a very insignificant part of a marriage after the initial period. It's the companionship, the sharing."

Getting older does not overly concern her. She is just more aware of it. "I know my age," she says. "I do not pretend to be younger or older. I just do what I have to do, to the best of my ability.

"You know, in China, we REVERE older people. When I was a child, we stood up when older people entered the room. When my grandmother started to speak, everybody shut up quickly and listened to her. Old people have great power and respect in China."

Nien has earned that respect from her younger friends. They admire her courage, dignity, and tenacity while in prison. Her voice is quiet, but her demeanor strong and her mind keen. All her mental faculties are intact. "My mind, so far, has not declined," she says gratefully. "I notice that I get tired more easily. I think I was more alert than I am now. Sometimes, especially when I'm tired, I get forgetful. I put my eyeglasses here in the living room, I do something, then I go look for them in the bedroom." She smiles indulgently.

"I have the beginnings of cataracts, but I can still see very well. I just had my eyes examined and my driver's license renewed. That's every four years. In four years, I may voluntarily stop driving.

"I have a hearing aid because my hearing is not as good as my eyes," she continues. "I usually don't wear it during the day, but at night I put it in when I watch television, so the sound won't disturb my neighbors. I love *Masterpiece Theater* on PBS Sunday night."

Part of her contentment comes from financial stability. She credits that to her traditional Chinese frugality. "I buy only necessities. I don't like to shop and I wear my clothes for years," she states emphatically. "Instead of throwing away food, I reheat it for another meal. I don't feel secure unless I budget."

That includes planning for the future. She's put her will in order and set up a trust with two successor trustees: a lawyer and the daughter of her best American friend, in case she gets sick and can't sign checks.

"I've also written a living will, going a step further than the normal one," she says. "It says that I don't want to be fed forcibly if I'm unconscious, and I don't want to be revived if I have a heart attack. If I have cancer or any other incurable illness, I'll let it develop and take its own course. My doctor has signed that will, and the minister and lawyer each has a copy. I'm completely relaxed.

"You see, I'm healthy now, and I think I'm emotionally balanced and physically healthy BECAUSE I'm not afraid to die. Not because I think I'm going to heaven," she adds quietly. "I leave it to God to decide. I do my best to be a good person.

"Death to me is rest, because in our life, it's really pretty exhausting." She laughs. "You get jammed in the traffic! Life is fun, but after a while, when I get older than I am now, the enjoyment part diminishes and the exertion part increases."

She loves her apartment, but recently was forced to consider moving. "Last winter, I was tired and depressed," she says slowly. "My legs were swollen because of a reaction to medicine, and I had to sit down to cut my vegetables in the kitchen. The joints in my right hand were all swollen from arthritis, and I couldn't curl my fingers.

"So I was thinking, I should look at assisted-living, where many staff members can always help me. Or I could have someone live here with me and turn my studio into a bedroom for them. But it's very hard to find someone reliable to stay," she says.

"So I am investigating," she speaks with new energy. "I'm Chinese, so I look very carefully at the expense! Some of these assisted-care places are $6,000 a month." She looks shocked. "I am looking, but I won't do it before a year or so.

"Besides," she laughs, "none of these places has Chinese food!" She breaks into tinkling laughter and we join in.

It's time to leave. We thank her for the interview. She gets up quickly, excuses herself, and returns with a small package that she presses into my hand. "This is for your birthday," she says. I had mentioned I was planning a birthday party. "But we just met!" I say. "How kind of you."

I open the package. It's a set of white, exquisitely appliqued handkerchiefs, made in Hong Kong. I'm overwhelmed. "You are so kind," I repeat. "Thank you very much."

"You're welcome," she says, taking my hands in hers. "I've enjoyed our time today. And I look forward to seeing what you've written about me. Please send me a copy so I can see it and check it for facts!"

I do, she does, and we've stayed friends ever since.

PAUL SPANGLER

Born: March 18, 1899,
  Mitteneague, MA
Profession: Retired surgeon,
  marathon runner, author,
  speaker
Home: San Luis Obispo, CA

I learned the value of physical fitness and feel so much better that I will never quit. I run seven miles a day, three days a week, and I work out with weights three days a week. Then I swim half a mile every day, six days a week. My running workout starts at 4 o'clock in the morning, the weight workout starts at 5 o'clock. I want to be the best long-distance runner in the world at my age. I want to be the best freestyle swimmer in the world at my age. I want to continue my lecturing as long as I live. And I want to keep enjoying my children and grandchildren.

I'm now in the years of enchantment and I'm enjoying them so much. I've written a book called *Life Styling for Health, Happiness, and Zestful Longevity*. I retired when I was 70 in 1969, but I've been preaching what the title of my book is by lecturing for 25 years. When I started my really serious training at age 67, I weighed 190. Today I weigh about 135. You live longer if you're slender. Overweight takes at least five to seven years from your life.

The best substitute for running is to get a flotation device around the waist, go in the deep end of a swimming pool, and go through running motions. It's really faster than jogging, because you're overcoming a lot more resistance in the water than in the air. You're not fighting gravity.

You've got to have goals to keep your mind and your body active all the time. If you don't, you just sit in the rocking chair and wait till the grim reaper comes and picks you up.

I'm in a barbershop quartet. I did it for 40-odd years off and on, and resumed it a few years ago, just to keep my voice in shape, because once I become a squeaky old man, I'm not going to want to talk anymore. I want to have the authority of youth when I lecture, because I want my listeners to accomplish what I've accomplished when they reach my age.

I look on the bright side of life. That's one of the principles in my talk. I tell the people, "There's two ways to go. One is down the road of active optimism. The other is down the road of passive despair. There's no in-between area."

I try to avoid old people as much as I can, because I want to be stimulated by trying to keep up with the kids. Mentally and physically.

Love is important at any age. And universal love, not only yourself, family, and country, but our neighboring countries. If we'd replace jealousy, greed, and hate with love, there would be no wars of any sort. It's hatred and jealousy and envy which are all against love, the opposite of love, and that's what's caused all our troubles. If you really love somebody, you're not going to fight with them.

"My mother always told us, 'Do as you'd be done by. Animal or person.' I have followed it to this day."

Georgie Clark

Born: November 13, 1910,
  Girth, OK
Profession: Owner, Georgie's
  Royal River Rats, a white-
  water river company,
  environmentalist
Home: Las Vegas, NV

Georgie Clark is single-minded. "The Colorado River is my life, always has been," she says in a high, squeaky twang. "The Grand Canyon is my home. Forty-eight years now." Her eagle-like eyes blaze.

Year after year, May through September, Georgie runs the river, guiding her rubber raft through rapids and falls, giving thrills to city slickers and nature lovers. On a good day, the waves crest at 15 feet, and when they hit, everyone laughs, screams, and holds on tightly. The sun soon dries the soaked boatload.

"I like it because I'm naturally that way —I like to MOVE and I like to GO." She speaks quickly, spitting out words. "I like the fact that there's a beginning and there's the end. And you meet different people all the time," she exclaims. "I like people and I like to give 'em enjoyment. I like to show 'em the river. They get a kick out of it." She pauses.

"That's the way I like it!"

It's a famous quote, her business motto, emblazoned on brochures and neon-bright tee shirts.

I book a seat on a trip in early May 1991. She writes me longhand on orange stationery: "I am looking forward to seeing you on the river. We can talk a lot then. Keep your notebook handy. I am so busy between trips that I can't arrange anything then. I only have three days between trips and work 4 a.m. until 10 p.m. to be ready for the next trip.

"I would love to be a part of your book.

"Sincerely, Georgie."

She's a tiny, sinewy woman with turquoise eyes and a platinum pageboy. Wrinkles line her tanned, leathery face. She shakes my hand with an iron grip and welcomes me to the canyon. "I hope you enjoy it," she says. I assure her I shall.

On the river, she is in perpetual motion. For five days, from 7 a.m. to 5 p.m., she steers and maneuvers her 37-foot-long raft, resting only for midmorning "egg breaks" and lunch onshore. She checks and maintains equipment, instructs her boatmen, oversees preparation of meals, and helps serve them. She talks with people, and after dinner, pours shots of her favorite blackberry liqueur into our coffee.

Always in command, she seems to be the last in bed and first to rise. At 4 a.m., she rouses the crew to start breakfast, serve, clean-up, then stow everyone's gear onboard for push-off at day-break. Once on the river, she stands silently at the stern of her raft, left hand on the outboard motor, right hand on a safety rope. Her eyes scan the river, picking the best spots to ride the rapids.

When we hit white water, she negotiates fast, efficient passage, avoiding whirlpools, skirting rocks, and twisting in and out of drops and waves.

It's a lot of work for an 80-year-old woman. But she loves it.

Georgie is a legend in the Grand Canyon. In 1945, she was the first woman to float down the river in a life preserver. She was the first person to take large boatloads of paying customers down the river, starting in the late 1940s.

In 1955, she introduced her own raft, the "G-boat," a trio of surplus rubber pontoons lashed together in a special configuration, for greater flexibility and less chance of flipping over. Her "G-rig," with a 30-horsepower Johnson outboard motor, is the biggest and safest boat on the canyon river. It measures 27 feet by 37 feet and holds 24 people.

"Everyone watches Georgie run rapids. That's part of the fun of the river," says Ron Hancock, long-time friend and boat-man. A tall, sun-reddened man with broad shoulders and ready smile, Ron motions toward a group of people watching from shore. Above them tower the red, craggy cliffs of the Grand Canyon.

Ron prepares to videotape our run through Hance Rapid, a 30-foot drop at the 76-mile river mark below Lee's Ferry, Arizona, the trip's starting point. "Hold on," he shouts. "Scream and holler and have a lot of fun!"

Georgie says nothing, but leans over the motor and peers out from under a red-brimmed hat, her hawk nose in profile, head cocked to the left, mouth in a faint smile. She steers to the right side of the river.

All around us is churning whitewater, and I see what looks like a big drop ahead. Suddenly the raft plunges and pitches, and we're in the middle of a trough. A sheet of water smashes the people in the bow, and they scream with delight. In the stern, we get pounded by a second wave and water shoots up through floor space. Everything is soaked, including Georgie. We look like river rats.

The people onshore shout, wave, and applaud, and Ron swings his camera toward them, capturing the end of another successful run. We check our gear to make sure nothing has washed overboard—hats, glasses, cameras, binoculars. We've been told to anchor everything inside our parkas and rain gear. Now it's time to take off the life jackets and let the sun dry our clothes.

Georgie's eyes never leave the river. She stays the course, squints into the dark blue water, and relaxes only slightly as we coast into a smooth stretch.

Ron's video will be sold at boat shows that Georgie attends in the winter to publicize her trips. She calls her company "Georgie's Royal River Rats" and her brochures include clients' quotes of praise. In the off-season, she patches and paints her rigs, revises the brochure, and buys supplies for the next season.

"I'm so busy, I never think of me," she says. "I'm so BUSY." Her voice has a tinge of wonder. "I don't spend time thinking anything about myself. I do what I want, with the good health I have. My sister Marie used to say if I gained a minute's time, I'd try to put an hour in it." She laughs a high, tinny cackle.

So you can laugh at yourself? I ask.

"Me? Oh, yeah," she smiles, showing irregular teeth. "For sure, for sure. That one I can do well." Her hands are dry and gnarled, her fingernails broken. "I'm all bones now," she laughs, looking down at her synthetic leopard-skin top and pants. "These were Marie's idea. I got motor grease on a red shirt once, and Marie got me a whole leopard-skin outfit. 'Wear these,' she said. 'If you get grease on them, it'll look like another spot.' So I have!" They've become Georgie's signature. A leopard-skin flag flies at the stern of her G-rig.

Tonight we're sitting in captain's chairs at campsite, a sand-bar that stretches 100 yards. Tamarisk trees with frond-like branches separate us from the canyon wall 40 feet back. The crew is preparing dinner and people are unrolling their sleeping bags. The sun sets quickly and soon we are in shadow. Georgie drinks beer from a can.

"I worked all my life. Born on it, raised on it," she says rapidly. "I'm a workaholic. If I'm not working, I practically feel uneasy. I'm used to doing things a certain way. And I always did manage to work for myself.

"I worked in real estate and at things where I could be my own boss. No matter what, even in the Depression, I was determined to work for myself, come hell or high water. I raised my own daughter when there ain't nobody around." She smiles and looks pleased.

Growing up poor made her strong. "We ate simple food: celery, beans, cabbage, and prunes. We ate rice, cucumbers, raw potatoes, baked potatoes, and tomatoes. All the things they say are GOOD for you now. We didn't have pies or cakes or anything sweet, because we couldn't afford it."

After marriage, she graduated from high school, gave birth to a daughter, and headed west to explore deserts, canyons, mountains, and rivers, including the Green, San Juan, and Colorado. She hiked, climbed, swam, and paddled. She attributes her stamina to good genes.

"You inherit things. I believe you inherit TERRIFIC," she says earnestly. "I don't need glasses and my hearing is good. I'm always active. I'm Irish and English on my mother's side, French on my father's. My mother used to say, 'That's French and alley cat.'" She laughs delightedly. "Of course, that makes you sturdy, because, anybody knows, animals or otherwise, these are the sturdy ones. Not if you're a thoroughbred, you'd never be sturdy. I like the mutts, I pick up the mutts." She grins.

Georgie always has had pets. Three cats and a dog live in her mobile home in Las Vegas, and she lavishes attention on them. "I feed 'em and pet 'em and let 'em sit in my lap," she says. "I always turn on the TV for 'em. The cats like to look at TV. Not for me, I don't watch. The first night I'm back from a trip, I stay up to keep 'em company, even though I'd like to go to bed.

"My sister used to accuse me of liking animals better than people, because I RAVED for them first," she goes on quickly. "My family's all dead: mother, brother, two sisters, and daughter. My father left us early on. My mother never talked agin' him. He was a Frenchman from France and she said he just simply should not have been married, that he was a party guy. So we didn't know anything about dads. When people today yak all this stuff about 'You should have two parents,' I just laugh, because my mother was so terrific."

She doesn't mention two former husbands. I read in her book, *Georgie Clark, Thirty Years of River Running,* that in high school, she married Harold White, the father of her daughter. Later they divorced and she married James Whitey. "'He eventually went his way and I went mine,'" she writes. "'Although I have been married most of my life, I'm afraid I've always been quite independent. I have always lived life my own way, no matter what my husband thought. Of course that's not the way to get along with a man, but then that was the way I have always been.'"

Her animals are her family now. "I like pets really as good as humans. Anyone can benefit from pets," she goes on enthusiastically. "It's too bad when people don't like animals, because animals, I think, are the BEST thing on earth. When I have a dog, I usually have a yard where he can run free.

"And cats," she exclaims. "I love cats because they will have freedom, even if they starve to death. I always say I'd be like the cats. I'll go sit on a fence and howl, even if I starve to death!" She laughs hard. "Animals treat you just like you treat them. You've gotta have the interest, put them BEFORE you. Whatever you get, take care of it." She looks fierce.

Georgie is a loner. Except for a couple of good friends, including her office manager, she keeps to herself. "I like to live alone," she says. "I don't even let anybody know the address. I don't NEED anyone, so I'm never lonely.

"My mother taught me to be self-sufficient. She always said, 'We're poor, there's no down.' And she never downed me. She told me to go for it! When I was thinking of going down the Colorado River in a life preserver and people said it couldn't be done, my mother said, 'Go for it! I'm sure you'll make it.'"

The smell of grilled meat floats over to us and Georgie excuses herself to oversee dinner. Hungry boaters have lined up with their cups and plates. Appetites run high on the river.

Later we talk about her daughter Sommona Rose, who was killed at the age of 15. "I named her after a French woman I knew," says Georgie in a loving tone. She describes how she and Sommona Rose did everything together: traveled, hiked, climbed rocks and mountains, even learned to fly together when Georgie trained as a pilot in the U.S. Ferry Command in World War II.

They were riding bicycles on the California coast when a drunk truck driver hit the girl, killing her instantly. The police tracked the driver, but Georgie declined to bring charges. "It wouldn't bring her back," she says quietly.

For a few weeks, she lived in depression. Then she met Harry Aleson, a fellow Sierra Club member and explorer. Aleson showed her slides of his hikes in the canyon country of Arizona and Utah. Georgie was hooked. A new world opened up and she suggested they hike it together. She and Harry became friends, and over the years, they covered many miles. Twice they floated down the Colorado River of the Grand Canyon.

"I was out here on the river 25 years when there was absolutely nobody here," she recalls. "All the people on my trips depended on me, period. There wasn't nobody else. There was no helicopters, there was NOTHING down here. The park rangers were not here. That was before the dams were built. These were long trips, one- and two-week trips."

At 80, she is strong in body and mind. She takes pride in not being emotional. "My mother taught us not to cry. We don't have that emotion. I don't have it about marriage or nothing. I was never one who had stars in my eyes. I was not one who grew up wantin' or being man-crazy. In fact, the men had to prove theirself to me!

"Oh, sure," she goes on. "I miss the people who've died, like my sister Marie, because we were peas in a pod. But there's no way I was going to cry, because I don't know HOW to cry.

"I don't go to funerals. I don't see funerals at all, because when people are gone, they're gone. They're out of it. You do whatever you want to do for 'em in lifetime."

Georgie has been "doing for" people all her life, starting with her older brother and sister. "We were always taught that no matter what, you helped one another and supported one another, good or bad," she says. She's helped Navajo Indians who live in the Grand Canyon. At Christmas, she persuaded friends and businesses to donate food, candy, and clothing, then trucked it herself to the reservations. "I like the Navajo," she says quietly. "I could've been a Navajo, lived as one.

"The Navajo feel the same way I do about life, about nature and sex. If they need it, they do it. That's that. They don't use all this build-up, with fancy dress and undress. This is RIDICULOUS. The Navajos never did such a thing. It flows natural. When I was young, I didn't even think of sex. If I wanted anything, I took it. If I didn't, forget it!" She laughs.

"There's no emotion in sex, there's no nothing. It's like eating. If you need it, you need it. If you don't, to heck with it.

"I keep busy," she says. "People need to be busier. If they've got time, they think about themselves too much. Then even any little thing, they can FEEL it, and that little thing gets bigger. If they got too much time on their hands, they're going to think about their ills. Naturally!

"A lot of older people don't have interests," she continues quickly. "They go into condominiums, things are done for 'em, they don't have the interest. This traveling around by bus and all, tours, any of this stuff, that's for the birds." Her voice is impatient. "I could have less interest in a bus trip than the man in the moon!"

At home in Las Vegas, Georgie drives blind people on errands. "I think of all things on earth, the worst is not being able to see. So my sympathy has always been terrific for them." She donates clothing and leftover food from the river trips to a local mission. "If I get two minutes, I do somethin' like this," she says.

She reads *U.S.News and World Report*, *Reader's Digest*, and *The Wall Street Journal*. "Not the financial stories," she says quickly. 'I'm not interested in that. I like their stories on the actual things in life. When they tell a story, it's really stated very carefully. They have a lot of stories on different things." Later, she confides, laughing, she uses the newspaper to line the animals' litter boxes.

Her religion is the Golden Rule: "'Do as you'd be done by,' my mother always told us." Nature is also a religion for her. "The Navajos are like that, the Navajos ARE nature," she explains. "Their original belief is complete nature. I could come on the river being a Navajo, because I've been with Navajos. I used to give 'em parties and get food and all for 'em, in the old days before there was civilization. I like the nature, I believe in nature, and I think everything's the way it's meant to be."

She's healthy, lives on fruit, vegetables, cheese, and bread. She takes no vitamins. "I think they would be an off-balance to you," she says adamantly. "I don't eat a lot. As a youngster, I didn't get a lot of food. None of us did. I never smoked, because I couldn't afford it."

She likes beer and an occasional glass of blackberry liqueur, but only at night. A new law forbids anyone to drink and operate a boat on the river. She says some river runners used to drink beer all day and became dangerous to other boatmen.

Georgie has a number of young friends in river-related businesses. But she believes most young people lack the strong fiber of her generation. "I look at kids today and feel sorry for 'em. They don't have a mother like mine, who taught me to be self-sufficient. They aren't bad. It's just a case of the times. Times change and they're going with the times. It's simply the different day they're raised in. They don't know different, so what would they do any different?"

She loves children and welcomes them on her trips. "I wish that more families would bring their children," she says. "We get some, but not as many as I'd like. Sometimes I'll get children of the Girl and Boy Scouts who hiked with me in the early days."

Georgie seems to be at peace.

What's the key? I ask.

"I see the good in everybody and just forget the bad," she replies. "I just forget it, pick out the good and leave the other alone, 'cause everybody's got good and bad faults. It just depends on the person who's judging."

When she turned 80, friends and admirers honored her. "Ted Hatch of Hatch River Expeditions put on a party, a great big party!" she exclaims. "They had 400, 500 people at Marble Canyon, at the Hatch Warehouse, and it was a real blow-out! No one will ever forget that party." She cackles.

"There was a guy with long blond hair in leopard-skin cape and tights who jumped out of a cake that came down from the ceiling. Then he took me on a ride in a Cadillac. I'm not so sure I liked that, because he liked to drink," she whispers. "That guy loves a WILD time, that guy loves a wild time." She shakes her head and smiles.

"Then he drove me up in the hills above the warehouse, and all of us watched some fireworks. They put on a real show. Yeah, it was SOME party."

Her eyes glisten and she grins.

Monk Farnham

> Born: December 27, 1908,
>   Riverhead, NY
> Profession: Writer, international
>   sailor (Guinness World
>   Record holder), hospice
>   volunteer
> Home: Henderson, MD

My greatest joy is the opportunity to bring adventure in the lives of people who haven't had the chance to do all the things I have. God keeps opening doors for me. I'm still exploring myself.

I'm young at heart because it was planned hundreds of years ago, in the long line of ancestors and zillions of spermatozoa put forth by them, among which I was just lucky enough to make contact in 1908 A.D. I'm reasonably sure that nothing happens by chance. We're all part of a great plan that's too vast for us to comprehend, utterly beyond the scope of our five senses. I write haiku:

> People without fear
> Have discovered for themselves
> The presence of God.

The quality of life, including our health, is pretty much what we make it. We continue to smoke, drink excessively, do negative things to our bodies. The paunches on Americans! And the hips on women! Fat is a national disgrace. No wonder the Japanese can knock us over like ten pins. They're lean and they're efficient. I say to people, "Get your act together. Get off your duff!"

"I believe that life should be lived so vividly and so intensely that thoughts of a longer life are not necessary."

MARJORY STONEMAN DOUGLAS

Born: April 7, 1890,
   Minneapolis, MN
Profession: Environmentalist,
   Everglades activist, writer,
   retired college lecturer
Home: Coconut Grove, FL

She doesn't mince words. "I have no idea why I've lived so long," she snaps, giving me a withering look.

She's agreed to an interview and I've flown in from New York. I rent a car, drive to Coconut Grove, and after making several wrong turns, find her home down a hidden road. Off to one side, in a grove of tall pines and palm trees, the English Tudor cottage looks like something out of a fairy tale, with leaded glass windows, steep roof, and gingerbread gables. She designed the house, had it built, and has lived there since 1926.

The wind blows quietly and the insects sing in the afternoon heat. I park on the yellow-grass lawn and knock at the door. There is no answer, so I walk in and explore. Plaques and awards crowd the walls and tables of the living room. Her signature straw hats cover a corner chest. I call her name. No answer.

I explore the rear of the house, and I find her asleep in a small bedroom. She is a tiny, thin, white-haired woman, covered in a pink blanket. I hesitate to wake her, but I must do the interview today.

I speak gently to her and she stirs. I explain who I am and she vaguely remembers that we have an appointment. "I'm just getting over the flu," she explains. "We can do the interview here."

I pull up a chair and begin asking questions. She answers, falling back asleep every few minutes. I'm concerned, but continue to ask questions. The answers become shorter as she tires. I feel terrible, bothering this poor woman, but I have to talk to her now.

"I can't write any more, because I can't see," she tells me. "I'm blind for the past ten years. Macular degeneration. But I dictate to a woman who is helping me with a book I've worked on for the past 25 years. It's about W.H. Hudson, who was a nineteenth-century environmentalist, naturalist, writer, and diplomat. He was one of the first environmentalists. Charles Darwin was the first." Her voice is dry and brittle, but has feeling.

"Hudson was born in Argentina and went to England when he was 33. I began researching his life when I was 78. I made several trips to Argentina and England. For the past 15 years, I've been dictating to a secretary and having the manuscript read back."

It's been tough going. She lost time when her first assistant and long-time friend Katheryn Witherspoon died. "That was a great shock to me," says Marjory. "But I got going again with another girl." Sharyn Richardson, her professional secretary, took over. Together they've finished the book, which is being considered by several publishers.

What keeps you going? I ask her.

"Why, I don't know," Marjory seems surprised. "What keeps YOU going?"

I love to write, I reply.

"I like to LIVE," she retorts tartly.

Where did you get your passion for life? I ask.

"How do I know where I got it? How does anybody know?" she says impatiently. Her father was founder and editor-in-chief of *The Miami Herald*, on which she worked as reporter, columnist, and assistant editor. "My mother and father were separated, so I didn't know my father until I was grown up. My mother died the year I graduated from college."

After leaving the paper, Marjory made a name for herself writing short stories for magazines, including *The Saturday Evening Post*. "It was the great day of American magazines," she says with longing. "Television has killed that."

She went on to write seven books, including the classic *River of Grass* (1947), which brought local and national attention to the Florida Everglades. Long after it became a national park, she continued to aggressively monitor its endangered birds and animals, the falling level of its water, and growing pollution. She founded Friends of the Everglades, which continues her work.

Now that she's completed the Hudson book, Marjory spends much of the day resting, listening to talking books, and welcoming visitors. A full-time aide cooks and cares for her. Old friends drop by, including Ms. Richardson, to work on Friends' business.

Are you proud of your Everglades accomplishments? I ask.

She hesitates. "I don't think proud is the word," she says slowly. "I'm deeply concerned."

Several times a week, her personal secretary Martha Hubbart comes to talk and read to her—loudly, because Marjory is deaf. She enjoys the local papers, mysteries, and animal books by the Scottish veterinarian James Herriot. Her brain remains quick and her wit sharp, according to friends.

I hear someone entering the house. A young, well-scrubbed man introduces himself as Michael Blaine, friend and part-time caregiver. "Marjory's just getting over the flu," he says protectively. "She's usually up and alert.

"She's very optimistic. She never lets anything get her down. She's lost too many people to death to dwell on it. Her interest in life keeps her going. She wants to know any current thing every day. 'What's new?' she asks me every day—about Russia, ongoing trials, everything."

The two met when he enrolled in a class she taught on Florida history at Dade Junior College. The friendship grew over long discussions about movies, a common passion. When she was in her eighties, Marjory took Michael to Paris on a vacation, a trip he remembers with great affection, especially the movies they saw.

I return to her bedside and tell her Michael is here. She smiles. He comes in and takes her hand. I continue to ask questions.

Do you have faith in today's young people?

"Yes, of course," she replies crisply.

Her advice to them: "Everything in moderation. You have to do things in moderation. You can't just go all out for everything." She speaks from experience. When she was young, she admittedly worked too hard on many projects, including her father's newspaper, and had two nervous breakdowns. A doctor told her she had to slow down. She followed his advice, left the paper, and recovered.

Always spare in her habits, she recently added ice cream and Ensure to her usual diet of solid food that the companion cooks. Marjory never took vitamins and wouldn't consider it today. "Not unless the doctor orders them," she says thinly.

She pays great attention to drink skimmed milk. "My father died of kidney stones caused by high cholesterol," she explains. "I vowed I would never drink whole milk or eat eggs. I do eat meat. I eat what I want," she says with a slightly defiant air. I don't bring up the high fat content of ice cream.

She takes no medicine, except two daily aspirins to keep the blood thin. Her blood pressure remains low. In the past she's taken calcium. "But I don't make a specialty of it. I feel pretty well, overall," she says. "I feel pretty well."

Is old age what you expected? I ask.

"I don't know, I don't think much about it," she replies quietly, starting to fade.

What about a sense of humor?

"Oh, yes," she rebounds quickly. Michael chimes in, "I remember a practical joke I played on Marjory once. I substituted a cheese doodle for her hearing aid. She tried to put it in her ear, then realized what was happening. She laughed so hard." Marjory nods and smiles.

Do you have any regrets? I ask.

"Oh, of course, one always has regrets," she says. "But it would be silly to let regrets govern your life. I mean, you can't live on regrets, you know."

She has no regrets about children. "I never wanted children," she says shortly. "I believe overpopulation is a major problem today in the world."

Throughout her life, Marjory relied on inner strength, not that of others. "Probably because of my family's situation and my mother's death," she muses. Part of her success, she feels, was doing things alone. Her brief marriage ended in divorce. "He travels the fastest who travels alone," she says, without emotion.

Boredom is never a problem. "I see to it that I am not bored."

Concerned and interested, Marjory keeps doing. She speaks at schools that are named after her. She accepts honors from dozens of organizations, including the prestigious Conservationist of the Year award from the National Wildlife Federation.

On her 93rd birthday, Florida Governor Lawton Chiles sent her a big, stuffed Energizer Bunny. "He compared it to her, saying she keeps going and going and going," says Ms. Richardson. "Marjory laughed at the joke after it was explained to her, since she doesn't watch TV."

During the 1992 presidential campaign, Hillary Rodham Clinton, a fellow Wellesley graduate, visited Marjory at her home and asked advice on environmental issues. At her 103rd birthday party, President and Mrs. Clinton telephoned congratulations and invited her to visit the White House. She accepted, and later that year traveled to Washington, D.C. to receive the Presidential Medal of Freedom from Mr. Clinton. "That was a great personal success to her," says Ms. Richardson, who accompanied Marjory on her three-day stay at the White House.

She once told friends she wanted to live to be 107, and recently revised that to 115.

"Her quality of life has dimmed," says Ms. Richardson. "But she doesn't feel she's lingering. She always asks me, 'Who's coming today? What's the news?' My daughter Dana comes and reads to her. It's a good experience for both of them."

Recently she noticed Marjory was more frail and told her, "You need to walk more, you're so frail." The 105-year-old responded, 'Why do you say that? I'm not frail!'"

She is still feisty.

"Marjory is reaping the benefits of her life," says Ms. Richardson. "She has so many friends and relationships that she created. She is just remarkable."

AVELINE

AND

MICHIO KUSHI

Born: February 27, 1923,
 Yokota, Japan
Profession: International peace
 activist, macrobiotic cook and
 teacher, author
Home: Brookline, MA

Born: May 17, 1926,
 Kokawa, Japan
Profession: International peace
 activist, macrobiotic teacher,
 author
Home: Brookline, MA

veline

I forget my age! I am thinking like a teenager. Sometimes in my dreams I dance with teenagers and jump rope with children. I'm not grown-up yet. I feel like 17 or 18 years old.

If I retired and didn't do anything, I think it's not so good. We just keep going. I don't know how long, but it's wonderful—everywhere we travel, we get so much energy from the people we meet. As I grow older, there's more appreciation for life, for nature, for food. And more acceptance of many things.

Modern technology is wonderful, but young people should also study traditional subjects, religious and literary subjects. Some young people eat too much commercialized food and take drugs. There is too much artificial—we must change and go back to nature. Change the food, discover food energy. Young people can change their lives and make something they want to do. Have the dream for life. And dream faster!

Michio

Life-wise, my age is infinite. Human chronology-wise, it's 66. Dream-wise, it's always about 22, 25 years old.

Young people should keep a bigger dream, not be afraid to fail. They should know how to eat and keep up health and maximum vitalities. Develop friendships, brotherhood, sisterhood, with anyone. If they dislike someone, that means they are showing their limitations.

Life is not for work. Life is play for one's own dream. Play with the dream, from morning to night, endlessly, until the last breath of life. No vacation, no workman's compensation, no retirement, no unemployment.

Do not sell your life, like selling a piece of sausage that you slice and exchange for money. Do not cut, do not slice life for that. If your dream is related to all peoples, then naturally you will get incomes, to be used for the same purpose. I've used all my money for the education of peoples.

Colonel Ellis with his grandson Tracy Mulligan, Jr.

"I eat right, I sleep right, and I take plenty of exercise.
I've always liked to walk and now it's more important than
it used to be."

EDMUND DETREVILLE ELLIS

Born: March 12, 1890,
  James Island, SC
Profession: Secretary, Class of
  1915, U.S. MilitaryAcademy
  at West Point, retired U.S.
  Army Colonel
Home: Chevy Chase, MD

Colonel Edmund deTreville Ellis has survived 101 years by working, surrounding himself with friends, walking two and one half miles a day, and remarrying for love at the age of 91.

An ex-cavalry man, he stands ramrod straight in the spacious entry hall of his home. Smiling broadly, he shakes my hand with a strong grip, then invites me to sit at the dining room table. His voice is dry and crisp, and in a refined South Carolina accent, he pronounces no "r's."

How are you? I ask.

"Pretty good for an old-timer!" He laughs amiably.

Dressed in a cherry-red cardigan, a white, open-neck shirt, and blue slacks, he sports a green, plastic-visored baseball cap. "That's to keep out the glare of the light." He indicates a lamp over the table. His hands and fingers are long and slender, and he wears a big West Point class ring. Fine, silvery hair stops just short of large ears, and his bright eyes are framed by dark, rectangular-rimmed glasses.

First things first. "I'm the oldest living graduate of the U.S. Military Academy at West Point," he announces, handing me a May 1991 issue of *Assembly*, the school's alumni magazine, with his photo on the cover. Inside is a long, laudatory story about him.

"For 30 years, I have served as class secretary," he says. "For the past ten years, I have also been class treasurer and scribe. It's a chore, but somebody has to do it, and I've been stuck with it for quite a long time." He smiles, eyebrows raised, eyes twinkling.

He enjoys the job. "Granddaddy loves people and thrives on their friendship and correspondence," says Tracy Mulligan,

Jr., who's joined us this morning. "He receives frequent visits and letters from alumni and their relatives, many from out of state." All provide material for his column, which he writes every two months on an old Royal manual typewriter.

Colonel Ellis takes great satisfaction keeping in touch with 16 remaining widows and many sons and daughters of classmates. The most illustrious were Generals Dwight D. Eisenhower and Omar Bradley, whose photos hang on the dining room walls, next to one of the colonel visiting President Eisenhower at the White House.

Photos also cover the big table at which we're sitting. Whenever someone visits, the colonel marks the occasion by having a Polaroid photo taken. He shows me some, describing each person in detail.

"My grandfather enjoys people," says Tracy affectionately. "Even though he lives alone, he is not lonely. He thrives on people. Look at where he's put his time over the years: visiting and correspondence.

"When he was younger, he drove to South Carolina and visited family and classmates along the way. After he stopped driving, at the age of 96, he started to receive visitors here. At least 50 people come every year." The colonel has helped many friends, including Army widows, to plan funerals and apply for Social Security entitlements.

At Christmas, he sends out handwritten cards. This year the total was 130, down from a high of 300. He writes a personal note on each one. He also sends birthday cards and receives many in return. Some lie scattered on the dining table, and he reads them out loud, clearly savoring their goodwill.

"You know, I'm also the oldest living graduate of the University of South Carolina," he tells me. Colonel Ellis received a B.S. and M.A. in civil engineering, then went to West Point. After graduating, he was selected by the War Department to attend Harvard Business School, where he received an M.B.A. The army then sent him overseas.

The discipline he developed in the military put him in good position to stay fit throughout life. A strict walking regimen sets him apart from most old people. Twice a day, he picks up a wooden cane and walks 110 times back and forth on the front porch, for a total of two and one half miles. He knows the distance exactly because he's measured it with a yardstick.

"I used to walk around the neighborhood," he says, motioning outside to an elegant, tree-lined suburb of Washington, D.C. "But now I walk on my front porch because I'm liable to fall, and if I fall, I'd like to fall on my own porch." He laughs shortly.

He's walked every day for the last 20 or 30 years, he can't recall exactly how long. Before that, he played polo and rode horses for pleasure. "Granddaddy," says Tracy, "remember how you used to ride standing up in the saddle at full gallop, during drills at West Point?" The colonel nods. "Yep," he says softly. "It seemed to be the thing to do at the time, just like so many other things. Just DO it." He raps the table gently.

"When Teddy Roosevelt was president," he recalls, "every army officer had to ride a certain number of miles in a certain period of time. We had to sign a statement every month about our exercise and physical fitness."

Besides walking, the colonel works an isometric spring machine for the upper body, doing 50 reps with each arm every day. He also does 100 arm raises and 100 leg raises in bed.

"I feel good," he says stoutly. "I have a very regular schedule. I get up at 7 o'clock, get my breakfast, go back to bed, rest, exercise, get up at 10 o'clock, get dressed, and walk outdoors, at least a mile and a quarter. After lunch I take my nap for about an hour. I'm in no hurry, I can nap anytime," he smiles. "Then I do some more walking, another mile and a quarter. In the afternoon, I read quite a bit.

"It's so important to keep a balance," he continues. "Because there are so many of my friends in the upper-age bracket who fall and break a hip or arm. I've been lucky so far. I haven't done that.

"About 7 o'clock, I have my usual supper and watch the evening news on television. I read and turn in about 11. I sleep very well indeed. I have to get up a couple of times a night, but that doesn't bother me. I go back to sleep right away. I find that I need more sleep since I got older." He shifts in his chair and sets his elbows on the table.

Colonel Ellis married for a second time when he was 91. "Several years after my first wife Laura died," he explains, "I fell in love with this lady whom I'd known for 18 years. Winnie Robinson was the widow of a West Point classmate of mine."

Why did you marry? I ask.

"I felt it was the proper thing to do," he says, somewhat surprised. "Falling in love has nothing to do with age." He and his bride moved to Florida where she had a home. They spent five years together before she died. "She was a little younger than I," he explains.

The colonel's first marriage was to his "Kaydet" girl, as West Pointers called a cadet's steady date. She died of a stroke, just shy of their 59th wedding anniversary.

Is it hard being alone now? I ask.

He pauses. "Oh, yes, it's difficult," he says huskily, eyes moist. "But I have to keep going."

Why? I ask.

"Because I feel I've got to carry on to the best of my ability." His voice is calm and steady.

He's glad that his family lives nearby. "I'm very fortunate that I have my son-in-law—my daughter died two years ago of cancer—my two grandsons, and six great-grandchildren. All live within five miles of me. I see them frequently." Every evening, one family member eats supper with him. They celebrate holidays together, and the colonel occasionally attends a youngster's soccer or basketball game.

Out-of-town guests invite him to dinner. "I'm a member of the Bethesda Naval Officer Club, so once in a while, someone takes me out there. In former days, I used to go to a lot of lunches and dinners of different organizations to which I belonged: the Veterans of Foreign Wars, American Legion, West Point Society, Harvard Business School Club."

Every Sunday morning, he telephones his sister Julia Ellis Hamlin, 100, who lives in a retirement home in South Carolina. He also calls his second wife's sister, who lives in Georgia. "It's important to keep these contacts alive," he states.

After retiring at the age of 60, Colonel Ellis indulged his love of travel. Every year for a month or two, he and his first wife packed up the car and took a driving trip. "We visited relatives and friends, mostly in this country, but some up in Canada and a little bit in Mexico. A couple of times we got back to

Texas, where I'd been stationed as a cavalry officer. We covered about 10,000 miles each time."

After his wife died in 1974, he continued to travel, making regular trips to South Carolina with Tracy. "I stay pretty close to home now," says the colonel. "I stopped driving several years ago, because of my age. I figured my reactions were not as prompt as they had been." His voice has no hint of regret.

"I keep walking. When I walk, I concentrate on that, of course. But I also think about things that I've done in my long lifetime, and about history." He points to two hefty books on the table.

"Those are the books I've written on my family history: *Dr. Edmund Eugene Ellis and Some of His Descendants*, published in 1966, and *Nathaniel Lebby Patriot and Some of His Descendants*, published in 1967." He asks me slide them over. "I took several months of several years working from the ground up, in New England on my mother's line, the Lebby line, and in South Carolina on the Ellis line. I did a lot of correspondence, too."

I scan a few pages of one thick chronicle. His mother's New England family dates back to 1625, his father's to 1690 in South Carolina, where they helped establish Beaufort, a town between Charleston and Savannah. His ancestors fought in the Revolutionary War. "I'm a Son of the American Revolution on both the Ellis and Lebby line," he says. "I typed those books, then had a professional retype them." He paid for distribution of about 400 copies, mostly to relatives and their children.

Books are a big part of the colonel's life. He reads voraciously, several books at a time, mostly about the Civil War, which he delicately calls "the late unpleasantness."

That sounds like a gentleman speaking, I say.

"Well, some of the family were killed in that war," he replies quietly.

He also reads magazines, including *America's Civil War*, *Civil War Times*, *American Legion Magazine*, *Modern Maturity*, and *U.S. News and World Report*. Every morning he reads *The Washington Post* and at night he watches TV news.

He is not given to self-analysis. Sometimes my questions puzzle him.

Are you flexible and easy to get along with?

He thinks, then answers, "I'm very flexible."

Flexibility is one way of staying young, I say.

Long pause. "Probably correct," he nods.

What qualities did you inherit from your parents? I ask.

Another pause. "I don't know how to answer that, except to say they brought me up correctly, I guess," he says carefully. "My father was a planter, growing Sea Island cotton primarily, and later beans, peas, and asparagus. My mother was at home with me and three other children. I guess she helped me to win that scholarship to West Point." His voice turns soft and dreamy.

How does it feel to be 101? I ask.

"It feels GRAND," he replies. "I never had the remotest idea I'd live to be 101. I came back from overseas in 1923 because of a disability. Doctors at the Walter Reed Army Medical Hospital found what the trouble was. It was some problem not generating the proper amount of acid in my tummy, and they gave me medication. Otherwise I wouldn't be here now. I still take one of the medications. Only one," he says quickly.

Do you have any aches and pains? I ask.

"I have no pain," he says evenly. "I feel very good. I take a pill for post-nasal drip and one to regulate atrial fibrillation. I don't take any aspirin."

Does a sense of humor help as you're aging? I ask.

"Oh, yes," he smiles quickly. Tracy adds, "A DRY sense of humor." Colonel Ellis regards me with a glint in his eye. I could swear he winked.

Can you laugh at yourself?

"Sure!" he crows. He leans back in his chair and laughs.

Tracy explains, "He's never thought about these kinds of questions. That's why his answers are short. He's not trying to evade you."

Colonel Ellis wants to show me his office, so we walk through a big kitchen and into a small sunroom that holds a bed, desk, typewriter, and black rotary-dial telephone. Here he handles correspondence, keeps files, naps, and sleeps. He goes upstairs to shower. "I usually have someone with me, like my housekeeper Berthine when I climb stairs, just to be sure. I really don't need it, but I try to be as careful as I can."

He praises Berthine's kindness. "She has a good head on her, too. She worked on Capitol Hill. She knows what I eat and wear. She also takes a lot of telephone calls for me from a lot of people who want to sell something, and she turns them off very promptly!" He smiles.

Meals are simple: oatmeal, figs or prunes, prune juice, and tea for breakfast. "I haven't drunk coffee in 30 years," he says. For lunch, he likes rice with beef or chicken, lettuce and tomato salad, tea, and pie or ice cream, preferably a mixture of chocolate and vanilla, his favorite flavors.

Supper is another piece of pie, milk mixed with malted milk, and sometimes ice cream. He watches TV news while eating. He doesn't drink liquor. "Not at my age," he says. "I used to drink a little, but I stopped. I figure it's best not to take any alcohol. I don't take vitamins, although I did once, at the insistence of my wife." He smiles fondly.

"And I used to smoke, but I quit in 1948, over 40 years ago. I think that had something to do with my being alive now. I was a light smoker. When I was a boy on James Island, South Carolina, I went through what they called rabbit tobacco, something we rolled up, like tea leaves. Later I smoked cigarettes, cigars, and a pipe."

He wears a hearing aid in his right ear, the one closer to me. "My other ear's gone, probably old age," he says. "My eyes are doing very well for my age. I've had no cataract surgery. I wear bifocals and reading glasses. I use two magnifying glasses to read small print, but I can read without them." To prove his point, he picks up a greeting card and strongly reads it out loud, his strong voice tinged with pride. Tracy is smiling.

I thank them and ask if I may come again. The colonel agrees, and a month later, I return. We spend the afternoon talking. He wears a light yellow cardigan with white shirt, dark pants, and the same green-visored cap. A tuft of white hair pokes over the visor, giving him a slightly rakish look. He is alert and interested.

We sit at the dining room table, covered with a white linen cloth, and neat stacks of mail, cards, magazines, and books.

How are you? I ask.

"I'm fine," he replies animatedly. "Yesterday a woman who's the daughter of an old friend came to visit, she and her husband. They live in California. I had a letter from her saying they hoped to get to this area. Her mother was my secretary in the Territory of Hawaii, at Schofield Barracks, about 30 miles from Honolulu. It was one of the largest army posts we had at that time.

"I also had a call from the son of a West Point classmate. He gave us some information, part of which I'll be able to get in the next *Assembly*. Then I received a note from a lady whom I didn't know at all, but turns out she's the daughter of a West Point classmate. Her mother-in-law is the one I wrote to. She's now in a nursing home. I'm going to write to her probably today or tomorrow, write to both of them." He looks eager.

As I ask questions, he listens patiently, his right ear close to me, elbows on the table. He twiddles his thumbs and looks into space, concentrating.

Is old age what you expected? I ask.

"No," he replies without hesitation. "I expected it would be harder than it actually is. Harder because of physical ailments and the necessity to go to a nursing home. I've seen enough of nursing homes in visiting friends. Old age is much better than I thought it would be."

Does time seem to pass more quickly as you get older?

"Yes. I have no idea why," he says shortly.

What's the best part of being old?

"Being in good condition, having my family around me, and being able to take care of myself." His voice is clear and quiet.

Do you believe in God?

"Yes, I joined the church when I was 12 years old. Presbyterian."

Do you pray?

"No, I used to, but I don't anymore."

Are you afraid of death? I ask.

"No, it's got to come sometime, just like being born, being married, and death," he says. "I do not want to have any prolonged sickness, though, like I've seen with so many of my friends, some in nursing homes. I've been very fortunate. I hope to postpone death as long as possible." He turns his head and smiles at me.

Do you have something in writing that says you don't want your life extended artificially?

"Yes, Tracy's dad has a copy of that."

The colonel also has typed a letter in case he's hospitalized. He gets up to find it among his papers and reads to me. "'If I have to be rushed to a hospital, please take this with me so the doctors will have something on which to start work.'" It includes his Social Security number, army identification number, and reference to medical records at Walter Reed.

Have you taken risks and chances in life? I ask.

He pauses. "Well, as a boy on James Island, I'd go fishing a great deal," he says slowly. "You never knew when a storm might come up, or heavy wind. We'd be out in a rowboat, occasionally fog came up, and you didn't know if you were heading out to sea or heading back home.

"Later, I took many a risk at playing polo, broke an arm on occasion. That's okay. It's a very strenuous game, and not too many played it. I was on the cadet team at West Point. I chose the cavalry and I played polo wherever I could, even in Germany. I guess we played the British teams." He smiles, lost for a moment in nostalgia.

"I quit polo when I was 50 years old because the horse went out. That is, the horse cavalry became mechanized. You couldn't get any more polo ponies, at least I couldn't, without undue course. I like polo very much. I think it kept me in physical condition. That plus riding over the jumps and all that sort of business."

Do you have any regrets? I ask.

"No, I took things as they came and did the best I could with what I knew at the time. Decisions have to be made at different times with the best information that you have available." He falls silent.

"Mail hasn't come yet," he says softly. Apparently the mail carrier is later than usual today.

What do you think of today's youth? I ask.

"It's not a lost generation, as some would say. It's coming along and taking over from the older generation. My grandchildren and great-grandchildren give me hope."

Have you any advice to young people? I ask.

"Get interested in various activities and keep busy, both physically and mentally. Education is very important." Colonel Ellis has set up a $500 scholarship at USC for deserving youths. Two or three students have benefitted every year since the late 1960s.

What do you say to old people who are discouraged? I ask.

"Get interested in something and keep your minds off the bad features." His voice is clipped.

Do you feel like a kid inside?

He looks at me incredulously. "Yep, sure," he replies with a straight face.

Really? I say.

"No, I'm just kidding you," he chuckles softly.

But you still have your spirit?

"Right."

And you don't give up?

"No, I keep going. I do what seems to be necessary at the time."

What is your greatest joy today?

"Being right here now!" he exclaims in a loud voice and brings a fist down on the table. "I live primarily in the present. The past is past. I live in the present and future."

MARTHA GRIFFITHS

Born: January 29, 1912,
   Pierce City, MO
Profession: Retired member,
   U.S. House of
   Representatives, former
   lieutenant governor of
   Michigan
Home: Armada, MI

My great passion in life is justice. The laws should be just and enforced in a just manner. That's why I attended law school and went into politics.

To age gracefully, you must find an interest in something and get up every morning to see if you are winning or losing.

Never move after you're 80! Oh, God! All at once you find a lot of stuff you thought was lost or you didn't know you had. Of course, you've got to go through it all.

I found some diaries that I kept when I was a kid. The day before I was 16, I wrote, "Tomorrow I'll be 16. Another year and what have I done? Nothing! I'm going to be better at SOMETHING than anybody else in this country, if it's only washing dishes!"

"We laugh at each other and ourselves.
We never go to sleep at night with any kind of argument."

DALE EVANS

AND

ROY ROGERS

Born: October 31, 1912,
    Uvalde, TX
Profession: Singer, actress,
    author, speaker
Home: Apple Valley, CA

Born: November 5, 1911,
    Cincinnati, OH
Profession: Singer, actor,
    businessman
Home: Apple Valley, CA

They sit close, side by side, on their office sofa. They finish each other's sentences. They laugh and talk at once. After 44 years of marriage, the King of the American Cowboys and Queen of the West still appear very much in love.

"I feel very fortunate to be here," says Roy in a soft, musical drawl. "Because last year I had a real close call. Not only an aneurysm, but right after that I had four straight colds and ten days of antibiotics for each one. The last cold turned into pneumonia. At one time I couldn't raise my hand, I was so weak." He smiles wanly and shakes his head. Dale nods with concern.

"I got so weak, I said a little prayer," he continues. "I said, 'Lord, if You got anything left for me to do here on earth, let me stay a while longer. If not, let's get out of here.' And that's exactly how I felt."

He speaks quietly and intensely. A small, wiry man with a baby face and blue eyes, Roy looks the quintessential cowboy in Western shirt and pants, and a fawn-colored hat pushed back on his brow.

Dale, also dressed in western clothes, adds quietly, "Roy prayed the night before he was operated on for the aneurysm. It was quite serious. They told me we could lose him, but they got him just in time. That's the same operation that killed Lucille Ball. They didn't get her in time." Her voice is sad.

During his recovery, Roy got a big boost from fan mail. Still incredulous, he explains, "There was an article in the newspaper that said I was sick and in the hospital. The first week I got 15,000 letters and 5,000 the next week. Somebody sent me a get-well card about the size of that wall." He points to a greeting card tacked on a long wall in the hall.

"Everybody in this company signed that card. I'll show it to you later," he says. "I read those beautiful letters and I felt that I was being bad by even THINKING about dying. Such beautiful letters that tears come to my eyes. And I read them hour after hour." His voice is hushed.

He recovered and now makes a point of taking it easy. "I don't make personal appearances or ride in rodeos and parades anymore," he says. "I don't ride horses anymore. I always say my bowling ball gets heavier and my horse gets taller every year." He chuckles. "People see those old movies and still think I'm 40 years old, but I'm not! They forget that time passes, and you're going with it.

"I'm tired out of making personal appearances," he goes on gently. "I am not trying to promote any kind of appearance. But Dale," he looks at her fondly, "she does her Christian work and she does a beautiful job on it. It keeps her going. If I could talk and ad lib like she does on Christianity...." He stops, a silent compliment hanging in the air. They smile at each other. "But I was raised on a farm and my vocabulary isn't that big." They both laugh. "It's harder for me to get up and just talk about things."

Dale used to speak and perform nearly full-time. Now she's cut back to one week a month. "I appear before religious groups," she says. "I've done things for abused children, retarded children, and senior citizens. The Lord is my life, my light, and my salvation, and has been for almost 45 years, shortly after Roy and I married. I had a son Tom from a previous marriage, and Tom was a very committed, faithful Christian. He was the one who made me commit my life to Christ." She smiles, showing movie-star perfect teeth.

"I was raised in a wonderful family," continues Roy. "But we lived way out in the country and never got to church very much. So I didn't know too much about it until I met Dale. She married me with three babies. I'd lost my first wife when the last baby was born. Dale was smart enough to know that she couldn't handle this unless she had the help of God. I've got to give God credit for taking care of me and having me meet Dale." They smile at each other.

"You talk about being young at heart," says Dale. "When I do concerts, there is a blind fellow, a terrific Christian and beautifully talented man named Ken Medema. He wrote a song called 'Lover of the Children.' It's a wonderful song and I sing it wherever I'm speaking." She recites the words with feeling:

> Walking in the sunshine, laughing in the rain,
> Lover of the children, make me young again.
> Climbing in the treetops, running down the shore,
> Lover of the children, make me young once more.
> Vigorous and daring but touchable and mild,
> Lover of the children, make me like a child
> Trusting in Your goodness, walking where You lead,
> Lover of the children, keep me young indeed.
> Make me young enough to know that alone I cannot go
> In the darkness of the night.
> Make me young enough to see that your love will never let
>   me go.
> Keep me open to surprise, put wonder in my eyes,
> Make my vision clear and bright, make me willing to
>   be led,
> And to follow where you bid me go,
> Fearing not tomorrow, trusting you today.
> Lover of the children, make me young, I pray.

"I'll be singing that next weekend in New Orleans at a Southern Baptist Women's banquet on aging," she says in a lilting drawl.

"You know, I wrote a book *Homestretch* three or four years ago. It was all about the fact that aging should be enjoyable and that we should be able to feel so much in the homestretch, from our backlog of experiences. It's all about the spirit of being young. Age is an attitude," she says firmly. "Not a chronological thing."

"It HURTS once in a while, too," chimes in Roy, referring to aches and pains. They laugh together.

Dale goes on, "It's getting up in the morning and thinking, 'What do I have to do today? What CAN I do?' Always keeping your mind thinking and active, but also prayerful, believing in the Lord. That's the subject of the book I'm writing now: *Celebrate Tomorrow*. Look toward tomorrow with anticipation instead of dread."

On a hot, spring morning, I've driven northeast from Los Angeles to the high desert and the mountain town of Victorville, site of the Roy Rogers-Dale Evans Museum, which opened in 1976. It's still early, but tourists are lining up outside. The museum is a history of the Cowboy Couple, filled with memorabilia, including their favorite horses Trigger and Buttermilk, mounted, in rearing positions; their rodeo and motion picture costumes, hit record albums and sheet music, comic books, even cereal boxes with their photos on them. There are several of Roy's cars, and one stands out: a long, sleek, lemon-yellow, 1963 Lincoln Continental convertible.

I find Roy surprisingly small next to Dale, who is bigger, with strawberry-blonde hair in a bouffant style. Both smile continuously. He wears a hearing aid whose batteries squeal from time to time, eventually causing him to swear lightly under his breath.

"The most fun thing I do now is wake up!" He laughs, eyes crinkling. "No, I enjoy coming over here to the museum. The first thing in the morning, I go in there and the people come in and they are just BEAUTIFUL. I shake hands with them and they take pictures. They all have cameras.

"We don't sign autographs, because once you start, you're there two or three hours. I quit that about six years ago." He pauses. "I prayed about how I was going to do it. The next morning I came in that back door down there, and this little girl about 12 come up to me and said, 'Mr. Rogers, can I get your autograph?' He mimics a child's shy, high-pitched voice.

"And I said, 'Honey, we don't sign autographs anymore. We shake hands with mom and dad and we try to find out where you are from and we take pictures....' 'Oh!' she said. 'You take pictures?'

"And that settled it," says Roy, beaming. "She was very happy that we took a picture with her and her mother and father.

And I've been doing that ever since. Every morning I go out there and take pictures till we get 'em ALL taken care of, and talk to them. It really perks you up for the day." He smiles gently.

"And real thrilling things happen for me," he goes on. "I've had men 60 years old, tears running off the end of their cheeks. They become five years old all of a sudden! And a lot of ladies the same way.

"Yeah, they remember you when they were kids, and I guess I impressed them. Sometimes those things grow with you all your life." He stops, lost in thought.

"A lot of people look at me and say that they can't believe I am 80 years old. A guy asked how it felt to be 80 years old, and I said that I didn't know, 'cause I just GOT that way!" He grins. "But I guess I'm very fortunate, even though I've had some rough things happen with my heart situation.

"Whatever I got left, I'd like to be UP and not be in bed." He is vehement. "I'd rather be dead than laying in bed some-place the rest of my life."

Roy has been diagnosed with congestive heart disease, a condition that sobers him. "I don't want to push it. I've had two heart operations in the last few years, and this aneurysm just last year. I take it day by day. I suppose whatever I'm supposed to have, I will ride it out and do what comes naturally, just living another day.

"I have so much to be thankful for," he goes on. "I saw my mom and dad getting physically older and how they aged and the things they could do. They were a very pleasant couple," he says sweetly. "My mom died at 76 and my dad was 89, so he did pretty good.

"I've got a wonderful family to brace me up, to give you something to live for. As long as I can stay healthy— I'm not the healthiest guy in the world, but I can still get around and try to pace myself. I sure can't run." He laughs. Roy moves quite easily, as I see when he gives me a tour of the museum warehouse.

They revel in their large family. It's their greatest joy: six children, 16 grandchildren, and 25 great-grandchildren. "We have so many in our family and most of them live nearby, so we have birthdays or family reunions two or three times a year," says Roy.

"We had a party a while back before Easter and 65 people were here, all relatives, and some friends from our church."

Their oldest son Roy, Jr., affectionately known as "Dusty," walks in and introduces himself. A blond giant of a man with a wide smile and take-charge attitude, he handles public relations for the family and museum.

"You know," Dale goes on, "you talk about attitude. It's the way you look at getting older. I mean, when I was a child, I thought that when I was 30 years old, I was going to be DEAD! To a child of six or seven, 30 seems ancient.

"The only birthday I ever minded when I came to Hollywood, was when I turned 30," she admits. "After that, it didn't make any difference. I don't feel any different today than I did then, except that I have learned a great deal and experienced a great deal. But I'm still the person I was at 30.

"To me, life is exciting," she says with verve. "We're living in some perilous days, rough days, morally, spiritually, and economically. But God is ABLE and He is still on His throne. There are those that would have you not believe it."

Do you talk with God? I ask.

"Oh, yes, of course," she replies quickly. "First thing when I awake in the morning, that's when I talk to the Lord. I talk to Him when I'm driving in my car, and at night, but not so much, because I'm tired at night. We'll have grace at the table and pray. Christ is my best friend. I can talk with Him about things I can't talk with anyone else about.

"I'm grateful for everything, even for the sorrows that I've experienced in the past, because they helped me grow. Yes, ma'am," she states emphatically, looking at me sharply. "You take a tree without storms and wind, and a tree doesn't grow. That's where the growth comes—they dig that root down DEEPER into the ground. And we should, too! I speak a lot to senior citizens, I mean people who are quite morose and some of them despise being old."

Roy adds, "Dale studies her Bible a lot. She knows it frontwards and backwards."

"I hope I am helping these older people," she continues. "I just pray I am. I pray that I will be USED, that God will use me. People ask me, 'Do you have a goal?' I say, 'Yes. I want to have a SERVANT heart, to serve others.' And that's what makes me happy—helping."

They receive a lot in return. Roy looks at a canvas in the next room and speaks with hushed awe. "That's a painting of Dale and me and Dusty. I think that's about the biggest one we've seen. A guy did that! He had to go to the trouble to make a big painting like that. They brought it in yesterday.

"People send us all sorts of things. A lot of the stuff in the museum are things that people have done for us. It surprises us, that there are so many of them," he says.

Dusty returns and hands a bit of yellowed newsprint to his father. "This is what I was looking for," says Roy excitedly. "It's a newspaper piece called 'The Value of a Smile.' People always ask me about why I smile so much. I tell them, 'It takes a lot more muscles to frown than it does to smile.' The American Mothers and the Missouri Mothers Association sent this to me." He gives it to me and I read aloud.

"'A smile is nature's best antidote for discouragement. It brings rest to the weary, sunshine to those who are sad, and hope to those who are hopeless and defeated. A smile is so valuable that it can't be bought, begged, borrowed, or taken away against your will.'"

I go on, "'You have to be willing to give a smile away before it can do anyone else any good. So if someone is too tired or grumpy to flash you a smile, let him have one of yours anyway. Nobody needs a smile as much as the person who has none to give.'"

He nods. "To me, that's the best description I've ever heard of a smile."

You smile a lot, I observe.

"Yes, I do smile, HAVE to," he replies cheerfully. "It's ME."

Dale and Roy describe their humble backgrounds and hard times in the Great Depression of the 1930s. "I think I'm the way I am because of the era I was raised in," says Roy. "I was born in the early era, the greatest era this country will ever have, from the days of the button shoes, the horse and buggy, through the Depression, right up to the man on the moon and computers. I like the earlier days better," he confides with a wink.

"Honey," he looks at me, "we didn't have ANYTHING. I came through the Depression without anything. Everybody was in the same boat those days. I signed with Republic Pictures, starting at $75 a week. Today you can't get somebody to mow your lawn for that." He chuckles and Dale nods.

"If you don't have any tough times," he goes on, "you can't appreciate the good times and vice versa. I thank the good Lord that I was born when I was, and that I got to see some of those experiences and live through them."

Dale speaks quietly, "I remember trying to get by on $5 a week for groceries in Chicago. I was always hungry and never able to buy enough to eat. It was just pitiful along Wacker Drive, by the Chicago River. People were homeless. After the banks all closed, people were jumping out of buildings, committing suicide." She frowns. "I had to SURVIVE."

As a teenager, Dale eloped with her first sweetheart. "I wish now I had stayed home and finished high school and taken some college courses," she says. "Dale did go to business school," offers Roy. "I had to quit high school to help support my family."

Things are different today. Their entertainment and business careers have made them millionaires. "I've tried to get everything in shape for the kids, in case anything happens to me," says Roy. "We've everything split equally among the six kids and it's all in trust. I'm ready any time the good Lord is ready for me. If he needs a cowboy up there, he'll have to get me a short horse." He laughs ruefully.

"Death is just a door," says Dale. "John Milton said that death is but the key that opens the palace gates to eternity. I'm not afraid."

"I'm not afraid either," says Roy. "I had this last experience with my heart and that's exactly how I felt. I stayed prayed-up all the time, and if it happened, why, it happens." He looks serene.

"I had a dream not too long ago," Dale continues. "I dreamed that I'd died. I was aware of what was going on, but I didn't feel any pain. I felt WONDERFUL. I'm not afraid. You know, the Bible says, 'He that fears is not made perfect in love.' I love the Lord and I love my family. I love life.

"When I'm traveling to speak or do a concert, people help me, which is nice. Not only that. When I get on a plane, I just take myself a deep seat and say, 'Lord, I am with you, whatever. If you want to turn this plane upside down, that's your business. If you want to get me where I'm going, that's your business, too."

Dale and Roy have pacemakers and monitor their health carefully. "I walk," she says. "We have a big house. I walk when I have to make connections on the plane. I also take vitamins, a LOT of vitamins. I do the best I can to eat right. Right now, I'm on a gout diet. I have a gouty form of arthritis, so I'm restricted to two ounces of red meat, twice a week. I don't miss the meat. I can have cheese for protein instead. I'm a great cottage-cheese person. The diet's working. I AM feeling better. And I take medication."

"Dale tells me I don't eat enough to keep a bird alive," says Roy, smiling. She looks at him affectionately. "I weigh 158 and that's low for me. I guess I used to be 165, 170 when I was working all the time. But when you get old and don't do the exercise you did, the physical work, what do you have to burn up? I just can't eat very much. I fill up quick!" He laughs cheerfully.

"I also take several types of vitamins, and I have certain pills that my doctor gave me for my heart situation. I don't do anything to push things since this last close call. And we don't drink or smoke. Neither does Dusty."

Dale excuses herself for her next appointment, and I ask a final question. Is being flexible important to stay young?

"Oh, yes," she says quickly. "We try to stay flexible in our everyday living. You don't know everything. You might think you do, but you don't. To me, life is a growing process."

"And a learning proposition," says Roy.

"I think we're supposed to learn as long as we live, as long as we have breath," she adds.

I ask to take a photo and immediately they move together like synchronized swimmers, striking a pose with their heads nearly touching, smiles bright and natural.

Roy wants to show me the warehouse. "Come on back and take a look. It's got everything you can think of." He leads me through rows of shelves holding movie reels, record albums, clothes, and gifts from fans: baseball bats, hats, artwork, and that huge get-well card that Roy likes so much.

Then he takes me to the museum, past the yellow convertible, letting one hand trail affectionately along the side. He put 100,000 miles on that car, one of about 50 that he owned in his lifetime, from sports cars to station wagons.

Do you always wear a western hat? I ask.

"When you're taking pictures, I do," he smiles broadly.

That's all your own hair, isn't it? I venture.

"Yup," he says. "Do you want to feel it?" He gives me a mischievous grin and takes off his hat, ruffling his hair. We both laugh.

What do you think of today's young people? I ask.

He heads back to the office, turns serious and shakes his head. "A lot of them are in big trouble," he replies. "It depends a lot on how they were raised. If they didn't learn right from wrong when they were little, they're going to choose whatever they want to do when they get to be teenagers.

He settles back into the sofa. "That's what moms and dads are for. There are a lot of single-parent kids that don't have the golden time they need when they're little. A lot of them end up in serious trouble. I feel sorry for them.

"I don't know what the answer can be except the way that Dale and I feel about our church. If you don't get the right guidance at home, at least you get it from your minister at church."

He doesn't like the amount of sex depicted on television. "There are a lot of pictures on TV I wouldn't even want Trigger to watch!" he exclaims, laughing and shaking his head. "It seems like the only thing left in the world is sex on some of those shows. They always talk about it, and a lot of kids are too young to know about those things.

"They're going to learn about it sooner or later, because they're human beings," he goes on. "But it's confusing to them when they're little. They hear it and try to put two and two together. Sometimes they get in trouble experimenting with something they don't know anything about. It's rough on the kids who don't get guidance from their parents."

Roy's voice becomes loving when he speaks of children. "We used to play a lot of shows for children in hospitals and orphanages," he recalls. "We adopted four children and a foster child. We also had a child of our own named Robin. She had Down syndrome and lived for two years.

"Dale wrote a book about Robin, called *Angel Unaware*. That book brought little Down syndrome babies out of the backroom," he says with pride. "We played a lot of shows, at Madison Square Garden, the Chicago Stadium, and before that book, you very seldom saw a little Down syndrome child in the audience.

"After the book came out, we saw those children ALL OVER THE PLACE. So it opened up the doors. A lot of people were ashamed of their Down syndrome babies, but we loved ours and maybe they did, too. They was helpless about doing something about it. So we decided we would keep Robin and do something about it."

Dale has written 22 books on family, religion, spirituality, and personal guidance. She also hosts a weekly television talk show *Date with Dale* on Trinity Broadcasting, a Christian cable network.

Roy's hearing aid begins to squeal again. "I've got a story to tell you about these little things," he says, removing both hearing aids carefully and placing them in the palm of one hand. They look like small peanuts.

"This friend of mine was telling a friend of his, who made them, about me. Well, he came over and wanted to make a pair for me. I said I didn't need any. I didn't have anything to compare it with, you know. This was about three or four years ago.

"Dale had been telling me, 'Honey, you should get some hearing aids or something.' I said, 'If you would finish telling me the story before you start walking two or three rooms away, I could hear you!'" He laughs. "She said, 'Well, you're using that as an excuse.' I said, 'Okay.' What could I do?

"So when this guy offered to make me a pair, I said, 'Okay, let him think I need them.' He called me after each pair and asked, 'How do you like the hearing aids?' I said, 'All right.' But I didn't put them in. I'd put them in for a little bit and then take them out.

"After about the fifth pair, I was beginning to get a little embarrassed. So when he called to ask how I was doing, I decided that I was really going to give him a chance. I put my hearing aids in and got 'em tuned up pretty good because I didn't want to be doing this in church. I got in there," his voice assumes a tone of wonder, "and I heard EVERY WORD the minister said." He laughs hard. "I didn't get sleepy or anything.

"When the choir started, I thought that I was in the middle of the Cincinnati Symphony!" He pronounces it "Cincinnata." He's been wearing them ever since. "They're small, you can't hardly see them little things. They have a teeny battery that lasts about a week and then you just get another one.

"These hearing aids open up a whole new world," he says. "It's like a blind person getting a pair of glasses. The world comes alive."

Are you still singing? I ask.

"Yes, I made a recording last year," he replies. "It was a big surprise to me. When I was honored at the Country Music Awards about three years ago in Nashville, they suggested that I make some records. I told 'em, 'I'm retired, I don't sing anymore.' But they heard me sing someplace and they wanted me to do an album.

"Well, to make a long story short, I made one, and it's still going." He sounds pleased. "I don't read music, so I had to memorize the songs. They got them to me early enough and I learned six new songs. Then I took some of the old songs, and I wrote a new one, because it sort of hits my time and place, meeting people out here in the museum."

Without my asking, he starts to sing.

> I feel like I've grown up with everybody that's alive
>   and a kickin' today.
> If it wasn't for you, there wouldn't be no me,
> That's exactly what I always say.
> I want to thank you for the many years of fun and the
>   love that always comes my way.
> I feel like I grew up with everybody that's alive and
>   a kickin' today.

"Then," he says, "I do a little yodel. Second verse.

> When I made my first picture, 'Under Western Stars,'
> They really were exciting days.
> Old Trigger was four and I was 26,

It wasn't work, just play.
Back in '39, it only cost about a dime to see a
    western every Saturday.
I feel like I've grown up with everybody that's alive
    and a kickin' today.

"I do another little yodel. Third verse.

It was a wonderful time for the kids growing up in
    an era learning right from wrong.
They used to ride the range on the little stick horse
    singing a happy song.
Many years have passed, they've all grown up,
The kids are married and moved away.
But if they keep coming by singing, 'Happy Trails,'
They are alive and living today.

"And I yodel once more."

His voice is clear and precisely on key. The song, "Alive and A Kickin' Today," is featured on the album *Tribute*, with country music singers Willie Nelson, Randy Travis, and Clint Black. Roy stays in touch with them all. "I'm raising some offsprings of Trigger, Jr., and I just sold one to Randy Travis. He just talked me out of it," he jokes. "I was keepin' it for myself, but I liked old Randy and he wanted it so bad that I let him take it!

"You know," he says, "I love to drive, too! My dad had an old Model T that I loved to drive. The last 40 or 50 years with Dale flying all over the place to all these shows a jillion times, things are booked so close together, there is no WAY you can drive," he says. "So you fly most of the time.

"Dale and I were talking, and she said her Aunt Estelle, who's 86 years old, had been sick and couldn't come to Dale's family reunion last year in Texas. Aunt Estelle's got a great sense of humor. I talk to her on the phone every once in a while. She's been to California and I just love her.

"Well, right after my birthday, right after we had a big Thanksgiving party, I says, 'Honey, let's get in the car and drive down to see Aunt Estelle.' Dale says, 'You're kidding, aren't you?' You know, it's 2,000 miles.'

"'No, I like to drive,' I said. So she said, 'Great.'

"We got ready and drove, and in two days we're in Crowell, Texas. The highways were unbelievable." His voice is tinged with awe. "You know the roads today, they're all freeways. You have to drive so fast, because the truck drivers would run over you if you didn't." He laughs.

"We spent two or three days with Aunt Estelle and had a wonderful time.   Then we came back by Carlsbad Caverns in New Mexico. Dale had never seen them, I'd seen them a couple of times. We visited a cousin she had in Phoenix, Arizona, and then came on back home. We was gone ten days and had a wonderful time." He smiles to himself and becomes quiet.

I realize that Roy is tiring, so I get up and thank him for their time.

"That's all right, honey," he says, shaking my hand firmly. "It was a pleasure. I hope you have time to go through our museum. It's full of interesting things." I do and it is. Especially the long yellow Lincoln Continental convertible that Roy likes so much.

JEANNE BEATTIE BUTTS

Born: June 27, 1904,
  Fort Montgomery, NY
Profession: Founder, Oberlin
  Senior Citizens Center,
  director, Intergenerational
  House, Oberlin College,
  social worker.
Home: Oberlin, OH

The best part of being old is feeling so free to be honest. I've never enjoyed opera particularly, and I used to think I should. Now, I just don't bother. I sure don't bother with people I don't enjoy. Time is more precious than ever and I must be selective.

I love young people. I have ten grandchildren and five great-grandchildren. They come to the family lake house in the summer and I feed them and give them a canoe and sailboat. When you feed people and give them a boat, why wouldn't they come? Young people keep you sharp. You can't be sloppy in your thinking or else they'll pick up on it very quickly. "Now grandma, that's just an assumption you're making!" they'll say.

I don't know depression. I have too much to do.

J.W. and Harriet Fulbright

"In my life, I haven't been too strenuous.
And I haven't had the idea that you shouldn't have anything to
drink or anything!"

J. WILLIAM FULBRIGHT

Born: April 9, 1905,
  Sumner, MO
Profession: Lawyer, retired
  member, U.S. House and
  Senate (1942-74), retired
  president, University of
  Arkansas
Home: Washington, DC

He deals with age by making fun of it.

"I'm just too damned old. I'm 85!" booms Fulbright jovially. His eyes crinkle under bushy, white brows and his smile widens, revealing a missing tooth. "I don't like getting old a bit," he says heatedly, then laughs.

My photographer and I are enjoying tea and cookies with him and his new wife Harriet in their elegant Federal home near Embassy Row in Washington. We sit on beautiful antique furniture upholstered in shimmery blues and beiges.

"Since my stroke last year, I can't remember names like I used to," he says irritably. "My speech has been affected. And my teeth are horrible. I'm very sad about my teeth." He makes a face. "One of them fell out this month in Korea. But I'm not going to whimper about it. What the hell can I do about it?" He laughs and lifts his arms expansively. Next week he's scheduled to see the dentist.

That's the last we hear about his health. The rest of the interview is positive, even ebullient. The senator is more interested in talking about work, friends, world events, and most especially, his new bride.

"Look at her!" he carols in a rich, gravelly voice with a thick Arkansas accent. He motions toward the slim, gray-eyed beauty. "Doesn't she look like a bride?" The former Harriet Mayor, 56, sits with perfect posture, smiling serenely. "Why, she's revived my interest in life! I smile all the time now."

He beams at her and continues joking. "You know, she's a grandmother," he whispers. "I felt better about marrying a GRANDMOTHER. Otherwise I'd have felt I was taking advantage of a young girl!" He grins. "This way, I thought,

'What the hell, it's all right, she's looking out for herself.'" They both chuckle. It's a second marriage for them both.

"She was executive director of the Fulbright Association, but I paid no attention to her. Then she got in front of a truck and got run over, and I felt sorry for her and had to pay attention." He laughs uproariously and looks fondly at her for approval. "She was in traction in the hospital and I thought, 'Anybody who would go to that trouble deserves my attention.'"

She shakes her head in mock dismay and straightens in her chair. "He very well knew I was alive before the accident," she counters with quiet dignity. "We'd had business luncheons and gone to receptions together. When I got run over and finally came home after a month in the hospital, I was hobbling around the kitchen on crutches. He said, 'I have a housekeeper. Why don't you come over here?' So I started coming for supper two or three times a week, and we became fast friends."

A romance grew. Two years after they met, Fulbright proposed. It was over the telephone at 8 a.m. "I was sitting here one morning and I thought, 'I'll call her up early, while she's bright and understanding!' What did I say?" He looks to her.

"He said, 'I'm sitting here all by myself, eating breakfast alone, and I don't like it. Marry me!'" She takes a deep breath. "I was absolutely floored. But I told him, 'It sounds like a nice idea. I'd like to talk to you about it.' So I came over that evening— and it's been wonderful ever since." She smiles benignly.

"She bewitched me," he exclaims. "How does anybody understand these things? And she's REMADE me. She's stopped my drinking. Well, almost." She objects good-naturedly. "That's right," he insists. "I haven't had a good drink but two or three times. And I don't smoke, except when I go to the club. I've not smoked in this house, have I?" he asks, looking at her eagerly. "That's true," she nods.

"It's a terrible change, a terrible change," he moans. She jumps in, laughing. "You see how he's suffering, poor man." He adds quickly, "It agrees with me. As a result, I've gained ten pounds. My clothes don't fit and I have a hell of a time. I've got to lose ten pounds. I've GOT to lose ten pounds." He looks down at his paunch.

Senator Fulbright is in his element: joking, story-telling, holding court. It's part of the dramatic *persona* he enjoys presenting, with a twinkle in his eye, a tongue-in-cheek, an affectionate glance. He is earthy, outrageous, charming, and eloquent.

Why are you still going strong? I ask.

He is silent for the first time. Finally Harriet says, "Well, he's the original jogger!" What about good genes? I ask. A positive outlook, good luck?

"Well, it's a little of all those things, I guess," he answers slowly.

Fulbright came to Washington from Arkansas. His parents had moved to Fayetteville so their six children could attend the University of Arkansas. Fulbright won a Rhodes scholarship, went to Oxford University in England, and returned to become president of his alma mater. He founded the world-famous Fulbright Scholarship Program, then entered Democratic politics. He is responsible for the creation of the Kennedy Center for the Performing Arts in Washington, D.C. He also became the Senate's most outspoken critic of America's war in Vietnam.

"I can't explain it," he says, looking puzzled. "I can't explain why the people voted for me for 30 years. Politics is a mystery to me. When you look at who's over there in the Senate today, doesn't it mystify you?" He gives a hearty laugh at my mention of Dale Bumpers, the man who ended Fulbright's reign. "Of course, I was disappointed," he says. "I didn't resign, I was defeated. Dale Bumpers is young and good-looking. He has hair. He's very attractive-looking." The elder statesman smiles magnanimously.

He, too, is attractive. Blue, blue eyes. Tanned face. Those huge eyebrows. Captivating voice. Strong physique. He watches his health. "Two or three times a week, I go to the Senate gym. I've been going up for 30, 40 years, to try to keep mobile. I do a little bit with the little ol' machines they have there, sort of press weights, but mostly bend to keep mobile." He speaks quickly.

"I've been moderate in living, you know. People who say you shouldn't have anything to drink or anything, they usually die, shrivel up like a prune, unless someone subverts them a bit," he deadpans, then flashes an impish grin.

He starts each morning by reading *The Washington Post*. "I spend entirely too much time doing that," he laughs. "It takes so long to get out of the house." Then he goes to work at the law firm Hogan & Hartson.

"I don't really claim to be a full-fledged partner," he explains. "But I go down to the office every day and I represent certain aspects in the area of foreign affairs.

"Just yesterday two men from Italy came in, clients of the firm. One of them had been a Fulbright student from Italy 30 years ago, so they asked me to go to lunch with them. I think they had fun and this man said he appreciated the program. Everyone I've ever seen who had one of those scholarships thought it was a great experience, just like I did when I had a Rhodes scholarship."

He also handles personal mail from Fulbright scholars. "Every now and then I get the most wonderful letters about their experiences," he says fondly. "It's very rewarding to have evidence of the program's effect on the lives of so many people. I respond to letters like that, because those people went to a good deal of trouble to write."

He often has lunch with clients or friends, then travels to Capitol Hill to work out at the gym. In the afternoon, he returns home to take walks with his wife in their tree-lined neighborhood. They watch the evening news on public television, read, and retire early. Occasionally they dine out or attend a party with colleagues and friends.

"He is a fun person to be with because he keeps up with things," says Harriet. "I love him to reminisce, but that's not the only thing he does. He thinks about things present and future."

Both stay active in the Fulbright program. Recently they flew to Korea and Japan to meet alumnae/i scholars. "In Korea," explains Harriet, "when a member of your immediate family dies, the unwritten social code is to stay in seclusion for at least six months, if not a year. But during our visit, people were coming out after two or three months, just to shake Bill's hand. It was more important to thank him for changing their lives than to keep this very strong code. It was amazing." Her voice is tremulous and her smile proud.

In Japan they attended an alumnae/i reception. "The Japanese are supposed to be incapable of expressing emotions," she continues. "People came up with tears in their eyes, hanging on to his hands, saying, 'I've been waiting for this moment for 10, 20, 30 years, just to thank you for changing my life.'"

For his work, Fulbright received the Onassis Prize for Mankind, a $100,000 gift. "That's the first prize money I'd ever seen," he says with surprise. "I gave most of it to George Washington University, the University of Arkansas, Oxford, and the Fulbright Alumni Association. I kept 10 or 15 thousand. I don't have a lot of money. I'm too old!" he exclaims. "What would I do with $100,000? I have everything I need, I don't need much, except my bride." He looks at her and smiles. "That's all I need."

His bride and people. "Yes, I like people," he admits brusquely. "What else is there besides people? How can you be in politics if you don't like people? How do you get votes if you don't like people? Did you ever run for office?" he asks. "You should try sometime, it's a good experience. It's different. It's not easy," he says quietly.

How about love? I ask. Is it important in life?

"Love is very important," he answers with conviction. "It's not much fun doing anything alone. The real pleasure I had in the Senate was talking with my wife about everything. She helped me. We did everything together. We were married 53 years. She had rheumatic fever when she was young and she died in 1985, just gradually, very sad, gradually faded away, a lovely woman." His voice trails off. "I have two daughters. They're wonderful girls and I go visit them in Florida and Missouri. Five grandchildren, too."

Fulbright misses his contemporaries. "Most of my old friends up in the Senate are dead," he reflects. "There are very few left of my vintage." A few remain, like Mike Mansfield, Senate Majority Leader when Fulbright was chairman of the powerful Foreign Relations Committee. Occasionally they get together for lunch. Fulbright also stays in close touch with his former administrative assistant Lee Williams and his wife.

With his sense of history, the senator has sympathy for today's young people. "I think they have an awful hard road because the older people have made such a mess of our government and community life," he observes crustily. "I don't like the inability of Congress to agree on a budget. I don't like our political system.

"Back in the 1940s, I got in trouble suggesting that we change to a parliamentary system. Everyone else has got it right: the French, British, Canadians, and Australians. Our system is a lousy, unworkable system. It's a perfectly hopeless system, and the whole world is laughing at us." His voice rises to a fever pitch and he scowls, brows bristling.

He advises young people to get a good education as a basis for everything else in life. "Take an interest in public affairs and change things," he says vehemently. "You know, Americans think they're the greatest country. They've grown up on, 'We're the greatest people in the world' and therefore don't need a change.

"We examine every issue and say this or that can be done to improve things, except our government, our society. It's always perfect, it's the best." He snorts. "We're pig-headed. We absolutely will not seriously talk about our own system. Part of the problem is that our country is too young to have any perspective."

My photographer asks if they would move to the patio and sit in the afternoon sun. They happily comply and settle into lawn chairs with fat cushions.

Are you a religious man? I ask.

"I used to go to church as a boy," he replies. "Mother was a traditional member of the Christian Church and taught Sunday school. In Fayetteville, Arkansas, church was as much a social as a religious organization. I sort of tried to figure God out and couldn't figure it out, so I stopped trying.

"I have no great religious belief," he continues. "But I certainly don't have any contempt for it. I think the Golden Rule is good. The good, practical principles of personal conduct are very good and very useful. If everybody would live up to them, it would make a better world.

"Whatever it's been, it's served me very well up to now." He leans over, takes his wife's hand, and smiles into her eyes. She puts both her hands into his and returns his gaze.

MAGGIE KUHN

Born: August 3, 1905,
  Buffalo, NY
Profession: Founder and
  spokesperson, Gray Panthers,
  founder Shared Housing
  Resource Center, social
  activist
Home: Philadelphia, PA

Older Americans have five roles. I call them the five M's. One—The Mentor. The Mentor is SO important, and in this period of SWEEPING change, to be grounded in a sense of history and see the evolution of change, is terribly important. Two—The Mediator. He helps to resolve conflict and disagreement, because he has that perspective and can listen. Like the elders in a tribe. Three—The Monitor. He watches the media, the people in public office, in city hall, the state house, and The White House. Four—The Mobilizer. He organizes groups. Five—The Motivator. He's linked with The Mentor. He encourages and gets people to be involved and to have confidence in social change.

There are three things I like about being old. First, I can speak my mind, and I do. I made a solemn vow on my 80th birthday that I would try to do something outrageous every week. Second, I've outlived my opposition. People who have put you down and said your projects would never work, are not here anymore. Third, I've been privileged, honored, and blessed to be able to reach out to others.

"I was born with a happy spirit that I inherited from my father. He was gregarious and outgoing. I look for joy in life."

PATRICK HAYES

> Born: January 30, 1909,
>   New York, NY
> Profession: Managing Director,
>   Emeritus and Founder,
>   Washington Performing Arts
>   Society
> Home: Washington, DC

He opens the door and greets us with a broad smile and hearty hand shake. "Hello, hello," he sings out. "Please come in. May I take your coats?" He carries our heavy winter wear to a closet and ushers us with great ceremony into a formal, sun-filled living room with a view of the city. "Please, sit wherever you wish. Make yourselves comfortable." My photographer and I settle in.

Mr. Hayes is a trim, pink-cheeked, silver-haired man, impeccably dressed in blue blazer, starched, striped shirt, silk tie, and polished, winged-tipped shoes. He arranges himself on an elegant, armless chair, looks at us eagerly, and awaits the first question.

Where do you get this enthusiasm? I ask.

"I like people," he replies animatedly. "I'm LOVING your being here. I'm glad you're with me. I've got an audience! We actors love audiences." He enunciates each word. "By myself, I'm as quiet as can be. I think in poetic terms, I think in terms of dreams, and I'm very relaxed. Then when I'm with you now, I'm on stage!"

He has a regal bearing and near-perfect posture, speaks with raised chin, and moves his arms in graceful sweeps. "I am not a professional actor," he says. "But my father was, and so I studied the craft. As a young man, I played on stage, in Vaudeville and in nightclubs. When I realized that I'd never be a Cary Grant or Jimmy Stewart, I snapped up the chance to enter the concert business." He laughs warmly.

Mr. Hayes became a professional concert manager, the best-known in Washington, D.C. "My job was to arrange concerts, hire the hall, engage the artists, arrange for tickets to be sold, and take care of the counting. Beyond that, there was the personal touch." He takes a breath and continues rapidly.

"I've always been in front of the concert hall as the crowds came in saying, 'Hello, hello!' I greeted people like the floor-walker in the department store. There I was, giving myself and getting it back." His face is radiant.

"Come over here, let me show you something." He jumps up and walks to a small table with a large book of embossed, cream-colored goatskin. Reverently he strokes the cover.

"When I was 70, the staff of the Washington Performing Arts Society, of which I was founder and managing director, gave me a surprise party. They presented me with this book, engraved by two English people at the Library of Congress. It's like the *Book of Kells* in Dublin." His tone is hushed.

"This will last hundreds of years. You must turn a page a day, so the pages don't mat together. You've seen the *Book of Kells*?" he asks. Yes, I reply, on my last trip to Ireland. He smiles and looks pleased.

"This book is a kind of valedictory from the board members and artists whom I brought to Washington. Each one wrote something." He turns each page carefully. "Here's Rudolph Serkin, Artur Rubinstein, Isaac Stern, Ashkenazy, Pinchas Zuckerman, Beverly Sills, there's a favorite! Alicia de Larrocha, Paul Taylor, Maria Callas. What eyes!" He lingers over her photo, then turns the pages. "Andre Watts, Victor Borge, an old friend, Leonard Bernstein, and Helen Hayes, my idol, bless her heart. Leontyne Price, an angel, an absolute angel."

For each person, he tells a story. For conductor Arturo Toscanini: "It was the biggest moment of my life, at a concert in Washington, May 1950. I always go backstage to greet artists, but this time I could not bring myself to go back for him, anymore than I would go back to call on the Pope. I stepped back when he passed by. I revered him."

For conductor Leonard Bernstein: "The last time I saw him was in August 1990 at the Tanglewood Music Festival in Massachusetts, his next-to-last concert. We went backstage to see him. He was weak, still smoking like a fiend. He embraced my wife Evelyn and, as always, said to me, 'Here's the Irishman!'

"We had a little chat and went our way, and that was the end. Here's what he wrote in my book: 'Every time we've met, it has been a ray of light for me, and so may it continue to be, world without end, Amen. There is something magical about the Irish-Jewish chemistry, isn't there?'" His blue eyes mist and he closes the book quietly.

After retiring in 1982, he continued to go to the office, acting as consultant. "Once in a while, in critical moments, I have input." He laughs easily.

"In life, phraseology means a great deal," he explains. "I never say to my colleagues, 'Why don't you do this?' I say, 'Have you thought of doing this?' or 'What do you think of this?' I provoke their thinking. Douglas Wheeler and his staff are doing a simply brilliant job. We have a stunning board of directors. I observe, I know everything that's going on, and I approve of it highly. I see what I created. It continues well, and it will be here long after I'm gone."

Mr. Hayes also does volunteer work. He's a board member of The Arena Stage and The Cultural Alliance of Greater Washington, both groups that he helped to found. He serves on the Speakers' Committee of the National Press Club and is active in the Harvard and Cosmos Clubs.

Several nights a week, he and Evelyn dress up and attend WPAS concerts. They have a special box at the Kennedy Center, and greet old friends and acquaintances. "After a concert or party, Evelyn and I come home and dish," he says enthusiastically. "'Dish' is an old-fashioned slang term, like putting everything on the plate to look at. It's lively small talk about people, events, and ideas."

Beyond work, faith keeps him strong. "More than I can tell you," he says softly. "All four of my grandparents came over from Ireland. I had a very strict Catholic upbringing and I was an altar boy in church.

"All this captures your spirit, to this extent. Once I was in a receiving line with the actor Gregory Peck. I introduced myself and said, 'I've admired you enormously. May I ask what led you to the theater?'"

His voice drops to a low chant. "'The Catholic mass,' answered Peck. 'I was an altar boy. I was in theater, I was in a costume, with the smell of lighted candles, incense burning, the ritual in Latin, the music, and I've just always been in the theater.' A lovely answer, don't you think?

"I can't say I was terribly religious in my early decades," he continues. "But as I've gotten older, I've felt some spiritual call. I pray every night and I go to Mass regularly on Sunday. I'm thankful for my health. I thank God for everything.

"I believe in God. Anyone who doesn't must have a strange angle to him as to how the universe is created, how this earth is rotating like mad, and yet we're sitting still, in the middle of it. And we couldn't just have happened." He sputters in indignation.

"We're human beings, we're bodies and eyes and ears and hearts and souls! There's no manufacturing plant for all that, except somewhere upstairs." He raises his eyebrows and smiles confidently.

"The essence of life is that we're put down here for a reason, to live a good life," he explains. "God gave us that life in the first place, and if you create something that didn't exist before and will live on after you, that's the ultimate joy. So that 20, 30, 40 years from now, I'm sure there will be a Performing Arts Society, Wheeler's grandson will be running it by that time, and there will be a public to be served and artists who need an instrument to handle them."

Mr. Hayes recalls a happy boyhood. "I had a stout heart and good health. My father gave me a happy spirit. My passion is life itself and happiness in life. I married the perfect woman for that. Evelyn is a concert pianist and music professor. In 52 years, we have never run out of topics for conversation.

"We also travel. We've been to Ireland many times, and every summer we go to Vermont, which we fall in love with all over again." They visit and entertain their three children, Bryant, Edward, and Elisabeth, who live in New York, Washington, D.C., and Paris, respectively.

Physically active as a boy, Mr. Hayes stays in shape by eating sensibly and taking vitamins C and D and cod liver oil. Every day he walks 20 blocks. Three times a week he goes to the gym and exercises on a weight machine and stationary bike. "I walk out of the gymnasium with a definite spring in my legs!" He laughs. In the afternoon he takes a nap. At night, he sleeps seven hours.

How do you deal with stress? I ask.

"I curl my toes," he replies promptly. "It's an old actor's trick, told to Helen Hayes during a run of *Victoria Regina* in the

1930s. You see, actors are always tensing the back of their necks and their shoulders. This actor told Miss Hayes to curl her toes back toward the arch, to get her mind off the top of the body. I curl them up toward the knee, too." He gleefully demonstrates, insisting he is doing it correctly inside his shoes.

He doesn't mention a close call in 1985. Daughter-in-law Gail Kearney reports that after he had an aortic valve replaced, the wound became infected. It took two operations to heal properly, and for three weeks he was in and out of consciousness. His wife and daughter stayed by his hospital bed, talking to him and playing news radio. After three weeks, "he woke up and was fine. His doctors call him a walking marvel."

Young people gravitate toward the Hayes. "That's the theory in academic life," he says, smiling. "Evelyn's father always had teenagers in his choirs and loved his advanced and best pupils. Evelyn feels the same way, and so do I.

"I go to the WPAS office every other day and I rejoice, looking at all these young people so eager at their work. There's fire there, fire! There's an old phrase in show business, 'Unless you have fire in the belly...!'" His face lights up and his eyes shine. "You MUST feel that passion. Something ignites it, another personality ignites it, just as your questions ignite me." He looks triumphant.

He has great faith in some of today's youth. "There are all kinds of young people," he says. "Lech Walesa, the Polish leader, spoke at the National Press Club and said, 'Every generation takes off from its own launching pad.' I believe that while all launching pads are similar, they are not the same.

"The difference is the timetable of movement, of decades," he continues. "Two hundred years ago, you and I would be talking on a farm. One hundred years ago, we'd be talking in an industrial society, with coal mines and cotton gins. The 1900s have been a fast-moving century with TV, technology, and the pace of the cities becoming almost too much. Those things affect people.

"The young people today are going faster than in the last century. But the pace of their lives doesn't change who they are. I would think there must have been a man like me 200 years ago, and I'm sure there will be a man like me 100 years from now. The circumstances around him may vary. He may dress differently, but he'll THINK the same way.

"The mind of humanity doesn't change that much. In every generation, there are those who lead by being educated. They are trained to speak well, to lead, to organize, to get things done, to invent things."

What is your advice to young people? I ask.

"Enjoy your work. Ten years ago I spoke at a commencement and said, 'Now, you're going out to become what they tell me are members of the "me" generation. Set out to be the best "me" on the block! You'll get a job and if you don't like your boss, QUIT at the end of 30 days. If you don't like your job, quit at the end of the year and go somewhere else.

"Of course, you must do diligent work, homework, and have persistence.' That's the kind of life I had, growing up in a small New England town," he explains. "The spirit of life, the way things were simple, honest, direct, and leisurely. The 1700s and 1800s were all that."

Mr. Hayes tries to live that philosophy by staying flexible and keeping a sense of humor. Most of all, he savors what he calls "the grace note." He looks at me intently. "You know, in music, there's something called the grace note." He lifts a hand and touches two fingers together. "It's an extra note, a little tiny note.

"I look for the grace notes in life. The little touch. Sometimes it's a gesture, it's a manner.

"When I get on the bus, it's so amusing. There's always a young woman who offers to get up and give me her seat. And I'm taken aback! I say, 'No, I feel fine.' She says, 'Well, I thought you might want to sit down.' I say, 'Did I look that tired?'" He laughs gently.

"That's a grace note. A gesture she made to me, a kindly thoughtfulness. More people should have it." He smiles at me and nods sagely.

LILLIE

AND

RALPH
DOUGLASS

Born: September 3, 1907,
  Rosh Springs, Indian
  Territory, OK
Profession: Pharmacist, retail
  merchant in Native American
  crafts, Methodist medical
  missionary, world traveler
Home: Sedona, AZ

Born: January 27, 1906,
  Anadarko, Indian Territory,
  OK
Profession: Pharmacist, retail
  merchant, missionary, world
  traveler
Home: Sedona, AZ

 illie

Look at what there is to do left in the world! We like to read, we like to talk, we like to go. Our family encourages us, our two daughters and their children and grandchildren. We've been married 67 years and we're still in love. We've had a wonderful life together. My husband has contributed constantly to that by being kind and considerate and gentlemanly. He also likes to drive a car or a trailer or motor home in all kinds of countries.

alph

A lot of older people get mad at each other when they get old. For some reason they don't get along. You have to have some love involved or you don't go ahead. I kiss her three or four times a day to keep her in a good humor. Every day I go to the post office and grocery store, do a bit of work in the yard, and then we have a Scrabble game or dominoes or cribbage. We like to play all kinds of games together.

Ruth, Skitch, and Rex, their Lakeland Terrier

"Don't look back and don't look forward. Look today.
Have something today!"

SKITCH
HENDERSON

Born: January 27, 1918,
  Birmingham, England
Profession: Pianist, conductor,
  founder and music director,
  New York Pops Orchestra
Home: New Milford, CT

Skitch strides onto the stage of Carnegie Hall and waves expansively to a glittering audience. He is a tall, silver-haired
man in white tie and tails. His orchestra of 15 years, the New
York Pops, plays "Happy Birthday" and he grins and bows in
appreciation. At 80, Skitch Henderson is receiving a stellar birthday tribute from peers, fans, and benefactors.

It's been a long journey from his native England to New York,
by way of Hollywood and a lot of small towns. His 60-year career
in music has touched many people, some of whom have gathered
tonight to honor him. Masters of Ceremony Liz Smith and Mike
Wallace introduce a host of stars, including Isaac Stern, Steve Allen,
Cyd Charisse, Tony Martin, Julius La Rosa, and Tony Danza. One
by one, they appear and tell personal stories about Skitch. They
call him talented, generous, funny, and amenable.

Amenable, explains comedian Steve Allen, because
Skitch graciously played "The Man in the Street" in Steve's
sketches on the old NBC *Tonight Show*. It was a tough job,
quips Allen, but someone had to play the straight man. The
audience laughs appreciatively.

The maestro basks in the warmth of his party. He thanks
each participant, embracing the men and kissing the women.
He taps his foot and sways to the music. Occasionally he con-
ducts while his guests sing—Martin's "Dancing in the Dark,"
La Rosa's "Where or When," and Danza's "It's Almost Like
Being in Love."

He also conducts an overture that he first played with the
NBC Symphony Orchestra. His body twists and weaves, leaning forward to pull sweetness from the violins, hunching over

to quiet the trumpets, and straightening up with arms flung wide to bring the musicians to a final crescendo.

Skitch Henderson is in complete charge, exuding self-confidence.

So it's a great surprise when he later confides, "My big passion is WORRY. Really!" He gives a short laugh.

He's swept into his conference room like a dashing pirate, handsome in open-necked white shirt, billowing sleeves, and snug black pants. His luxuriant hair is slicked back and a silver goatee frames his pink face rakishly. He takes my hand in his huge one, shakes it warmly, and in a deep and resonant voice, welcomes me to his office at Carnegie Hall.

The moment he sits down, he says that he has one hour for me.

I take no offense. I know that he's busy. I've just glimpsed him bent over a music score in the next room. "The Little Drummer Boy," he explains. "I'm conducting it with the Harlem Boys Choir at a Christmas concert."

I come back to the question, Do you really worry?

"Yes, I WORRY," he repeats earnestly, looking hard at me from under large, bushy eyebrows. "I'd like to say it's doing the very best I can, which I ultimately try to do. I can't think of EVER resting in a four-poster bed without the crank going in the brain, trying to figure out what didn't work the night before, or what I have to face three weeks from now. Why didn't that work with some orchestra and it works with the next one?" He shrugs his shoulders.

"It's not that it's unhealthy," he goes on. "But it's a kind of middlebrow existence—the constant worrying about what's around the corner."

His major worry came in 1986 when the Pops was three years old. "The first two years were wildly successful," he says. "Then suddenly the next year, we led a foul year." He leans forward, face serious, voice low. "Admission fell down maybe 9 percent and our marketing people became very nervous. I thought, 'God, am I going to fall off the cliff again?'

"Then attendance came back up," he straightens and smiles. "It's been a solid platform since then. This season's series is sold out. The last 15 years I've had my concerts here at Carnegie

Hall once a month and our concert series is sold out every year. We are a success, we're ALTOGETHER a success." His voice rises and he thumps the table with his fist. His grin shows perfect rows of pearly teeth.

"My staff and the orchestra, they charge like tigers," he says. "And they're PROUD." Skitch's *basso profundo* grows warmer. "They talk to each other about how well they played, which I love. You can't BUY that. In the last ten years, 95 percent of the orchestra has been constant with me, here or on tour. Every other year, we tour the Orient and Florida." At ten concerts per tour, that seems a grueling schedule. Skitch insists that the orchestra loves it, and that inspires him. He plans to keep it up.

He also wants to expand the Pops' children's programs in New York City schools. "I started these programs because it was time I paid my dues and gave back," he explains. "I just made up my mind these last few years of my working life that I want to really work in the schools. It's important that schoolchildren be exposed to music and play music that's easy and contemporary.

"First we have 'The New York Pops Salute to Music.' Every year some of our musicians volunteer and give instrumental lessons to 120 junior-high kids. Then we bring the best kids in to play with the Pops. Oh, yes, they play in the performances," he notes my surprise. "I just had two percussion players do Ravel's 'Bolero' with us. I mean, who could HAVE that experience when you're 12 years old?" He throws up his hands in excitement.

"Our second program is 'Kids in the Balcony.' That gives schoolchildren who've never heard an orchestra a chance to attend a concert. The schools pick the kids and bus them in. We give them free seats. The kids have to be clean and presentable. They have the most FANTASTIC time." His voice quickens and he trips over his words. "When I stand on that stage and hear the roar that comes from that top balcony, it's just unbelievable."

His third program involves rewriting music for children to play in schools. First Skitch polled children on what kinds of music they'd like to play in their bands and orchestras. Then he gathered a group of arrangers to write the music.

"It's simple, contemporary music for kids," he says. "I got the idea at a meeting with about 600 city music teachers and visits to conduct school bands. I was so APPALLED by the music they had to play," he groans. "I found that a lot of that music was copied out by the teachers." He shakes his head in disbelief.

A young office assistant enters and places a plate of small, yellow cookies in front of us. "Would you like one?" he asks, blue eyes twinkling. I accept, and the first one explodes with buttery-coconut goodness in my mouth. "You'll never get thin on these," I tease. He laughs loudly. "My wife Ruth makes them and they're delicious. I just can't resist." He tosses down a couple and grins in satisfaction.

Is work your greatest joy? I ask.

"Yes, it is," he says, after a slight pause. "I suppose I should put my life at the farm with Ruth first." He sounds a bit sheepish. "But I think she would agree with me." Ruth and Skitch have been married for 41 years and she keeps a solid anchor at home in rural Connecticut.

When they bought a 200-acre farm, she oversaw conversion of an 1830s dairy barn into their new house. Next door she established The Silo, a cooking store/school and art gallery that draws guest chefs and visitors from around the world. At Christmas, Ruth sets up a huge evergreen tree that reigns over holiday festivities. Skitch is proud of her work and says I must visit them at the farm to take photos.

"Ruth was a golden wand in my life, because she came along at almost a crossroads for me," he says lovingly. "Radio was ending and television was beginning. She's German and she brought me the great German culture, the art, the education in the schools. She had that basic knowledge that we're fighting for our kids to have now. She's just been an incredible support system."

Skitch also speaks fondly of his mother, a church organist. "She got me started in music. She sent me to the London Conservatory of Music when I was six." Later he attended the Paris Conservatory.

"My mother was my best friend. She died when I was very young. My father couldn't understand that she would thrust me into the field of music. He thought playing music was the most ridiculous thing in the world, that boys should go out and get a job or drill an oil well. So I had that dichotomy when I was young.

"My father sent me to live with his sister in Minnesota. I ran away right away," he says easily. "That's how I stumbled into Hollywood."

Stumbled? I ask. It sounds like you had a guardian angel.

He pauses and smiles. "Yes, I think somebody watches you," he says, thoughtfully. "I believe that you keep your fingernails clean and blow your nose and—that's it." He relaxes, leaning back in his chair.

He returned to England to serve in the Royal Air Force. During World War II, he met Bing Crosby. "He told me I shouldn't be flying planes in North Africa," recalls Skitch. "He said it was too dangerous for such a talented musician!"

Crosby pulled some strings and got Skitch transferred to what is now the U.S. Air Force. When the war ended, Skitch returned to Hollywood and worked as piano accompanist for Crosby, Frank Sinatra, and Peggy Lee.

Later he joined *The Tonight Show* as orchestra leader, conducted the NBC Symphony, and in 1983, fulfilled his dream of founding The New York Pops.

Along with success comes touring and guest-conducting. Skitch is on the road six months of the year, most recently in Savannah and Montreal. The physical travel has become "too much," he says. "But I'm not letting up. You know why I really take these jobs?" he asks in a stage whisper. "Because you can't be a SNOB." He pauses dramatically and fixes his eyes on mine.

"I don't think you can sit and say, 'I'm a star and I live in New York and I'm working Carnegie Hall, and screw the world.'" His voice booms. "I spent so many years trying to get my foot in the door as a conductor of other than Tinkertown orchestras. Now I have the ECSTASY of working with Swedish Radio, the Oslo Philharmonic, Hamburg, Berlin, Munich! It takes so LONG to get there." He takes a deep breath and sighs.

Sometimes Ruth accompanies him. "She came when I toured New Zealand and she often goes with me when I tour Germany because she has family there," he says.

They keep August free. "That's MY time," he says emphatically. "Ruth and I have some property in Vermont. I sold my airplane last year, but I'm still an avid glider pilot and we have a WONDERFUL soaring club in Sugarbush. I go up there and soar and talk to the birds. Very quiet." His voice trails off and he closes his eyes.

Suddenly he looks at his watch, stands up, and ends the interview. We shake hands and he reminds me to telephone Ruth for a visit to their farm. As I leave, I see him working on his score.

A week before Christmas, I drive to Connecticut on winding, country roads through woods and small towns. With some difficulty I find the farm. Ruth, a striking beauty with short, silver hair and bright red lipstick, answers my knock at the sliding-glass doors. I enter a huge main room with a two-story vaulted ceiling. Skitch waves from the kitchen table, where he's just finishing some editing and Ruth offers me a mug of hot coffee.

We sit down on big, comfortable couches and I marvel at the multitude of red and green decorations. She acknowledges her handiwork and enthusiasm at the holidays.

A beautiful Steinway baby grand piano, covered with framed photos, sits in one corner, and I can't resist. I ask Skitch if he would please play something, and he graciously agrees.

Settling onto the piano bench, he stretches his long legs to the pedals and waits a moment before starting. His hands ripple up and down the keyboard, his head bends slightly, and his body moves with the rhythm. The music floats through the house and I think, what a spectacular treat to hear him make music.

We settle in for a talk and Rex, their eight-year old Lakeland Terrier, jumps up and nestles in Skitch's arms. The Hendersons are preparing for the arrival of their children Heidi and Hans Christian and their children, for a Christmas celebration. "Heidi's children are seven and eight, and Hans' are teeners," says Skitch. "They come to the farm because that's the PLACE for them to come. They can run around, tear up the world if they want, or sleep in, if they want.

"I get along with them very well. I get along with them because they are in awe of my MACHINES. Yes, exactly!" He grins. "I take them for rides on the tractor. That's my grandfathering.

"I don't want to be a doting grandparent. I just want to be their FRIEND. Sometimes they come to Pops rehearsals and I bring them up to sit on the stage of the orchestra, so that they experience what a big orchestra sounds like. Of course they want to play the drums right away." He chuckles. "Everybody wants to play the drums."

Skitch looks robust. He says he feels good and doesn't think about his age. It was quite different when he was 50. "Then I was conscious of growing older, very conscious. Isn't that funny?" he muses. "'My God!' I thought. 'Will I live through 2000?' His face contorts slightly.

"Then in my sixties, I looked at the age factor a bit, looked at the calendar. That was all." He flicks a hand.

"Now, in the past 20, 25 years, I never think about it," he says. "In fact, I beg Ruth not to give me any more surprise birthdays." He looks at her and they smile.

"On my 70th birthday, she gave me an unbelievable party, just an unbelievable party!" he exclaims. "EVERYBODY came, people and artists whom I loved, not necessarily whom I've worked with, but artists I really worshiped, from afar even, in the opera house." He has always loved opera. "The party was wonderful, it was wonderful. But I told Ruth, 'Please don't do that again.'" He sighs gently.

He doesn't feel different from when he was a youth. "Does that make any sense?" he wonders out loud. "I feel no difference at ALL. I still worry about how I dress and if my shoes are shined—the things I worried about when I was 18 years old, when I was trying to feed myself in Hollywood!" He guffaws.

"You know when it kills me?" he asks impatiently. "When somebody in the orchestra calls me 'old man' or something like that. I know it's not a form of derision. They just say, 'Well, you're older, you have all this—experience.'" He laughs. "I want to say to them, 'I have the experience, but you don't HAVE to say I'm a senior citizen.' He pretends to look hurt.

"Now that I'm older, people do not treat me differently. Except headwaiters!" he jokes. "Nobody else does in New York. You know that. In Des Moines, they'll open the door for you, but not here." He looks at me knowingly.

Age has not made him slow down. It's actually helped him maintain a fast pace, because he knows he has a limited number of good working years left. "Old people tend to get pushed around," he says. "At my age, it would bother me terribly to

have somebody push me around. I guess that's why I keep working!" He raises his eyebrows in understanding.

I ask about patience. He sighs.

"I used to be always polite and try to figure out a way to
get along with somebody I didn't agree with or they didn't agree
with me. I'd always figure a way to round the corner. But I
don't anymore.

"I can be—not obnoxious," he picks his words carefully.
"But forceful. That's a kind word. They used to call me Hitler
at NBC!" He roars with laughter. "I didn't find that out until
they tore up the music department and disbanded the NBC symphony orchestra."

Skitch plays as hard as he works. Collecting antique tractors and steam engines is his hobby. "I love my toys because
they help me relax," he explains. "When I'm really frustrated,
I can go and mess around, cleaning the boiler in my steam
engine for four hours, and I LOVE it. When I first came to
Connecticut, my neighbor Arthur Miller, the playwright, talked
to me about diesel fuel. That was his first lecture to me. A very
important thing! Diesel fuel to keep the tractors going."

His favorite "toy" is a 1954 Massey Ferguson steam
engine, which he installed in his front yard. "I just bought a
1954 Allis-Chalmers restored tractor," he goes on. "And I have
an International Harvester tractor.

"I love machinery, because machinery is sound, it's smell,
and it's precision, just like MUSIC is sound and precision.
Instead of an odor, machinery has an aesthetic odor. It has a
pleasure to it—if it works. And all my engines work!" His
voice is rhapsodic.

"You know, if I hadn't been a musician, I'd have been a
machinist or a pilot. I still fly—I just passed my flight physical
six months ago. My doctor says I'm in good shape. But stress at
work does take a toll. Once in a while, the blood pressure starts
creeping up, and then I'm very careful with my diet—for a while."
He winks. "I eat everything. Ruth's a wonderful, wonderful cook.

"I'm really a barbecue soul," he confesses. "In the fall, I
work with some orchestras," he speaks *sotto voce*—"I don't want
to be too public about it, but some orchestras I love to work

with simply because of the barbecue stands in their cities! Very FAMOUS barbecue houses.

"Other than barbecue, though, I do eat carefully, most of the time. Oh, sometimes I'll take vitamins," he says offhandedly.

Several years ago Skitch broke his back when a wagon fell on him. "I thought the CRASH had come," he says sadly. "I was flat on my back about three weeks in one of those iron maidens.

"Then this wonderful young woman walked in." His voice warms. "I don't think she ever said hello, just barked at me, 'Get out of bed.' 'I can't,' I said. 'If you can't, I leave,' she said. 'You want to get out of bed and say hello to me?' You know, that's a cruel thing to say." He makes a face. "But I got up and with her help and therapy, I just knitted back together. I didn't need surgery."

Do you exercise? I ask.

He rolls his eyes upward and laughs. "I worry and sweat so when I'm working that I don't exercise."

Conducting is a type of cardiovascular workout, I offer. His eyes light up and he nods appreciatively.

Prompted by his wife's behavior, he stopped smoking years ago. "I used to smoke only cigars," he explains. "But when I married Ruth, she smoked more cigars than I did."

Really? I ask.

"Oh, sure, the German ladies smoked," he says. "That kind of turned me off. So I quit smoking. I still have a good humidor," he adds proudly.

"And I never drank. I have an occasional glass of wine. I was lucky. With all the catastrophic societies and people I've worked with, I never fell off that trolley. Somehow, I kept straight ahead."

Skitch has a yearly physical, eye exam, and dental checkup. "I'm lucky to have my eyesight," he says. "I don't wear glasses. When I'm conducting, I just won't back up, and I have to read scores all the time. They're pretty hard to read." He knocks on the wooden table. "I've been fortunate."

He'd like to travel less. "I wish there were a magic way that somebody could wave a wand and you'd be on the podium at St. Petersburg tomorrow," he says longingly. "A good example: I'm here on a Friday night with my orchestra. Next morning I rehearse with a symphony in Canada. That's hard. It's hard for your mental process. If you show up for your first rehearsal, you should know what you're doing!"

He needs only six or seven hours of sleep a night and doesn't nap. "If I take a nap, it's hard for me to crank up. Bob Hope used to talk to me all the time about naps when we played the fair circuit with Jack Benny. Hope would say, 'I can sit any place and nap, and that will save you.' But I never learned to do it. If I sleep solidly for half an hour, it takes me two hours to get going again." He grimaces.

Skitch wakes up slowly in the morning. Lying in bed, he plans the day. It's a far cry from former times when he hit the ground running. "I think I'm old enough now to know that I might fall down," he cracks. "Each morning, I always try to re-construct what has to be that day and what I didn't do yesterday.

"I never make lists. My wife goes CRAZY because I don't make lists." He laughs. "I generally remember things, and I have a great young staff at the Pops."

I ask what he thinks of American youth?

He frowns and speaks with urgency. "It's easy to say today's kids are going down the tubes, because too many of them ARE. But it's not their fault. It's OUR fault. It's whoever we are," he says fiercely. "It's what we've handed them or what we've failed to hand them.

"You have to seize the opportunity. I did, when my mother encouraged me in music. That's one reason I set up the children's programs at Pops. I wanted to give these city kids an opportunity."

He was baptized Lutheran, but is not religious. "I don't go to church, but I'm drawn there," he explains quietly. "All the years when I was on the road and lonesome, I used to go to the Catholic churches, because generally they had an organ and a choir. There was something there that held me together. When we moved to Connecticut, I surveyed the organs in the churches. And that's my wand of togetherness. I just want to go sit in the back of the church and contemplate." He smiles serenely.

"I believe in God. Oh, I'm sure I do," he says quickly. "I prayed a lot during the war like everybody else. I was scared to death! I knew there was something, something that kept me together. Now, occasionally I'll pray. I'll tell you when."

He leans toward me and becomes intent. "Sometimes when I'm with a strange orchestra and really have a catastrophe to face, and I'm not sure I know exactly what I'm doing. I will sit in my dressing room and look to somebody—and it must be God." He sounds a bit surprised at his own words.

Do you meditate? I ask.

"I've thought about it many times," he answers. "Especially the last ten years, because we play Japan every other year I have gone to the temples there, and I think—I don't know what it is—but there's SOMETHING." His voice grows soft. "There's a spirituality that somehow rests on your skull. You can't walk away from it, if you continue being around a certain kind of a—and I use the word advisedly—a 'cultured' Japanese. It's a different life from ours."

After taking photos, I thank him and Ruth for their hospitality and compliment him on his sense of humor. He is visibly pleased. "You can't be in the music business if you don't have a sense of humor," he laughs. "You'd be a maniac! Because the things that go on, on and off the stage, just with orchestras! The TRAIN WRECKS that you have, the musicians that you play with, and the soloists that you play with."

Eccentric? I ask.

"That would be the kindest word I could say," replies Skitch.

"I can't imagine a nine-to-fiver having a life like we lead," he goes on. "We're gypsies. We travel. I'm on the road all year, really. I'm lucky now that the last 15 years, I've had my concerts at Carnegie once a month. So that brings me back. That's been a wonderful solidarity platform.

"If I had a wish now, I'd wish that our orchestra were 50 years old! I'd like to be remembered as the person who made The New York Pops a huge reality. I want this band to be a city institution.

"And I have NO plans to retire," he adds impetuously, flashing a huge smile.

HELEN KEARNS RICHARDS

Born: November 25, 1899,
   Gunnison UT
Profession: Matron and
   volunteer, Church of Jesus
   Christ of Latter Day Saints,
   radio broadcaster, teacher
Home: Salt Lake City, UT

Every day I do something. My husband died about five years ago, and after 67 years of marriage, I decided I had to organize my life. For the first time, I was absolutely free to do what I wanted to do. There is a satisfaction that comes from knowing you can do the wise thing. On Monday, I wash and clean house. Tuesday is Temple Day: I do ordinance work in the church. On Wednesday I visit four or five friends who are in nursing homes. They inspire me. That's the spirit of service. Sometimes I bring my prune cake. The rest of the week, I visit shut-ins, meet with church study groups, and see my family. I play the piano nearly every day to give myself happiness. On Sunday I go to church.

I can drive, but not at night. I like my independence. I don't want to impose on others. I have lots of friends, four children, 14 grandchildren, and 23 great-grandchildren. I'm never lonely, never bored.

Time passes so quickly. Up to age 90, I felt I had unlimited time. Since then, I've felt an urgency to get things done.

I'd like to live as long as I'm useful to my family and friends. I want to contribute and make a difference in their lives.

You go through different stages. I remember a stage in which I loved to shop and travel. I'd always be looking for things to bring home. Now I don't want to be burdened with things. I've got more than I need. I'm always thinking, "Whom can I give this to? Who would like this?" I remember the great actress Helen Hayes saying, when someone offered her a gift, "I'm at the 'de-thinging' stage." That's where I am.

My secret is to turn away from the mirror! Then you forget how you look. I don't FEEL old at all!

"Love is very important,
as long as you've got integrity going with it. If it's just love for
selfish reasons, that's not going to help you."

THEODORE HESBURGH

Born: May 25, 1917,
   Syracuse, NY
Profession: Catholic priest,
   social activist, President
   Emeritus, University of Notre
   Dame
Home: South Bend, IN

Father Hesburgh moves fast.

He runs up stairs for exercise. He flies around the world to meetings. He attacks mail, research papers, newspapers, and magazines with fervor. When he finishes work, he ploughs through books for pleasure.

"I learned early on that I wasn't the kind of person who could be satisfied doing just one thing," he says briskly, sitting in his office at the University of Notre Dame. A compact, barrel-chested man with wavy white hair and a smile that crinkles his eyes, Father Ted, as he's affectionately called, wears olive slacks, an olive plaid jacket, and a color-coordinated tattersall-checked shirt. Like many Catholic priests, he no longer dresses exclusively in clerical garb.

"I'll be succinct," he says, setting the tone of our one-hour interview. "As far as I can remember, I've always had about four or five major jobs at the same time. I founded five institutes and worked on each of their international boards. Now I'm chair of the advisory board of the peace institute." The Kroc Institute for International Peace Studies is based at Notre Dame, along with the four other institutes on human rights, third-world development, ecology, and ecumenism. "Basically, the ecumenism institute works to get religions to stop fighting each other, like they're doing in Yugoslavia and the Middle East," he says dryly.

His latest job is working for peace in the Mideast. He was appointed by the U.S. Secretary of State to the Anti-Incitement Committee, a group of Americans, Israelis, and Palestinians who work to implement the Wye Plantation Treaty.

"Our problem is to keep the thing from blowing up," says Father Ted. "Now that Israel has a new prime minister, I think we're going to be quite successful in getting that treaty totally implemented. As soon as Ehud Barak puts his government together, we're going back with some joy, because we have a man who believes in peace.

"Up to now, I've been running back and forth to Jerusalem like a yoyo," he says. "I was over there three times in about three months. It took a lot of time, effort, and NERVE, because the tension was very high. It really kicked me in the head!" He looks surprised. "But I felt this was a special call on peace."

His schedule is grueling. "You leave here on a Sunday morning early and don't get over there until 3 p.m. Immediately you've got a meeting, then dinner, then prepare for the next day's wrestling match, trying to keep peace." He takes a long breath. "They literally told us, 'You're trying to keep us from hating each other.' I said, 'You're darned right! Because if you keep on hating each other, you're going to wind up killing each other, and then there won't be any problem.'"

He leans back in his chair behind a desk piled neatly with papers. Floor-to-ceiling bookcases cover the walls, and tables hold family photos, statues of the Virgin Mary and St. Paul, a large crucifix, and model airplanes. Classical music plays softly from a vintage radio.

Father Ted is looking forward to his next trip to Latin America. "We have a good number of alumni in Guatemala, Salvador, Honduras, Nicaragua, and Panama. Our ambassador in Honduras is a Notre Dame guy. Every so often, I go in and tell them what's happening in the university and talk about world problems. I've been doing it for years. This'll be a two-week trip."

Travel is second nature to him. He flies regularly to Washington, D.C., for meetings of the U.S. Institute of Peace. That job is a presidential appointment which he's held for ten years. He also flies around the country to speak at Notre Dame fundraisers.

When he's home, Father Ted stays in close touch with 50 world organizations that tie into his institutes. "Half the mail I receive is from this network," he says, motioning quickly to desk papers. "They all publish stuff and they're all looking for money." He smiles ruefully. "I funnel everything I get to our director, so we don't reinvent the wheel. If someone else is doing it, you can take their results and not duplicate."

He often guest lectures on topics he says he knows "a little about," including a class, "The Civil Rights Revolution." Father Ted was a charter member and served 15 years on the U.S. Civil Rights Commission.

"I rather enjoy those lectures," he says. "I can still GET the students, I think. You can sense that—if nobody's going to sleep." He chuckles. "You've got to have your heart in it." Teaching is his first love, the first job he had at Notre Dame in 1945.

He continues to receive honorary degrees from institutions of higher learning, a total of 141, a world record, documented in the *Guinness Book of Records*.

With all his contacts, he's often asked to be honorary chair of fund-raising groups. "I'm on over 50 of these groups," he says.

So you're far from lazy? I joke.

He pauses imperceptibly. "I'm fundamentally lazy, but I've conquered it!" He laughs triumphantly.

"When you're retired," he continues, "everybody figures you have nothing to do. So I probably turn down 50 invitations a month. At one point, I made up my mind not to socialize or play golf or bridge any more. I don't have time. My relaxation is new projects, facing different challenges.

"Reading books is my recreation. I have a dozen or so that I've half-finished, one on Pope Paul VI, who was a good friend of mine, and one on Amundsen, the Antarctic explorer. I don't read them until my work is done, and that's sometimes 2 a.m."

He eagerly relates his new formula for retirement. "Do as MUCH as you can, as WELL as you can, as LONG as you can! Don't gripe about things you can't do anymore. The last part is the most important, because there are so many things you CAN do. I could say, 'Oh, I have a terrible eye problem, I can't read like I used to.' But instead I say, 'I've read two books in the past three weeks.' You have to look at the positive side.

"Some people retire, go to seed, die the next year," he goes on sharply. "They just turn it off. Maybe they miss the activity. The phone isn't ringing anymore, the mail isn't coming in. But I'm lucky. I'm here at the office, things are going on, kids are in and out, the mail comes in every day, a stack two feet high in two weeks. That's what will be here when I get back from Latin America.

"And the phone's ringing all day long! I got a call from a Notre Dame graduate, a woman student who's trying to get into a Chicago law school. She says there's a great Notre Dame guy at this school, and would I put in a word for her? Sure!

"The first day she calls, the second day I call him, the third day she calls to say she got in." He lowers his voice and looks paternal. "She needs a little boost.

"That goes on a thousand times. You're like everybody's grandfather. You're THERE, they know you're going to listen and give them the best advice you can. It's mostly just standing with them. My old friend Charlie Sheedy, a dean here at Notre Dame, says, 'You know what life is all about? Just showing up.'"

Once Father Ted took a vacation. It turned into a year of travel around the world with Father Ned Joyce, his friend and fellow educator. They were both 70 years old and had just retired from 35 years at Notre Dame, Hesburgh as president, Joyce as executive vice president.

"I wanted to do this as a clean break," says Father Ted. "And this was about as clean a break as you could get." He throws back his head and laughs. "Driving an RV out west— neither one of us had ever been in one of those before, or prepared meals. We each lost ten pounds, but that was good. We both needed it!

"We took a little airplane over Alaska," he relates with relish. "We went down the Amazon in a ship. We worked on the QEII as chaplains and sailed around the world. Then we went down to Antarctica for Christmas." From detailed notes he kept, he wrote *Travels With Ted and Ned* (1992).

He's aware that he's aging and gives it a positive spin. "I'm feeling great," he says. "Oh, sure, you get a little creaky as you get older and my eyesight isn't as good as it was. I have macular degeneration in my right eye, and it's getting worse. But I can see peripherally, and I can still read. I've got a wonderful doctor at Johns Hopkins University. They're the best in the world, the Wilmer Eye Clinic. I got my cataracts taken care of there. Now I get check-ups every six months.

"Apart from that, you thank God for 82 years of terrific health and no problems, and you go on from there. Someday the old 'bod' is going to give out. When that comes, it comes. It's no big deal." He shrugs and smiles broadly.

"The biggest thing about health is really mental," he continues. "I had an EXCRUCIATING pain in my back and I ran into a book by a guy at the Rusk Memorial Hospital in New York. He said it's mind over matter. He explained how the mind creates a lot of these things to distract you from doing OTHER things that you ought to do. So you just admit it, believe it, and every time the pain comes up, you deny it!

"I talk to my brain. I say, 'Knock it off, I've got other things to do.' As a result, the pain is practically gone." He smiles with satisfaction.

Just to be safe, he does back exercises every morning.

And he prays. "I pray all the time," he says. "The fundamental core of my life is the priesthood. I say Mass every day here in my chapel." He indicates a room next to his office. "I say the prayer 'Come, Holy Spirit' throughout the day. I have a lot of faith in prayer because there are so many things you can't solve any other way. I think the good Lord does hear it. He said, 'Knock and the door will be opened.'

"When I was young, I thought the greatest thing a priest could do was be in a parish. I did that during World War II in Washington, D.C. It was very satisfying, like being a doctor in an emergency room.

"Then I got into university teaching and began to see the long-range effect on people's attitudes and values. I still get letters from kids I taught 50 years ago, saying, 'I never forgot what you said and it's really carried me through a lot of problems.' He fixes his eyes on me. "I don't remember," he says. "I don't remember what I said. But at least, there it is!" He smiles warmly.

Father Ted wanted to continue teaching, but his church superiors had other ideas. In 1949 he accepted the position of executive vice president and in 1952 he was named president. His social activism blossomed.

"I do a lot of stuff you may say has no relation to priesthood. But I think working for justice and peace has A LOT to do with priesthood," he explains. "Even as president of Notre Dame, I say I had 14 different jobs. Many of them were presidential appointments."

His reputation grew. Students would point to a campus statue of Moses, his finger raised to the sky, and say, "There he goes!" referring to Father Ted's frequent trips away from school. At a recent toast/roast, he heard one friend tell an old joke, 'What's the difference between God and Father Ted? God's on campus more often.'" One alumnus told me, "He really was an American ambassador for the Catholic Church."

Father Ted is unapologetic. "I never TOOK a job which I felt I couldn't honestly do it as a priest and as an educator. I turned down a lot of interesting jobs because of that. President Lyndon Johnson asked me to head up NASA, the National Air and Space Administration. I've been a space and aviation buff all my life.

"But I refused, because I felt it would be inappropriate for a priest. NASA was going into a $6 million Apollo program to land on the moon, and I could just see some Baptist down in Georgia saying, 'That damned priest turned me down on my contract and gave it to some guy in Massachusetts!'" He laughs heartily.

"The important thing is that your life is in some kind of order. And mine was. I was a priest of the Congregation of Holy Cross and I had these three vows of poverty, chastity, and obedience. I'm perfectly conscious that if I'd followed my own inclinations—teaching—I would not have done or had the opportunity to do practically everything I did in my life." He looks quietly satisfied. As a young man, he studied in the U.S. and Italy, learned several languages, earned advanced degrees, was ordained, and became a working priest.

He lives simply. Home is a room in Corby Hall, which houses Nortre Dame faculty. "I have a small room, like a Motel 6—minus," he says. "A bed, dresser, closet, a shower, sink, and john. It's all you need. There's a study I can use in the dorm, but I don't, because I have this office."

Located in the main campus library, the office keeps him in touch with students. "Around here, you're not allowed to get old, because every time I come into work, I get a big confab in the elevator with the kids," he says happily. "I always ask them what they're studying, and we get into an argument. They're very friendly, if you're friendly with them."

He runs into students on his daily walk to the Grotto, a campus shrine. "I'll say, 'Hi, how's it going?' They may say, 'Okay,' in a subdued way. I say, 'Hey, wait a minute, you don't get by with that. What do you mean, "okay?"

"'Well, things aren't all that great,' says the guy.

"'Do you want to talk about it?' I say.

"'Well,' says the guy, 'my girl just told me she didn't love me.' I say, 'Well, that's no reason for jumping in the St. Joe River. It's cold!'" The St. Joseph River runs through South Bend.

"I say, 'Did you ever stop to think that maybe that's one of the best things that happened to you lately? Because you think you love her. But if SHE doesn't love you and you put your lives together just because you love her, and it's a big disaster, well, it's a lot more honest for her at this point to say she just doesn't love you.

"'Let me tell you something,' I say to the guy. 'There are more women than men in the whole world. And there are millions of very attractive women who would be wonderful life companions. The greatest thing they can do for you is to say, "I like you, you're my friend, but I don't love you." That's a favor. It's a blow to your pride because you think you're God's answer to all women. But for that, you've got to be grateful.'

"Then I say, 'The sun will come up tomorrow morning and the birds will continue to sing, and a few weeks from now you'll meet another girl who's even more attractive than the one you think you love. And maybe she'll love YOU. If she doesn't, pray God she tells you before you go overboard.'" He pauses and looks at me sharply.

"It's an encounter with the kids, ships passing in the night. I don't know the kid's name. I'll probably never see him again. But it's part of a symbiosis of young people and older people living together. Sometimes you can put their horizon out there in a way they can understand. It's your perspective."

He lives his job of educator. "Education enlarges everybody's potential," he says fervently. "Learning languages is important. Every language allows you to be a different person. Every language opens up a whole world. Don't worry about pronunciation—just be a ham, be an actor, and launch out,'" he booms. "Whether you pronounce it right or not."

As a student in Rome, Father Ted was determined to learn French, Italian, and German all at once. He forced himself to memorize ten words in each language every day, then use them in conversation. He achieved his goal.

"People ask me how I learned Spanish? I always say, '*Como un niño, oyendo y practicando, sin miedo y aun sin verguenza.*' 'Like a child, listening and imitating without fear and even without shame.' Just do it!" His eyes snap and he looks slightly impatient.

"Great chunks of my life would not have been possible if I couldn't operate in another language," he continues with gusto. "The Ecumenical Institute in Jerusalem—we put that together entirely in French, with an international committee. There's always some guy who knows only French, so you've got to run all the meetings in French, or else double them by translating everything. It's much easier to do it in a language that everybody understands.

"And Italian was very useful, because at times I had a lot of work around the Vatican." Father Ted was the Vatican representative to several groups, including the International Atomic Energy Agency. He also served as counselor to four popes, including the current Pope John Paul II.

He likes being around young people. "They have enormous wells of good that you can bring out, IF you give them the right kind of advice," he explains. "They are capable of great heroism. The greatest heresy handed out to young people today is that they can't make a difference, the world is too big, too complicated, politics is bad. You've heard it all.

"I say to them, 'You CAN make a difference. I'll give you a whole list of individual people who made a difference. You just pick a lady like Rachel Carson. She wrote a book called *Silent Spring* and today we have all over the world an environmental movement that we didn't have before.' That book had an ENORMOUS effect on the world.

"Even the kids who are lost can be saved. You've got to have confidence in them. You've got to love them fundamentally, because if you don't love them, you can't touch them at all, and they know very quickly.

"When I had the freshman residence hall at Notre Dame, I had 330 freshmen. On the day they arrived, the first and most important thing I did was to learn their first names. If you don't know their first names, you're out of the ball game right then and there." He looks at me intently.

Besides getting a college degree, Father Ted advises students to do what they love. "I tell them to learn what you want to do and like to do, because as a professional, a person does best in what he likes to do. If you're going to be a doctor or a lawyer, teacher, priest, health worker, social worker—these are all professions. A professional is a person who's at the beck and call of anybody who needs what he has to offer. It's not a matter of money or prestige or power or anything else.

"If someone knocks at my door here at the office, he gets in. He gets in right away. That's always been my policy. If you're available, it's amazing how much you can do for young people."

Above all, he believes that one must try to be a good Christian. "That's terribly important," he says. "Love thy neighbor as thyself. And be a good Samaritan. It's not enough just to be compassionate to the problems that are so endemic throughout the whole world today, enormous problems affecting millions of people. You've got to be committed to do something about them." He speaks forcefully.

"For example, you drive by an accident on the highway. If you're a doctor, you might say, 'Gee, that's tough, that car looks really banged up.' But you don't stop because you might be sued for malpractice or something. That's a terrible thing that's happened to our society." His voice becomes sad. "People are impeded from reaching out to other people because of other consequences.

"When you get to the end of your life and appear before God in judgment, the only thing you've got to offer Him for your life is what you've given away of yourself, or your means. You enrich yourself to the extent that you empty yourself.

"We have a tradition at Notre Dame where students volunteer, here and abroad. Seventy percent of the students do volunteer work now," he says proudly. "That's up from a single volunteer when I came here. We'll get 100% someday," he states assuredly.

Are you more patient as you get older? I ask.

He pauses, one of the few times he doesn't answer quickly. "I think older people tend to be a little MORE impatient, but I watch that, I try not to be," he says quietly.

"The biggest thing is not taking yourself too seriously, because you're not WORTH taking that seriously, I don't care who you are. If you take yourself too seriously, you put yourself in the middle of everything, which is egotism."

He speaks carefully. "It's also important to not let anything intrude on your inner peace of spirit or peace of soul. I've always tried to practice that. I can be in the middle of a really tough situation and I'll be at peace, simply because I'm doing all that I can. I've always tried to follow the advice, 'Don't worry about things you can't control.'

"If the main university building burns down, so it burns down. You build another one. There's no sense falling apart about it. Or if you lose a finger or a hand, no point in getting all that excited about it. You've had it all these years, be grateful for it." He speaks matter-of-factly.

"Don't let people get you rattled and don't get rattled yourself," he goes on earnestly.

"Do FULLY what you're doing. Don't worry about what you're going to be doing an hour from now, or what you just finished doing. You make decisions—I make them fairly quickly—and you put down your money and take your choice. Then it's over. You go on to the next thing."

His no-nonsense attitude extends to a health regime. "I try not to eat as much as I used to. Sure, I eat meat, but less than I used to. I exercise every morning, because I have a bad back. I do exercises for stretching the back, then I do 20 bends to the floor, 75 half push-ups, and 20 squats. A squat is something you need as you get older," he explains.

"You just have something to steady yourself—it can be the back of a chair, the post of a bed, almost anything. You squat literally to the floor, as far down as you can go, then you get up again. You don't pull yourself up, you use the back of your leg muscles. Those are the ones that start to atrophy as you get older. What you're getting at here is keeping your muscles alive, when normally they would dry up. I get those exercises out of the way right after I shave and before I shower.

"I used to climb 100 stairs every day, whenever I was at my office," he goes on. "Now I do only 60 or 70. I found I was puffing a bit and thought, 'Let's not overdo it.'" He smiles. "Instead of getting off the elevator on the thirteenth floor, I now get off on the ninth or tenth and climb up to the thirteenth. People spend a lot of money buying machines for that! I've got it built in here." He taps his chest. "That's very good exercise to get the heart pumping, kind of blows out the valves. I also walk about half-a-mile just about every day around campus."

He drinks moderately and smokes cigars. "I give them up for Lent," he confides. "It's nothing! I don't inhale. And there's no place you can smoke anymore. At the end of the day when I come back to my office, I can have a smoke. Cigar smoking is the best way to give up cigarettes. I used to smoke about two packs of cigarettes a day, but I quit in 1970. Yeah, my lungs are clean," he says easily.

Every few years —"as little as I can," he laughs—he goes to the Mayo Clinic in Rochester, Minnesota, for a medical check-up. "I haven't had any major illnesses," he reports. "I've been very fortunate. I haven't missed a day's work in all these years.

"As far as sleep, I get as much as I can get. People kid that you don't need sleep when you're older. That's baloney. Normally I'm up until about 2 a.m.. You can't get anything done around here, during the day because of phone calls, meetings, drop-ins, homework, and reading."

When he and Father Ned traveled, they went to bed early. "I sleep like a rock," he says. "I don't need pills or anything. Sleep is the easiest health thing in the world. It lets your body renew itself."

He voices some concern about his eyes, but immediately returns to a positive note. "I've had 82 years of wonderful eyesight. I've read probably 16 hours a day all my life. So I've gotten more than the mileage you'd expect. Sure, I read a little slower. But you've got to be a realist. What is, is!"

"Be grateful for what IS and HAS BEEN, and hope for the future," he advises. "Hope is a great virtue all your life, especially as things mature. If there's trouble reading, I've always got this." He touches a magnifying glass on his desk. "If I need more light, I've got this." He points to a halogen lamp. "It's great, it's terrific. So why worry about it?" His voice is impatient.

Father Ted keeps current every morning by tuning into WBBM Radio, a Chicago all-news radio station. Then he turns on television to watch CNN (Cable News Network). He reads only *The New York Times*. "You read that every day, you're up on current events. It's really the paper of record. I don't read the local papers or even the Chicago paper.

"I used to watch the television network evening news when I could, but I find CNN much more effective. I can catch it every hour during the day. Occasionally I enjoy Ted Koppel at 11 o'clock on ABC. But with my kind of a busy life, you can't do it all the time."

TIME has been a favorite since 1937. He regularly reads five or six other magazines, and selectively reviews ten more professional journals and publications from his 50-member organizations. "In the age we're living, it's important to stay abreast of current events. Otherwise you can't work in it and judge it—and BETTER it."

Has age mellowed you? I ask.

"I think I am much more liberal today than when I was younger," he answers. "I was probably stricter with people when I was younger. I'm a soft touch today, but that's because you begin to see that people have a lot more good than evil in them, and you take account of that.

"I think I am more optimistic today than before," he goes on. "I realize that if everything is in order—rules, regulations—if it all had to be done with precision, then you could run the world with a computer. 'This set of facts, this person did this, Bingo, put them in jail!'" He snaps his fingers and looks officious.

"As you get older, you say, 'Well, this student got in trouble, but—first of all, he's young, he didn't know what he was doing. Second, he wasn't malicious about it. Third, he probably had a couple of drinks and he wouldn't have done it if he was sober.' So the real lesson is to tell him to watch his drinking, rather than kick him out of school."

With abiding faith, Father Ted views death with humor and equanimity. "If I could pick a way to die, I'd just as soon die in an airplane crash," he says with a laugh. "The advantage there is that you've got time to say, 'Lord, I'm on my way, open the door!' It would be a lot EASIER to die quickly. But you don't know how you're going to die.

"Death is not an ending," he says. "It's a beginning and it's a much better beginning than an ending. You can really say, 'You ain't seen nothing yet!' Because the Lord himself said He couldn't find words in our language to describe what God has prepared for those who have loved Him in life.

"People should look forward to it. In fact, there's a word in the canon of the Mass which says, 'Look forward with joyous hope.' That's a pretty good combination of words to the coming of our Savior, which happens when you die. You meet your Savior and enter eternal life. That gives you enormous possibilities that are so good, you can't even describe them.

"It's going to be one of the greatest surprises of all time," he continues animatedly. "You're going to be able to do things you can't do now. I've got a small planet out in the asteroid belt named after me, and I expect to visit it after I die."

I raise my eyebrows and smile.

He nods and his voice lightens. "When you die, you can be someplace in the spirit, just by thinking about it. You can't do that if you have to haul a BODY around. When I die, I'm going to do some pretty inter-stellar travel, I hope—among other things," he adds quickly.

He rises, signaling an end to the interview. I thank him and he shakes my hand firmly.

"God bless you," he says.

RUTH WARRICK

Born: June 29, 1916,
St. Joseph, MO
Profession: Actress, Unity
Church teacher
Home: New York, NY

Retiring is anathema to me, partly because my work is something I love. I've been playing Phoebe Tyler in *All My Children* for years on TV. I can understand that somebody who's screwing a bolt or hammering something would want to retire and try something else in their lives. But not when it's a creative force you're using. The creativity is your life blood. That's the strongest thing that keeps you going, using all your faculties.

As you mature, you let go and drop a lot of the things you thought were absolutely *de rigeur*, that you had to do, or had to have, or had to say. It's like shedding a skin. I think it's important to keep an open mind. Don't indulge in hardening of the categories. That's just as vicious as hardening of the arteries.

When I was young, I had low blood pressure and my doctor said, "I'm going to tell you something to do, and you'll probably hate me, but if you can do this the rest of your life, it will add a lot of years and energy to you. Take your warm bath or shower, whatever you please, then turn the cold shower on, full blast. This will make your circulation go and it's as good as running a mile, because it really gets your heart going." I did, I stayed with it. I warn people that I sometimes scream and yell. They say, "How long do you do it?" I say, "About a minute."

There's no way we can exhaust everything there is to learn, to know, to enjoy. If you let yourself be bored, then yes, you are bored and you'll probably become boring. Be helpful to somebody or be available for an emergency. Get a group around you that becomes more than casual friends.

Remember that your body has a perfect pattern in it. We're born with that, it's part of the sacred nature of your being. Although part of a pattern may get out of whack now and then, if you do a healing meditation and ask for recovery of that part of your anatomy and believe that it is done to you, it can be. Honestly, it can be. The world is full of that kind of miracle.

We have a saying in Unity: I go to meet my good. It's out there waiting for you. Sometimes you have to go find it. Dance, care, laugh, sing, and be joyful. When we can laugh and sing, it's much easier. We're put on this earth for that.

I love what the Chinese say: long-lived, not old. The demographics of our country are swinging in that direction so powerfully, I think we're going to have to use older people in a lot of jobs. There are not going to be enough young ones to do them all. Young people need our counsel. A mature person probably understands about caring more than anybody else does.

"Mother used to say, 'You take your hide to the marketplace yourself.' That means you have responsibility for your life. Live it well, period."

HILDEGARDE

Born: February 1, 1906,
  Adell, WI
Profession: Singer, pianist,
  entertainer
Home: New York, NY

Hildegarde stays young by sheer will and discipline.
"I keep on DOING," she says in a strong, throaty voice. "I keep at the piano. I just retired from show business, but I play and sing at area hospitals and nursing homes. My friend Maurice Chevalier once said about aging, 'I prefer it to the alternative! To dying." She laughs shortly. "I agree with him.

"People should do what they have a talent for, or volunteer. I often sing at the Mary Manning Walsh Home uptown and the Mt. Carmel Home in the Bronx. I just call them up and say I'd like to come. They APPRECIATE it. I perform all alone at the piano. I'd like to start going to a home on Staten Island and give of myself to them.

"The people at the homes are younger than I am, but they look so old, and they can't understand that I have all this," she says. "I sing and play and joke for one and one half hours. They know my age and just don't know how I do it.

"I always say, 'Lord, help me to be youthful, vital, and useful. And bless my face.'" She laughs unabashedly. "Because that's the first thing you see.

"I also go to hospitals for the veterans. I'm so effective with those boys." At 90, "The Incomparable Hildegarde," as she is known in show business, still brings joy to audiences with her sublime nightclub act.

At home in her East Side apartment, she sits with regal posture, camera-perfect blonde hair, and a dazzling sequined pantsuit.

Her living room is filled with paintings, prints, and *objets d'art* in crystal and porcelain. Framed photos of celebrity friends cover her piano.

Until a year ago, Hildegarde performed in shows and cabarets around the world, including New York's Carnegie Hall,

Town Hall, The Russian Tea Room, and in London at The Palladium, the Prince Edward Theater, and Pizza on the Park.

At age 89, she formally retired at a Town Hall Tribute to Oscar Hammerstein, where she sang "The Last Time I Saw Paris." She recorded a CD, *The Other Half of Me—The New Songs of Bernie Bierman*, and received lifetime achievement awards from MAC (the Manhattan Association of Cabarets and Clubs), Bistro (U.S. and Canadian Nightclub Associations), and the Daniel D. Tompkins Foundation in New York.

"I think it's time to step aside and let the youngsters take over," she says, referring to Margaret Whiting and Julie Wilson. "Sixty-nine years is a long time in show business and I've decided to retire. My junior partner Bill Wright passed away from AIDS this year, and that affected me deeply. I decided I just didn't want to break in a new pianist or deal with rehearsals, dress fittings, and the anxiety and stage fright anymore. That's enough, I've had it." She speaks quietly, with dignity.

I express surprise that she has stage fright.

"Of course, all the time!" she cries. "We never know whether we're going to be good or not. We never know how audiences are going to accept us. It's really an anxious time."

It's also a magic time when she and the audience connect. "You get in front of an audience, you give something of yourself, and you want them to forget themselves," she explains. "No matter what their problems are, I like to have them in my world. In MY world.

"Of course, when I'm finished, that's when it's sad. They say, 'Oh, that's finished,' and leave. That kills me."

Work keeps her vibrant and inspires her to stay in shape physically and mentally. "Show business is all I know," she says. "I achieved it on my own, with hard work and great support from my mother. She was my first piano teacher. When I was a girl, she told me, 'If you want to do something in your life, you have to practice and apply yourself, and don't just think of the boys too much.' And I did.

"I practiced, I worked hard. I knew what I wanted. I wanted to get into show business. I got better as I went along and one job begat the other. I was never out of work.

"I could have married and had children. But there was a drive there. I had a talent and I had to express it. I was good." She states it as a fact, not a boast.

Would you please play something for me? I ask.

She acts surprised, then delighted. Apologizing for her voice, a bit hoarse from a cold, she walks over to her Steinway concert grand piano and sits down on a bench. Lightly running her fingers up and down the keyboard, she asks, "What would you like to hear?"

I request her signature song, "Darling, Je Vous Aime Beaucoup."

She smiles and says it was written by her agent Anna Sosenko in 1933, as the two of them were bicycling in a British War Memorial Cemetery in France. It tells of an American boy in Paris falling for a lovely *mademoiselle*, wooing her with his few words of French.

Hildegarde begins to sing softly.

> Darling, *je vous aime beaucoup,*
> *Je ne sais pas* what to do.
> *Vous avez* completely stolen my heart.

Her voice is warm and flirtatious.

> *Matin, midi, et le soir,*
> *Toujours* wondering how you are?
> That's the way I felt — right from the start.

Her hands ripple up the keyboard.

> *Ah, chérie,* my love for you is *très, très fort.*
> I wish my French were good enough,
> I'd tell you so much more.

She lingers on the last word, then resumes singing.

> Oh, darling, *vous êtes très jolie,*
> *Qu'est-ce que* c'*est vous* do to me?
> Absolutely, *je suis* in a trance.

Her voice becomes shy and coquettish as she begins the second verse.

Tout le temps j'espère que vous
Dream of me *un petit peu.*
Ah, chérie, je pense this is romance.
Quand nous sommes alone and you are in my arms,
Je remercie le bon Dieu pour all your lovely charms.
Dites moi, Do you love me, too?
Je suis happy if you do.
Darling, *je vous aime beaucoup,*
I love you, yes I do.

She ends slowly, pulling out the last line to a breathy sigh.

It is a superb performance. Thrilled, I applaud and she acknowledges it with a slight bow of the head. Again she apologizes for her voice, but I insist it sounds wonderful.

"Even though I don't feel my best," she confides, "when I talk with you, I've got something. I've got SPIRIT. It's always there. It's been that way since I had my first show business job in 1926. I've been dedicated because I had to express myself musically. It was a drive. It was a career. I made money and I helped my parents."

Onstage she shares generously. Offstage, Hildegarde is a very private person. "I don't need too much social contact," she says softly. "All my close friends are dead. Yes, I go out, I love to dress up, I love to go to the theater and symphony. Occasionally friends come over, we'll have drinks and I'll take them to a restaurant for dinner.

"But I'm sort of a quiet, introverted person," she says. "I enjoy staying home and reading a good biography or autobiography. I like fiction that has a good, strong story, like Danielle Steele, Taylor Caldwell, or Irving Stone. I read to relax. I think reading is more important than watching TV. You can form your own picture in your brain. Keeps you working up there!" She touches her head and smiles.

That ease with being alone stems from a strong faith. Raised Catholic, Hildegarde wanted to become a nun when she was 18. "But the priests talked me out of it," she laughs. "They said, 'You've got a personality, you've got a talent, you belong in show business.'" That clinched it for her. She jumped at a theater career.

"I've always been very religious," she says fervently. "I believe in taking care of the soul before taking care of the body. The soul is immortal, the body will die. You take care of the soul, this great something that is in you, and it either goes upstairs or downstairs or in the middle, which is purgatory." She laughs. "I prefer to go up, to heaven, RIGHT AWAY.

"I try to go to Mass every day. When I was on tour, I would always find a church. Always, always, always. If you're Catholic, you jolly well have to go to Mass and holy day services. Otherwise, that is a sin. It's not gray   it's black or white.

"I say the rosary daily," she goes on. "I say it for the collapse of Communism, I say it for the Pope, for the poor souls in purgatory, for all my friends, my relatives, and for the people I'm estranged from, if that's possible." She stops to reflect. "I think I'm estranged from a few people." She chuckles.

"I pray a lot. I say, 'All right, God, what is your will for me?' I abide by it, although I might stamp my foot." Another laugh. "I say, 'Come on, that's not the way to answer my prayers.' Well, He's my Father. I've always been that way." Among her awards is the highest papal honor given to a layperson: Lady of the Equestrian Order of the Holy Sepulchre of Jerusalem.

Hildegarde tends her body as carefully as her soul. "I've always taken care of myself. I believe if you don't dominate nature, she dominates you," she says sharply. "Every day I have a routine, a discipline. I even do isometrics with the face twice a day to keep the muscles from sagging. If you exercise the body, you have to exercise the muscles of the face."

You haven't had a face lift? I ask, marveling at her tight, firm face.

"No," she says, turning to show me the profile. "It's pretty good for 90." She laughs.

I compliment her on her eyes—no drooping lids.

"Really?" she says. "Well, I blink! I try to remember the eyes when I'm doing the face exercises. I blink, blink, blink." She smiles at the image, then looks at me. "You have a pretty smile. You have pretty teeth. Take care of them," she admonishes in a motherly tone. I thank her.

Her autobiography *Over 50...So What!* (1962) details her health regime. One reason she takes such good care is that her mother, father, and a sister died of cancer. Another sister had colon cancer and survived.

Hildegarde visits a doctor and a gynecologist twice a year for check-ups, an eye doctor every year, and a chiropractor when her lower back aches. "I believe in chiropractors," she says. "They work!"

She took vitamins before they became popular. "Natural vitamins every day of my life, since 1950," she says proudly. "I had a friend in Milwaukee who taught me how to do it. It makes sense because I'm on a diet—I always watch what I eat—and I don't get all the nutrition I should. So I get it from vitamins. I take a handful every day."

Junk food is out. She eats simply, avoiding red meat in favor of fish, fowl, and veal. "I don't eat the 'whites,' like sugar, salt, and white bread. I eat a lot of fresh vegetables. I actually eat very little. That's what keeps my weight down."

She weighs herself every day and if she's gained a pound, she immediately cuts back. "My weight is 130 and I'm going to stay that way," she says staunchly. "I take no alcohol, except a glass of white wine at dinner."

Her daily routine, she jokes, is "very peculiar." She gets up around noon, a habit acquired from years of performing at night and going to sleep late. First she drinks a glass of juice with a tablespoon of rice bran, and puts on a favorite face cream. "Then I lie down, say the rosary, and do my facial exercises," she says. "After that I have a piece of fruit with my vitamins, 14 different kinds. Down they go! That holds me for quite a while.

"Around 4 o'clock, I have two pieces of toast with soy-bean margarine from the health food store. That holds me for three, four, five hours. You see, I know how to spread it out, spread out the eating. When you're hungry, you eat. And I'm never really hungry.

"Late, around 7 o'clock, I may take another piece of toast while I watch *A Current Affair* on TV. That and the 10 o'clock news are the only things I watch. I read *The New York Post* every day. That takes two hours. The print is clear and bright."

At 10 o'clock, she eats a salad, followed by broiled meat or fish and a cooked vegetable. If she's performing, she eats dinner before going onstage, "to give me strength." Later, she may have a small bowl of cereal before going to bed.

She aims for eight or nine hours of sleep. "When I have that, I feel SO good," she says brightly. "I walk with a good, snappy clip. But if I don't get that sleep, I feel like Grandma Moses." She laughs.

"Sometimes I wake up prematurely, with songs surfacing in my head, and then I lose two hours' sleep. But I say to myself, 'Don't go back to bed. Get up, get in circulation, do your chores, go to your appointments, keep on going.' I never humor myself about this problem."

Even though New York City water is reputed to be excellent, Hildegarde drinks only bottled water, Mountain Valley Water of Hot Springs, Arkansas. It came to her attention when the company president attended one of her performances.

"John Scott, the president of Mountain Valley Water, was a friend of mine," she says. "He came to see my show at the St. Regis Hotel in New York. I had to drink some water onstage, and I made a face. The next day he sent over a case of his water with a note: 'Here, you'd better try this. You won't make a face.'" She throws back her head and laughs.

"Now I drink it all the time. They even made me the company's vice president-at-large. It's the best water in the world, just remarkable. This water has no bacteria in it. I praise it every time I'm onstage."

She is not as enthusiastic about exercise. "But it's necessary and I do it every day. I go to the door and stretch to 50 counts, so I feel tension in the whole body. I'd like to do it in a class with others. There's one just across the street in the Turtle Bay Club." She points out the window to another building, where I see people exercising, boxing, and lifting weights.

She pushes herself to go outside and walk. "Otherwise I'd feel too isolated and confined, and I don't like that," she says. "I like to walk 20 blocks a day, which is a mile. Sometimes I can't make it, and sometimes I do more. I like to visit the Metropolitan Museum of Art and the Museum of Modern Art."

Do you wear sneakers? I ask.

"No, I wear shoes that have Cuban heels. I do have a pair of sneakers," she adds quickly. "But it just goes against me to wear them, because I'm always dressed nicely, and when you wear sneakers at the bottom, that clashes. Yet everybody does it today. It isn't pretty." She looks at me archly.

"I do enjoy fashion. If I hadn't been in music, I'd have liked to be in the fashion business. I have gorgeous clothes for my performances." Hildegarde was famous for luxuriant, full-length gowns that highlighted her wasp waist. She always wore long, white kid gloves and carried a handkerchief.

Work and constant travel made it difficult to maintain romantic relationships. "One thing I regret, I didn't marry," she says softly. "I had a lot of love affairs. I was in love with Maurice Chevalier. HE was young at heart." She pauses.

"Teri Garr's father Eddie was one of my lovers. I had a big, big thing with him. We almost got married, but then I went my way and he went his way. He met Phyllis, a Radio City dancer. Their daughter Teri Garr is a very lovely person. When she was eleven, all three of them visited me in Los Angeles when I played the Statler. Now she's on the cover of *People* magazine!" She smiles fondly.

"Marriage never worked out for me," she goes on. "I love children. When I see a baby, something happens to me in my heart, and I say, 'Oh, gee.'

"Some people do it all. Today the Hollywood people seem to do it, but not when you're traveling like I did in Vaudeville. It's impossible. It just wasn't meant to be. I was given a talent and you have to obey that."

At one time, she wanted to be a painter. "See this?" She motions to an oil portrait on the wall. "That's St. Cecilia, the saint of music. I did that when I was 18. My teacher was Sister Angelica, a Dominican nun at St. John's in Milwaukee. She told me, 'You've got such talent, you must pursue painting.'" Hildegarde smiles.

"At the same time, I was musical. I said, 'No, sister, I'm going to go with music. I think I can make more money that way.' I had to think of that. I had to help my family."

Hildegarde graduated from high school and attended Marquette University Conservatory of Music in Milwaukee for two years. "It was run by Jesuit priests and was a very splendid university," she says. "I started with classical music. I wanted to be a concert pianist, but I just didn't make that. So I went popular and became good at it. First, as an accompanist, then I went out on my own.

"I stayed two years at conservatory, but then I had an offer that was too tempting not to accept. It was to play with a traveling piano group, 'Gerry and Her Baby Grands.' I was 20 and it was 1926.

"I went to the Palace Theater one afternoon and I saw four white baby grand pianos on the stage and four beautiful girls dressed in white colonial costumes and white powdered wigs." Her voice grows rapturous. "I saw their act and was thrilled with it. I thought, 'If I could be one of those girls, get into show business and out of Milwaukee.' I wanted it BADLY. I auditioned for Gerry and she offered me a job in her second group. It was the only offer I had and I grabbed it!

"My mother encouraged me to take it. She said, 'You go to have your career.' My father said, 'No, she'll never make it in music. She should be a stenographer.' And mother said, 'She is leaving! She's got talent, she's got a chance to go in show business with Gerry, and she's got to GO.'

"Mother wanted to be an opera singer. She had a gorgeous voice. Her mother wouldn't allow it, because she thought to be in opera was sinful. She said the voice was meant to use in church, only for God. So mother wound up an organist. She taught herself how to play the organ. She never had a lesson and yet she read difficult music, Gregorian music, when she had her choir in Milwaukee.

"Well, finally, when I had been with Gerry for a while, we appeared in Milwaukee. Father was dying of cancer and I asked if he'd come to see me. I had a box for him and he said yes.

He saw me and was SO proud. I looked up to the box and said, 'How are you doing, Father?'" She smiles to herself. "Later he told me, 'To think that I never gave you much credit for wanting to be in music! I was wrong about you and music.' That was a few months before he died."

Hildegarde never regretted her decision. "We're all destined for something. Some people become nuns, priests, doctors. I had to be in show biz. I obeyed my calling. I worked hard and used the talents God gave me. I think we all should.

It's a sin to waste talents. We all must use talents, no matter what field we're in." She speaks passionately.

She invites me to see her apartment. It's exquisitely furnished with velvet-cushioned chairs, classic tables, and cabinets that hold statuettes, goblets, and chalices. On the walls hang prints and paintings, one by French artist Raoul Dufy, and memorabilia: awards, programs, magazine covers on which she appeared, and a *New York Times* ad for Bonwit Teller department store.

"That's when Bonwit had big mannequins of me in their windows. I'm very sentimental, I have to keep everything," she confesses. "So I frame everything. That's the only way you save it. Otherwise, it deteriorates."

On the piano are autographed photos of Harry Truman, Ronald Reagan, Eleanor Roosevelt, Mamie and Dwight Eisenhower, Pat and Richard Nixon, and Nelson Rockefeller. "Here I'm dancing with Conrad Hilton," she says with affection.

"Here's Noel Coward, Tallulah Bankhead, Cardinal O'Connor, and my piano teacher Isador Achron. There's Irving Berlin, Fritz Kreisler, Maurice Chevalier, Alice Faye, and me, onstage at Carnegie Hall for my 80th birthday.

"That's King Gustaf of Sweden. He was a big fan of mine in Paris. And Michael Feinstein, he's a darling. We both appeared in London at the Prince Edward Theater. I followed him. He's given his life for his artistry, too."

She points to several photos of her family. "Here's one of us in 1947," she says lovingly. "Mother sang and played organ, father played violin and the drums, a strange combination. My sister Honey played cello, sister Germaine played violin, and I played piano. We had little trios at home. People came and listened to us. It was very sweet. We were full of music, all of us." She smiles gently.

Hildegarde takes me into the kitchen. The walls are covered with dozens of envelopes. "They're from a fan," she explains. "He's hand-painted each one. I offered to go to the president of Hallmark Cards and have him work for them. But he said no, he didn't care for that sort of thing." She sighs. "I just don't like to see talent wasted."

Affixed to the wall are spiritual messages: "God bless this house," "Trust, believe, and you will receive," "Do not fear, do

not fear what may happen tomorrow," and "Let Go, Let God."
She taps the last one. "That's a tough one," she laughs.

"I believe in every one of them. I especially like Plato's
definition of music." She reads, "'Music is a moral law. It
gives a soul to the universe, wings to the mind, flight to the
imagination, a charm to sadness, and life to everything.' It's
quite something," she murmurs. Her taste in music runs the
gamut, but she leans heavily to the classical, especially sym-
phonies. "Chamber music," she states, "has no character."

You seem very positive, I observe.

"Sure, I see some of the dark side of life, but I don't let it
bother me," she says with conviction. "I just go along my merry
way. What happens, happens. It's meant to be. I cooperate
with destiny.

"Whatever length of life God gives you, you have to
accept. Maybe I will die next year, maybe I will die at 95. But
I'm prepared. I've arranged with my church to give me Last
Rites. And I'll arrange for my church to get me cremated. It's
all taken care of in my will."

She is vehement about not wanting to linger. And she wonders if euthanasia is not a better way. "I'm sorry that euthanasia is not allowed in my church," she says. "I wish it were,
because it must be terrible to linger and suffer, and eventually
die anyway. If it's six months or a year, let the doctor be able to
give you that final...." She breaks off, looking troubled.

What is your advice to young people? I ask.

"Work hard to make something of yourself," she says
immediately. "If you have talent and want to get places, you'll
jolly well work. You can't just sit back and say, 'It's coming to
me.' You've got to go out and GET it.

"Keep in mind that a career is really a love/hate thing. Ask
anybody," she says. "My manager Anna Sosenko was wonderful. She was tough in business, but we got the respect. Sometimes we'd fight like mad. I didn't like what I had to do.
Sometimes I didn't like to work at my career. I thought, 'I hate
this, I hate it, I hate it.' But I listened to her and without her, I'd
never have become famous.

"You must have inner resources," she continues adamantly. "And perseverance. Many a time I wanted to give up because I wasn't doing too well. My mother said, 'Uh, uh. Now, come on!'

"I remember one time I was in Europe and told her, 'I need $95 to get home on a German ship.' Mother said, 'I won't send it to you, you just see it through.' She did not send me that money. She just said, 'Face it, you can make it.'

"And I did." Hildegarde laughs triumphantly. "I did."

JOHN HENCH

Born: June 29, 1908,
  Cedar Rapids, IA
Profession: Artist, senior vice
  president, Walt Disney
  Imagineering
Home: North Hollywood, CA

My eyes are still good. We artists use our eyes and change focus all the time. Focus is purely a muscular problem. When we look at something and make a drawing or painting, we change that focus rapidly back and forth.

I love my work. I've been here at Disney for 53 years and I've never really been bored. If you don't love what you do, you're at a continuous disadvantage. If you don't like your work, if it seems degrading to you, you can still do it if you dedicate it to something else, either a person or an ideal. It can be a reason bigger than yourself.

"I just keep on livin'. Keep on doin'. When I get old,
I'll let you know."

EVELYN BRYAN
JOHNSON

Born: November 4, 1909,
  Corbin, KY
Profession: Pilot, flight
  instructor, airport manager
Home: Jefferson City, TN

I'm flying 2700 feet above ground in a Cessna 152 airplane with an 84-year-old woman at the controls.

It's something my mother expressly forbade me to do, but I trust this pilot, a 5 foot 1 inch, pear-shaped woman, dressed in salmon, pink, and orange.

Evelyn has a steady hand, keen eye, and a perfect record of 45 years with no accidents. "Mama Bird," as she's affectionately known, easily guides the plane above the green hills of Eastern Tennessee, sweeping her eyes across the horizon, back to the instrument panel, and monitoring all systems.

"Don't worry, I won't do anything fancy," she laughs, tossing her full head of white hair, when I tell her I get airsick in small planes. "We'll just have a nice, quiet ride."

She takes us toward the Great Smoky Mountains, passing over manicured countryside, studded with farms, grazing animals, and tiny patches of water. The plane bounces gently in a few air pockets. It's a clear and sunny afternoon, with some small cumulus clouds in a bright blue sky. I exclaim at the miracle of flight.

"Oh, mercy, it's wonderful!" she quickly agrees. "It's a whole new world, flying is. You just can't get in an airplane and fly around and see the beauty of this world, and not just be so FASCINATED with it.

"And it's FUN to fly," she goes on. "You get away from everything up here. You still have troubles, but you forget 'em for a while."

We can see a long way, I say. Does that keep things in perspective?

"It sure does," she nods vigorously. "See that little thing down there that kind of comes out? See that white house toward the lake? That's my house." She points out other landmarks.

"Every day I'm anxious to get up, get up in the air, and go to work," she says. "Every day I go up, I see something I hadn't seen before. Maybe it's a house just sittin' there I hadn't noticed 'em building it. It's just fascinating." She speaks fast, in a musical Kentucky twang.

I hear her through headphones. She started using them several years ago, after developing laryngitis from shouting over the noise of the engine and propeller. "I strained my vocal chords while I was teaching," she explains. "So now my voice is a little fuzzy."

I'd like to keep flying, but after half an hour, Evelyn turns back toward home, the Morristown, Tennessee City Airport. She lands smoothly on the runway and taxis to the parking area where other small planes sit in neat rows. After turning off the motor and shutting down all systems, she easily jumps out of her seat and hits the tarmac.

I slowly unfold my body and stiffly alight, putting one foot gingerly on the ground, then the other. It takes a minute to regain my balance, but Evelyn is already walking briskly among the planes, explaining each one to me.

When the tour is complete, she takes me inside to a conference room, and offers a snack of cheese and crackers. She tells me she's been flying since 1945 and teaching since 1947. Evelyn is in the *Guinness Book of Records* for the most flight hours logged by a woman.

The last 16 years, she's served on the Tennessee Aeronautics Commission, which distributes state money to 75 local airports. She is also on the board of directors of Silver Wings Fraternity, a group of pilots who soloed over 25 years ago. She attends meetings of the UFOs, the United Flying Octogenarians. "We have some people way up in their 90s who are still flyin'," she reports. "Out of 100 members, seven are women."

She's especially proud of membership in the 99ers, an international group of licensed women pilots who first met in 1929 and elected Amelia Earhart president. "We have about 8,000 members and it's quite a going organization," Evelyn says. "We give scholarships to help ladies advance their flying."

She's managed the Morristown airport for 46 years, and "I'm getting paid for it now," she states proudly. "I became a city employee. I get about $16,000 a year." She used to own a flying service that transported passengers and did rescue missions. Now she concentrates on teaching.

"Teaching people to fly is SO rewarding," she says. "'Cause you take somebody that knows nothing whatsoever about an airplane. Then one day, you get on an airline and there's a captain's name of somebody you taught to fly." She laughs delightedly.

"There's so many of 'em have done that," she says. "There's a girl here in town that I took through everything. She's a copilot on American Airlines now. And a whole lot of the boys! One of them is vice president of U.S. Air. Another's chief pilot for U.S. Air over in Charlotte. There's just DOZENS of 'em." She smiles with motherly affection.

"It would be terrible to have a job you didn't love," she goes on. "The thing of it is to try to find the niche you should be in, and do something you enjoy doing. Money is important, but just enough to eat, pay the rent, pay the insurance, and all that kind of thing. I don't have a lot of money and don't expect to ever have a lot of money. I get along okay."

Evelyn works at the airport seven days a week, administering, teaching, and taking students up for their FAA flight exams. She's done more than 9,000 exams. She also teaches air and space workshops at several Tennessee colleges.

"Mama Bird" is a nickname coined by a devoted student. "She's nearly as old as I was," explains Evelyn. "But she sent me a card on Mother's Day and called me 'Mama Bird.' Said it's 'cause I looked after the students like they were baby birds or somethin'. And I DO. I keep real close touch on 'em. Make sure everything goes right." She nods her head smartly.

Evelyn has a reputation for being tough, especially on the flight exams. "Some people say I'm too hard," she remarks. "But I don't ask the people to do anything the FAA don't say I have to ask 'em to do. Some instructors, you know, don't like to maybe get in so DEEP."

By law, flight instructors may teach only eight hours a day. The rest of the time she handles airport business. "Like scheduling changes," she says, wrinkling her nose. "Suddenly things just pile up. I'll come in, find the schedule book, and somebody's got me booked for three people at the same time." She lifts her arms and looks heavenward, then smiles with a twinkle in her eye.

Twice a week, she stays late while the local Explorer Scouts and the Civil Air Patrol meet at the airport. "I'm so busy that I really don't have much time to bother about bein' alone," she says. She's been married twice. Both husbands died.

"Last week I soloed a lady who's 64 years old," she goes on. "But most of my students are between 16 and about 40. They generally come at about 15 1/2, so they can solo on their 16th birthday. You can't solo until then," she explains. "The 17th birthday is the first time you can be a private pilot.

"I've never been without students and I've never even been down to two or three," she says with pride. "I've always had lots of 'em. Most everybody that flies, flies at least once a week, but some fly more. I average 15 students at a time."

She knows that working at a job she loves helps her feel young. "I don't believe in sitting down doing nothing," she scoffs. "Don't sit down, you might not get up!" She laughs high and long. "I've noticed that people that retire and just sit down, don't last very long. I'm plannin' on living to at least a hundred. Get Willard Scott to wish me a happy birthday on *The Today Show*." She chortles.

Why 100? I ask.

"Well, I just think that'd be a nice age," she says breezily. "It'll be in the next century. It sure will."

You look about 60, I say.

"Well, thank you," she says sweetly. "I never think about being old. It just doesn't occur to me. 'Course I know I am, but it just doesn't occur to me. If there's anything I want to do, I do it.

"People ask me, 'When you gonna retire?' I say, 'I'm not old enough to retire. I'm just 84.' There's no one telling me to retire. The FAA, sometimes those inspectors might like to. But there's not a one of 'em in the office down there that could follow me around all day. I KNOW that." She laughs.

"There are no age requirements for pilots. You just have to pass the physical each year. My health is perfect. My doctor who gives me my physical says he feels like he's not doin' a good job. He can't find anything wrong with me." She smiles brightly. Evelyn's mother lived to be 91, her father about 75, the best she can recall.

With age, she's gained a few pounds. Now she weighs 125, up from 100. But it doesn't bother her. "I'm active and all," she says. "And I don't get great gobs of food. I eat mostly fruits and vegetables. But I do think as you get older, you get a little weight anyway. Evidently." She pauses and laughs.

Her breakfast is cereal. Lunch is a package of peanut butter crackers, usually on the run. "There's a dentist in town who tells me, 'I've been eatin' an apple a day, but I'm gonna quit and start eating peanut butter crackers, so I can get along as good as you do.'" She chuckles. "For dinner, I microwave one of these Healthy Choice frozen dinners. You get a meat, a vegetable, and a dessert. I don't take vitamins. And I don't take any medicine."

Her friends are all younger than she. "I don't associate with anybody my own age 'cause they're too old," she declares. "They don't do anything but complain and tell about all the pills they take, and goin' to the doctor, and this hurts and that hurts. I KNOW it hurts. But I hope if I ever get in that shape, I won't talk too much about it. You feel really sorry for these people, but you can't do a thing about it." She looks distressed.

Evelyn has had injuries, but always bounced back. She fell while being inducted into the Hamblen Women's Hall of Fame for Flight Instructors, one of over 30 honors she's received. "Since then, once in a while, the knee takes a spell hurting and I'll take an aspirin," she says. "But it's not anything regular." She goes to bed at 9 or 10 p.m. and sleeps eight hours. Some years ago, she can't recall exactly when, she had cataract surgery and lens replacements.

With so much work, what's home like? I ask.

"I'm not too crazy about housework," she says a bit guiltily. "If I ever retire, I'll take the first six months to clean house." She laughs. "I'll tell you a good example of what happened cleanin' the house. It's been three years, I was vacuuming the floor and the closet in the bedroom. The door was open and I just bumped it with the vacuum cleaner and the next thing I know, this big, full-length mirror hit me in the head, cut my head, blackened my whole face, blackened my eye, and knocked me down.   I say housework's very dangerous!" She laughs uproarously.

"A funny thing, I went to the Aeronautics Commission the next day lookin' like that, 'cause I don't miss any meetings. Somebody said, 'We'll be adjourned,' and one of the members said, 'Not till Evelyn tells us how she got that black eye.' 'Course it was a whole black face." She laughs again.

Evelyn doesn't have children, but she adores her two stepgrandsons by her second marriage. When they were teenagers, she taught them both to fly. Michael, the elder, lived nearby until recently, then married and moved to Florida. "We don't see them but 'bout once a year," she says. "Chad graduates from college this spring and then he's going to get back to flying. I think Michael may, too. He just got his physical renewed."

She and her first husband W.J. Bryan wanted children, but were not able to have them. "We had three or four of 'em born dead, and one lived five hours," she says softly. "So it evidently was not meant to be." Now she considers her students as her "children."

She also taught school before she got married. "I was about 19 years old at that time and I taught for two years. I DO like people," she acknowledges. "I don't know of anybody, I couldn't point out ANYBODY I don't like. Just couldn't do it, 'cause I like everybody." She shrugs her shoulders and grins.

Today a group of schoolchildren is visiting the airport. Evelyn gives them a cheery welcome, leads them onto the tarmac, and describes some of the 52 planes in the parking area. She pokes her head into one plane and explains the instrument panel, then takes questions. "Oh, sure, I enjoy kids," she tells me later. "But there's so many of 'em, you can't even get a chance to find out who any of 'em are.

"Like the other day, just about eight or ten were in here, and I had each one of 'em tell me what their name was. 'Course, I didn't remember a one of 'em, but they don't know that!" She laughs, a bit embarrassed.

It amuses her that people obsess about youth. "You see it on TV. They're gonna put all this cream on and they're keepin' the wrinkles away, they're gettin' so old. And these models are about 20 or 25!" She erupts into laughter. "I get so tickled at 'em. And all these people that are showin' to go on a diet is real skinny girls. I don't see how anybody believes all that."

And yet, she sees nothing wrong with plastic surgery. "Well, that'd be nice," she says thoughtfully. "It sure would be nice to get yourself lookin' a whole lot better. If you got the time and the money and willin' to do it, have at it!"

But you're not interested? I ask.

"Well, no," she replies. "I don't have the time or the money. I got lots to do, though," she says brightly. "Want to keep workin' and doing it. I want to keep teaching and go to Aeronautics Commission meetings in Nashville."

She moves easily. Her walk is brisk and she crawls nimbly in and out of planes. "That's quite a task sometimes," she laughs. "The small planes, you know. I probably walk out to the hangar two or three times during the day. That's just out a little piece, about a hundred yards. I guess the most exercise I get is when I solo somebody down that end of the field. Then I walk back up here. It's a mile, you know. Then I touch my toes every mornin', a few things like that, but nothing like I should." She throws a knowing glance at me.

Evelyn doesn't smoke, and she is hard on people who do. "Both my husbands died of cancer and they were both heavy smokers," she explains. "My sister died of cancer and she was a heavy smoker. I really believe that smokin' causes that. People keep smoking, they think it'll happen to other people and won't happen to them. I always give people lectures against smoking." She looks unapologetic.

She has deep spiritual beliefs. Every Sunday morning she goes to the 8:15 service at the Morristown Baptist Church. "I've had plenty of things happen that were hairy," she says, referring to flying experiences. "And God got me through them. Yes, ma'am, God's got me through a LOT of tight spots, a lot of 'em. I can think of several times when something went wrong and I just called for His help, and I got it.

"One time I had a problem with a throttle, and I said, 'God, please help me.' And it was just almost like somebody took my hand and pushed it and opened that throttle.

"Then one day I was comin' up the highway, I had an employee that, really, I'm tellin' you, he just really bugged me. I really felt resentful toward him and I was prayin' to God to please help me get over this resentment.

"Then, I never did know such a thing was possible, right here. You know these old rubber suits like it goes divin' in the water? It was like I had one on and it started comin' up through here, up over my head, out over my arms and my hands, like someone was pullin' off this rubber suit of resentment. It was comin' off over me.

"And I was so HAPPY and I felt so GOOD." Her voice becomes melodic. "I didn't know physically you could feel that good. And I just loved everybody. I've never been resentful of him or anybody else since.

"Then one day I was just walkin' across the ramp and I don't know what it was, I said, 'God, if everybody bothers you as much as I do, how in the world can You hear us all?' And just as plain as somebody was walkin' along beside me, they said, 'Through the Holy Spirit that dwells within you.' I heard that just as plain as day. I mean, out loud PLAIN." She looks at me with raised eyebrows.

"I pray off and on all day, you know. My God and I are buddies. Flying like I do, I feel really closer to Him. Flyin' all over the country, I don't see how anybody could get up there and look down on this world and not believe in God. It cannot be here by accident. No way, this big explosion. If there was a big explosion, it's the way He did it. Nobody has said how He did it, so whatever it is, it's how He did it.

"And as far as death, I'm not afraid," she continues quickly. "I'm not in a big hurry for it, but I'm not afraid. I don't want to be kept alive through life support. I think that's terrible that people are forced to do that, kept alive with machines. No, no, that's not for me. I hope it never happens to me." She takes a quick breath.

"Reincarnation? I know my first husband believed in it. I think we do have guardian angels. And I believe mine might be him. I think there's a heaven and I think maybe I'll see all my family and all someday." She is relaxed.

Evelyn remembers exact dates: marriage to her first husband lasted 32 years and eight months. After he died, she remarried. That lasted 12 years and three weeks.

"Oh, I've had lots of love," she says with a smile. "I don't have anyone to run around with now, and I miss that. I wouldn't advise anyone to get married with the idea that if it doesn't work, we can get a divorce. Because you'll sure get one if you go into it with that sort of attitude. You have to go into it with thinkin', 'This is for life and I'm gonna really enjoy it.'" She speaks firmly.

She's equally adamant that young people should get all the education they can. She received a college degree from Tennessee Wesleyan. "Even if you're workin' on something like flying, for instance, mark that for a career," she says. "Most airlines require you to have at least two years college, and some require four. Even if you don't know exactly what you want to do in the future, be preparing! Get an education.

"Or somethin' will turn up that maybe you'll specialize in before you get through. You may not know the first year or two in college, everybody doesn't. But after a while, things begin to open up and you'll have a goal. Always have a goal, always work towards it." Her eyes sparkle with enthusiasm.

It's late afternoon and she's scheduled a flight lesson. "I'll be back in an hour and we can talk some more. Just make yourself at home. Here, take a look at some of my scrapbooks," she says, pulling out two huge leather-bound books. While she's gone, I scan hundreds of news clippings and photos about her work, awards, and honorary degrees.

Later she tells me that George Prince, a pilot whom she trained, is writing her biography. She is genuinely puzzled that anyone would go to the trouble. I say that she is special. She laughs it off.

"Are you hungry?" she asks. "Let's go to dinner." We eat at a country buffet restaurant, where she chooses vegetables and salads. In minutes she's finished. "You'll excuse me," she says. "I've got some things to do at home." I see her to her car and she tucks a few jars of homemade jelly in my hand. "Please come back again, anytime," she says warmly.

Every few months, I telephone to check up on Evelyn. Tonight, she's bubbling over with enthusiasm.

"Dan Rather's TV crew was here last week and filmed for NINE hours," she says breathlessly. "I suppose they'll end up with about three minutes." She laughs. "They're doing a story on older people who are still working. I felt real honored."

What happened? I ask.

"Well, I took the interviewer up in a Cessna 150," she says. "We flew around and just chatted the whole time. And the most INTERESTING thing happened. We were being filmed by a camera taped up on the instrument panel, right in front of us. The interviewer had a little monitor on his lap." Her voice is full of amazement, then drops to a whisper. "I made a REAL good landing. I was surprised at myself." She laughs.

"Then they wanted to see me teaching someone who hadn't flown very much," she continues. "So we got a girl student who'd had just one lesson. She came over to the airport and we went up in the plane, and the camera was up there, too.

"Then they wanted me to do a little more teaching. So one lady student came out and we went up in her Cessna 172. She started lessons when she was 66, so that fit in good with the story." She takes a quick breath.

"Then the interviewer and I went up again in late afternoon, and another plane followed us and took pictures of us. We landed and just barely got out on the ground before a big thunderstorm hit."

That's quite an adventure, I say.

"Oh, yes," she says, delightedly. "We had a good time."

RICHARD
ERDOES

Born: July 7, 1912,
  Frankfurt, Germany
Profession: Artist,
  photographer, writer, Native
  American expert
Home: Santa Fe, NM

My wife Jean and I have more young friends than old. We relate to them and they relate to us. We share interests. One reason we get along with our three kids is that we have shared interests. Jean and I are proud to have instilled a love of the outdoors, for climbing and roaming and hiking and sitting with the Indians. We have young people from all over the world coming here to visit. Everybody winds up in Santa Fe.

Never stop! If you stop, you're dead. If you stop going, if you stop hiking, if you stop making love, if you stop whatever, you're dead. Just keep going and don't start sitting down. Don't worry about anything.

I get a kick out of old age. People are deferential to you. You can be as eccentric as you want and everything is forgiven to you. So I enjoy old age.

"I'd like to live as long as possible, just a little beyond my wife, whenever that is. We're a team."

GEORGE JONES

> Born: August 20, 1897,
>   Oberlin, OH
> Profession: Professor Emeritus
>   of Botany, Oberlin College,
>   curator, Oberlin Herbarium
> Home: Oberlin, OH

Work and love keep George Jones young at 95.
His work is teaching. He's taught at Oberlin College for 80 years. He collects plants for the college herbarium and keeps them in good order. Every spring he gives a campus tree tour on Alumni Weekend. He leads Sunday morning nature hikes which several thousand people have enjoyed over the years.

As much as he enjoys work, his greatest love is Mary, 92, his wife of 70 years. Together they look like a happy American Gothic painting. "I enjoy her sleeping in my arms," he confides. "We belong to each other.

"We belonged to each other a full year before we were married. We wrote to each other every day during our engagement. I was overwhelmed by her. She was a student in one of my classes at Oberlin." He smiles, blue eyes shining.

Since Mary is not well, he stays close to home. They work together in the garden, he on the vegetables, she on the roses. Pink, white, and red roses twine up their clapboard home on a quiet street lined with tall trees and green lawns.

Inside they do chores together. She cooks, he helps with the dishes, and in the evening, they sit side-by-side in soft, worn armchairs, reading, talking, and dozing. Their cat Kittypuss sleeps on Mary's lap.

Dr. Jones is an institution in Oberlin. Friends call him a living treasure. When I first meet him, he offers a rough calloused hand of welcome. He looks like Santa Claus: short and round, with a barrel chest, tanned face, white hair combed straight back, and merry eyes. His plaid flannel shirt, comfortable pants, and soft shoes bespeak a man at home in the out-of-doors.

"Hello," calls a light, sweet voice from the kitchen. I see a small woman with a kindly face and white hair pulled back into a bun. "My wife Mary," he introduces us. "She's canning tomato juice. We had more tomatoes than we could eat this year." Mary wears an apron and stands over a steaming kettle. The smell of cooked tomatoes floats our way.

We sit down in the living room and Dr. Jones starts talking about Mary and how they met, courted, married, and had a family. He's kept their romance alive by writing rhymes to honor her on birthdays, anniversaries, Valentine's Day, and Christmas. He recites one, his voice full of gentleness and emotion:

> I love our children dearly,
> But their greatest values lie
> In being vehicles of praises
> For the apple of my eye.

She overhears it from the next room. "I like 'em all," she calls appreciatively. She's saved every poem he's written.

"Marriage can be fun, if you work on it," he says in a soft, husky voice, his fingers folded together in a ball. "Three things seem necessary. First, pick out the right partner, which is not always easy. We did. Similarity of family code is very important. Physical attractiveness is not enough, though it helps.

"Second, both must work at it. We've done that. Skill at making my rhymes helps." He smiles self-indulgently. "Both husband and wife need to enjoy DOING and SAYING things to please the other. She knows that she is, but she likes to be told. He does, too.

"The third requirement is live long enough. Sometimes that's not your decision. I think I can say with honesty, we've never had a real quarrel. We've sometimes agreed to disagree." He cocks an eyebrow. "She loves TV and I can't stand it. Drives me to DRINK. But I don't drink," he adds quickly. "She says she's the luckier of the two of us. I know I am." His tone is no-nonsense.

Marriage is an institution that he highly recommends. "An unmarried person is relatively wasting his time," he scoffs. "Make the necessary contact! Being married is well worthwhile."

As you get older, is love more important? I ask.

"It's always important," he says resolutely. "We're helping each other now. We're a team.

"You're not so productive after the age of 95," he goes on. "I'm slowing up. I used to walk for half a day at four miles per hour. I hardly make three now, maybe two and one half. I get tired. But I'm generally in good health." His eyes are good, his hearing is a bit gone, and he took care of prostate, hernia, and skin cancer problems years ago. Recent back trouble has cleared up.

"I still mow the lawn, an acre of grass, with a gas mower," he reports. "I can fix things. I shovel the snow off our walks and our neighbors' walks. I've often said I'd like to die of a heart attack while I'm shoveling snow." He smiles.

"Do you know the best way to shovel snow?" he asks.

I shake my head.

"I'll show you."

He gets up and walks out the front door. Picking up a garden shovel, he puts one of his big hands over the handle, the other under it, rather than both hands under. "This way you can shovel a lot longer," he says, shoveling the air.

I try it and it does feel more natural.

May I see the vegetable garden? I ask.

"Sure," he says cheerfully. We head toward the backyard and walk by carefully cultivated rows and plots. "The garden is getting to be kind of laborious," he admits. "This year I sowed three patches with lima beans, potatoes, quite a bit of sweet corn, tomatoes, and pod beans. The rabbits ate most of THEM." He laughs easily.

"Then soybeans for the rabbits, zinnias at the borders, and some roses. That's her job," he says, inclining his head toward Mary in the kitchen.

Soybeans for the rabbits? I ask.

"Yes, they like them," he answers.

Do they leave the other crops alone?

"Hm, sometimes," he says, smiling.

He allows that he has some arthritis in his hands, but it doesn't hurt most of the time. "I can't close a fist, but I can still hold a hoe," he says, holding up a hand and demonstrating. "And I can still push a wheel hoe quite a distance. That's my exercise. I have plenty of exercise in the garden.

"Every other day I walk to the botany lab. In the summer I collect plants, then prepare them for lab use in class." It's a job he's done for years. Although he officially retired in 1963, at the age of 65, he's regularly asked to help out in classes. He fully enjoys the work and the students. "Quite a few of the kids relate to me," he says simply.   He advises choosing a career they enjoy. "Money is not as important as love of your work."

This spring, he invited fourth- and fifth-grade children from Prospect School to see his garden. Tales of rabbit visitors piqued their curiosity. "They all seemed very much interested," he says. "Being with young people feels very natural to me."

We walk back into the house and he settles into his favorite chair, where I take photos and he tells me about his family.

He and Mary have two daughters, four grandchildren, and four great-grandchildren. They visit once or twice a year and stay for a week. "THEY do the cooking," he says, smiling. Then he turns serious.

"We had a son who died when he was 20, in a tree-trimming fall. It was very hard to lose him. He had quite a sense of humor. One time he said, 'You know, a sense of humor gets you somewhere.' But that wasn't strong enough," says Dr. Jones. "I believe that a sense of humor gets you LOTS of 'wheres.'"

Where do you get your wit? I ask.

"I don't know," he says slowly. "Maybe from reading. I prefer the classics to modern literature. Over there are a few of my books." He motions toward a huge bookcase. I see volumes of Rudyard Kipling and George A. Henty.

"Henty was an Englishman who wrote books for boys," he explains. "The books are very highly moralistic and romantic, always showing gentlemanly behavior." Mary comes in from the kitchen and sits down in her chair. "He reads those books over and over," she says tenderly.

Some of today's young people could USE a good dose of Henty, he suggests. "Most young people are good, solid citizens. Some are lost, but they were lost before.

"In my youth, we didn't have the problem of drugs. I grew up in a highly moral family. The family code was no alcohol, no tobacco, no gambling. My older brother indulged in all of these and died of cirrhosis of the liver during middle age." He speaks without emotion.

"I've never swallowed anything alcoholic," he goes on. "When I was a little boy, I tried smoking corn silk. Horrible! I did use tobacco once," his voice drops to a whisper. "I had ringworm on my leg, caught it from a dog. Mother made a nicotine poultice from chewing tobacco that cured the ringworm." His straight face breaks into a grin. Mary smiles, too.

Chocolate is a major weakness. "I've eaten at least two tons of sweet chocolate in my lifetime," he states without remorse. "I used to eat about half a pound a day, but cut that in half. Now I've stopped eating it altogether. I've lost seven pounds and have to lose some more." He pats his ample stomach and laughs. Every Christmas, he hand-dips chocolates for presents, setting them to harden on a special marble slab he keeps just for the occasion. It's a tradition he began in 1935.

The rest of his diet is quite normal, he insists: a variety of food, including meat, and a daily multivitamin. He sleeps about nine hours a night, with no naps.

His good health, he believes, is helped by a deep faith in God. That's been part of his life for as long as he can remember.

"We are members of the local Congregational Church. I was treasurer for 20 years. Mary and I pray at home. We have grace with each meal, and at the end of the day, in the evenings, we alternate saying prayers. We say, 'Thank you for our extraordinary good fortune.' He looks at her across the room and she smiles back. He speaks quietly, picking his words carefully.

"Early on I realized that praying for something didn't necessarily produce the results. Prayer is not asking for something, but trying to get RIGHT with God. Prayer tries to make you react the way God would want you to react, thinking about things with God listening. If you can see you've messed the thing up, you can be sorry.

"I believe in a gentle God," he says. "I don't believe in a hell. A God who is like a father wouldn't tolerate such a thing."

Dr. Jones is not afraid of dying. He takes it philosophically. "I'm not certain, but maybe there is an afterlife," he says, furrowing his brow. "Death is kind of puzzling. If there's an afterlife and most people have a chance, how many people are there and where is it?" He chuckles.

"My next-door neighbor and I were talking over the fence one day about Sputnik. I figured heaven is in the seventh dimension and that's all unlimited space. At the same time, it must be pretty boring." He brightens. "But pretty nice to spend the rest of eternity with my wife." They look at each other lovingly.

"It seems kind of a waste of the good stuff if you die and that's the end of it," he continues. "There's a quote from the school of Dr. Bosworth, that if there isn't an afterlife, it means a little piece of lead, a bullet, that got into somebody's head, would end all that the person accumulated and all his character. That doesn't seem very economical." He sounds miffed.

"I never thought I would grow so old," he muses.

How old do you feel? I ask.

"There's a French dictum, 'What age do you feel in your heart?' Some people are quite old at 50. I wasn't. There's no need for a mirror, although I look younger than I am. When I got my driver's license renewed, the girl at the Department of Motor Vehicles said, 'You really are 93? You don't look it.'" He seems pleased.

Does your age make others treat you differently? I ask.

"Yes, some of the regulars on the Sunday hikes seem to be solicitous," he admits. "I don't mind. Once my shoelace came untied and one of them got down and did it." He smiles affectionately.

"I'm a little surprised I feel as well as I do at this age," he says. "I can still climb a tree." Last year a Scotch pine tree died on his property, and he started to fell it. "My next-door neighbor said, 'You're up pretty high on that extension ladder.' I'd already cut some branches. He had some people cutting his tree, so I had them do ours.

"You know, I was asked to retire. Then this fellow David Benzing, professor of biology, had too big a class. After collecting plants for him for several years, I started helping. I still am." He pauses. "It's not unpleasant to be needed."

We agree to meet on his next nature walk.

Sunday morning at 9 a.m., a small group of casually-dressed men and women gathers in the parking lot behind the botany department building. I join them as Dr. Jones drives up. "Well, where would you like to go today?" he asks. After some discussion, we agree on a spot and carpool to dense woods several miles outside town.

It's cool and shady. The sun breaks through in spots as we traipse slowly through the undergrowth, close to a meandering stream. We are like children following the legendary Pied Piper. Our leader picks a tiny sprig from a green plant and holds it aloft. We look closely.

"What is it?" he asks.

Someone knows and gives a name. Dr. Jones agrees, then identifies it by official name, both English and Latin, and describes its seeds, leaves, habitat, and length of life.

We continue walking, talking quietly, climbing over tree stumps, crossing puddles, and asking questions about nearby plants: forest ferns, Jacks-in-the-pulpit, evergreens, and mountain laurels. He answers them all, giving us the scientific names. Although he carries a small reference book, he rarely consults it. Often he refers to plants seen and identified on earlier walks. Some faces light up with recognition. A few people take notes in small, well-worn books.

Going up a small rise, we leave the forest and enter a field of tall grasses and wildflowers, a piece of land left natural by a farmer. In the tangle of stems and blossoms, we tread lightly. A bird calls and we glimpse a red-winged blackbird. "They like these grasses," observes Dr. Jones. "You'll see them all around here."

It's nearly noon. The sun warms us and we shed shirts and sweaters. Dr. Jones keeps his plaid shirt on. Someone passes around a water bottle, another a pair of binoculars. The professor talks about blue cornflowers, wild daisies, and hollyhocks that dot the field.

We're not sure where we are, but as we walk, he spots a familiar road. "Oh, yes," he says. "I know now." He takes us down a hill that leads into the woods, and half an hour later, we're back at our starting point.

It's been a good walk, a learning journey, and we thank him.

"Well, I hope you enjoyed it," he says. "We went a good distance today." One man jokes, "Not half as far as the other time."

Another says, "Remember that day when we kept going and somehow got lost?"

Dr. Jones' eyes sparkle. "That was a good day, too," he says, smiling. "We always make it back all right.

"And I always learn something new from my students."

LUCILLE LORTEL

> Born: December 16, 1905,
>   New York, NY
> Profession: Theater owner,
>   producer, actress
> Home: Westport, CT

I have so much to do yet. It bothers me that I haven't done it all. There's a lot of unfinished business and I never seem to have time to get it all done. I think I'm always ahead of what I want to do. I have many ideas that pop up.

There are so many joys in my life. I'm pleased with the play *A Walk in the Woods*, which was a struggle. We had one of the great stars Alec Guiness wanting to play it in the London run. It was a great joy being able to go to Russia with this wonderful play.

I call the theater my family. I call the theaters my children. The White Barn in Westport is one child and the Lortel Theater in New York is my other. I regret now that I didn't have a family. That's my fault. At the time I felt that children would hamper me. Then, when I wanted to have them, my husband didn't.

I just take risks without thinking. If I like something, I get very enthusiastic about it. I think my enthusiasm, more than a play, makes people interested.

If you love what you do, go ahead and stick to it.

"I make friends with a lot of people.
I like the janitor as well as the millionaire."

ETHEL KEOHANE

> Born: March 30, 1901,
>   Carlisle, KY
> Profession: Champion
>   Tournament bridge player,
>   retired executive medical
>   secretary
> Home: Wellesley Hills, MA

I read about Ethel in *The New York Times*.

Bridge columnist Alan Trescott called her "the *grande dame* of American bridge." When she was 90, she held the most master points—about 12,000—of any American her age. When I interviewed her at 91, that total had risen to 12,300.

Trescott called her "a living monument to the importance of enthusiasm and willpower." Ten years earlier, Ethel had been in a car accident and broken nearly all her bones. "The doctors did not expect her to live, but they were wrong," he wrote. "They said she would never walk again, but were wrong once more, because she devoted every waking hour to exercise and rehabilitation. She quickly returned to the tournament circuit with undiminished zeal."

I was intrigued and telephoned her in New England.

"Well, sure I'll talk to you, if you think I'm important enough to put in your book," she answered, somewhat surprised. "My goodness, you must have dozens of people more interesting than me." I assured her that I did not.

We set a date and I drove to Massachusetts. Her two-story white house was on a quiet street with manicured lawns and gardens, just blocks from Wellesley College.

Ethel answered the back doorbell, shook my hand vigorously, and invited me into a 1930s, formica-filled kitchen. "Did you have a good trip?" she asked. "Let's have some tea."

A short, skinny, pleasant-faced lady with curly red hair and bright blue eyes, she sat me down at the kitchen table, put the kettle on, and stacked some cookies on a plate.

"My husband Billy and I designed and built this house shortly after we were married. He died some time ago. I love it and I want to stay here." She does her own housekeeping and leads a busy life, traveling to bridge tournaments in the U.S., playing in local tournaments, and meeting friends for lunch, dinner, and bridge games.

"Come see the house," she says, and leads me through a spacious, classically-furnished living room, into a sunroom flooded with light and filled with glass tables that display a huge collection of shiny bridge trophies. I exclaim over them and she makes a modest comment.

"Let's go upstairs and sit," she says, taking me to a second floor study, buttercup-yellow with wicker furniture. She plops into an armchair and puts her feet up on a stool. "Have one," she says, pointing to a jar of butterscotch candies on the shelf behind me. I take one and hand her the jar. "My favorite, I just love 'em," she exclaims, popping a candy into her mouth.

What keeps you going? I ask. Her energy seems boundless.

"I'm CURIOUS about life," she says quickly, in a singsong twang of her native Kentucky. "I want to live to see EVERYTHING. I want to live to see a woman become president of the United States. I've got to wait to see that. I'd like to see a good businessman become president. Then we wouldn't have all these deficits." She makes a face.

"I want to live to see more exploration in space. I think there are things in other galaxies and I want to live to see this. Oh, heavens, yes, there's more than just our earth.

"I love life," she goes on. "Every day I just think, 'Ooooh! I look forward to it, I just love it. And I don't think I was ever depressed in my life. I can't remember such a thing.

"Oh, and please call me Ethel," she says. "No one calls me Mrs. Keohane."

Her passion is playing tournament bridge and she does it several times a week. "It keeps me young, it keeps me pepped up," she explains. "I'm always learning. I get the MOST pleasure out of playing bridge. I learned to play in 1940 because my late husband played four nights a week, and I knew I'd never see him if I didn't learn." She grins and takes another butterscotch.

"Bridge is a challenge. You have to match your wits against some of the best in the country. I tell you, the Jewish lawyers make fine bridge players. When you can play in a national tournament against people who are really fine players, you LOVE beating the best. If you can outbid, outplay them, you just love it. Over the years, I've made so many wonderful friends."

Ethel drives to tournaments, except those in Florida, to which she flies. "In June, I was at a regional in Hyannis, then in Toronto for the nationals in July." She ticks off her schedule. "This fall I'll go to the nationals in Orlando. I just came back from a tournament in Albany."

Unlike professionals, she takes no money for playing. Her group, the American Contract Bridge Association, with 200,000 members, holds charity games and donates proceeds to medical research, including AIDS.

Ethel can afford to play the circuit because a former bridge partner, whom she "looked after for years," set up a trust fund for her. "Every year I play the national tournaments, several regionals, and the sectionals. Nationals are the top, they're three times a year. People come from foreign countries. Last time it was about 30. Per capita, the U.S. has fewer players than most countries. Finland has the most.

"This Sunday I'm playing in what's called the Grand National Masters Pairs." She takes a breath and goes on rapidly. "But I don't play every day like some people. I couldn't do that. I'd hate it."

You speak quickly, I say.

"Oh, yes, I always talk fast, although they claim that Southerners have a drawl. I always talk fast. I think I want to get it over." She laughs delightedly. "I talk too much, too fast. I do, I do."

She points to a bookcase over my shoulder. "Those are all my books on bridge. My boyfriend, he's 92, he's written a couple. I try to keep up on the latest bridge conventions and things. I've always played with the best in the Northeast, but I don't have a partner now. I lost my favorite woman partner in the car accident in 1981. I'll meet a new one in Florida this September at a regional tournament." Her voice is full of anticipation.

The accident happened when Ethel was driving home on the New York Thruway. A tire blew and she hit a tree. Her prognosis was poor, but she rallied in the hospital. "The reason I recovered so quickly," she explains, "is that I was fascinated with what they

were doing in the Intensive Care Unit. Everything they did fascinated me. I just took an INTEREST.

"Not only that," she goes on. "One of my bridge friends,
the minute he heard about the accident, took the next plane out
and stayed with me the whole week. The first words I heard
was his voice, 'Ethel, I love ya, I love ya, I love ya! And you're
going to make it!' I can hear that now. Then his wife came and
stayed with me, 'cause he had to work. When I got ready to
come home, they were both just wonderful to me."

She spent seven weeks in Intensive Care, five more weeks
in the hospital, and seven weeks in rehabilitation. "I heard that
they didn't think I had a chance. Then I heard I wasn't going to
be out of bed again," she says sourly.

"At the hospital, they put a little walker beside the bed,
then they lifted me into a wheelchair and said, 'See if you can
stand.' They were amazed when I took two or three steps. They
couldn't believe it. The head nurse came and said, 'I've heard
this and I don't believe it.' And I said, 'Why not?'" She shrugs.

"When I came home September 3rd, I was in a wheelchair,
but getting around the house all right, so I decided that by the first
of December, I wanted to get rid of it. And I did. After that I had a
walker. And at Christmas, I had a little cocktail party here.

"I did some exercises and they had someone come in for a
month or so, every two, three days. In December and January, I
went on two of those three-pronged canes. I did that for a month or
two and decided that one cane was enough. Then I got rid of THAT.
In the meantime, I went to Bermuda at the end of January.

"I think the surgeon would rather I walk now with a cane,
but I've been without a cane nine or ten years." She walks with
a noticeable limp, and climbs stairs one at a time, resting on
each landing. The limp is partly a result of corrective surgery,
gone awry. "The knee's stiff and they set this leg crooked," she
explains, without anger. "It's made a difference. It's kind of
hard. Oh, they did a good job," she dismisses it.

Did you ever get discouraged? I ask.

"No," she replies, "because I was getting BETTER. You
don't get discouraged when you're getting better. Now, if I were
dying by inches of cancer, I might. But I was getting better.
There's nothing to be discouraged about.

"Not only that," she goes on. "I didn't have one friend who didn't have something wrong with them, and I now said, 'It's my turn.' That's the way I felt, it was my turn." She grins with satisfaction. Until she was 80, Ethel considered herself healthy and never lost a day of work to sickness. She had her first physical exam when she was 71.

Determination helped speed her recovery. So did support from friends. "I have so many wonderful friends," she says. "Three of them wanted me to stay with them until I got well. I have a friend in North Carolina, not the boyfriend," she adds quickly. "Anytime I telephone, he'll come up and stay with me. Anytime I need his wife, too. They're good, they're really nice friends."

Ethel's current boyfriend is Garton Churchill, an old friend whom she first dated in 1924, when he attended Harvard Law School. They went their separate ways, married other people, and stayed in touch. Later they played bridge as a foursome. When their spouses died, they became bridge partners. "We've been friends, he's just like a relative almost," she says warmly. "He came from Ohio. He's 92, he's not well now, he can't hear anything." She speaks matter-of-factly.

The phone rings and the answering machine picks up. "This is Ethel. I can't come to the phone now. Leave a message and I'll get back to you." Her tone is brusque and professional. "I'm very busy," she says, pointing to the desk calendar, pencilled in with lunches, dinners, bridge games, and tournaments. Firmly, but pleasantly, she tells me that she has only so much time for me today, but when I'm back in town, we'll have lunch together.

Before joining the bridge circuit, Ethel worked full-time. "I always worked," she says. "I had a good life, but I worked most of it. There's nothing in the world like working. Nothing! There's such a sense of satisfaction in it. Work you enjoy is the best thing in life. And my brain NEEDS the exercise."

She attended junior college, took a business course, then became a bookkeeper for a doctor. After marriage, she took 12 years off, but grew bored. "It was only social life. It was all right, but not for me," she groans.

Returning to work was a necessity, "We needed the money. We had a second mortgage on the house by that time." She took a job as secretary at Harvard Medical School, and later as administrative secretary in Children's Hospital for Dr. William Lenox, "a man who's in *Who's Who in Medicine*," she says proudly.

"The two of us started alone and we built that office into a big unit. I had five secretaries under me. We had technicians and three EEG machines. We had doctors come for EEG training from all over the world, from Germany, Japan, Finland, Switzerland, Italy, Greece, and South America. I still keep in touch with quite a few of them," she adds affectionately.

"We were busy and I was in charge of everything. I loved it. I just LOVE, love that kind of thing." Her eyes sparkle. "I kept things going. Oh, yes, I kept them going.

"Then I was forced to retire. They throw you out when you're 65. But they didn't throw me out until I was almost 67." Actually, she admits, she retired because her husband retired. "He was eating two dinners a day and calling me at the office three or four times a day. I had three phone lines coming into my desk, and I didn't know what I could do. He wanted me home. He needed me. So I retired." Her voice has no bitterness.

The office kept calling her. "When I was 79 years old, the chief of the unit pleaded with me to come back, PLEADED. 'But I need you, Mrs. Keohane, I need you.' I said, 'No, no way.' That's kind of nice, isn't it?" she asks me, smiling with a faraway look.

"They also offered me part-time work, anytime I could come in. You know why?" She lowers her voice. "I always gave more than I was paid for. It wasn't me, it was what I GAVE. Giving is important."

Where do you get your energy? I ask.

"I was an unwanted child," she answers immediately. "My mother favored my older sister, and when she died, at age five, mother told me, 'The wrong one died.' Ethel laughs good-naturedly. "My mother used to say I'd get something in my head, because I'd never LOOK like anything." She laughs again.

"I have a sister-in-law and we're just as different as day and night. She's a mama's baby and my mother didn't like me very well, so that made a big difference.

"My sister-in-law said to me, 'Ethel, you always had to get out and DO things. But I was protected at home.' It's true, her mother did everything for her. She thinks I'm the greatest person in the world because she's had me take the place of her mother. There's no question about it."

Ethel and her mother remained good friends. "My mother, her name was Lunah Belle, lived to be 96. She did the best she could through the years, tried to help us," she says fondly.

"She had a big house in St. Petersburg, Florida, lived on the first floor, and rented the upstairs. At age 95, she was still washing her kitchen walls. Ninety-five and washing kitchen walls! She said her maid didn't like to do them." She shakes her head and laughs. "Mother was a little bitty thing, smaller than I am."

Working in the medical field made Ethel appreciate good health. "Health is the most important thing in life. I don't care how much money you have, if you don't have health, it's no good. And you can't DO anything good, if you don't have health."

She launches into a tirade against the public school system and its lack of health education. "Do you think that half the kids would be smoking and on drugs if they'd start 'em in kindergarten on health education?" She fumes, eyes blazing. "Believe me, they wouldn't. Teach them with their fingers or toes or eyes, teach them about the heart, lungs, taking care of them. Show pictures, LOTS of pictures!

"Show this beautiful baby and then show it through life and how it went on drugs, and say, 'Look. And here is the other one, both beautiful babies. This one did not take drugs.' It could be worked up to really be something," she says enthusiastically.

"Pound it in. But don't get some old doctor, poor old thing, 50 years old, or 40 or something. Get a young man, the younger, the better. Maybe some pretty young women doctors and medical students." She cocks her head and smiles.

At 91, Ethel has kept her quick mind. She credits it to strong genes, playing bridge, and watching *Jeopardy* every weeknight on television. She almost always gets the answer before the contestant, she reports.

Occasionally she forgets people's names. "But I think that's due to lack of effort on my part," she says shortly.

These days, she finds she must pace herself. "If I hadn't had my accident, I would have as much energy as I did at 50," she laments. "I never thought about reaching this age. Those things I never think about. Never!

"Once in a while, you see someone who's 108 years old. Willard Scott has their pictures on *The Today Show*. I think, 'Oh, my goodness, wouldn't I be awful? How many more years is it that I have? Seventeen, 18 more years?'" She leans back and chuckles.

Through no fault of her own, she has lung problems. "I inherited pneumonia from my father," she explains. "I've had pneumonia three times and I'm inclined to have bronchitis. I never smoked, but when they take x-rays of my lungs, they say, 'You've never smoked? Are you sure?'

"My lungs look like I'm a heavy smoker. You know why?" She pauses dramatically. "PASSIVE SMOKING. Passive smoking in the bridge tournament rooms. They're not allowed to smoke anymore, but the playing rooms used to be BLUE—blue with smoke. Your eyes would ache, oh! I think my lungs will always be the way they are."

She has regular oxygen treatments and recently bought a portable oxygen machine. "It's the most interesting thing." She opens a small suitcase to show me. "My doctor doesn't know I have it. He says I don't need to be on it now. But on these muggy nights, I know I do, because I get choked up. That's why the air conditioning is important. Anything medical, I'm right in there." She beams.

To save her breath, she bags dirty clothes on laundry day and throws them down the basement steps. "Why should I carry it?" she says indignantly. "I just toss it and make as little work for myself as possible." She still carries firewood up from the basement. "I walk better than I stand," she says. "I can't go somewhere and just stand, like a restaurant line. I have to sit."

Except for her lungs and a heartbeat skip, for which she takes medicine, Ethel says she's in pretty good health. Two cataract operations have been successful. She wears glasses for reading. Her hearing is keen. Her hands get sore from arthritis, but she feels no real pain. "Oh, yes, I take vinegar and honey," she remembers. "Every morning, one tablespoon of each in a cup."

Her diet is spare, a holdover from childhood. "I like beans," she says brightly. "Any kind of beans, 'cause that's all we had when I was growing up in Kentucky. We couldn't afford anything else." She laughs. "Those little navy beans. I've never been a meat or bread eater. I eat mostly fruits and vegetables, and I love cheese. I eat a lot of cheese and yogurt."

For lunch she has fruit, cheese, or a peanut butter cracker. "Very small, I don't like lunch very much. I have an early dinner. If I'm home alone, I may watch *The Golden Girls* on TV, and eat some tomatoes, green beans cooked southern style, an ear of corn, a potato boiled, some dessert.

"I have all my teeth, that's something," she announces proudly. "When I was in the hospital, a male nurse brought a little bowl for my false teeth. I said, 'I don't have any.'" She laughs gleefully.

At restaurants, she sometimes orders a cocktail. "I'll also have a drink after bridge games," she says. "We never ever have anything between games, because it affects the bridge. Usually my friend and I have connecting rooms, and she and I will get together and have wine and cheese or candy and cookies. I like wine. Tonight I'm going out, so I think I'll have a bourbon sour, a little on the sweet side." She smiles in anticipation.

On nights out, she's home and in bed by 11 o'clock. On nights in, she goes to bed at 9 o'clock. "I like eight hours of sleep and usually I sleep right through the night," she says briskly. "I was having a little trouble with waking up, and I found if I got myself something to eat, I went right back to sleep."

Once she took vitamins. "I found some vitamin E up in my cupboard a week or so ago, and thought I'd take it. But I don't take vitamins normally. I think they may help, but I don't know if I need them. My internist hasn't said anything about it."

Ethel concentrates on the positive. "You have to think what I CAN do, not what I cannot do. I'm so thankful I can do what I do. I am so very fortunate. And I never talk about, 'Oh, I have this most awful cold,'" she whines. "That's just awful. People really are not interested in your ills. No, they're not," she says sharply.

"Do everything you can do for yourself. I've seen some old people—anything someone can do for 'em, they won't do. I don't think that should be so.

"Get out as much as you can, do as much as you can. Do everything you can possibly do for yourself. When someone starts to do something for me, I say, 'I can do that!' There are a few things I can't do, but I can do this, I can do that."

She acknowledges it's pleasant to be treated well because of her age. "They're good to people in wheelchairs," she laughs. "Boy, are they good. I go to St. Pete alone in a plane, and at the airport they bring a wheelchair, transport me to the bus, and I go straight to the hotel. Of course, I give them a tip," she adds.

"At the recycling place here, where I take my junk, the last time a lady said, 'Oh, may I take that for you?' I said, 'Oh, I thank you, certainly, thank you. You're the first person who's ever said that.' The men don't, and one or two of them practically knock me down, getting past me. They never say, 'May I take this in for you?'" She looks peeved.

Ethel enjoys being with people of all ages. "I did something I'd never done before," she says. "I played bridge three mornings in a row this week with a man 48 years old. He worked as an engineer, to great acclaim, and now he's semi-retired. He lives with a girl, they've lived together since she was 20 and he was 30. They don't want to get married. We were out together last night. I DO enjoy these people."

Is it important to have a male companion? I ask.

"No, not for me. Not a bit," she says, without hesitation. "People said after my husband died in 1972, 'Would you think of marrying again?' I said, 'Good heavens, I can't even get a man to live with me, much less marry me.'" She laughs. "I like company, but I don't care if it's male or female, particularly."

She misses her husband less and less. "But often when I drive up to the house, I think, 'Oh, I wish he were there.' The first week or two after he died, it was awful hard and I found myself getting out two plates, two cups. Now I don't miss the cooking part. Ugh! I don't like to cook. My husband always thought I was a good cook, but I didn't like it. You gobble it down too fast and there's not as much appreciation as the work that went into it."

She doesn't miss having children. Early in their marriage, she wanted them, but her husband did not, because of the high mortality rate of women giving birth. "Women were dying like flies in the early 1930s, when we would've had ours," she explains. "I think they were oversedating the women. We hardly had a friend who wasn't affected. One of my classmates hemorrhaged and died.

"I had my husband almost in the notion," she goes on. "Then I went out with some doctors' wives to a luncheon. I came home and said, 'Now, Billy, one woman has a two-year-old and a new baby and she's just thrilled.' About a month later, my friend told me the woman had died. My husband said, 'See, her husband was a doctor and her father was a doctor and they couldn't save her. I don't ever want to hear one more word about it.' And that was it.

"My physician knew how much I wanted children, and he talked with my husband twice about it. He wanted to talk to him again, but I said, 'No, don't, because you've tried twice. It won't do any good.' The physician told me, 'You'll mind a lot now, and you'll continue minding for quite a while. But you'll mind less and less, until after a while, you'll be glad.'

"Well, I am glad now, because when I see some children, a lot of them are just kind of waiting around until their parents die for that 25 cents. I've seen children just paw over their parents because of this," she says hotly. "Some children are a nuisance, and their parents are a nuisance to them. If I had children, they might be after me, 'Mommy, you've got to give up your house, you just can't be there alone.'" She cackles. "No, I don't miss that."

One of her young friends recently died of AIDS. "John, dead of AIDS! Oh, lawdy, I call him young. He was 48," she cries. "I'd promoted him in our unit. I wanted someone to clean nights and he was a young boy going to Boston College. Shining! Everything was shining after he cleaned. I trained him as an EEG technician, promoted him to head technician.

"About three years ago, he told me, 'They give me two years.' He came back to the house, he looked a little drawn. He got worse. He worked up to three or four months before he died." She shakes her head sadly. "They've got to do something about this epidemic."

Ethel isn't afraid of death, but fears being incapacitated. "It's like they ask the woman if she's afraid of flying and she says, 'Oh, no, I'm afraid of crashing.' So that's it. This lying in a bed in a hospital or something, and dying by inches, that's bad.

"Some of the nursing homes, I understand, aren't that desirable. My sister-in-law just goes on, day after day, about it, says she'd rather they shoot her than put her in one. I had to put my mother in a nursing home. First I got nurses round-the-clock at her home. She wouldn't let them do anything. Oh, it was awful.

"I was working at the time. The doctor said she should be in a nursing home. She was there about two and a half, three months. The doctor called me and told me she wouldn't take her medicine and said, 'What do you think?' I said, 'If she doesn't want it, don't give it to her.' He said, 'That's the way I feel. Let her die in dignity.' He said it might prolong her life a week or so. I said, 'Oh, goodness, no. I don't believe in that.' She went quickly after that.

"That's the way I want to be treated. When I'm going, let's go quickly." She sits up in her chair and pounds the armrests.

"I'm happy that I can live at home. I do NOT want to live in a retirement place, I'm not ready for one." she says vehemently. "I can take care of myself and my own house. I have a handyman who helps me, but I do all my own housekeeping, except for help two hours a week. I like things to look neat." Her house is spotless and everything is in place.

"I'm not afraid of living alone, I'm not the least bit afraid of anything," she goes on. Twice her house was burgled and jewelry stolen, so she installed an alarm system. Now she has an inside "panic button" and a portable one. "But I never think about taking it with me when I go out," she confesses.

What do you think comes after death? I ask.

"It's kind of hard to know what to believe in, isn't it?" she says quietly. "If there's reincarnation, maybe I could come back as a butterfly or something. Maybe a worm," she jokes.

"I'm not very religious. I was brought up a Methodist and I was on my knees most of my life, so I decided when I got older, I wouldn't go to church. And I don't, if I can help it. When my cousins come visiting from Kentucky, I take them to their Christian Science services.

"I do believe in God," she continues. "I'm just not fond of all this stuff about Jesus. I think he's a smart man and all, but I just don't want to hear so much about it."

What's the best part of being old? I ask.

"I can say and do anything I want," she says happily. "If I do something, they'll say, 'Well, that's because she's old, the poor old thing.' Used to be, I was kind of prim and proper, but now—oh, I can say anything.

"A couple from New Hampshire was coming to visit and couldn't find a place to stay anywhere near that was decent and affordable. I had two double beds in a room, and so I left a message on their recorder, 'I have an extra bed and Doris can have one bed all to herself,' inferring that Bruce could stay with me.

"I kid around like that, you know. At night when they got into bed, he called over and said, 'I didn't think this was the arrangement!'

"Oh, Lord, I wouldn't have said anything like that when I was young. Oh, no. I couldn't have!"

MICHAEL
WERBOFF

Born: December 10, 1896,
  Ukraine
Profession: Artist, portrait
  painter, teacher
Home: New York, NY

The birth certificate has nothing to do with age. I was asked several times, what is my formula to be so long-lived? I said, "Just don't give in. Think young, surround yourself with a lot of young friends, and they will make you feel young." I have some friends with young children and when I come to them, they never let me sit with the older people. They always ask me to their table. I'm always very, very grateful for this.

I feel comfortable with young people and they feel comfortable with me because I never try to teach anyone any kind of philosophy. I have used that with my pupils when I was teaching. I have never criticized my pupils from my point of view, always from their point of view. And I found if you treat young people as your equals, not as their superiors, they are very responsive.

I learned early in life, thank God, not to be jealous, not in my romances, not in my professional life. Jealousy doesn't change anything. I have always been tolerant. I never interfere with somebody else's beliefs and feelings. And after I went through the starvation period in Russia, between 1918 and 1922, I learned that worrying doesn't help anything.

My understanding of age has changed quite a bit. When I was 16, I was taken into a studio of an artist who was beginning to be well-known and I said, "When I'll be that old, I'll try to do as well." That old was 32.

I started to think about age only when I was 50, and only because people were telling me, "Well, Mr. Werboff, half a century! Formidable date!" I said, "I don't know, because I just now was reminded of it."

I don't think of age even now. I'm 95 and I have no feeling of being old. I'm going to shock you, because I cannot imagine myself even as a middle-aged man. I have the same enthusiasm of living as I was having in my late twenties and early thirties. I'm still painting and doing better than before.

I have a very simple philosophy of happiness. Make the very best of what you have got, with the hope for the better. Strive for something, but be very pleased with what you've got. Don't stop.

"There is a beautiful saying: 'You have to stick your neck out
 to move forward.' And another: 'If you don't say anything,
you end up doing nothing and being nothing.' I believe that."

ELISABETH KÜBLER-ROSS

> Born: July 8, 1926,
> Zurich, Switzerland
> Profession: Psychiatrist,
> author, social activist
> Home: Headwaters, VA

Elisabeth wraps us in a cocoon of warmth and good food as soon as we step into the kitchen. She's making Christmas cookies and the aroma fills her Virginia farmhouse.

"Come in, come in, put your coats over there, I'm baking," she greets us in a sing-song, Swiss-German voice, husky and strong. "How was your drive? Did you find me okay?" she asks.

We shake hands, and she smiles broadly, showing a missing tooth. Short and pear-shaped, she wears blue jeans, a sweatshirt with "Arizona" emblazoned on it, and rugged boots. Her face is lined with wrinkles and covered with huge-rimmed glasses. When she looks at you, her eyes lock on and pierce like skewers.

We would like to take a photograph right away. "The light is good in front of the house," says my photographer Ann Hawthorne. "No, no photo today," Elisabeth dismisses us. "I broke this front tooth and have to go to the dentist to get it fixed. You'll have to come back another time." We look at each other in surprise, but accept her decision. We don't want to get off on the wrong foot.

The kitchen is low-ceilinged, dark and homey, filled with hanging pans, rustic furniture, and old stoves. Elisabeth sets an old-fashioned metal coffee pot down on a long picnic table and invites us to sit on benches. Over coffee, cookies, and cigarettes, we spend several hours talking. She and Ann smoke. "I don't even ask anymore," Elisabeth waves a hand airily. "I do it anyway!"

She talks almost nonstop about her life, beliefs, and passions. Quick and thoughtful, she crafts her replies with unusual words, often switching verb tenses in mid-paragraph. Because of her accent, we must listen carefully. When I ask her to repeat a word, she graciously obliges. She pronounces all her "w's" like "v's" and runs her sentences together.

"When you live alone, with NOBODY to talk to and share anything, it's quite lonesome," she says, without sadness. "I have MILLIONS of people who LOVE me and they think it's love, but it's not," she scoffs. These are people who have read her classic book *On Death And Dying* (1969) and attended workshops on how to cope with death. Elisabeth spent years traveling around the world to give workshops. Now she's trained staff to take over. She drops in to give an occasional talk on spirituality.

Most of the time she works on pairing AIDS hospital babies with adoptive parents. She also advises groups setting up a new kind of nursing home, in which old people mix with young children. As a medical doctor, she continues to treat patients and make house calls. Her evenings are devoted to correspondence. She receives a quarter of a million letters every year. "It's my big headache." she laments, with a smile. "I answer all the letters from people who've been hit by tragedy or death."

As a defense mechanism, she lives by herself. "I've CHOSEN to live alone," she explains. "I've HAD to. Otherwise I'd be flooded with so-called friends. You learn soon to differentiate who is a friend and who is not. Do you know how many people say, 'I love you?'" She pauses dramatically. "Baloney! It's not, 'I love you.' It's 'I NEED you for something. If you write a foreword to my book—or do this or that.' That has nothing to do with love.

"God! You should see my room," she shudders. "I have about 75 manuscripts that I'm supposed to read before December 11th. They all want forewords, a little blurb. I do much too much," she exclaims with distaste. "If they send it without asking first, I send it back now. I used to have two rooms full of unrequested manuscripts, from floor to ceiling. People don't have the courtesy to ask first," she mutters.

Who are your true friends? I ask.

"My ex-husband Dr. Ross, our two children, Dr. Ross's six-year-old daughter, and my staff here," she replies promptly.

"We are OLD FRIENDS," she speaks warmly of her former husband. "Nothing has ever changed since I failed with my marriage. I go cook for him at Christmas." She brightens. "At any occasion I have, I do. He lives in Phoenix right now. He's dying, he's not doing too well." Her tone is resigned.

"He has a daughter, a six-year-old child, and she is my absolute FAVORITE child. I spoil her ROTTEN." She flashes a big smile. "I don't know what to call her! She's the half-sister of my children, and my children love her dearly. My daughter Barbara, who's 27, she's a child psychologist, terrific with kids, fantastic. My son Kenneth is 29, he's a photographer and loves what he does. He and I have a dry sense of humor.

"I saw both of them at Thanksgiving and will see them at Christmas. When we're together, we shop until we drop. My daughter likes that, my son doesn't. He's a typical man." She smiles kindly.

"Help yourself." She pushes the coffee pot toward us. "I can always make more." We refill our white china mugs. Elisabeth checks the oven. "Agh!" she cries. "See, I should not do two things at the same time." A faint burnt odor rushes out. "That's all right," we chorus. "We'll eat them!" She shrugs her shoulders and places a plate of slightly over-baked cookies before us. We devour them. She smiles dubiously, sits down across from us, and lights a cigarette.

"I always wanted to live in the country," she continues. "But my husband's specialty kept us in cities, so we were doomed to live in New York or Chicago or Denver. I had no choice. When he left, my choice was to buy a farm and do what I love to do." She bought a 300-acre farm in the Shenandoah Mountains of western Virginia and began to work it.

"It took me five years to put this place together. It hadn't been farmed in 15 years." She planted a big garden and collected cows, chickens, sheep, llamas, a donkey, a beloved St. Bernard dog, and cats. The cats must stay outdoors. "No animals roaming in the house!" she barks. "That we don't want."

Sometimes country life is a struggle. "I live alone on a farm, and you can't function that way alone," she says bluntly. "You need a man, a strong man, to lift the bales of hay. I have trouble after my stroke." Elisabeth hired men to help with the chores, but doesn't believe it's the ideal situation.

Lack of money is a constant worry. Workshop fees cover only a fraction of her costs. She manages the rest with book royalties, speech fees, and donations.

Her age is a factor. She acknowledges that her energy has diminished, but insists that aging has benefits that she fully appreciates. "I LOVE to grow old, I LOVE to be old, I have NO hangups about old age," she says with renewed gusto. "I would not want to be 40 again, or 50. I would like to be 70 or 80, if I'm functioning as much as I am now. My eyes and ears are good and I sleep all right—five or six hours a night.

"The only disadvantage of old age," she chuckles, "is that you have to go to the bathroom all the time in the middle of the night, and you can't sleep until nine or ten in the morning. I always thought it would be great if I didn't have to get up to open the chicken coop and could sleep until nine or ten. It would be heaven. Now that I can actually do that, I can't sleep anymore! It's a small thing, not important." She flicks a hand.

"Yes, I smoke and I drink coffee, and I eat beef once in a while, and I HATE macrobiotic diet," she says defiantly. "I do everything NORMAL. If there is a nice Christmas meal, I still like a glass of red wine. In Switzerland, my father had a gorgeous wine cellar, and with every meal we had a glass of wine. It's like you Americans drink Pepsi or Coke. I never had a pop in my life, never, ever, ever." She sounds proud.

"But I eat very little. When you are alone, you don't eat. You stop cooking. If you have a family to cook for—yes, I'd eat, but now I do not make big meals. That was my problem. Now I have to be sure I cook one meal a day. So I make soup." She looks satisfied.

Aging has another plus: the worst is past. "You don't have to go through all the nightmares of life," she says blissfully. "Those are behind you, you've learned all your basic lessons. You've learned that there are very few people you can trust, but those few are the REAL friends.

"And you know to differentiate who's a friend and who says, 'I love you,' and has nothing to do with love." She gives us a long, hard look. "You learn a LOT of things on your path and I'm glad to have that behind me. It was not easy."

Elisabeth was born in 1926 and would like to live until 2003. "2003—this is my fantasy! If I go early, I watch everything from the other side," she says happily, referring to her belief in an afterlife. "That's no problem. But I don't want to live much longer than 2003. Because between 77 and 78—yuk!" She spits out the words. "I don't want to be that old.

"You're like this: you drop everything, you can't chew anymore, and you can't work in the garden anymore. You just sit in a rocking chair and live alone. That's not pleasure. I'm only 64 ½, not 77 yet. As long as I'm 77 and happy and can do, I just put in my request to take me at 77.

"You know," she goes on quickly, "I was paralyzed totally from a stroke. Three years ago last August I couldn't speak. I had to climb on all fours, to the top of the mountain every day, yes!" She sees our look of disbelief. "I climbed above my log cabin and sang at the peak of my voice to get my voice back and be able to move again. And I sing TOTALLY off-key!" We all laugh. "But nobody hears me," she whispers cheerily.

"Within a month, I was able to talk and lecture again and walk around. Now my health is good, I'm fully recovered, except for names. And that's a blessing. Now I can say, 'No, I don't remember that. I had a stroke.'" She strikes an innocent pose, then smiles.

I say, Please don't tell me that when I call you to check a fact.

"I might," she answers mischievously.

She's pleased that she no longer conducts her workshops. "I don't miss it," she says easily. "When it's time to leave, I have no problem letting go. I think I've done my share. I've hand-picked and hand-trained people to do a lot of things. I have six assistants in every workshop. They're not the same as when I gave them, but they're good. We have workshops here and in Europe, Australia, New Zealand, everywhere."

Her main project now is adoption of AIDS babies. "I wanted to specialize in pediatrics when I was starting out in medicine," she explains. "Now I'm working with AIDS baby groups everywhere, many in America. I have an organization in Arizona with a computerized system and 154 families ready to adopt.

"But we can't get the babies out of the hospitals," she laments. "They get $1,000 a day from the government for research and they don't want to release the babies and give up that money." Her voice rises in frustration. "We've been able to get only one AIDS baby out of a hospital in three years. Now we appeal directly to the pregnant women who have AIDS or are HIV-positive. We try to avoid that they get into hospital."

Studies show that HIV-positive babies can become negative if given constant care and touching. "That's why all these AIDS babies in Romania die like flies, because nobody touches their skin," she rails. "If these babies are MARINATED in love, if they are touched all the time, then they have the chance to become HIV-negative. I tell that to everybody. I have two babies born with AIDS and now they are HIV-negative." She nods triumphantly.

"I want you to see my AIDS baby room," she says quickly, jumping up and opening a door. Beds, tables, and chairs are piled with gifts. "Every one of my AIDS babies gets a handmade quilt, a handmade sweater, a handmade doll, and a handmade stuffed animal," she says. "That's my hobby, to make CARE packages.

"We have a woman in my workshop who makes quilts for every single AIDS baby. She already sent out three thousand quilts. Every time I have another group of AIDS babies, she sends me some more. Now they sent two or three thousand quilts to Romania."

She points to a group of hand puppets. "These were made by a 26-year-old Swiss woman before she died. They're a masterpiece and took lots and lots of work. Those are knitted things," she indicates a pile of sweaters. "Some come from Switzerland, some from Germany. They're very European." She picks up a stuffed animal. "This, my sister made. Those chairs and rocking horse were made from a long piece of wood. And the sleds!" She touches a wooden sled with shiny runners.

"I turn a lot of people on, I'm a good catalyst," she says unabashedly. "I tell people what they can do for these babies. If they can't adopt them, at least they can do this."

Her fondest wish is to adopt an AIDS baby, but she knows it would cause a furor in her ultraconservative Virginia neighborhood. "I cannot have an AIDS baby here," she says flatly. "If I would adopt one single AIDS baby, they'd burn my whole farm down. They've already made Ku Klux Klan cross burnings on the property. What this has to do with AIDS babies, I'll never understand. I teach that you should not respond to negativity, so I have to practice what I preach. Sometimes it does get difficult.

"This farm would make an ideal place for AIDS babies," she goes on. "I raise enough vegetables for 100 people, enough fruit, enough everything. But the people here are afraid. When we tried to rezone five acres of my farm for the babies, there was a public meeting. One person said, 'We are reborn Christians, but if you ever, ever call for an ambulance, we will not respond!'

"Another person got up and said, 'We are reborn Christians, but if you ever send any of those kids to our schools, the doors will be locked.' Every sentence began, 'We are reborn Christians, but....'

"In time, I lost my cool and said, 'You are a strange kind of Christians. If Jesus would be walking on the earth now, then he would take all these AIDS babies and love them.'" She sighs and wonders, "How can you talk to people like this? It's hopeless. They are like 200 years ago. They intimidate me, but it goes in one ear and out the other. They shot bullets through my windows." We gasp. "Luckily I wasn't inside at the time," she says.

"Then I kept getting flat tires. I stayed up one night and saw them drive by in their trucks. They threw pieces of glass and rusty nails into my driveway. The next day I laid something down so that all the glass and nails went through the slits. They just couldn't get to me. Instead of hating them, I outsmarted them."

Her other big project is organizing what she calls E.T. centers. "E.T. was a being of unconditional love," she explains, referring to the movie about an extraterrestrial who visits earth. "E.T. is my favorite! My E.T. centers are nursing homes that WORK, not like the ones we have in this country. These are homes for the elderly, with toddlers. It's a day-care kind of set-up where the parents leave their children for the day and don't worry, because they're in good hands. It helps every generation.

"The old people don't have to pay. But they do have to pay," she adds quickly. "There's never anything for nothing. Their payment is to pick one child—a redhead or a black-curly-head or whatever they like the most—and to spoil the child ROTTEN. Not by buying things for the child, but by taking them on their laps and telling them about good old Ireland or Scotland or whatever they have memories of.

"Touch them again, old people NEED to be touched," she says. "Children like old people's wrinkles and pimples. They play piano on them." We laugh. "They DO," she insists. "Two-, three-, four-year-olds. They like it and they touch it and they don't find it icky. Children are absolutely fabulous if you don't ruin them. Most kids get ruined too early. They get spoiled with all these electric book toys and all that stuff.

"More and more of my workshop people are starting something like E.T. centers. I've been talking about them for 15 years. You should skip the mother, because if children are raised more by the grandma, at least part of the day, they don't develop all these mother-daughter problems. If you skip a generation, you have NO problem."

Care Costel, the first E.T. center, opened a few months ago in Colorado Springs, Colorado. Each home is different. "Everybody does what feels natural," says Elisabeth. "I'm in touch with most of the people setting up the centers. I have no requirements, except that the old people should not have to pay.

"I think if somebody contributed to society for seven decades or more, they're entitled to a WONDERFUL old age in an environment which is nice, with some of their furnitures, and a cat or parakeet. I'll never be able to take my St. Bernard dog in there," she laughs. "But they should have something living.

"In the E.T. homes, old people get patched again. They NEED to be patched again. The old people give the children total, unconditional love. Those children have all the foundation for a positive life because they got it very young in life. Then when they have a mother and a father who is a grouch and gives conditional love, they have grandma or grandpa who loves them UNCONDITIONALLY. You only need one human being one hour in your life, early in life, who gives that kind of love, to give you the foundation."

Ann gasps. "That's it, that's exactly what my grandparents gave me. May I tell you something, Elisabeth? Twenty years ago in college, we studied your book *On Death and Dying*. You gave me such a gift. I was able to help my grandmother die. It changed my life and gave me her life. As her brain cancer was getting worse, you could see her closing doors."

Elisabeth nods. "Yes, the world shrinks."

Ann says, "My grandmother always kept ME, though. We'd be in the room talking and talking and talking, she'd be sobbing and crying or laughing. Then someone would walk in and she'd just—the curtain would go down. She could not deal, did not want to deal with it. She'd already let go of people. After they'd leave, we'd be back into it. She talked to me about everything."

Elisabeth smiles. "That was the biggest gift you could give her."

Ann replies, "It was wonderful. Thank you."

The doctor replies, "Thank you for sharing." It's a heart-felt thanks, not a platitude.

Elisabeth's work means everything to her. "When it comes to work, I'm young at heart," she states emphatically. "When it comes to play, I'm lousy. I never learned how to play because I never really had a childhood. I've NEVER learned how to play. Never, ever, ever! I'm one of triplets and we played and played, the three of us together, but that wasn't much fun. We had to play the same games.

"I love my work now, but I don't know how to play. What other people say is play, to me is icky. I love to garden. In March, when I put my seeds out in the greenhouse, every day I go and look. I love that. I go hiking. I have animals. That's my company.

"I get excited when I can deliver my baby lambs in February and March. All my cows are pregnant now, my llama is pregnant and my donkey is pregnant. So I'm looking forward to spring, when I can be with my animals. THAT I'm happy about. When the plants are coming and I see the first snowbell—that makes me happy.

"Deer come to my home, I had three deer here in the drive-way this morning. I'm not a city person. Now I have a place in the country. It's not WHERE I want to live, it's HOW I want to live. The people here could be much nicer, but the immediate neighbors are adorable, and they're all patients of mine.

"One woman had lupus. Two had sleeping sickness and one woman has a stroke and sits at the window for 16 years. Those who've gone through the hardships of life are ador-able, and I visit them and make rounds twice a week. We get along terrific."

Other patients telephone Elisabeth for advice. "They may have herpes or venereal disease or symptoms that could be AIDS," she says. "They call up, but anonymous. They say, 'What do I do for this and this and that?' I tell them, I always answer their questions. You have to practice and to preach."

Children are her favorite people. "I've worked with children almost exclusively the last 15 years and I just love them. They're honest, they're not phony-baloneys yet. If they're sad, they cry, and if they're mad, they get real mad. They tell you what they think of you in your face, whether you like it or not. They're honest. By the time they go to first grade, they become phony-baloneys.

"In many cases, children deal with death more naturally than adults," she says. "You know, the children who've had the privilege of watching grandma die and bring some tea to her or play some music. Then when grandma dies, they have no hangups.

"But when they think of themselves dying, they're always afraid of being buried. That's because they see that we dig a big hole, put grandpa in a casket, and nail it closed. Then we put him in that hole and put dirt on top of him. That's like the ultimate! Adding insult in injury.

"But I tell them, 'Don't worry, it's not your grandpa. It's just a cocoon, not a butterfly.' I have this adorable model for children and they love it. They understand it much better than grown-ups. They say, 'Grandpa is about to fly already, you can put all the dirt on top of him, and it doesn't hurt him.' Beautiful! I love that.

"Grown-ups are afraid. They say, 'Are the children going to see butterflies and think it's grandpa?' And I say, 'No, children are not that stupid.'" She sounds exasperated.

Not surprisingly, Elisabeth has no fear of dying. "I have not been afraid of death for 64 ½ years, because in Europe, in the old days when I was a country doctor, EVERYBODY prepared for death. They didn't have these hang-ups, they don't have this embalming nonsense and rules like you have to have a silk pillow and shoes that fit for the deceased.

"In the old country, they made their own caskets and buried them on the farm, exactly the same way they do here in this part of Virginia. The prolongation of life, it's not my cup of tea anyway," she says vigorously. "I would not want to live on a respirator or be resuscitated. All this, just to live another week or month? If I get another stroke, I won't call anybody."

A friend knocks and enters the kitchen. "Beryl, when you want some soup, it's ready," calls Elisabeth. "When you have a chance, can you fill up the car? Before I forget it. Is anybody going to the center? Soon? Would you call them? I want these ladies to see the center. You're not in a hurry?" she turns to us. "You have half an hour to see the center?" Of course, we say.

A staff member takes us through a big new building next door. The large main room is round and airy, with groupings of chairs and sofas. On the periphery are bedrooms, bathrooms, study areas, children's play nooks, and a kitchen. Wall-to-wall carpeting and comfortable furniture lend warmth. Here workshop leaders teach Elisabeth's techniques for dealing with death and the five stages a person goes through: denial and isolation, anger, bargaining, depression, and finally, acceptance.

We return to the farmhouse to find Elisabeth taking more cookies out of the oven. "Now, come and I'll show you my log houses," she says, donning a jacket. We dutifully follow her out the door and up a gently sloping mountain. She moves with energy and enthusiasm.

It's late afternoon and the sun is warm. "Can you guess what this is?" she asks, stopping at a small building.

"A root cellar?" says Ann.

Elisabeth nods and we duck into a room fitted with shelves holding potatoes, onions, turnips, and hundreds of glass jars. I see canned peaches, applesauce, cabbage, cauliflower, peas, and tomatoes.

We stand in amazement. "Take one with you!" she exhorts us. "I have anything and everything. What else do you like? Take some. Have some. You're welcome! That's zucchini. Do you know how to make ratatouille? Take one of the tomato, then you cook that with rice, cook it for an hour. What do you like? Take one. Look, I'm living alone." We leave with arms full.

Last year she put up 2,000 jars of produce. "In December, one tomato in Staunton, that's the city nearby, one tomato cost $3.05. One tomato!" she exclaims in disgust. "And I thought,

'This is the time to help the homeless, because they don't get any vegetables.'

"I went over to the food bank and offered them a thousand jars of homegrown, homemade, wonderful, right-from-the-garden vegetables. You know what? They cannot take it because it's not government-inspected. That's America!" Her voice crackles with indignation. "That's America. People die of hunger and you cannot give it to them.

"I invite the guys who work here to have lunch. Yesterday I made a DELICIOUS vegetable soup and I hoped they would eat it. I said, 'Lunch is on the table, you stop working, you come and eat now.' But they don't have time or they don't make the time," she sighs. "It's their problem, not mine. They have to choose how they live.

"So I freeze it. I have five freezers that are so stacked full, I couldn't put one more soup there." She laughs.

She never stops doing. Why? I ask.

"My big fear was always that I would be bored." Her voice drops. "I'm not a good person for being bored. I keep busy all the time so I'm not bored. I've had lots of super experiences," she says, referring to supernatural experiences, feeling at one with spirits of people who have passed on. "It makes my life a bit colorful," she smiles knowingly.

We continue walking up the mountain and reach a log and mortar cabin. "I built this for my sister Eva, the ski instructor, the mountain climber," says Elisabeth. "She visits one month out of the year. These are 250-year old logs. I had to demolish a log cabin within 24 hours—they were selling it—and label everything and move it here. I reconstructed it into a new shape. Eva did all her own chinking. The first year I built it, the second year I furnished it, the third year I put in electricity.

"My sister always wanted a log cabin," she continues. "And she likes a BIG shower. So I built her a big, American-style shower. Do you want to see it?" She opens the door and takes us upstairs to a big room that is shower/bathroom/kitchen, with a wood-burning stove in one corner. "Eva loves it," she says. "I hate showers." A picture of the Matterhorn, a reminder of their Switzerland, hangs prominently on the wall.

"Come," she says, "before it gets too dark, I'll show you my house. It's another log cabin that I built. The chinking was very hard work, I did it myself." We enter a large, high-ceiling room with rustic furniture and a fragrant Christmas tree. Smoke wafts out from a fire in the stone fireplace. Music is playing softly.

"Without music, I couldn't live," she says with fervor. "Because I have no human being to talk to." Rows and rows of cassette tapes fill a bookcase. "Country music for a long time was my absolute favorite." Tonight it's easy listening.

She throws a few small logs on the fire. It burns day and night, she tells us. The hearth is covered with antique pots and kettles. On the mantlepiece sit pine cones, wreaths, candle molds, kitchen utensils, and a crucifix. More treasures crowd the tables.

"That's my Noah's ark, from Guatemala," she indicates a carved wooden miniature. "That's an eye of God," a woven square of yarn to protect a house from evil. "That's my horoscope," she nods at a drawing. "I'm a Cancer, a homebody." Pictures, weavings, and rugs hang on the walls. Plants and crystals are scattered about. "I love rocks, plants, and animals," she says. "I gave a big amethyst to Kenneth and he loves it.

"Come, I'll show you upstairs." She climbs quickly and apologizes for unpacked suitcases from her last trip. In a bedroom, she indicates a group of antique dolls in one corner. "Since I was nine years old, I've had a doll collection," she explains. "I also collect thimbles." She touches a wooden case mounted on the wall. Each niche holds a tiny thimble. "I have 4,000 thimbles. Everywhere I travel, I buy one. They're small, I can put them in my pocket. I like the old ones. I have every kind of material, from bone to ivory. This ivory one is from the Eskimos," she points.

"Come and sign my guestbook," she says, leading us downstairs. We ask her to autograph her books. "You'd better bring them fast. After that I turn into a pumpkin," she jokes, referring to the setting sun.

She has more to show us. "Which one was I?" she asks, picking up a framed photo with three children, seemingly identical. "This is us when we were 2 ½ years old, so you know what a problem we were."

We guess wrong. "That's all right, I could never figure out which one was me either," she says easily. "Really!" We all laugh. "Erica and I looked exactly alike. We have hundreds of pictures and I don't know which one is me. Eva was bigger."

Elisabeth, Erica, and Eva are triplets. They have one brother. By the time the girls were four years old, they'd become such celebrities that their parents moved from Zurich to the village of Meilen to escape the publicity.

Elisabeth felt the sting of being raised a triplet. "We had everything materially, but as a triplet, you are nothing, absolutely zero. I could have dropped dead, they wouldn't have even known which one died," she says dryly. "And I'm not exaggerating.

"We were so totally identical. We had to wear the same clothes, the same shoes, the same bedspread, the same dolls. We were like cloned objects. That's why I hate photography, because we went to school and everybody took pictures of the famous triplets. We had to sit on identical night pots!"

Like Eva, Erica visits for a month every year. "Because Erica was paralyzed for many years, she can't do any of the activities outdoors. When she was little, she would sit in a darkened room and read. I could never read a book. I had ants in my pants," she laughs shortly. "That's why I can't meditate. I'm a doer. Erica's a reader and philosopher."

After their father died, the four children made a pact to invite their mother to a new country every year. "And we kept that pact," says Elisabeth. "My brother invited her to India and Pakistan. He lived out there. One sister invited her to England and the other, I think, to Spain. I invited her to America."

She takes a deep breath. "We drove all the way from New York to Colorado, to my first house. When we got there, the family hadn't moved out of the house yet. So my mother looked on the map and said, 'We are THAT close to California. Could we go out to California?' So we packed the one-year-old child and put him in the back of the car and left the U-Haul in front of the house and we went to California!

"That was my mother. She lived it up AFTER, when she was a widow. She deserved it. I think I got the best from both parents," she muses. "Love from her, discipline and learning from my father."

Night is falling, but she doesn't seem anxious for us to leave. We relax on living room sofas and enjoy the warmth of the fire. I notice Southwest Indian objects, including statuettes of eagles. The eagle, I say, is a creature that soars and sees things in perspective.

"Well, that's the most important lesson I'm trying to teach families who lose one, two, three children," she replies. "They think it's the end of the world. But if they look at it 20 or 30 years later, they see that because of this tragedy, they are today who they are. They would have never gone to this point.

"Of course, you can't say that to somebody who's just lost a child," she says. "Otherwise you'll end up without your teeth. But you must see things in perspective. Otherwise you won't survive."

She picks up a feather-and-bead headdress and holds it aloft. "My Indian name is Standing Eagle. I'm an Indian, I'm a Pipe Woman, and I'm very proud of it. When a white woman gets the sacred pipe, that's an experience. They also gave me this pipe and totem pole with people's faces on it." She handles her gifts lovingly. "That made me more proud than my M.D. degree. I also got the Sacred Heart of a Snake from the Australian Aboriginals. So I have three medical doctor degrees, three kinds of shamans: the Aboriginals, the Indians, and the White Man."

She treasures her Indian connection. "I feel very, very comfortable with American Indians," she says. "There's so much we haven't learned from them and now we have a chance. We eradicate them, like the Australians eradicated the Aboriginals. Now they're sorry they didn't learn anything from them. They went on manhandling until there wasn't a single Aboriginal alive on the whole island of Tasmania. We didn't do much better." She speaks with dismay.

"The wisest people you can ever meet are the Hopis," she continues. "Have you ever studied the Hopi prophecies? You really have to go to the Hopi country and talk to a shaman, who will take you to those stone carvings where the whole prophecy is written IN ROCK.

"And everything is true," she says excitedly. "Everything they predicted hundreds and thousands of years ago has become true, including the AIDS epidemic. Just like if you study 'Revelations' in the Bible. We understand them. A lot of people read them and don't understand them. Or Nostradamus. The Hopis have predicted everything.

"And they all come to the same conclusion: the 1990s are the last decade of change, and if we don't change, it's going to be a disaster. If we change enough people, then it's going to turn FANTASTIC. The Hopi prophecies are fabulous and have been there for hundreds and hundreds of years.

"In the spring, I'm going to the Hopi Hospice Training Center near Albuquerque, New Mexico. The whole group, all the students and I, put it together."

Elisabeth documented her spiritual journey in an autobiography *The Wheel of Life: A Memoir of Living and Dying* (1997). She emphasizes the word "spiritual," as opposed to "religious." When she was a girl, she attended the Swiss Protestant Church every week for 12 years, but left, out of disgust. "The minister beat his children and then preached goodness every Sunday," she tells us. "What hypocrisy. I couldn't take it."

Her family was chagrined, but she felt justified. She developed her own belief system, which includes daily prayer asking God to help people on her special list. "You learn to be honest and practice what other people preach," she says. "You make booboos and you learn. All the religions teach basically the same thing: love thy neighbor as thyself. Unconditional love, that's the only thing that's relevant.

"After you die, nobody asks you how many mink coats you had, how much makeup you put on, how pretty you looked, how many mansions you built. All they ask is how much love you've been able to give and to receive."

Is receiving as important as giving? I ask.

"Yes," she says emphatically. "I learned that from my mother. My mother NEVER learned to receive. Her biggest fear in life was to be a vegetable. We told her, 'You end up a vegetable if you don't learn.' And she never learned it. If a neighbor would bake a pie on a Saturday, next Saturday she had to make a pie and give it back to her. Always like this.

"Then she ended up with a stroke. And for four years, she was unable to move one-tenth of an inch of any part of her body. She didn't say a word, and she was totally conscious.

"I went through all stages of anger with God: He's a monster and why does He let her suffer like this, after she spent her life loving?' About two years after she died, I got it. It was like an enlightenment: God is the most generous man in the world. He allowed my mother to GIVE for 75 years, to give and give and give, and only demanded she learn to receive for four years.

"She had no choice. Somebody had to clean her rear end, somebody had to feed her, somebody had to brush her hair, somebody had to wash her. She had no choice, she had to learn it the hard way. She died after four years like that. She was in Switzerland, I was in America. No mourning left now." She cuts off abruptly.

"So now I'm trying not to fall into the same trap that my mother did. I'm absolutely sure that if somebody had given my mother an overdose like this horrible organization, the Hemlock Society—they don't know what they're doing. They cheat people out of the last lessons that they learn. Absolutely. I'm TOTALLY opposed to it. My mother BEGGED me to give her something and I said, 'I absolutely cannot do it. As bad as I feel for you, I cannot do it.'

"And I'm glad I didn't," she says with conviction. "I'm not in favor of artificially prolonging life *ad infinitum*. I think it's ridiculous. But to shorten somebody's life with an overdose is a no-no. Because many, many, many of my patients learn the biggest lessons in the last year or so of cancer or AIDS or whatever they have. We are not doing them a favor. We are doing it out of pity and out of the wrong motivation. It is not love, it has nothing to do with love."

Are you learning to receive? I ask.

She pauses and looks at me hard. "I'm IMPROVING, let me put it that way," she says slowly, smiling. "I'm not doing too well. But I'm not half as bad as ten years ago. Every day I learn a little more."

Her credo is simple. "If you want to live a full life and grow old gracefully, you need three things: a lot of work, a lot of humor, and a lot of faith. If you have that, you're okay."

Do you have faith? I ask.

Another pause. "Well, it's shaky most of the time," she replies quietly. "I have faith in certain types of people who work on themselves. People who just sit on their rear end and don't want anything to change, I don't have much faith in them. But maybe in a century or so." She drifts off.

"You have to work on your unfinished business," she comes back, fiery. "The more you get rid of unfinished business, the more your spiritual side opens up. People who have the guts to work on their unfinished business—at the end of my workshops, 94 percent of these people have the biggest increase in spirituality. It's something you have to WORK on.

"You don't work on it to BECOME more spiritual," she explains. "But that's automatic when you get rid of your crap. DON'T use that word in the interview," she adds sharply. "When you get rid of your grief, your hate, your revenge, your greed, all the negative stuff, that will be replaced with love. And I mean real love, not phony-baloney love.

"Most grown-ups in America have not developed a spiritual side. They don't even know what they want to be, or how they want to spend their life. They float from one thing to another to another. And that's a pity, because they miss out a lot."

The real hope, she says, comes in the next century. "The nineties are the decade of change. So I have to live until after the year 2000. I'm not very interested in getting very, very, very old," she admits. "I'm eager for the transition. If I had no children, I would be very happy to die tomorrow."

What do you think of today's young people? I ask.

"A lot of young people have been raised with not enough discipline, and this is the biggest, biggest problem," she answers. "That's why they go drinking and go on drugs. Anytime something is difficult, they need some dope or some drug to make it through. If they'd been raised with natural emotions and with enough discipline, they would be a SUPER next generation. But they've been spoiled rotten. If they cry, they get what they want. How the hell they can grow up as a whole person?" Her tone is angry.

Elisabeth believes everyone must follow his dreams in order to grow and blossom. "You must do what you LOVE," she emphasizes. "People work in an office every day and they can't wait until they retire. They just work to pay the taxes and they never LIVE! It's stupid. They should do what turns them on.

"Look, I told my father, who ran an office-supply company, 'No, I'm not going to work in your office. I'm going to do what I want to do, even if I have to make a ten-year plan.' I was the only child who spoke up. And I'm very glad I did, because I would've ended up in an office as a bookkeeper or something, and I would've been a GROUCH and miserable and unhappy all my life long. I learned that from HIM. He was a very outspoken man, very honest.

"If you do what you love and are good at it, and if you make half of a living, then you don't have to worry. Do you know how many doctors on their deathbed look sad? I ask them, 'Why are you so sad?' They say, 'Well, I've never really lived.' I say, 'What the hell does that mean?' They say, 'Well, I made a good living, but I never really lived.' I ask, 'What would you like to do?' They say, 'Well, my father was a doctor, my grandfather was a doctor, it was understood that I would study medicine. They would be very proud of me.'

"That's 'I love you IF....'" she says tartly. "That's conditional love. These people became doctors to please the family. Maybe this man wanted to be a dancer or a carpenter or something, and he never, never fulfilled his dream of his life. It's a totally wasted life. Totally! No matter how many people he helped. If he helped with bitterness and resentment, it's not worth it."

After Elisabeth decided to become a doctor, she implemented a ten-year plan. Every day from 6 a.m. to 12 midnight, she worked as a medical lab technician. She earned enough money to attend medical school in Zurich, and after receiving her M.D. degree, she and her husband emigrated to the U.S., where she became a psychiatrist.

"You know, if you want to be a doctor, BECOME a doctor," she says firmly. "Even if you have no penny, you FIND the money somehow. Somebody will help you if you are on the right path. You will run into somebody who helps you with what you need. Not what you want, but what you NEED. You always get what you need, always. I'm absolutely convinced of that.

"We were down to $5 when we had to build this center," she motions next door. "We had to put the roof up, otherwise the whole building would have been ruined. And out of the blue, we got a gift of a few thousand dollars. That gave me enough pep to go lecturing again and get the money together.

"We never build anything unless we had the money. That's a Swiss disease," she laughs wryly. "I learned that from my father. But I'm glad I never made any debts. You don't buy a car until you have the money together.

"When I had my stroke, I had no debts. The farm was paid off, my house was paid off, everything we built was paid off. So if I would have dropped dead and they could have never finished it, at least what was there was paid for. That's a very good, very good philosophy." She looks satisfied.

It's 6 p.m. "Do you want a plate of hot soup before you hit the road?" she asks. "Aren't you hungry?" Yes, we say, and walk down to the farmhouse with her. She dishes up vegetable soup thick with salsify, carrots, celery, and onions, and sets a plate of salami and bread before us. Dessert is homemade applesauce.

We eat and talk for two more hours. Elisabeth describes knitting scarves to raise money for workshop scholarships. She tells us about her sisters' visits, and the neighbors' conservative attitudes. She discusses plans for Christmas, just a few weeks away.

"You haven't seen my Christmas tree yet?" She leads us into the living room filled with the smell of evergreen. "I haven't put the candles on it. You never have electric lights on a Swiss Christmas tree. But here you have to do both, otherwise the fire marshal comes." She laughs loudly.

"I always make a big fuss about Christmas. Monday is Christmas at the office and I can't wait. I've made all the packages. I have all my Christmas gifts ready in September. I HAVE to be organized. I buy things when I find something exactly right, then wrap them. But every Christmas I have to open up those damned packages to put in something I find at the last minute." She makes a face.

We return to the kitchen for fresh coffee. For a moment she is silent, then bounces up from the bench.

"Your grandma!" she says to Ann. "That makes me happy, that story about your grandma." We all smile and nod. I recall that when my father was dying, I tape-recorded him while he could still speak. "You taped him?" exclaims Elisabeth. "That's wonderful.

"My father left his singing for us. He made a record 30 years ago in Switzerland, a record of his own singing. It was a big deal. He went to a studio and sang all our favorite songs that we used to sing every night. He made a record for each one of us. At Christmas I play it. I even sing! He died 30 years ago, exactly. Kenneth was one year old when he died."

It's time to leave. She wraps a CARE package for us: soup, bread, cake, apple pie. "You take the pie with you," she insists. We don't argue. We thank her for a wonderful day together. Rarely does a person give us so much time for an interview. She hugs each of us hard.

We'll see you again, I say.

"Oh?" she says.

To take the photograph, I remind her.

"Oh, yes. Come back and take my photograph with the animals," she says enthusiastically. "I'll get the llamas and the donkey ready. Come in the spring when the lambs are born and you can take my picture with the lambs."

The thought delights her and she breaks into a girlish smile.

J.R. SIMPLOT

Born: January 4, 1909,
  Dubuque, IA
Profession: Chairman Emeritus,
  J.R. Simplot Company
Home: Boise, ID

Honey, I got places I go every day. Usually I drive to the club for lunch and play a few hands of gin rummy with some friends. Then I drop by the office to see what's new with the company. I founded it and ran it until I was 85. My son Scott is chairman of the board now. My other children are on the board of directors. In the evening, my wife usually has plans for me.

I've always been active. I rode horses, I ran, I could do a day's work with a shovel or pick. I built miles of trails up there at McCall, Idaho, and kept 'em open. Took all the timber and rocks out of 'em with a pick and an ax and a saw. I used to walk two and one half miles a day, but don't do that anymore. I move around all right. I skied up until a few years ago, even after I had my hip replaced. Hell, I'd just ski like a pro. I got down that mountain in nothing flat. I loved it.

I don't eat a lot of food. Over the years I tried to take care of myself, keep the weight off. But I didn't pay a damned bit of attention to what I ate. I don't know if that was smart, but I'm still here.

You've got to take risks. I've had my neck out that far all my life. You're not going to get very far unless you've got some gambler in you. It's tough enough that the best are out there competing. You're not going to get a good one if you try to play cinches. It isn't in the cards.

It's very, very important to get all the education and get good at something. Get good at something you like to do, stay with it, and polish it. Try to make something happen every day. I've taken on more damned jobs than any man my age ought to have. And I'm still going!

"Home and family have always been my priority, and health has always been up in the top. But my main value has been to do what you like to do BEST and try to do it BETTER."

ART LINKLETTER

Born: July 17, 1912,
  Moose Jaw, Saskatchewan,
  Canada
Profession: Communicator,
  entertainer, businessman
Home: Bel Air, CA

Arthur Gordon Linkletter makes a business of telling people how to age well. He flies around the country and gives a speech, "Stay Alive All Your Life, Die Young as Late as Possible."

It's a mission that he thoroughly enjoys. "I talk to conventions, universities, annual dinners, and to senior developments, everything from small seniors clubs to big retirement communities like Leisure World and Sun City," he says. "One of my greatest joys is standing up in front of an audience who've come to hear me, and talking to them for one and a quarter hours about life!

"And I always tell them the same thing." His blue eyes twinkle. His voice is strong and silky.

"At your age, you have a lot of negatives surrounding you and you have to work harder to maintain the status quo. You can't brush off health problems. You do the best you can with them."

He ticks off the requirements. "Get a GOOD doctor, get a good pharmacist, have yearly checkups, and observe all the basic rules of good health: rest, sleep, good food, exercise, non-smoking, nondrinking, and a regular schedule.

"Get your eyes examined every couple of years, have a thorough gastrointestinal checkup every three years, plus x-rays when you need them. Get your flu shots and your pneumonia shots every couple of years, and spend time doing things that you took for granted."

That's a lot of work, I observe.

"When you get older, you can't be a sissy," he warns, referring to his book *Old Age Is Not for Sissies*. "You can't just let things happen to you. You've got to MAKE them happen.

"And you have to begin cultivating new, younger friends BEFORE you need them," he warns. "Otherwise you're going to find yourself with a narrowing circle of good friends. You can't really make close friends out of kids who are 25 or 30, but there are lots of successful people I deal with in their 50s and 60s." His face is animated.

"I also tell my audiences that you have to do something for someone ELSE. That's the most important thing you can do. Be a giver, be a volunteer, be a foster grandparent. Be somebody who joins a group that's taking care of part of the highway and cleaning it up once a month. Or go back to school and spend some time with younger people in night courses. Just for the fun of it!

"Of course," he adds with a smile, "you learn to live with aches and pains. Some people never learn to live with their sorrows. They clutch them to their bosom. That's not good. You're robbing yourself of your life."

He sits behind a big desk in his modest Beverly Hills office. Behind him stands a big Mickey Mouse doll. The walls are decorated with plaques, honorary doctorates, and photos of his family, along with celebrities including Nancy and Ronald Reagan.

Art's schedule is rigorous and he thrives on it. A tanned, calm, fit man with bright eyes, silver hair combed straight back, and a perpetual look of bemusement and wonder, he makes 75 major speeches a year and dozens more to smaller groups. He calls himself a communicator.

"In all of 50 years I've been in radio and broadcasting, I'm probably best known for interviewing children, aged four to ten, on my television program *House Party*. But in the last five or eight years, I've moved over to the really large-growing segment of our population, which is over 65. In another 10 or 15 years, there are going to be more than 100,000 people over 100 in this country."

These people are his target. "I'm basically half schoolteacher and half preacher and half sales manager," he says without blinking. "That's three halves. And when people say, 'Would you like to live your life over again?' I say, 'There wouldn't be time.'

"I write, I speak, I broadcast, I teach, I motivate, and I'm interested in words, because with words, you think," he looks at me hard. "Without words, you don't think. The more words you have and the more facile you are with them, the more your mind is working."

He's written 23 books including *Drugs at My Doorstep*, *Kids Say the Darndest Things*, and *Confessions of a Happy Man*. The past 25 years, he's talked to young people about the dangers of drugs. After his daughter Diane died during an LSD experience, he became deeply involved in the anti-drug crusade.

He plans to keep working as long as he lives. "I can always write," he says. "If I can't write physically, I can dictate into a tape recorder. Or I can speak from a wheelchair or anything else. Yes, I'm lucky," he says. "I'm in a profession where you can do that. Many people can't do that, and I understand.

"When I speak to older people about adapting to old age, I do not intend to hold myself up as the one they should emulate, but merely an example of what is possible," he says gently. "Some people are sick, some people are poor, some people are not talented in a way that would fit into old age. But there's always SOMETHING you can do. You can volunteer to help somebody else."

For years, Art hosted popular radio and TV shows, including *House Party* and *People are Funny*. His interviews with children are legendary. He liked them, took time to know them, and truly listened to them, so they spoke candidly. The resulting humor was tremendous, and audiences howled. Art uses that fascination with people to talk to adults and inspire them.

"You know, I've always had this passion for life," he says, leaning back in his chair and rubbing his hands together. "I don't know where it came from, but I was always the one volunteering for everything. All the way through school, when I was a hobo—yes, I was a hobo—and when I went to work, if anybody said, 'We need somebody to....', you fill in the blank, I would be there with my hand up.

"I find it was not in order to be rich or famous or powerful," he explains. "It was to BE. I never had the idea I would be any of these things. I turned out to be all of them, but not intentionally. It was because I just had a zest for life. And to do BETTER.

"It might have been genetic, except, of course, I was an orphan, abandoned. So I don't know anything about my parents.

I had no conditioning by environment because the people who adopted me, Mary and Fulton John Linkletter, were old, poor, fairly uneducated, working-class people, highly religious, not at all business-oriented and with no grasp of the possibilities of life. They lived a very narrow, constricted life. And yet, I always had the exactly opposite feeling." He sounds incredulous.

"It shows the importance of what is INSIDE of you, rather than what is PUT ON you, at least in my case," he concludes.

Part of it is a sense of humor. "Of course, I see fun in everything," he says, very seriously. "I'm basically a humorist. Not a comedian but a humorist. Wherever I go and whatever I do is tinged with humor, and it makes people laugh." He smiles with a glint in his eye.

Do you see humor in yourself? I ask.

"Oh, of course, FIRST! As a public speaker, I nearly always start with something that is funny and slight poking goosefeathers at myself."

Who helps you keep your sense of humor?

"Probably my wife and my family," he replies thoughtfully. "But it's internalized. I feel just as funny in a board of directors meeting of a multinational corporation as I do talking to a bunch of kindergartners. It's different material, but it's the same attitude. I see funny things in everything."

He's delighted that he's so healthy and busy at his age. "I suppose the biggest surprise the last 30 or 40 years has been that I never have come to a sound barrier of age that I thought, 'Oh, gosh, here I am in male menopause.' There never was a time when I said, 'Well, I'm old now.' I hear that from people: 'Oh, my gosh, I'm 60 years of age.'

"I'm always so busy," he says. "I have so many projects, things to do, places to go, IDEAS.

"I've given more thought to 80 than any other age," he continues. "But not daunting thought. I tell everybody how old I am, which is violating all the rules of Hollywood. In fact, I'm very proud to be 80 and in such good health.

"But seeing so many older people who are sick, as I visit hospitals and nursing homes, I've also come to accept the fact that there IS an end to everything. The only thing I've done recently in anticipation of anything is to write a living will, which

I think everybody should have as they get older. If I'm sick and hopeless, I don't want to be hanging around with artificial means of ANY kind, drugs or electricity, some new-fangled device." He speaks with concern.

Art is not afraid of death. "But," he adds quickly, "I always remember what Woody Allen said. 'I'm not afraid of death. I just don't want to be there when it happens.' I love that." He grins. "I'm sure if I were confronted with some terrible disaster, I would be afraid of it, because it would be terrifying. But the thought of just passing away from being sick doesn't bother me."

He thinks of himself as a kid. "I'm a kid at heart. That's why kids talk to me on the air, because they see a child in me. I'd like to be a kid today, I'd like to be a kid anytime," he says happily. "I'm ready to go back and do it all over again.

"I'm a kidder. A very important part of my interviews with kids for 26 years was the five or ten minutes I spent in my office with all the doors shut and the four kids and me on the floor. Oh, yes," he notes my surprise. "They had to see me up close. We fooled around and I had to see which ones were going to respond to me."

Do you sit on the floor and play with your grandchildren? I ask.

"Oh, sure, sure," he croons with a faraway look.

Art and his wife Lois have three living children, seven grandchildren and eight great-grandchildren. They get together several times a year for holidays and family meetings. "Most of the family lives in California, scattered from Northern to Southern California, and we have one up near Seattle in the San Juan Islands," he says.

'I go up there, lease a yacht, and we all get on the boat and sail up through all the islands. We drop anchor and have picnics. We're a VERY close family. Never a day goes by that I don't speak to at least two or three of them, EVER," he says with satisfaction.

"Last Mother's Day, we had a whole bunch of them together at our house. Lois and I have been married 56 years. She's a major part of my life. Our family has been the center-piece and the family gets more important the older you get, because they're the ones you can count on.

"I will say something that most people will disbelieve, or if they hear it, they will scoff at it," he says quietly. "But in 56 years, Lois and I haven't had more than a couple of serious arguments. Even those were not name-calling or 'to hell with you' kind of thing. They were serious disagreements about whether we should move or what we should do about the family.

"Some people think that you're not really in love unless you have violent altercations and that lovemaking comes out of that. I disagree, only because I don't understand it. I very seldom get angry.

"At home, I'm basically the one with the sense of humor, so anytime anything begins to build up, I can kid about it and Lois can appreciate it.

"She's always been a mother and a housewife. She's never had career aspirations. Her children were her life with me, and we always put each other VERY high on the list, so that the children weren't more important than we were. My greatest joy is being with my family."

His family meetings began seven years ago, to keep everyone up-to-date on finances. "We have a family trust," he explains. "I put into a central organization various kinds of money and properties, and that's all reported on at meetings. Anyone can ask any questions he wants. I want everyone to understand the RESPONSIBILITY of having wealth.

"They're all being well-educated. That's the main thing I want to leave them, although there's plenty of money to go to them. They all know what's coming and why and how.

"We're having our next meeting in two weeks in Wickenburg, Arizona. There'll be 27 of us. We'll take over a big bed-and-breakfast place, and we'll have fun and games and cooking and cookouts," he says with a big smile.

"We'll also have guest speakers on various subjects: negotiating, family problems, insurance, real estate, and the stock market. We'll have some games, like guessing what the interest rate will be in six months and what the Dow Jones averages will be when we meet next."

Art schedules three meetings a year, often in Santa Barbara or Palm Springs. The family traditionally spends the week before Christmas skiing in Park City, Utah.

Skiing? I say. Do you still ski?

"Oh, sure," he says casually. "Skiing is like bicycling. Once you do it, you've got it. I do it six weeks every year, all through the winter. I finished my last skiing in April, at Vail, Colorado. My wife and I spent a week up there skiing at 11,000 feet, coming down the steepest hills you can POSSIBLY imagine. One of my greatest joys is standing on top of Black Diamond at 10 o'clock in the morning, with all the peaks rosy and white, knowing I'm going to go down a steep, exciting hill."

What other exercise do you do? I ask.

"Well, every day after breakfast, before I come down to the office, I go out in the backyard and have a romp with the dog. Throwing the ball with Charley, he's a big German Shepherd. Then I have two, ten-pound weights that I do a lot of upper body work with. I do 50 to 100 pushups, which is 1,000 to 2,000 pounds pushing up.

"Then I have a stationary bicycle and I do ten minutes of rapid riding. I have an electric walker for indoors and I do 10 to 15 minutes on that. The main thing is to exercise regularly. That much persistent exercise can do more for me than anything. I don't break into a sweat.

"If a man of 30 years of age did this same exercise," he explains, "he would get about 10 percent help to his body. I get 50 to 60 percent help. That's how much more you get it, because you need it.

"I have a swimming pool and I do 8 or 10 or 15 laps. In the winter, I don't swim because the pool gets too cold, but from April on, I swim almost every day. I'm a very good swimmer. Then, of course, the surfing in Hawaii, which I go to every year. I'm a board surfer."

How do you stay up on that board? I ask.

"It's very hard," he acknowledges. "I started when I was about 20. It's like riding a bicycle, you never lose it. You lose a little dexterity when you first go out. The main thing about wave riding is reading the waves. And I've been doing it all my life. You know," he smiles, "I'm amused. I see people go out and rent a surfboard, rent an instructor, and he takes them out there and stands waist-deep.

"When a wave comes in, he gives it a push at JUST the right moment, and they go right in, the very first time. They're not standing up, but they're on the board, and they go in. Then he gives them another push," he makes a "sh" sound. "And in a little bit, they stand up and go in. They just think it's wonderful.

"Then the instructor leaves—and they never catch another wave. Ever. EVER. Until they learn." He grins. "It's like everything else, and I've been doing these things a long, long time.

"I played four-wall handball until I was 50 years of age," he adds, "in national tournaments. That's one of the hardest sports there is. You can hit the ceiling, back, front, side of the room.

"Once in a while I'll miss my daily exercise, but I always get at least four or five times a week. If I'm on the road, I do calisthenics in my bedroom. I think exercise and healthy food are very, very important, because your enthusiasm, your vitality, everything in your life, depends upon the battery. If you don't keep the battery charged, what can you expect?" He lifts his hands and shrugs his shoulders.

"It there's nothing wrong with the heart as it's born, if there's no disease or abuse, it can still be GREAT at the age of 75 or 80."

The last year and one half, he's taken medicine to lower blood pressure. His doctor says the condition is purely genetic. "Because I've always been moderate in my living," says Art. "I never smoked, never drink alcohol. Oh, I've had a drink, but I don't DRINK," he says.

"I keep my weight down to a moderate standard, you might say. I'm a few pounds overweight, which is best, by the way. People live longer who are five to eight pounds overweight. Oh, yes, it gives them a little extra edge of energy or substance. I don't know why, but that's the fact."

He's had no serious health problems. "I've been blessed in many ways," he says. "I am not nagged by problems of eyesight, as most older people are. I don't wear glasses. I read, drive, and pass my driver's test. I've never had any teeth problems, which is also a problem of older people.

"In other words, as you get older, you not only have all the little things about health that happen as you wear down, but you lose a certain amount of energy and you certainly have other things.

"For instance," he goes on with relish, "it's well known that every organ in your body, except your heart and your brain, have diminished since you were 30. Your heart, generally, if it's good, is good. And your brain has so many billions of cells, even though you lose a lot, there are so many you haven't used that are waiting to be used, that you don't have any problems, unless you have a neurological ailment."

He takes no vitamins, but eats a variety of fruits and vegetables and very little fat. "I eat meat very seldom, maybe once every ten days. I eat dairy products, and I love desserts, so I eat them regularly. But I eat only a very small portion, and I THINK about it.

"Most Americans are so busy talking or gulping it down, that they don't really taste it," he goes on, enjoying his subject. "I eat my dessert the way I would eat something I might never taste again. I find that by putting my spoon or fork down between bites, it is a wonderful deterrent to just gulping.

"I enjoy mealtime," he continues. "I enjoy the company, the ambience, and the food. I am not a fancy-food eater. I like beef stews that my wife fixes, I like salads. I have been a member of many, many famous food societies and I have eaten fine food. But I am not that kind of person. I do it because it's fun to be associated in that business."

Art spent the first quarter of his life doing a variety of odd jobs, working in dams and offal coolers, being a waiter and a sailor. "Back then," he says, "I did a lot of tough things and I didn't mind it at all. I didn't really know about people being poor because everybody I knew was poor. I had no vision of what it was to be rich. I never even thought of it."

In high school, he joined the debating team and honed his speaking skills. At San Diego State College, he became interested in radio, and began a series of jobs that took him from local to network level at meteoric speed. Along the way he invested in various businesses, which now make up Linkletter Enterprises.

"My company encompasses a number of businesses that I run," says Art, "including asbestos removal, real estate, ranching, oil and gas, toys and games. I've been in 74 businesses in the last 50 years. I'm very curious and I'm very interested in things, and I get involved in people. I believe in PEOPLE and so I BET on people.

"And now that I am rich, I don't flaunt it," he says quietly. "I don't take it for granted. I LIKE it. I still have to struggle after all these years, and I've been very well-to-do for 50 years, but I still catch myself occasionally looking at the right-hand side of the restaurant menu, to see what the prices are." He smiles.

"There are some poor kids who got rich and they love to just spend money, not exactly flaunting it, but kind of as an exercise. They have four cars and a yacht and their own airplane. All the people I know, practically. I don't.

"One time Sammy Davis, Jr. and I were talking in the back lot of NBC. I was one of those who gave him his first public appearance on my show, so we were always good friends. He says, 'Art, you have a Lear jet, haven't you?' I said, 'What makes you think I have a Lear jet?' He says, 'Well, everybody has one. You can afford it, can't you?' I said, 'Yes.' He says, 'Well, DO you?' I said, 'No.' He says, 'Well, why don't you?'

"I said, 'Why do I want a Lear jet? It's very, very expensive. I can use my money better in some other ways. Do you have one?' He says, 'Oh course.' I said, 'Why do you have one?' He says, 'Because FRANK has one.' Frank Sinatra. Absolutely true story. It's partly a desire to show off that you're successful. A lot of my friends have Rolls-Royces."

What do you drive? I ask.

"I drive a nice Cadillac," he replies. "It's a very good car, American-built, and it's very comfortable. But it's not a Rolls-Royce or a $100,000 car.

"One time I was talking to Danny Thomas, when he was building a huge home up here in the hills not too far from me. I said, 'Danny, you have a lovely house. Why are you building this HUGE castle?' He said, 'Art, when you've got it, flaunt it.' He was very honest about it. He said, 'I've made it, and I want to show everybody how much I've got.'

"I told him, 'Well, that's fine. I've no objection to that.'

"My house is a very nice house," Art goes on. "But it's far from what I could have, if I wanted just a BIG house. I don't want a big house. My house has more than enough for what I want."

Are you grateful? I ask.

"Oh, yes, all the time," he says quickly, with feeling. "I can't BELIEVE what's happened to me. When I get up, I'm in this beautiful home and these beautiful gardens. I overlook the whole city of Los Angeles, I have a giant panorama. I have all the good things that I have, I just really can't believe it.

"I like the way I've lived my life," he says. "As you're young, you're impatient with people who don't agree with you. I've traveled all over the world, I'm one of the most traveled people you'll meet. My whole life, since I've been doing well, has been spent in visiting places.

"As you go through India and China and Pakistan and Tibet and all these strange places, you get a huge tolerance for everything. Because you see millions of people living entirely differently and satisfactorily, with a set of values and cultural differences that are at great variance with your own."

Do you think that people are basically good? I ask.

"Yes, I do," he replies. "I also believe that everyone has weaknesses and no one is perfect. You cannot project on some individual your demands for perfection and expect them to be met.

"I associate with EVERY kind of person," he says. "I like every kind of person. I'm around young people. I'm on the Board of Regents at Pepperdine University, and I'm out there regularly, speaking to incoming freshmen on the definition of success in life. I'm talking to special groups on the meaning of family in life and how important family is. I speak on positive things to young groups.

"I have great faith, great faith in young people. The best and the brightest are better and brighter than anything I've ever seen before. Unfortunately, the lost souls are more lost. But they're the ones who get the headlines, generally speaking.

"I've just come back from an annual meeting of the Horatio Alger Society in Washington, D.C. One of the main reasons we exist is to give scholarships. We give millions of dollars in scholarships to kids who have nothing, but are deserving. We only gave about 50 or 60 complete scholarships this last year. But they were selected from 50,000 entries. Every year we go through those, and the stories of these nominees are just heart-warming."

Education is priority. "A good education today is more important than any time in the history of the world," he states emphatically. "A liberal arts education is very, very important, because the next 50 years are going to be dominated by information and communication.

"I think for most people, it's best to get a general education, a bachelor's degree, because it's going to be like calisthenics for a particular skill later. A computer school is narrowing a young person's opportunity to grow. Yes, it's giving them a leg up and it's better than nothing, by far. But it's not a real liberal arts education, so that you can engage in conversation about other subjects than the one you're primarily assigned to."

As a boy, Art was active in the YMCA and Boys Club. "Those young physical education directors taught me camping and swimming," he says. "My father was crippled, had only one leg, so he never was into any hiking or sports. I became a junior lifesaver, a junior club leader, a camp counselor, a YMCA switchboard operator, and the champion pool table and ping-pong table player.

"I intended to go to Springfield College in Massachusetts and become a YMCA secretary. You see, I had a whole bunch of surrogate fathers who were YMCA secretaries. After I was successful, I went back to Springfield College and gave them a speech. They awarded me an honorary doctorate. I observed that they had a very small swimming pool. So I gave them an Olympic-sized swimming pool, and I've paid them back all my life.

"I do more things for the YMCA and, of course, I've been active in the Boy Scouts. I have all their top awards. So I've stayed active with kids as a way of repaying what kept ME out of trouble." He grins.

Art recalls his parents with great affection. "My father was a shoemaker and I remember all through my youth the smell of leather, and talking to my dad with a cheekful of tacks and nails. I remember all the religious part, which was very, very strong, because being a visiting evangelist, he spent ALL his spare time preaching and helping people poorer than we were.

"My parents lived until they were almost in their eighties. I was about 22 or 23 when they died. I was just really getting going when they passed away. I remember my father had mixed emotions about my first big success.

"I went from local broadcasting in San Francisco to network on the West Coast in radio. My sponsor was the Roma Wine Company. Of course, as a strict, old-fashioned Baptist, he had to cluck a little bit about the wine. Except, of course, like any good Baptist minister, he can repair to the Bible and find where Jesus turned the water into wine at the wedding, or where Paul said, 'A little wine is good for the stomach.'" Art laughs.

"So I invented a slogan for the wine, which he loved. At the end of the program I said, 'Roma Wine. Don't drink it, SIP it. That's the way to enjoy good wine.' And, of course, he never heard the last phrase."

His parents' religion resurfaced years later. "I was not a devout Christian until the loss of my daughter Diane on an LSD trip 22 years ago," he says. "Then I began to speak, teach, and motivate young people about drug abuse. I became very involved with Teen Challenge and other religious organizations, as well as psychological, psychiatric, and sociological props to help fight drug abuse.

"And I found that the religion, when it was properly structured, was better than all the others. I could SEE it, I could FEEL it."

He prays, on occasion, and thinks of God as "a buddy. I don't go to church or say grace regularly, but I do speak at many banquets where grace is said so that I'm constantly listening to it.

"I was brought up in the business of talking to God like you'd speak to a dear friend down the street on the phone. 'We're troubled, we look to you for help, is there anything we can do?' That kind of thing, instead of the pontificating and the theses written by clergymen."

Art doesn't have a specific view of death, but believes there is a continuum. "I don't see a mythical heaven with white streets," he says slowly. "I think that it's something that you do. To me, hell would be going someplace with nothing to do! I think there's SOMETHING to do after we die and I'm ready for it!

"If there's nothing, if I thought there was nothing, and obviously everybody has doubts at times because it's a leap of faith and nobody can prove anything, it wouldn't make a bit of difference in the way I treat other people or the way I observe honesty or decency or humaneness.

"In other words, my life is not in preparation to earn heaven. The trip is your life, and you have to do the best you can."

He stays current with the news because he's genuinely interested and it helps him in his work. "I couldn't live without it, I just LOVE the newspaper. Every day I read *The Los Angeles Times* from beginning to end. I read three or four magazines every week: *TIME, Newsweek,* and *Inc.* for business news, along with *The Wall Street Journal.* I fly so much, I see something I like and just buy a magazine.

"I get some of my news from television, the documentary type, PBS. But news departments in television do nothing for me, except give me a few images. Not enough depth, it's all surface, and it's too many 30-second bites. I sometimes watch the nightly network news, but I don't make a point of it. I'm more apt to look at *20/20* or *60 Minutes* or *Prime Time* or in-depth interviews by people I respect, like Bill Moyers. I look at PBS a lot. I LOVE National Geographic television.

"And I'm a GREAT sports fan. I like basketball and football." His voice warms.

"You see, I have to keep up with events because being a speaker, speaking on eight to ten different topics, I'm constantly updating my thinking and rearranging my priorities as to what I'm going to speak about. I pick up ideas or examples or new discoveries. Just this morning, I was fascinated by a little item about the discovery of metallic substances in our brains.

"These are little, tiny, wee bits of things about one-millionth of an inch across, which are the same kinds of things they find in the brains of pigeons and which are used for navigational purposes through the magnetic planes of the earth.

"I'm a student of the brain, because I'm chairman of the board of directors of the John Douglas French Alzheimer Foundation and on the board of the Center for Aging at UCLA," he explains.

"I'm dealing with doctors and I go over to the laboratories every month and see the newest CT scans and MRI scans of brains. I see how the brains develop, and how, by using them, the ganglia and all the little branches off the nerve cells stay alive. Because it's absolutely true." He pauses dramatically. "If you don't use them, you LOSE them."

Would you have liked to be a doctor? I ask.

"No, I might have been a psychiatrist," he replies. "I minored in psychology in college. I majored in English."

Art is concerned about older Americans who retire. "After 65, probably 85 to 90 percent of people are retired. So, if you're not working at something and are not needed, if you're not fitting into a pattern of future operations, you are, by definition, unnecessary.

"We in this country are generally defined by what we do," he goes on. "I'm a homemaker, I'm a realtor, I'm a bus driver. When people say, 'What do you do?' and you say, 'Nothing,' that's basically very negative.

"You can kid about it and say, 'It's great to be retired,' because you can just sit around and criticize everybody else and do nothing. But that's negative.

"You know, this Horatio Alger Society—I was initiated in 1975. It has about 300 or 400 members who are very successful. But the requirement to be a member is that you started with nothing. Very poor with no friends, no family. I mean no influence or money.

"We call ourselves the most rejected people in the United States because we've had so many rejections. We've had so many failures. In fact, I was thrust into life as a failure, because when you're born with no parents and no name in a tiny town in northwest Canada, that's really starting at ground zero. The best that could happen to me was that I'd break even.

"Every successful man has had many failures, and failure is growth." He enunciates each word. "Failure is an education, which is more important in many ways than success. Because you remember all the grisly details of your failures and you analyze them and you painfully go over what you did wrong or what went wrong.

"A success quite often is flags flying and you march down the boulevard and nobody cheers and nobody asks any questions and that's it. It just happens. Every successful man has turned failures around to the positive, not used them as excuses.

"I think everybody is self-made," says Art. "But the only ones who brag about it are the ones who succeed. You hardly ever hear a man say, 'Look, I'm a failure and I did it myself. I didn't need any help from anybody. I failed.' No!

"Persistence is a very strong element of success. Persistence and enthusiasm and planning. You HAVE to have goals," says Art. "A great French philosopher, whose name escapes me, said, 'There is no fair wind for a ship that has no port.' Everybody has to do some work.

"I love the story about the old farmer who was being visited by an evangelist in the old frontier days. Riding through the forest, he came upon this beautiful little farm. He stopped to congratulate the farmer on what a lovely place it was and how good God had been to him.

"The old farmer said, 'Well, God IS good to me, but you should've seen this place when HE had it.'" Art laughs.

"YOU've got to work," he says. "I think people who work will surpass, nine times out of ten people, people with talent and brains and intelligence and education and breeding and background who WON'T work."

And now, he must return to work. He shakes my hand warmly, poses for photographs, and thanks me. The phone is ringing and his long-time assistant Lee Ray is standing at the door, looking anxious. I put my tape recording equipment away and by the time I look up, 20 seconds later, he is out the door to his next appointment.

MARY SHERWOOD

Born: May 1, 1906,
  Hartford, CT
Profession: Founder, Walden
  Forever Wild, naturalist,
  forester
Home: Storrs, CT

'm at my typewriter at 7 a.m. every day to run Walden For ever Wild. This is a national organization. Our goal is to get Walden Pond changed into a state sanctuary. I work at it full-time. And I'm glad to do it. I feel it keeps me from being one of these teeter-totter old ladies doing nothing. When I'm typing and working, I forget myself. As far as I'm concerned I'm still in my thirties or forties.

I was the first woman forester in the U.S.A., which probably means the world. I was trained and got my degree in forestry from the University of Connecticut at Storrs. I did advanced work at Cornell University, then became a junior forester for the state of Wisconsin. I ran a forest museum and did field research and trout stream ecology studies.

I have so many interests, I need nine lives to do them all. I'd like to be a geologist. I'd love to be a top-flight astronomer, because I'm fascinated with outer space. I always say that when I die, I'm not going to heaven, I'm going out in space and explore the whole universe. It will take me all of eternity to see it all. Every new thing that the modern telescopes discover, I write and put on my list.

"I like old people. I like their kindness and their experience and what they've done in life."

SARAH NEWCOMB McCLENDON

Born: July 8, 1910,
  Tyler, TX
Profession: Journalist, social
  activist
Home: Bethesda, MD

Veteran news reporter Sarah McClendon is still going strong. At 88, she can't walk on her own, but she still covers Washington full-time with the help of friends who escort her and push her wheelchair. Best known for her tough questions at presidential news conferences, she also monitors CNBC, MSNBC, and C-Span channels on television from her one-room apartment and office in an assisted-living Catholic home.

"I'm NOT retired," she snaps when I ask how long she plans to work. "Today I was talking to the phone company, trying to get my telephone in order, so I can continue to send my stories. Some days there's one story, some days they're six." She runs her own news service, picked up by American newspapers, and writes a monthly newsletter *Sarah McClendon's Washington Report*.

She's been a reporter for 54 years.

"I still keep up with delegations and Congress and other things in Washington." She speaks quickly in a heavy Texas drawl. "I'm still going back and forth to the White House. The president's been out of town a great deal lately, so I check the White House every morning, and if he's there, I go down.

"I have an escort, someone to roll me in and get checked through security. I have a seat in the White House briefing room that's been assigned to me for years, so I use that." Her books *My Eight Presidents* and *Mr. President, Mr. President* describe years of covering the White House.

"We also go to as many receptions as we can," she says, referring to Steve Bassett, her long-time friend and most frequent escort. "We're going to a party tonight at the Cosmos Club."

News in Washington is generated at social functions and Sarah is a familiar figure on the party circuit. Petite, red-haired, with red lacquered nails and colorful silk dresses, she's often surrounded by a group of men, chatting and laughing.

She works 18 hours a day, cornering public officials, asking hard questions, practicing what she calls citizen journalism. "That's news as it affects citizens, all of us," she explains crisply. The masthead on her newsletter proclaims: "Purpose: To inform the American people so that they may keep a citizens' watch on government. Guidelines: The people have a right to know."

Sarah attends presidential news conferences and her questions are acknowledged almost every time. For daily White House briefings, she relies on C-Span coverage. She also gets information from contacts, press releases, and phone tips. After she types the story, she faxes it to subscribers.

How many do you have? I ask.

"That's a trade secret," she says shortly.

"People always talk about my energy," she goes on, running her words together. "I'm really working hard and enjoying it. I'm thoroughly enjoying life and I can't wait for the day to open again. So I get up and start to work, usually 6:30 or 7 in the morning, and go to bed at about 2, 1:30 or 2 in the morning.

"I'm very fortunate. I've had very good health and very good energy. Sometimes I drop off to sleep, take naps during the day. I don't intend it, I don't plan a nap, but I drop off to sleep, usually for half an hour." She laughs heartily.

"I don't require that much sleep, but I get sleepy during the daytime and wherever I am, I nod, and that's very bad. People object to that very strongly, so the doctor gave me some medicine to carry with me.

"If I start nodding at a banquet, I can take these pills. You can buy them over-the-counter, but they're not cheap. Honestly, I've been like this for YEARS. Every time I went to a banquet, I couldn't stand this. I guess it's from moving around a lot and then you suddenly sit still.

"And preachers!" she cries. "I can't stay awake in church! I just can't stay awake during that sermon. I don't know why." She looks apologetic.

A self-confessed workaholic, Sarah kept going after she fell and had to move from her downtown apartment to a nursing home, then a rehabilitation center. "At the V.A. home, they let me go and come whenever I wanted to," she explains. Sarah was a WAC in World War II.

"Most of the time, I was out. I went to press conferences as much as I wanted to, to the Capitol or the White House, whichever I needed to do that day. I always had someone take me. We took taxis and just folded up my wheelchair in the back seat. I had a fax in my room and sent all my stories that way."

Your spirit and voice are strong, I say.

She clears her throat and softens slightly. "My voice doesn't seem to be as clear as it ought to be. It's been worrying me about my throat. I cough a little bit. I wanted the voice to be clear and lovely, so I could make more speeches. I didn't think people want to hear a foggy voice." She laughs.

"I've always been asked to make speeches. I have one or two speaking dates coming up, one on October 31st, when I'll be honored by my junior college alumnae association. It's the first college I went to, in my hometown, Tyler, Texas."

Until recently, Sarah traveled regularly to speak and autograph her books, usually at women's and veterans' meetings. She maintained good health with the help of a hip operation in 1985, when doctors inserted a plastic rod for support. After she fell a year ago, she jostled the rod loose. The doctors weren't sure that an operation to reset the rod would work, so they left it alone.

"I got through about five days of pain and I haven't had any pain since," she says. "But I can't stand by myself. My legs don't work. I'm in very good health, except I can't walk." There is no bitterness in her voice. At home she uses a walker. She goes to church in an electric cart. The wheelchair is for work.

"Bartholomew House is the BEST place to live," she says. "They're wonderful to me. Everyone who lives here can get around on their own. If I need help, I just call on this internal phone and they send somebody right down. You see," she points to the window, "there's a patio and fish pond outside, and the church is right across the parking lot. I don't belong to this church, but I am Catholic and I do go to church here.

"The Archbishop told me years ago that he was going to build nine places for the homeless in Washington. And this is one of them. It's brand new. This type of thing is assisted living, which was needed. As he put it, 'assistance with dignity.' I would add, 'a place for people with dignity who need assistance.'

"All the meals are provided and many services. The meals are splendid. I eat everything, everything they offer. I don't drink wine, but I do take coffee and tea. I always have a good appetite." Sarah is 4 feet 10 inches and weighs 95 pounds. Her one complaint, says daughter Sally, is that there aren't enough men at the home. The one man who lives there always sits at Sarah's table.

Do you take vitamins? I ask.

"Oh, they give me seven or eight pills in the morning and three at night," she answers. "My V.A. doctor's prescription transferred here. I don't know what they're for. They don't tell you. You try to find out, I've been trying to find out for a long time.

"Some of them are vitamins, some are for bone. I take a lot of calcium and it collects in your feet, makes you have swollen feet, so I work on not having swollen ankles. I elevate my feet when I sleep."

She joins group exercise twice a week. One class is designed for people in wheelchairs. "The other gets me out of the chair," she says, "and it's very strenuous. But I don't mind doing it. I walk to and from the dining room with my walker three times a day, and I reckon that's as much as I did in physical therapy at the nursing home."

She wears glasses to read. "I guess I had cataracts and two operations on that," she says absently. She's hard of hearing in one ear and owns a hearing aid. "But I can't see that it does much good," she comments tartly. She voluntarily gave up driving in 1992 because she didn't want to drive at night.

Sally and her husband David MacDonald live nearby and visit. "Sally's a linguist, a very excellent teacher of English as a Second Language," says Sarah proudly. "She likes to mix with people. She ought to be in politics! My granddaughter Allison works for a lawyer and was recently married. She's very happily married." Her voice turns warm as she picks up a wedding photo of the couple with Sarah in the middle.

It sits next to a photo of her with President Clinton. Photos with other presidents and dignitaries cover the wall. Some have autographs. President Bush, Sr. wrote, "To Sarah, It's true. Everyone knows it's true. I still love you. Keep the questions flying. Sincerely, George Bush."

Sarah actively participates in the American Legion, the Paralyzed Veterans of America, and the Battle of the Bulge Association. Mr. Clinton appointed her to a committee to study the feasibility of a World War II Memorial in Washington. She's also a vocal member of the National Woman's Party, which supports passage of the Equal Rights Amendment.

Her social life has included interesting men, one being the late actor E.G. Marshall, who escorted her to many White House parties. She misses him acutely. "I was very, very fond of him," she says softly.

"I always look for that mental connection. I'd rather be with anybody who's thinking and got something to contribute in the way of mentality. I don't go around with somebody who's boring, I'll tell you that. I'm kind of like my daughter. She says she doesn't suffer fools at all." Sarah's marriage, she tells me, "was not a happy one" and ended early in divorce.

"I wish I were married now, because I really need a companion very much," she says longingly. "I'd like to be really in love with somebody right now. All my boyfriends have died or become ill."

Immediately she's back in a fighting mood. "I don't believe in stopping or retiring," she says. "I'll never retire. Every old person should be allowed to work as long as they can, as much as they can. We don't know from their experience what they might contribute to everybody else's life.

"Older people can contribute a great deal to their country, if their country would let them." Her tone becomes defiant. "I see so many people who are just brilliant who could carry on jobs, who could at least advise a government.

"Old people deserve more respect. I was taught by my mother to respect older people and take care of them and be kind to them. That was a good thing that she taught me. As a newspaper reporter, I've been very respectful of older people. I've written a lot about them.

"I love reporting, I'm so GLAD I got into it," she says, face glowing, hands moving. "I started to be a lawyer. One of my teachers told me I should be a reporter. I said, 'I don't believe I'd make any money as a lawyer at this point, so I'll try being a reporter.'" She smiles. "Well, of course, you don't make any money as a reporter, either, but you invest in your country. You invest in society. You invest in yourself.

"I'm working on stories that other reporters are not working on, for various and sundry reasons. And isn't it grand that somebody is working on those stories? Because they ought to be OUT." Sarah specializes in women's issues, health, poverty, homelessness, the army, and the Veterans Administration. "And security matters. I've found scandals in the government. Oh, yes! I'm writing stuff about the CIA that they don't want anybody to write about.

"You know, I'm very nasty to get along with when somebody tells me that I shouldn't write that story and they're not going to give me any information. I'm really nasty." Her facial expression is neutral but the voice is seething.

"I'm innately timid," she reveals. "I have to MAKE myself do things. I have to make myself do things that I think ought to be done. Somehow or other, when I start doing it, I get strength."

You don't give up, do you? I ask.

"No," she shakes her head slowly. "I spend some hours every day worrying about how we can tell the American people, so they'll know more about their government. My passion in life is the United States government and I want this country to survive and go on and be successful. There are lots of people planning now for it to go, and not only our enemies, people in other countries, but some people in this country. A lot of it stems from people being selfish and naive.

"I think a lot of young people today don't get a chance to hear history, don't get a chance to have families sit down with them and recall things," she continues. "People are so desperate trying to make a living. I know children not getting to go to college."

She established a fund at the University of Missouri, another alma mater, to help students study news reporting in Washington for a semester. "The goodness of young people is

THERE, if you give it a chance to be brought out," she says fervently. "I think there are a lot of good teachers who are having a good influence on children."

I listen to her stories of investigations, "my scandals, I call them." She mentions people who write to her, asking help in solving problems with the government. "These are people who've fallen through the cracks: veterans, widows of vets, people who've experienced age discrimination, sexual harassment. I help as many as I can."

Where do you get your strength? I ask.

"I believe very strongly in God," she replies. "I don't know what in the world we'd do if we didn't have Jesus Christ. My gosh! All the terrible things that would happen in the world. And I pray. I've always found that prayer is just talking to God.

"I'm not afraid of dying," she goes on. "I view death as a great stoppage. I'm not going to let any undertaker make money off me!" She laughs. "I've got myself set up with Georgetown University Medical School to take all the transplants they can and see what made this woman tick!

"Now, have you got everything you need? I have some work I must do. Thank you for coming and please come again." She waves and picks up a ringing phone. "Yes, this is Sarah McClendon. Thank you for returning my call. I want to ask you some questions." And I hear her firing them off as I walk down the hall.

It's a reassuring sound.

RUSSELL MEYERS

Born: Feburary 25, 1904,
   Brooklyn, NY
Profession: Retired
   neurosurgeon, Seniors
   champion athlete, writer
Home: Pensacola, FL

My principal avocation is writing my *magnum opus*, a book *Orientation for Neurology, Psychology and Psychiatry*. It keeps my mind agile and challenges me. I try to write every day and I've been at it for about 18 years. I have to remind myself that people like Dostoevsky and Isaac Newton had to write 27, 35, 40 drafts of what were going to be their great gifts to mankind. So I don't let the time factor upset me.

Every Monday morning I go to a meeting at the West Florida Medical Center. The doctors in the neurological sciences present a case and anyone in the audience may ask questions or offer ideas. This keeps me up-to-date on what's happening since I retired. All the doctors are younger than I am. I consider that to be indispensable to remaining young-ish.

My wife Polly also keeps me young, because she's very childlike. She gets a kick out of Christmas, like a seven-year-old. I tend to be a loner, but she's very gregarious. She has a wonderful sense of humor. She also does an enormous amount of reading and keeps me informed about all the modern lingo. Love is the most indispensable component of living and to have a love and have it reciprocated—I have that in Polly. At my age, you love more than you think you ever did when the hormones were motivating you in other directions.

I jog and walk three miles a day, five or six days a week. I was a runner in college, but between the ages of 20 and 64, I didn't exercise daily because I was working and doing research. At 64, I started jogging. At 75, I resumed taking part in competitions, with the International Masters Program. That's like an Olympics for seniors. I broke world records in my age group several times for the 110 and 440 meter hurdles, the 100 and 200 meter sprints, and the long jump.

The most important thing is to be open-minded, open to information from anybody and any source that may add to your knowledge. If you're open-minded, you'll be more tolerant of your fellow men, less biased and shut off. Listen to anybody, listen to the janitor. He may have something to tell you about aeronautics that you wouldn't have suspected.

"When I was a child, I just adored older people. They were
so interesting. I loved their stories."

Ruth Schick Montgomery

Born: June 11, 1912,
  Sumner, IL
Profession: Author, retired
  journalist, spiritualist
Home: Naples, FL

Ruth Montgomery is in love with life.

"Oh, I'm SO interested in everything that's going on around me, I can't WAIT to get up in the morning and read the newspaper," she exclaims in a light, musical voice. "I'm still a reporter at heart and I always turn on CNN when there's a hearing or ongoing story. I have a desire to know EVERYTHING. I have such a curious mind."

Lest she sound too prim and proper, Ruth admits to smoking cigarettes, drinking martinis, occasionally swearing, and hating to cook and exercise. She also does something that some people consider unusual: she communicates daily with her Spirit Guides. They are spirits of people, usually relatives or friends, who have died.

She's spent the second half of her career writing books, which her Guides "dictated" to her. Starting in the 1960s, 12 of her 16 books have dealt with metaphysical subjects. All are classics in their field, including the most recent *The World to Come* (1999), which contains predictions about life in the twenty-first century.

A small, slight woman with deep blue eyes, short, ash blond hair, and a sweet smile, Ruth is a journalist who covered politics in Washington, D.C., before being assigned a story on the metaphysical world. Full of skepticism, she did research, both in books and personal experiments. Gradually, the amount of evidence was so overwhelming that she became a believer.

"The Guides communicate with me through automatic writing," she explains. "First I quiet myself, through meditation. Then I hold a pencil on a piece of paper, or put my fingers on the typewriter." She starts to write words that she says the

Guides are telling her. She has no say in the matter and no idea what she's writing until afterwards, when she reads it. She is a channel, a conduit for the Guides.

The Guides' main message is simple. "They say that our life on earth is a training school, that we come back again and again to learn lessons and relearn lessons that we had forgotten in previous lifetimes. The purpose of all of us is to help others and LOVE.

"The Guides also say that we should realize that every single one of us is a part of God, that God manifests in every living thing. So we shouldn't judge others harshly, because we haven't walked in their shoes. We should remember that they're a part of us, too, because we're all a part of God."

Ruth sits curled up in her favorite easy chair in an elegant apartment overlooking the Gulf of Mexico. She lights a cigarette with a pink Bic and takes a sip of her martini. It's the Christmas season, and to celebrate, she's set a huge red poinsettia outside on the patio, bathed in rays of a pink setting sun.

Over the years, Ruth and her husband Bob came to believe what the Guides said. It took her a while, she admits, because she was a journalist and required proof. But research won them over. After Bob died in 1993, she began hearing from him, too.

"There's an awful lot of Bob's and my conversations in my new book," she says. "We were married 57 years. I miss him terribly, but thank heavens for our firm belief in eternal, active life. The Guides have told me of at least two previous lifetimes where they say Bob was my husband, once in England and again in Biblical Palestine. Sounds like we're in a rut, doesn't it?" She laughs merrily.

"He's told me, through automatic writing, what he's doing on the other side. That information will help other widows. Oh, yes, he's fine, wonderful," she says breezily.

Bob Montgomery served in the Navy, then as consultant to the U.S. Senate Appropriations Committee, and as deputy administrator of the Small Business Administration in Washington, D.C. Ruth was a Washington correspondent and columnist for *The New York Daily News* and the INS (International News Service). After retirement, they moved to Florida in 1987.

"I swore I'd never do another book," she says, referring to her last. "But I was overruled, by the Guides and by Bob." She laughs indulgently. "The Guides kept saying I should write this book and Bob, who had always said, 'Don't write another book,' changed his mind on the other side. 'You should write it!' he told me.

"I don't think it's by any means my best book, but so many fans want to know what my Guides are saying about the forecast shift of the earth on its axis, and what's going to happen in the next millennium. The Guides say the next hundred years are not going to be as bad as expected, because of all the spiritual work that's already been done here on earth."

She completed the book in six or seven weeks. "It didn't take long because it's made up of bits and pieces of things I got through automatic writing over a period of years. I bought a computer for it." She sighs heavily. "It took up practically all the space in one room and it was just ridiculous.

"I wish I could work a computer, but it's beyond me. I just couldn't get used to it. It was hopeless. I got sick, I lost quite a bit of weight, and I finally returned it. It cost me $500 to return it. Then I went back to my old IBM Selectric typewriter. Oh, but that typewriter looked GOOD after the computer." She laughs. "The kids today do it right. They learn early on computers."

Ruth spends a great deal of time answering fan mail, using a lap desk and penning a line or two on the letter itself. "It's just too much trouble to go to the typewriter," she says. "And people seem to like handwritten replies.

"I used to get thousands of letters every year, and I still get quite a bundle every week in a big brown envelope from the publishers. So many of the letters start out, 'Dear Ruth, Forgive me for using your first name, but I feel like I know you. I've read all your books and they've brought such comfort to me.'

"Or they'll say, 'Since reading *A World Beyond*, I have no fear of death,' or 'I was just tortured by the loss of someone and now I'm accepting it.' They're WONDERFUL letters.

"People have written asking what the Guides say about something and I try to respond. Sometimes they enclose a dollar bill for postage and that's very thoughtful. As a rule, I now reply only to those letters with enclosed stamped, self-addressed envelopes. I just don't have the time to address envelopes. I get so many letters from people overseas. That postage can get expensive.

"I receive a tremendous volume of mail from young people, some even from grammar school, who have read the books that their mothers and fathers acquired. They ask very intelligent questions, and some write that they are doing school essays on psychic matters discussed in my books.

"Several young people have even done their masters' theses on my books," she continues. "I used to receive a lot of mail from soldiers overseas with APO addresses. Many others write from prisons, where they've found my books in prison libraries. My books have been translated into 25 foreign languages, my publishers tell me, so I receive letters from every continent." She speaks gently, without a trace of boastfulness.

Every day she sits at her typewriter, enters a meditative state, and waits for the Guides to come in. "I have a hard time remembering to do it at the same time every day, which is the best way to do it. So I have a little timer that I set one hour ahead of the time. I do love the Guides. They help me so much to understand what's going on."

Her life may be metaphysical, but she remains fascinated with earthly news, watching CNN during the day and TV networks at night. "My favorite station is this little remote control, right here by my fingertips." She holds it up and smiles. "When they go into ads, I skip to another network. The button I use the most is the mute."

She also reads the local newspaper *The Naples Daily News* and *TIME* magazine.

Keeping current is part of staying young, she believes. "I have a friend who is remarkable in her endurance and youthfulness. She's older than I am. But she never knows much that's going on. She doesn't read the papers and she doesn't listen to the news much. She's interested in all the neighbors and she's a very good person. But it appalls me that when you bring up something, she says, 'Oh, I don't know anything about that,' or 'I'm not interested in that.'"

Ruth is adjusting to living in a new apartment. "I just moved here in January and the move wore me out," she exclaims.

"Everything's unpacked, friends came over and put everything away, and now I can't find a damned thing!"

Twice a day she exercises to recover from a fall three months ago. "My refrigerator has one of those ice makers that comes out in front," she explains. "I was making my martini that evening and some of the ice fell on the floor. I stooped over to pick it up and I slipped on the floor. I lay on the floor for three days and three nights. It was the most traumatic event of my life!" she moans, then laughs.

"I finally got into a room with a phone and called someone. An ambulance came and took me to the hospital. The doctor said I broke my pelvis. They couldn't operate. I was in the hospital a week, then a nursing facility for several weeks, and now I'm home. This is not an assisted-living apartment, but after what happened to me, the management made a new policy to make daily phone checks on older people who ask for it.

"Oh, yes, I have healed just fine," she says airily. "I apparently knit well. I have no pain any more. I've graduated from a walker and now use a cane, but nothing in the apartment. I've been awfully lucky. Next I'm going to work up to walking outside on the sidewalk.

"I don't ever want to move again!" she declares. "I left my penthouse apartment with four bedrooms and five baths. After Bob died, I felt it was too big. This apartment is smaller, three bedrooms, two baths."

Ruth hopes to resume painting. "When I moved, they lost a lot of things," she says, without anger. "The paints and easel didn't make it. I'll get back to it." The apartment walls are lined with many of her oil paintings of blue Gulf waters, renditions of Old Masters, and portraits of her and Bob.

She lights a cigarette and takes a draw. "Yes, I'm still smoking," she laughs without shame. "I don't know how many I smoke and I'm not confessing! I've quit several times and gone back to it. I was without cigarettes for two and one half weeks when I was in the hospital this spring. But I did go back to it.

"I'm lucky, I've lived beyond the normal life span. I don't know how long I'm going to keep going." She sounds surprised that she's made it this far. "I don't like food, you know. I don't like to eat. I'm a Gemini, an air sign, so maybe I live on air! I do love the wonderful fruits down here in Florida. I never did much cooking. I didn't know how to cook when I got married. I was a vegetarian.

"When I was an itty bitty child, I saw my grandmother wring a chicken's neck and its body was just flopping around. After that I never ate anything that had been alive. Bob was a meat and potatoes man, so I decided if I had to cook meat, I might as well eat it. I tried to plan healthy meals. But now I do nothing."

Her health is generally good, with occasional aches and pains. "I was always rather frail. I was never a strong, muscular person. So you just take it as it comes. I do take a multivitamin and calcium. But I need to put on some weight," she acknowledges.

"The one thing that does distress me is that my eyesight is getting worse. It's macular degeneration. My brother had it and two of my cousins had it. My right eye, the stronger eye, is fine. I asked my doctors if I should be careful of my eyes," she goes on. "And they say, 'No, USE them.'

"So I continue to read and work crossword puzzles and watch TV. Fortunately, my distance vision is fine. I don't have to wear glasses for that. To drive, I use glasses, because they made me, to give me my license."

She drives a cream-colored, 1989 Cadillac Seville. "I just love it!" she enthuses. "It's the only time in my life I ever had a love affair with a car. When the men in my building saw the car in the garage, they begged me to buy it. I told them they'd have to take me with it. It had only about 4,000 miles, so you can see why they were interested." She grins and winks at me.

Growing old doesn't upset her, but she doesn't want to lose her eyesight or become senile. "I pray that neither will occur," she says. "But if it should, I'm sure that God would provide the tools to deal with that. I want to live as long as I can be useful and active, and not a day longer. But that's up to God in His infinite wisdom."

She views medical mishaps as positive experiences. "When I was on a television tour with one of my books, I think it was *Here and Hereafter*, I fell and broke my shoulder and arm in five places. The doctors could only fit it with a heavy hanging cast, and I had to sleep sitting up in a rented hospital bed for six months. At the end of that period, we flew to Mexico for a vacation, and that's how we happened to move to Cuernavaca for five years. Bob and I had a lovely time.

"Then 14 years ago, I had a lumpectomy and received daily radiation for five weeks. When that was finished, we flew to Naples, Florida for the first time, and fell in love with it. We bought a penthouse overlooking the Gulf of Mexico. The Guides were right when they wrote, 'Our stumbling blocks are stepping stones.' Something good comes out of every ill, if we maintain a healthy attitude."

On the inside, she says, she feels 16. On the outside, she feels 40. "MOST of the time," she adds with a smile. "Who was it said, 'Youth is wasted on the young'? I think that's my favorite expression. It's frustrating when you think of the energy, the vitality, and the eagerness that you had when you were young, and what you could do with it NOW, when you have so much more wisdom and knowledge.

"But we have to keep looking forward," she continues. "I don't try to preach to old people, but I try to get them interested in helping others, so they're not immersed in self-pity. I think the very fact that we have such an exciting time to live in and such exciting prospects for the next round when we go into spirit, it sounds almost LYRICAL.

"Here we are, not encumbered by bodies, and we can be any place that we think about." Her voice rises in anticipation. "We can be with anybody we want to. We don't have to be with people we don't want to. This is all according to the Guides. And yet, we're serving God, we're worshiping God in both spheres.

"They say it's much easier to be good on the other side because we don't have these bodily temptations. I'm getting a little old for bodily temptations," she laughs. "I think it's an exciting prospect. Nobody should rush it, because we've been given this marvelous opportunity to be in this exciting, beautiful, wonderful world that I simply love. But we should have no fear of so-called death.

"Make the most of it while we're here," she exclaims. "Be kind to everybody. Try to keep from criticizing. That's difficult because as we get older, we see so many things that we don't approve of in other people. But remember that we're all one, and every one of us is a part of all these other wonderful people and wonderful plants and wonderful animals.

"Take each day as it comes and get out of bed eager to confront it and participate in it."

She admits that it can be hard. "I find myself so despairing about the crime and greed and lack of morals that are being reported all over the world. But I think every generation sometimes despairs of the generations coming along behind them.

"My mother, in her old age, would do the same thing, shaking her head and saying, 'I've lived too long.'" Ruth smiles gently. "I'm starting to feel the same way."

She worries about what she calls a lack of morals. "My personal opinion is that the invention of the birth control pill had a deleterious effect on the morals of the younger generation," she says. "I feel that the pill freed many high school and college girls of the fear of becoming pregnant. This, in turn, loosened the moral fiber of both boys and girls.

"I was a virgin when I married at the age of 23," she goes on. "It was not from lack of opportunity, since I had dates all the time. Some of my best friends were not virgins, but that did not influence me. My parents imposed no rules on me, and I don't remember ever discussing sex with them. But I knew they trusted me. I could not have had sexual relations with a date and then come home to face them. They were good and I wanted to be good, too. It was a question of ethics.

"Perhaps the saddest challenge for today's youth is drug addiction," she says. "In my youth, it was smoking cigarettes that made us feel grown-up, although I did not begin that lousy habit until I was a senior in college. And since prohibition was the law of the land, we avoided dating boys who would take a drink.

"I hope that the new crop of youngsters will see the damage that drugs have done to others' lives and turn away from the false lure of drugs." She speaks pensively.

What about AIDS? I ask. Might it make people return to old-fashioned values?

"I hope so," she says strongly. "It's the only good thing that could come out of that horrible disease that is killing so many talented young people. I cannot understand an age that makes a hero out of a sports figure who proudly admits that he had unprotected sex with hundreds of women who were unknown to him, except for one-night stands. Did he care nothing for the possibility of siring hundreds of fatherless children? Was he sorry only because he acquired the AIDS virus? It blows the mind!" Her voice rises indignantly.

"I think the younger generation has some wonderful, brilliant people, many of whom are more intelligent and better-educated than my generation. They set an example for all of us." The key, she says, is education. "It opens slumbering minds to exciting knowledge of all ages since the world began. It lifts us out of our puny selves and causes our spirits to soar."

Ruth has set up a scholarship for journalism students at her alma mater Baylor University in Waco, Texas. "Every year I get a lovely letter from whoever is awarded that scholarship," she says. "It's remarkable to hear what it meant to these students to get financial help. And you know what? Baylor has now established a Ruth Schick Montgomery Media Resources Room, full of computers! Very wry," she comments, considering her view of computers. In her will, she's left funds to sustain that room.

How should a young person pick a profession? I ask.

"Do what they love," she replies quickly. "Because we have talents when we come back to this earth, talents that we developed in previous lifetimes. They weren't just handed to us on a platter. God didn't say, 'Look, I'm going to give you a beautiful voice, you go down there and see if you want to sing.'

"We DEVELOP those talents. They're part of us and they're part of the nature we've been ever since we've been little sparks cast off from God. I think we should use those. Of course, it's essential that we try to make a decent living, so that we take care of family. You should do what you want to, but figure out also how to make a living at it.

"That's why—here I go, disapproving," she apologizes. "I don't approve of those saffron-robed monks in the Far East, because they could be making a living and still worshiping God. They don't have to go around with a begging bowl all the time, expecting other people to support them.

"That's how I feel about people here, that they should be intelligent enough to figure out a way to make a living," she says. "There are a lot of people who quit their jobs because they want to be writers. They sit at home and write and sometimes get food stamps.

"Well, I worked a full day every day and in the early days, six days a week, before there was a five-day week. And yet, I had time to do the things that I enjoyed. In the later time, that was to write books. And I was still working. I wrote my first four books while I was still doing a daily column. When I look back now, I wonder how I did it.

"But I worked evenings and weekends. That's why my husband threatened to leave if I ever wrote another book." She laughs.

She enjoys young people and would like to associate with more of them, but Naples is a retirement community, she says, and there are not many young people in her building. She stays in close touch by telephone with her three nieces, a nephew, and a grand-nephew, who is a senior editor of *Esquire*. "I'm very proud of them all," she declares. "They are well-educated, hard-working, creative, and fun to be around."

Occasionally she gets together with a friend's daughter or granddaughter.

Do you regret not having children? I ask.

"After several years of marriage, Bob and I both went to specialists to see why we were not having children." She speaks without embarrassment. "They could find nothing wrong with either of us, so I think it was just not in the cards for us, in this lifetime. Certainly I would never have had the time to write the books, which have touched so many lives, if I'd been rearing children.

"I guess my BOOKS have been my children," she brightens. "Although I miss the love that comes with children, I do not miss the frantic worries that my friends have had with children and grandchildren in this drug-infested age." She shakes her head sadly.

Her books, she emphasizes, are creations of the Guides, not her. "I don't try to take any credit for the way my books have influenced the lives of so many tens of thousands of people, because it's the Guides who made that contact. They changed me and they fortunately changed other people. I give full credit to them."

Her first book *A Search for the Truth* dealt with life after death, life on the other side. "Then the Guides said, 'Now we will talk to you about reincarnation.' I told them, 'I don't believe in reincarnation.' They said, 'Just investigate it like you did this other.'

"So I began investigating it, and with their messages, to augment my research, I became firmly convinced that nothing dies, that we go on, and that we come back in another body, into different circumstances."

After a period of agnosticism, she came to believe in God. Now she prays regularly. "I have no formation in my mind of what God is, just a knowingness. When the Guides spoke to me about how we each are a part of God, it made sense to me. Every single night of the world, the first thing I do when I go to bed is pray directly to God.

"I always thank the Guides and I always ask them to bless specific people by name, my family, of course, and a few friends. Then I ask God to bless everyone and if there's something tragic occurring in the world, I ask God to bless those people, too. I always ask it in Jesus' name, Amen.

"And I always ask God to bless the Guides: Arthur, Lily, and the Group, because I remember Arthur wrote, 'Your prayers help us even more on this side than they did when we were there.' Arthur and Lily have been the constant guides. I've never known names of the others, but they're all apparently helping. At one point, Lily said, 'Our Group is now complete. We are 12."

Ruth's contact with the other side helps her accept the prospect of death with equanimity, even anticipation. "I view death as the next exciting newspaper assignment," she laughs heartily. "In the newspaper business, we never knew from day to day what wonderful, exciting thing we would be covering the next day.

"And I feel the same way about death. In fact, death is a redundant word, because I feel we'll still be us, that I'll still be myself. I'll simply be in spirit rather than in body. I think that when our bodies wear out or when we've completed our mission here, we just go on.

"I'm not looking forward to death, because I love this plane and I love my life," she says quickly. "I think I've been so blessed and so fortunate. But I'm not afraid of death, because it's going to be exciting to see just how much of what the Guides told me is true."

She drains her martini, gets up, and thanks me for my time. "Please stay in touch and be sure to send me a copy of your piece, so I can proofread it."

I promise.

After transcribing her interview, I send her a copy. Within a week, she sends it back, filled with pencilled edits. I acknowledge all the changes.

Over the years we correspond and talk on the phone. She continues to receive messages from her Guides and relays pertinent information to me.

MARGARET
CHASE SMITH

Born: December 14, 1897,
  Skowhegan, ME
Profession: Professor, retired
  member, U.S. House and
  Senate, author
Home: Skowhegan, ME

I don't celebrate my birthday. I just forget it. People make so much of it. I say, "Why do you get so excited over one year nearer death?" They think that's terrible. I'm realistic. If people didn't keep publishing it in the newspaper and talking about it, it'd never occur to me that I was any different from you. Of course, I'm very well physically. That's the important thing.

I'm retired. But if this is retirement, I wouldn't know what a vacation was! I work as hard as I ever did, maybe harder, because I'm here, I have no privacy, the library is attached to the house. The library is for my papers, it's the history of my career. We have quite a number of people coming for interviews, and we have a good many students, from the second grade through high school and colleges.

I go out and talk to them two or three times a week and answer questions. I think it's very good for those young people to get an idea of what research is and how important history is.

I tell them that education is something that cannot be taken away from them and for them to get all they can while the getting is good and the teachers are there to help them.

I never have time enough to do all the things I want to do. I'm up and ready to dictate letters by 7 a.m. I think nothing of it. I've always been an early riser. If you don't get up, you don't get anything done. I keep a pretty steady pace and pretty complete schedule every day. I'm a very regular, ordinary person who crowds every single minute as full as I can with things I need and want to do. I enjoy people very much. I've always been curious about people.

If you start in something and find it is not to your liking, find what you do want and change. Don't do that too often, but do it until you become settled. Don't work at something you're not happy in when something else is available.

I have a great belief in God, but I don't wear it on my sleeve. We all have a purpose in life. I often say that we all have a spot on the wall. When that spot comes, it's time to finish our mission and go on to something else.

"I get hundreds of letters from children across the country and I try to answer. I'd like to be doing some other things, like composing and writing poetry. But when it comes to children, it's very difficult to ignore them."

GORDON PARKS

> Born: November 30, 1912,
>   Fort Scott, KS
> Profession: Photographer,
>   writer, musician, movie
>   director
> Home: New York, NY

"Some mornings I wake up feeling 21 and some mornings I wake up feeling 85," laughs Parks in a gravelly rumble, his mahogany face cracking into dozens of wrinkles. "It all depends upon the vitamins I take the day before and how much I did the previous day.

"Oh, yes, I take vitamins," he says, surprised at the question. "I know a lot of people don't believe in them, but I'll tell you one thing. I ran out of vitamin E recently and I didn't have the energy that I used to have. So my doctor said, 'Don't get the 400 I.U.s, get the 1000 I.U.s, take 1000 a day.' And I feel better since I've been doing that.

"I just bought another thing called Age Control, all herbal, and supposed to be very good. I've taken only three of them, so I don't know whether they're going to COLLIDE with the vitamin E." He smiles at his choice of words.

"And occasionally, I'll take vitamin C."

His body is small and wiry, honed by years of skiing, tennis, and jogging. He has a luxuriant mustache and thick white hair that curls onto his shoulders. A baseball cap turned backwards gives him a boyish look. He wears an olive velour pullover, unzipped halfway down his chest. When he walks, he glides, cat-like.

"I don't think of age," he says quietly, sitting at a paper-strewn desk in his living room. "To me, it's just a number. That's why I'm two months ahead walking now. Yeah!" He nods vigorously. "My surgeon says I shouldn't be walking as well as I do now.

"I had both Achilles tendons repaired seven months ago," he relates. "I had to learn to walk all over again. Now I can't even find my cane. I don't know where it's at." He glances casually around the room and chuckles. "So that's a good sign."

Parks is anxious to resume the sports he stopped during recovery. It was on a three-mile jog that he tore his tendons. "Now I want to give myself plenty of time for healing," he says.

He watches his diet. "Since the hospital, I've been eating a lot of fruit, a lot of fish," he says. "I don't drink much. The doctor wants me to have a steak once a week while I'm playing tennis. But I'm not doing that yet. I do ride a stationary bike. I did five miles the other day, which was not bad." He puffs up a bit, then smiles.

An internationally-known photographer, artist, and musician, Parks has agreed to an interview at his home on the East Side of New York, near the United Nations. After the apartment concierge announces me, I ride up in the elevator and get off on Parks' floor. I find his door ajar, and knock. No answer. I knock again and wait.

Still no answer. I enter and call his name. After about a minute, a man I recognize as Parks walks slowly in from another room and says, "Hello." He shakes my hand and invites me into a spacious living room, furnished in earth tones, with huge windows facing the East River. The cream-colored walls are covered with art and photographs.

I admire one painting that looks like a Van Gogh. "No, that's by Gloria Vanderbilt, she gave it to me," he says warmly. "I'll tell her what you said. We're very close friends. She'll say, 'Really?'" He smiles, delighted at the prospect.

"Yes, that's a Chagall," referring to another beautiful painting. "It's signed. I lived in the south of France for two years. I loved it, I loved Paris, too." His eyes close and his voice trails off. The only sound is classical piano music on his stereo.

He rouses himself and waves a fluid hand toward the floor. "All these piles of books on the floor, we used them in preparing my new book *Half Past Autumn: A Retrospective*." It accompanies an exhibit touring American museums for the next five years, a gathering of 57 years of his prize-winning photos, poetry, prose, and other art works. Already it's received rave reviews in Washington, D.C.

"I'm going to give a lot of these books to kids at a school that they just named after me in New Jersey," he explains. "Books they could never expect to see otherwise, some of them very expensive books." The Gordon Parks Academy in East Orange is a public elementary school specializing in radio, animation, film, and television.

The curriculum mirrors Parks' work, which is steady and prodigious. Starting in the 1930s, he used his camera, he explains, as a weapon to fight racism, poverty, discrimination, segregation, and crime. He was the first successful African-American film director with major hits: *Shaft, Shaft's Big Score!* and *The Super Cops.* He's written four autobiographical books, several volumes of poetry and nonfiction, and a novel about the nineteenth century painter J.M.W. Turner. He's also composed classical, blues, and pop music, and a ballet on the life of Martin Luther King Jr.

"Does this bother you?" he asks, starting to fill his briar pipe. Not at all, I say.

A flame catches the tobacco and sends sweet smoke into the room, which is already warm. "I smoke more than I should," he admits easily. "I stopped before the operation. But then I was in a wheelchair and I needed SOMETHING. You know, the confinement was too much." He grimaces. He smokes two tobaccos, one English, one American.

The pipes come from his father. A photo of Andrew Jackson Parks sits nearby in a bookcase. He is a mirror image of Gordon and smokes the same kind of pipe. "My father never said much to me during his lifetime. But I felt a lot of love from him. He was a quiet, very quiet man. Mostly he said, 'Boy, did you feed the hogs?' 'Yes, sir,' I said. 'Did you curry the horse?' 'Yes, sir.' 'You'd better feed the chickens.' 'Yes, sir,' I said. And that was about it.

"If I said 20,000 words to him during my whole lifetime, I doubt it. But he was a wonderful man. Nothing but love. He only tried to switch me once and he gave up." Parks chuckles. "So my mother had to finish off the job. And she was an expert. She could wield a switch like a baton." He shakes his head and smiles.

His mother Sarah Parks wears a long, white, Victorian dress in her photo. "That love we had, pulled me through," says Parks, his voice soft and husky. "The love I got from my mother and father, my brothers and sister. I never saw my mother and father have an argument once in all my lifetime. I never saw any of my brothers and sisters have a violent argument. It was always pretty even.

"Yeah, I keep their pictures close," he says reflectively. "If I've got a serious decision to make, I consult them."

He's been married and divorced three times and remains friends with his ex-wives. "Why not?" he says with affection. "They gave me the best of their lives and I gave them the best times of my life. So if I need them, they're there. If they need me, I'm there.

"Gene, my third wife, comes by and goes out with me now and then. Here's a picture of her, just recently." He points to a photo behind him. "And Liz, my second wife," he points to another, "and her 27-year-old daughter Shirley. She comes by and takes me to jazz concerts.

"My first wife Sally lives outside Washington, D.C. All three of them were at the opening of my exhibit last September at the Corcoran Gallery. Yeah, they were photographed by *The Washington Post*, all together with me and my children, smiling, everybody smiling." He laughs. "Oh, yeah, absolutely. Love and friendship, that's what's propelled me."

Parks is devoted to his three children, five grandchildren, and three great-grandchildren. His first-born Gordon, Jr., was killed in Kenya while directing a film. His older daughter Toni lives in England. Son David is in Texas and daughter Leslie lives across the river in Brooklyn.

"She just had a child and brought him over last Sunday. It was great," he beams. "I keep in touch by phone with everyone else and see them when I can, occasionally on holidays, but not as often as I'd like.

"They'll all converge upon St. Paul when the show opens there, because I have lots of nieces and nephews in St. Paul." He plans to play his latest work, a piano sonata that he premiered last month at the Kennedy Center in Washington.

"I got very well reviewed by *The Washington Post*," he says with quiet pleasure. "I wrote the first movement after Gordon, Jr. was killed. Then I was encouraged to go ahead and combine that with the rest of my children, which I did. Now it's in four movements, one for each child, in the key of F sharp. The worst key ever!" He laughs.

"My regret is that I don't have a big house up in White Plains anymore, where all of the family can get together. But this coming summer, I hope to rent a house for about three weeks and have everybody there under one roof." He pronounces it "ruff," true to his Kansas roots.

"I miss my children and not having them around," he says wistfully. "Although they make a LOT of noise." He grins. "It's sort of lonely without them. I skied with my two sons and played tennis with them a lot, so that part I miss. Now I play mostly with the pros. They can put the ball where I want to hit it," he jokes. "I played in a lot of celebrity pro tournaments, and I enjoyed, I learned a lot from them."

He's a bit taken aback at the warm reception he recently received at the Gordon Parks Academy. The 400 students and staff honored him at a Gordon Parks Day. "It's very difficult to describe my elation," he explains slowly. "The school is 95 percent African-American. These children have seen my books, read my books, and just want to meet me. They had a big program, played some of my music, and did skits of me as a child. There was a whole stack of letters and drawings they made for me. It was a wonderful day.

"You get a lot of energy talking to those kids," he continues. "Sometimes when I go to colleges and speak to young people, I learn more from them than I expect they learn from me. They have new ideas and fresher pursuits.

"You know, I didn't finish high school." He pauses a long time. "But I did go to high school where we had a teacher, a white teacher whom I mention in this latest book. She was Mrs. McClintock. She was our advisor, the black kids' advisor. And she told us not to spend our parents' money going to college, because we were all going to end up as maids and railroad porters. The poor woman really believed what she said. She was trying to be helpful, I suppose." He lowers his voice.

"When I got my thirtieth honorary doctorate, from Skidmore College, I dedicated it to her." He laughs, not unkindly. "I got two or three more this year. A lot of the doctorates are down there on the floor." He motions toward stacks of leather-bound books under a hall table.

His work has inspired children to write from across the country. "It's the busiest time in my life, really," he says in amazement. "I've got hundreds and hundreds of letters piled up here. I have an assistant, but some of the letters are so personal, it's hard for someone else to answer them. The kid wants to know if he should become a movie director or play the piano or become a photographer or writer, so you have to answer 'Jane' or 'Joe' and say 'I would do this,' or 'I would do that.'

"It's very difficult. They ask what I think about a certain character in one of my novels. It's very difficult for somebody else to sit down and write what I think about a character in a novel. But I can't say no to these kids.

"And you see these books all over the place? They keep coming in, people wanting me to write forewords to them. And I say, 'Okay.'" He sighs gently.

"Then someone has an exhibition and they want me to write a foreword for the exhibition. I just don't have time to do it. I want to get on with my own work. There's a lot I want to do myself."

He'd like to concentrate on poetry and music. "Writing poetry and composing music keep me away from depression," he says. "When I feel depression coming on, that's the easiest way to get out of it.

"I may write another book. Two companies are after me to direct films. I would like to do a film of my last novel, based on Turner's life, but I'd have to do it in Europe, and it would be very expensive because I'd have to spend time in England, Venice, Wales, France, and take a crew. Oh, yeah! It's a year's work," he says.

"Then some people send me scripts to read," he continues. "But I don't want to do a film unless it means something to me. I don't want to do it just for money. I've already done money films like *Shaft*."

He leans back in the chair and puffs his pipe languidly. The smoke drifts around us. I ask to take his photo.

"Do you really have to take a photo? I'm not at my best," he protests. I assure him he looks fine.

"Okay, you're the photographer, you're the boss," he says, removing his baseball cap and smoothing his hair. "I haven't cut it since the surgery. Tell me where to look."

Straight into the camera, I say.

He seems relaxed on the other side of the lens. I shoot him in front of his parents' photos, then ask him to play the piano at the other end of the living room. Twilight is settling on the river and barge lights start to twinkle.

"What do you want to hear?" he asks.

Your sonata, I reply.

He plays smoothly, with no music. He says he hasn't written the piece down on paper. All the better to improvise, I say. He agrees with a grin. The melody sounds vaguely Russian. "No surprise," he says. Serge Rachmaninoff is his favorite composer.

"I think Rachmaninoff has been the greatest influence in my life," he muses. "I don't know why. I just like him. I play his tapes all the time. You know, I nearly ran over him once in a car." His eyes brighten and voice quickens. "My God! I would have made history if I'd run over Rachmaninoff.

"He was crossing Fifth Avenue at 42nd Street, by the New York Public Library. He was walking against the light. It was snow and sleet and slippery, and he just seemed to ignore the traffic. I recognized him and wheeled into the curb. He just sort of walked on across the street, with a taxi driver screaming things at him." His voice is airy. "He was a sort of hero of mine."

Parks returns to his sonata and finishes a jazzy last movement. He's elated to play again. For months he couldn't use the piano pedals, on doctor's orders, because his Achilles tendons had to heal. To keep his sanity, he continued to compose the sonata on his electronic keyboard.

You mean it's not finished? I say.

"Oh, no," he exclaims in mock horror. "This piece will never be finished. It's like poetry. You go back and reedit and say, 'Ah!' You discover something that you play with much better. You substitute it for something else, or you add to it."

His eyes gleam. "I expect they're planning on getting me to try to play it in New York, too, when the show opens here. Time-Warner is going to be behind it."

He rises from the piano bench and returns to his desk. I take more photos with his parents' pictures in the background. He almost smiles in one of them.

"What kind of camera are you using?" he asks.

A fully-automatic Fotura, I say.

"Fancy!" he answers.

What do you use? I ask.

"A Nikon, the first camera I bought," he replies. "I like to be in control. I don't buy new equipment. You're not in control with it. The new cameras have so many gadgets on them."

I ask if he would please take my photo. He agrees and I hand him the camera. He cradles it and shoots a few pictures quickly.

Parks checks his desk calendar, ruffles through a pile of papers, and holds up some letters. "NOW, at my age, I get love letters," he says incredulously. "Love from people I've never met. You'd be surprised at some of these letters. People write me, people who've never seen me. They say they've read my works and it changed their lives. They feel me there." He touches his heart.

"Here's a girl who wrote me a bunch of her poetry. She calls me her adopted godfather. She says her mother just gave her my book *Arias in Silence* (1994), a book of my painting, photography, and poetry. She says she had tears in her eyes."

He reads from the letter. "'It was a beautiful moment and Mom shed a tear. She gave me your book. Awesome. I love it. Well, I guess if I don't finish this letter, I'll never mail it. I'll leave you with a couple of pages of my newest creations. With much love and admiration, Julie, your honorary goddaughter.'"

He falls silent for a moment. "So there are things like that, sort of get to you."

It makes him think. "You look back and realize all these things you've done, the accumulation of all these things, and it's a little mind-boggling," he says. "You don't realize it's hap-pening. They just come one by one, all the awards and so forth, and now there's not room for them. But they came one by one, through trial and error, and I appreciate it.

"One of my deepest regrets," he goes on, "is that my mother and father are not here to see that I've tried to fulfill their wishes. Oh, yes, I believe they know. My sister Gladys whom I loved dearly, said when she died, 'I will tell Mama and Papa about what you're doing.' And I believed her."

He says that God helps him out. "I have a kinship with It." He touches an index finger to the side of his head and nods. "Um, hm! I don't let it get to me too serious." He laughs. "But I believe there's a connection."

He also believes in ghosts. "Oh, yes," he says seriously. "When I was writing my novel on Turner, Old Turner himself used to come to my bed at night and urge me to get up and write. Really! He seemed concerned that I wasn't giving his book enough time."

Parks spent eight years writing that book. "Well, you have to know Turner," he says. "Turner would say, 'Give me your life!'" He laughs good-naturedly.

At 85, he plans more projects. He has no concern with aging. "I don't feel sorry for myself, the way some old people do," he says lightly. "And I'm still talking to you!" He grins like that's a sign he's alive. We laugh together.

"I'm still interested in making a film about the Russian writer Pushkin. And Russia wants my photo exhibit. But it's going to be tied up in the U.S. for five years.

"I'm looking forward to using a new pair of skis that I got, which are faster than the ones I had. I do downhill skiing at Vail, Colorado, every year. In the spring, I want to go back to the tennis courts. And I want to start running again, when the doctor says okay." He is visibly excited.

What's your greatest joy? I ask.

He chooses his words carefully. "My greatest joy is to get up every day, the sun is shining, and I know I can either go to the piano or I can go to the camera or I can go to poetry, and do what I want to do. That, to me, is the most enjoyable part of waking up every day. And talking to a good friend, one of my children, my grandchildren. They are a WONDERFUL mob. Here, let me show you."

He pulls out his latest book and turns to a section with family photos. I see a range of people in a close group.

"We are all colors in my family, a kaleidoscope." He touches the picture lovingly. "Through marriage and other ways, we are a mixture of American, Cherokee Indian, Chinese, English, French, Israeli, Scottish, Swedish, and Yugoslavian." He raises his eyebrows. "I feel like a citizen of the world. Yeah, a citizen of the world."

He smiles contentedly.

RUTH CHRISTIE STEBBINS

Born: May 19, 1891,
  New York, NY
Profession: Homemaker, world
  traveler
Home: Tucson, AZ

This business of hip-hooraying being 100 years old—I say any body who goes when they're 80 years old is the lucky one!

After my husband died 20 years ago, I felt things had come to an end. I had to adjust to a completely different lifestyle. I'm living with my daughter Barbara and if it weren't for her, I don't know where I'd be. We get along beautifully, we always have. But I want her to live her life and get the most she can while she's still able to get about and not be hampered.

People ask me how I got to live so long? I always quote Eleanor Roosevelt, who said, "Genes!" Unless you abuse them most dreadfully during your life. It's the way you're made. Period.

I loathe exercise. I even get squeamish when I look at one of those aerobic programs on TV. I was always a walker. I think you derive as much benefit from a good, brisk walk as any one of those aerobics exercises. I'm dead against jogging. You're doing miserable things to your body when you jog, coming down hard on your feet.

I'm not a bit afraid of death. If I knew I was to go tonight when I went to bed, I'm ready. I'm definitely ready. I don't think there's life after death. You take all of nature—plants, trees. They grow and when they die, that's it. They've given their time. I can't believe that everybody's who's ever lived is up there waiting for me!

I think young people today are horribly lazy. They've been made that way primarily because they've been given too much. They've reached the point where they demand it. If they get married, they want everything just as fine as their parents who've worked 50 years to get where they are. They want it all to start with. That's too bad.

I read, I watch TV, only selected things, mostly public TV, and I eat three good meals a day. Barbara's an excellent cook, so I eat well. I don't go out. She has a lot of friends coming in. There's a coming in and going out of this house all the time. I never feel isolated. Her friends are so lovely to me, so considerate, make so much of me! It's very nice. I visit with them a little bit and then I disappear, because after all, they came to see Barbara, and I can't take too much of that sort of thing. I get too tired.

I've taken life as it comes. I haven't tried to push it and be something else. I haven't aspired enough to go ahead and get and do. That may be why I've survived this long. I have been content. I haven't fought life, wanting something else, something more.

I'm very proud of my children. I adore my grandchildren. Two of them are coming to that awful one hundredth birthday business. As far as I'm concerned, it's just another day. They say, "Look how few people get to be 100." I say, "These days, it's as common as can be." And it is!

"I always liked older people.
I respected my elders, their wisdom.
I learned at an early age that if I went to an older person,
I learned."

LES PAUL

> Born: June 9, 1915,
>   Waukesha, WI
> Profession: Musician, song
>   writer, inventor
> Home: Mahwah, NJ

At 88, he is a pop music icon.

Decades ago, Les invented the electric guitar and still plays weekly to standing-room-only crowds.

Every Monday night, he drives into New York City and takes the stage at the Iridium, a Broadway nightclub. He and his trio— "kids half my age," he jokes—play two sets of mellow, jazzy music, including his signature piece, "How High the Moon."

The fans love his intricate improvisations. Between sets, they line up for autographs, which he signs enthusiastically, on napkins and items presented to him: postcards, photos, sheet music, record albums, even a T-shirt worn by a comely young woman.

A consummate gentleman, Les asks her to turn around and signs his name on her back. They both laugh.

"Hey, how're you doing?" he gives a hearty handshake to a German tourist. "What kind of guitar do you play?" The young man, clearly thrilled, replies, "A Les Paul electric." Les smiles warmly. "Gee, that's nice. Enjoy it."

He jokes and banters with the crowd during sets. "You want to hear THAT old tune?" he laughs. Then he invites anyone to come on stage and perform a piece. "You're something else!" he tells a young man after his lively guitar rock number. "I'd hate to follow your act." The youth blushes and grins.

After the show, Les invites me to his tiny dressing room. He sips beer from a bottle, leans back in his chair, and asks me about myself and the book. We have a mutual friend and an interest in music, so talk comes easily. I say I've always enjoyed his music. He laughs in appreciation.

"I can't express how much I look forward to WORKING every week," he says. "I can't express how much my trio means to me. They are so much younger than I am! The bass player is quite young and the guitar player is half my age. We all look forward to Monday night. It's almost like we're being GIVEN something, rather than working a job."

Quiet and well-spoken, Les is a slight man with fair skin, freckles, and light blue eyes that dance when he gets excited. Wispy red hair combed straight back gives him an elfish look. He wears a royal blue turtleneck and pressed, faded jeans.

"I never at one moment EVER stopped being grateful for all the people who like what I've done, or like me or my music," he goes on. "I love to be with the people. I love to hear their negative comments or their constructive criticisms. I LOOK for 'em.

"Yes, I look for 'em!" he says. "My son Les, Jr. is my engineer. He videotapes each set and I watch the videos at home. Every week I come down here and say, 'I'm gonna try again. I didn't get it right last week, so I'm down here this week to get it right.' And I enjoy it."

He plays guitar despite gnarled fingers. Diagnosed with arthritis 20 years ago, he despaired of ever playing again. Then he hit on a new method.

"I jam the pick between two fingers of my right hand," he demonstrates. "Then I use two, not the usual four fingers, on my left hand. Those two left fingers are my only good fingers now. In some ways, I play better than when I had use of all my fingers." He looks up and shrugs his skinny shoulders.

Les also survived advanced heart disease. In 1980, he had quintuple-bypass surgery, a new technique at the time. On doctor's orders, he stopped smoking and drinking. He radically changed his diet and started to exercise. By the time he went for a post-surgery checkup, he'd lost 45 pounds. "My doctor didn't recognize me," he laughs. "He really didn't know me! I've kept to that health plan."

Les did one more thing. Before he left the hospital, he made a list with two columns, labelled "positive" and "negative." He asked himself, "'Where am I happiest?' With all the different hats I wear, where am I happiest? And I was surprised to find out it was playing in nightclubs.

"NOT playing for presidents, or the Queen of England, or 50,000 people at a slug," he tells me. "Those were not the important things. It's playing in an intimate little nightclub, like this one, that I'm the happiest. I like playing the guitar with the real people, the rock people who have been loyal fans, the newcomers, and people coming in from different countries." Many fans are Japanese, who have followed his career and collected all his records and CDs. They tell him so when they shake his hand.

Before the Iridium gig, Les played at Fat Tuesday's downtown every Monday for eleven years. He loves his schedule. "It gives me time to do creative work at home the rest of the week," he says. He practices and experiments in a state-of-the-art studio that he built.

Where do you get this zest for life? I ask.

"Mother lived to be 101 1/2," he says promptly. "She had all the get-up-and-go, all the energy, UNBELIEVABLE energy. When she had her one hundredth birthday party, she leaned over to me and said, 'Lester, do I still have my marbles?' Ha! I said, 'Yep, you've got 'em, Mom.' She was just sharp as a tack, just like a lawyer. So quick.

"I was always very enthusiastic about most everything I got into," he continues. "I had to know why, when you throw the switch, that light LIGHTS! It's a curiosity. It's a curiosity where you not only want to know, but you CAN."

Do you want to live to be 101 ½, too? I ask.

"Absolutely," he says, without hesitation.

If you have all your marbles, I add.

"If I have all my marbles," he laughs, "and if I'm enjoying myself fine. If it so be that things aren't that fortunate, then I would like to check out. I don't see any sense in being around if it's just lingering on." He sips his beer.

"I feel like a million bucks, better than I did before the surgery. I feel young, I feel real young. I smoked five packs of cigarettes a day for ten years, from the age of 65 to 75. I stopped that after the bypass. I stopped drinking. I'll drink a little now, I allow myself two beers a week. I went on the Pritiken Diet. I'm very careful not to wander off on some flaky diet. I eat oatmeal, and a lot of popcorn! No saturated fats," he says crisply.

What about plastic surgery? I ask.

"I don't believe in it," he says. "I think that if the body is growing old, your face should go with it. I think the whole body should grow old together." He smiles at me, eyes flashing.

Les is rarely idle. He needs only five hours of sleep every night, sometimes less. "Just this last week I didn't sleep for two days, because I was busy," he says nonchalantly. "At home, I'm building a second recording studio, writing my memoirs, and always practicing to keep up my musical skills.

"I surround myself with young guys like Jimmy Page, Billy Joel, and George Benson," he explains. "I'm in a studio with all young players. I've done a country album, a jazz album, a rock 'n' roll album, and a blues album. They're all with young guys, except the jazz album.

"I learn from the young guys," he says excitedly. "I learn from my son Les, Jr. He's divorced, has three children, but lives with me. He'll ask me something, some advice, and I'll take a deep breath. Because I want to tell him, 'Look, I tried that 40 years ago, it don't work.' But it will work NOW, see, because he does it a little different."

His passion for work can take over, and Les has to watch it. "I get terribly busy, which is selfish," he admits. "Which is selfish," he repeats gently.

Does your current lady love understand?

"Oh, I make sure she understands," he replies, not unkindly. "We've been together 20 years. She understands."

Arlene is a little younger than Les and lives down the street from him. "She has a home and I have my home and we just see each other," he says. "Never get married! Never get married. It spoils everything."

He and Arlene like to take motor trips, often spontaneous. "Once we drove to the Pennsylvania Amish country. It was a beautiful autumn day and we stopped to get some food at a store and have a picnic by the highway." He warms to his story.

"We saw a young Amish guy, this red-faced, healthy-looking young person, trying to make out with a little Amish girl." He grins. "We saw these young people all jump into a car. All the rules they make—these kids were breaking them." He laughs delightedly.

"Another time we were on a trip and all of a sudden, I said to her, 'Hey, I need to get my exercise.' I walk a lot and ride a bike three or four times a week. I said, 'I'll tell you what. I'll take my walkie-talkie with me and I'll talk to you.'

"She let me walk two miles. A trucker came by and said, 'Can I help you? You got a problem?' I said, 'No, I don't have a problem, I'm just out hiking.' Then another person stopped, because she got the car parked two miles down the road and she was sitting there. 'Do you need help?' he asked. 'No, I'm fine, thank you,' she said. That's what we do. We have a wonderful time.

"If you're lucky enough to find somebody, you can share and enjoy yourself and be happy around 'em. You can benefit by your life in the past, too, and do the things that you didn't do. If you're fortunate enough to figure that out, you can actually be terribly happy." He leans back and takes another sip of beer.

So love and sex exist in old age? I ask.

"They're anything but over. As of last night, anyway," he laughs lightly. "I'll tell you something about love. My late wife Mary told me once that she was stunned at how many things came to my mind and were successful, whether it was writing a song or inventing something. 'Where in the world do these things come from?' she asked me.

"I thought about it perhaps two seconds and just blurted out, 'First you have to be in love. And second, you'd better believe in God.' And that's the truth," he says firmly.

"Being in love is a lot more than having someone around to sew a button on your shirt. I had a girlfriend that I used to hang out with, and we had two things that she just didn't understand. One was that pride was almost a disease. It's something that you have to be careful about, because pride is not always beneficial.

"The other thing was sharing. There's SO much in sharing," he says.

"Yeah, hang onto love, because love is important. You can love your work and you can love your partner. You can love your parents. There are SO many things. You can love music. You know, love is quite a word." He grows pensive.

Is love more valuable as you grow older? I ask.

"Sure, because you appreciate it more," he replies. "You don't know where you're going after you die. And I wish some son-of-a-bitch would come back and tell me!" He laughs. "But nobody comes back, you know." He wags his head at me.

"Although," he adds mischievously, "I beg God, Whoever, to let me come back and finish my job. You have so much to do and so little time to do it in. The days aren't long enough! Time seems to pass faster as I get older. I don't know why, it just does," he says softly.

He's not afraid of death. "When the time comes, I doubt if we're going to the pearly gate up there," he says. "I doubt that God's going to be sitting there, and that I'm going to have to meet some people that I'm so glad NEVER to see again. I don't think so!

"I do believe in a supreme being or power," he goes on. "Einstein did. And Edison did. I believe everybody has to say, 'Hey, this much you know for sure: it started with NOTHING. Who made nothing and then put something in it?" He stares into space and falls quiet.

Les doesn't go to church, but prays privately and often gives thanks. It's part of life, he says. "I never ask God for help, but I'm always thanking Him for what I've got. I don't ask Him to help so the Yankees will win or something like that," he says quickly. "Although I was at a Catholic hospital once in Pittsburgh," he chuckles. "And the nuns were praying for the Pittsburgh Pirates to win. I told them, 'I'm a Yankees fan and you have the edge on me. I have to go around the hard way, you know?' But then the Yankees won! That was something."

Les has cheated death more than once. "I had a bad car accident back in 1948," he recounts. "My chances of living were nil. Walter Winchell went on the air, saying I wasn't gonna make it. Others said I wasn't gonna make it. It didn't look good. At one point, I knew that I had a choice of letting go. My fingernails were hanging on the outside of the Empire State Building, and I said, 'All I've got to do is let go—and it's over.'

"Well, I didn't. I chose to fight." His face assumes a bull-dog look.

"It's terribly important for a person, especially an older person, to want to live their life the most productive and happy they can. You've GOT to have a positive attitude. And you've got to be grateful for what you have, okay?" He raises his eyebrows. "You've got to thank God for what you've got and quit complaining about what's wrong. If you don't believe in God, then thank WHOEVER."

Les acknowledges his old-age problems. "You live with 'em," he says briefly. "I have about a million of them! I wear a hearing aid. I take anti-inflammatory medicine for arthritis. I take a pill for gout, one for blood pressure, and I take aspirin. There are days when you just feel extra, extra good." His eyes flash and he smiles broadly. "Most of the time it's hard to beat me down, because in about two minutes, I'm up fightin' again!" That bulldog look returns.

He tells me that he was a serious child. At nine, he decided he wanted to be a musician and mapped out a career. At eleven, he began studying guitar. He persuaded his school principal to advance him two grades at a time and he attended summer school. By 13, he had acquired the equivalent of a high school education.

He left home to take a radio job, moved to New York, then to Hollywood, where his career took off. He wrote lyrics, composed music, invented the technique of over-dubbing, played nightclubs, and made records and movies with his wife Mary.

"I said to Mary once, 'Work is the most helpful equalizer in the world.' I'm a worker. So was she." Les shakes his head sadly. Their marriage ended after 14 years. "She said she couldn't keep doing the very hard work, the strain of singing and performing, the strain that especially a female can be under. It's very tough," he says softly.

"It means you have to look right, ALWAYS. You have to climb four flights of stairs at 6 o'clock in the morning, with no rest. You have to forfeit so much and have to give so much, just to stay on top. It's rough for any female. It's tough for a male.

"We had five children, four are still living, and five grandchildren. All of them live nearby," he says. "They come to see me perform. I wish they'd come more often to the house for holidays. It's hard for my children even to get the wives together. In the old days, it was sort of an unwritten rule. I'm very old-fashioned that way."

Mary and Les stayed close friends until she died in 1977. He retired for ten years, but got bored and returned to music at age 65. "It's the best thing I ever did, because it kept me alive and perking, in touch with young people. There are some great young players out there. I don't always agree with their new

music, but young people have to have artistic freedom, the freedom to choose their own music."

Most of the young people he meets impress him. "Very
few people you interview stress this point," he sits up in his
chair and jabs a finger at me. "About how much GOOD the
young generation has done.

"When rock 'n' roll music came in, the older generation
said, 'That trash, that junk!' I looked at it entirely different. I
said 'They're on MY side. They're taking my toys, my electric
guitar that I developed starting back in 1927, 28, and they're
playing with them.

"Thank God, they are!" he laughs happily. "I'm proud of
that. I'm grateful that I was the one lucky enough to think of
'em and bring 'em about, so they can play with 'em. The kind
of music that comes out today is something else. But that's up
to you. I say if the shoes fit, put 'em on. But if they're not your
shoes, they're gonna hurt your feet. You've got a knob on the
radio, turn it off." He tilts his head and smiles.

"I think YOUNG and I understand where these kids are
coming from," he says. "I'm genuinely interested in them. It's
when you turn off, when you turn 'em off—then you're done."
He is emphatic.

"Young and old, from nine to 90, come to the club to hear
my music. A nine-year-old kid sits here and I say, 'Hey, fella,
what are you doing here?' He says, 'I'm studying guitar.' I say,
'Do you have one?' He says, 'Yes, sir.' I say, 'What kind do
you have?' He says, 'What else? A Les Paul guitar.' I say,
'Bless your heart. You know, you study and someday you'll be
great.' He says, 'That's why I'm here. I wanted to come and
see the master.' I say, 'I don't know if this is the right place to
see that, but I'll do the best I can.'

"I'm a role model for them," he says matter-of-factly.

With all his work, Les keeps up with hobbies. He's a long-
time ham radio operator with the handle "Red," and enjoys
talking to people all over the world.

"I love to read and listen to books on tape. I'll read a book
on Einstein, something by Joseph Campbell, the Bible, anything
about Major Armstrong, he's the man who invented FM. And

Norman Vincent Peale, his book *The Power of Positive Thinking*. Brilliant man, brilliant man.

"In life, there are two things that make me tick. You've got to BELIEVE, and you've got to be in love. If you don't have those two things, you don't have much to live for. I don't care what you believe in. But you'd better believe in SOMETHING.

"Being happy is not having nine of everything," he goes on enthusiastically. "It's not having four cars in the driveway. Being active and being excited over something new, and appreciating what you have—THAT'S it!" he cries. "I could be happy if I had a cave in New Mexico and I pulled that rope up after me with a girl and a bucket of water, with no electricity.

"I'd be happy," he repeats. "I can be happy anywhere."

JOHN LAUTNER

Born: July 16, 1911,
   Marquette, MI
Profession: Architect, visionary
Home: Los Angeles, CA

I'm completely open-minded. Wherever I am, I try to contribute something better to the universe. That's one of the things I loved about Frank Lloyd Wright. I apprenticed with him for six years. There's no doubt he was a genius. He was WITH the universe.

I've had my neck out all my life. If I didn't have my neck out, I couldn't have done anything. Nothing! I never succumbed to the business, the codes, all the conforming things of life. I'm totally concerned with real contribution of ideas and improving human life, creating anything good. I can't understand the "Me Generation."

What helps me philosophically is Buddhism. I learned that when I went to Bangkok. Everybody was happy. I looked at the taxi driver and said, "What the hell is wrong? Everybody's happy!" He said, "Nothing is absolute, nothing is forever." That's my main hope.

As I get older, I'm better as an architect. Absolutely. Architecture is a very unique thing because it includes everything in life. There's no end to it. The longer you work with it and the more you think about it, the more there is to do. I work all the time.

The only friend my age is Ingo Preminger, the brother of Otto. We've known each other for 50 years. He's in Austria most of the time. Twenty years ago he told me, "All this society wants is to be held blameless." That's it. I want to be held responsible. That's the difference.

Frank Lloyd Wright said it best. Joy in work is man's desiring. We are just here to sing it. That's the essence of life.

"I'm fortunate, because it happens that my field of interest is such that I can continue working and getting satisfaction."

LINUS PAULING

Born: February 28, 1901,
  Portland, OR
Profession: Research scientist,
Nobel Prize winner, author
Home: Big Sur, CA

Linus Pauling, 91, stays young by working and looking for answers.

"I think we've made the greatest of all our discoveries just the last couple of years," he says, seated at his desk piled with papers and books. "We are in the process of preventing people from dying of heart disease and strokes, by taking vitamin C and lysine. Have you read my latest papers?" he asks with enthusiasm.

Pink-cheeked, blue-eyed, smiling, he eagerly hands me a copy of "Lysine/Ascorbate Related Amelioration of Angina Pectoris" (1991) and "Solution to the Puzzle of Human Cardiovascular Disease: Its Primary Cause is Ascorbate Deficiency Leading to the Deposition of Lipoprotein and Fibrinogen/Fibrin in the Vascular Wall" (1991).

I gladly accept them. I've admired Dr. Pauling's work since 1970, when his book *Vitamin C and The Common Cold* became a bestseller and, as a young reporter, I interviewed him. He made an instant impression on me and I became a convert to vitamin C.

He wore a black beret then, and still does. Why? I ask.

He sighs. "I just got used to wearing it, perhaps when I lost most of my hair. I was bothered by drafts." He laughs softly. A fringe of white hair curls from under the beret into bushy sideburns.

"The main reason was that my wife made my fedora over into a pork pie hat, back about 1926 or 1927. Our good friend Robert Oppenheimer liked my hat and I think I gave it to him. He became famous for wearing that pork pie hat." Oppenheimer was a fellow scientist who was important in the development of the atomic bomb.

"The trouble with the pork pie hat was that if I went indoors someplace, I had to put the hat in the checkroom. But with the beret, which I started to wear a few years later, I could just roll it up and put it in my pocket, so that I never have to check it." His voice has a trace of triumph.

I feel drafts, too, I say. I even sleep with a hat. Do you?

"Oh, yes, I wear a nightcap," he replies comfortably. "For quite a while, my wife made red flannel nightcaps and put a tassel on them. But the ones I have now, I've made myself and they don't have a tassel.

"I remember we went to a play at the Pasadena Community Playhouse, a workshop where students put on small plays, and one play was about Voltaire. There's one scene in which he was in his nightshirt and nightcap. Voltaire!" he exclaims.

Dr. Pauling keeps his beret on during our hour and one half interview. He wears a red-and-yellow plaid shirt, purple tie with navy squares, black sweater-vest, and dark jacket and trousers, stretched over a big frame and broad pair of shoulders.

We sit in his cluttered office at the Linus Pauling Institute of Science and Medicine in Palo Alto, California. Bookcases cover three walls. The fourth has a big greenboard with chemical equations, molecular structures, names of people, and phrases, including "Ascorbate stimulates production of lymphocytes," written in chalk. I take a photo of him standing in front of it. He seems pleased, smiles broadly, hands holding onto his coat lapels.

His speech has an unusual musicality. Sentences often start mid-tone and end on a high note. He speaks in clear, measured phrases. "It's probably my Oregon accent," he explains. "It's a reasonably pure sort of English. Good place, Oregon. They had good schools," he recalls with affection.

His manner is gentle and demeanor professorial. It's not surprising, since he was a college professor and is Professor Emeritus of Chemistry at Stanford University. He's been called the chemist's chemist, and is regarded as one of the two greatest scientists of the twentieth century. The other was physicist and mathematician Albert Einstein, who knew Pauling and called him "a real genius."

For his work in developing the modern theory of the chemical bond and molecular structure, Dr. Pauling received the Nobel Prize in Chemistry in 1954. He also deduced the structure of the alpha helix, laying groundwork for the later discovery of the double helix structure of DNA. He has written hundreds of scientific papers, 14 books, including *Vitamin C, The Common*

Cold, and The Flu (1976), *How to Live Longer and Feel Better* (1985), and is working on several more, including an update of *Cancer and Vitamin C* (1979).

My questions about aging interest him intellectually. He ponders them and answers with great care.

How long would you like to live? I ask.

"I was just on a radio program this morning in which I said my estimate was, by taking the proper amounts of vitamin C and following other health practices, people could live 24 years longer, perhaps even 32 years longer, and be 100 or 110 years old at death, instead of an average 75."

He wouldn't mind living to be 100. "I've accepted two invitations so far to birthday parties on my one hundredth birthday," he says, without blinking. "One is at Cal Tech, the other one is here at the institute."

What drives you? I ask.

"I'm just so INTERESTED in my WORK, just as I have been for 70 years," he says, leaning toward me. "It was 70 years ago that I began my graduate work. But even before that, when I was studying chemical engineering at Oregon Agricultural College, I'd developed a great curiosity about the nature of the world." His blue eyes glitter.

"When I was eleven, I began collecting insects and reading books on entomology. When I was 12, I became interested in minerals and got books on mineralogy from the library. The next year I became interested in chemistry and began carrying out chemical reactions in my laboratory workshop in the basement of our home.

"I have a great curiosity about the nature of the world. Curiosity keeps me going. Today I'm sending in another scientific paper for publication. I can get satisfaction from my work." He relaxes and sits back.

Are you proud of your work? I ask.

He pauses a moment. "Yes, I have to admit that, in part at least, I'm responsible for a great improvement in the health of people. And my institute has made it possible." Founded in 1973, the Linus Pauling Institute has conducted groundbreaking research on the effects of megadoses of vitamins, especially vitamin C, in fighting and preventing colds, cancer, and heart disease.

Dr. Pauling practices what he preaches. Ever day he takes 18 grams of powdered vitamin C, two grams of lysine, 50 milligrams of vitamin B, 30,000 units of beta carotene, 800 I.U. of vitamin E, 200 micrograms of selenium, and a vitamin-mineral tablet with 400 I.U. of vitamin D.

Recently he was diagnosed with prostate cancer, and last week he made it public. "When they told me, I wasn't afraid, just sort of interested," he says quietly. "I didn't have any trouble when the cancer was diagnosed. I thought, 'Well, here I am, at 90 years old, and almost all men by the time they're 60 or 70 have enlarged prostates and prostatic cancer.' Even if they don't die of it, autopsies show that practically every old man who dies has already started prostatic cancer. It's a slow-growing cancer.

"It probably started BEFORE I began taking large amounts of vitamin C," he guesses. "My vitamin C is probably what postponed the development of this disease by 20 or 25 years. I never expected that I would live forever and, of course, I never expected that I wouldn't begin to have the increased incidence of disease that's characteristic of old age. With nearly all diseases, the chance of getting the disease at a given age doubles every eight years in chronological age."

He takes the drug Flutamide to control the cancer. "My urologist is monitoring the dosage. I don't know much about drugs, you see. I've concentrated on orthomolecular substances. But I know enough to know that some drugs are quite effective in controlling diseases. Two of my sons are monitoring my care."

Dr. Pauling believes in conventional medicine. "I never said that high doses of vitamin C take the place of conventional therapy of disease," he explains. "I always say, 'Take a high dose of vitamin C as an ADJUNCT to appropriate conventional therapy."

His health has been good. He walks with a sprightly gait. Recently he broke a leg and was in a cast for two months. Now he's healed and back to work full-time. He prefers to stay at his ranch in Big Sur, high above the Pacific Ocean, where he can work without distractions. In Palo Alto, he meets colleagues, directs lab experiments, sees visitors, answers mail on an old portable typewriter, and gives speeches and commencement addresses.

"This Saturday, I'm giving the commencement address at the University of California at Berkeley," he tells me with enthusiasm.

"I've decided to say to the students that they should try to get a broad background of knowledge, like I did, not just narrowly limited to their field of specialty.

"They must also THINK, and think about the possible relation between some piece of information and some other piece of information that may come from outside their narrow specialty, and see if they are related to one another in ways that could be significant for the solution of the problem they are working on."

That is the scientist speaking, I say. What other advice would you give young people? Are love and marriage important?

"All my life, they were very important to me," he nods, smiling. "I would tell young people to pick out the right person, get married young, and STAY married. Don't waste your time the way young people are, looking for some significant other.

"I was married for just about 59 years, not quite, two months less. My wife died ten years ago. Her name was Ava Helen Miller. In Chile, she was introduced as Doctora." He pronounces the word with a Spanish accent, drawing out each syllable. "She had been given an honorary doctor's degree, Doctora Ava Helen Miller de Pauling.

"My wife really dedicated herself to achieving a mode of life for the family that would permit me to concentrate on the work that I wanted to do. She had very well-defined principles. She was thoughtful and very smart. She finished high school in three years in Oregon, and I often thought she would do better on intelligence tests than I." He smiles affectionately.

"She affected me a great deal by talking about what she was thinking. She was one of the organizers of Women's Strike for Peace, and she was responsible for getting me to do something about nuclear weapons and world peace."

Dr. Pauling led a worldwide effort that resulted in 13,000 scientists signing a petition that led to the 1961 nuclear test ban treaty. He wrote the book *No More War! (1958)*. Both he and his wife received peace awards for their work, and in 1962, he received the Nobel Peace Prize.

He was also honored by the American Humanist Association in 1961. He gave a speech to the group about the scientific derivation of basic ethical principles. Ethics, not religion, is the key, he insisted. "I started out by saying that I think that I am a

man like other men. If I cut myself, I hurt and I cry out with pain.
I see another person cut himself and cry out with pain, and I
assume that person is also hurt, has the feeling of being hurt.

"I would like to have other people behave in such a way as
to keep my suffering to a minimum. It is accordingly my duty to
behave in such a way as to keep the suffering of other people to a
minimum. This could be expressed in the words, 'As ye would,
that others would do unto you, do ye also unto them likewise.'

"My conclusion about minimizing the amount of human suffering as a basic ethical principle is really not a new one," he
continues. "Other people have expressed it in various ways, The
Golden Rule. I consider it to be a scientific principle of ethics."

Do you practice it? I ask. Are you a gentle man?

"Yes," he replies slowly. "I think so, yes. One of the people
here at the institute, in a discussion of a colleague, said to me,
'You treat everybody in the same way, no matter what his or her
status is.' So I have some EVIDENCE." He laughs.

He does not believe in God. "I have faith in the universe,"
he says. "Who was it, I've forgotten, made a comment, 'I accept the universe,' and the comment was, 'Well, you'd better!'

"And I have faith in myself.

"Of course, there is no God," he goes on. "As a boy of
eight, I read the Bible through and went to Sunday School.
The things we learned just didn't seem to make much sense to
me. I may even have formulated the argument that if God is
all-powerful, why is there so much suffering in the world? I
didn't just sit down one day and start resolving this problem.
After a while, I realized that this just seemed like some sort of
mythology to me, and not interesting."

He worries about the future of the world. "I think that things
have been getting worse," he says. "I've spoken on this a number of times, once at a symposium in Sweden. I pointed out that
all over the world, the rich are getting richer and the poor are
getting poorer. The rich nations are getting a larger and larger
share of the world's wealth, at the expense of the poor nations."

He has faith in the younger generation. He sees brilliant
young people in his work. "They're just as smart as ever, probably brighter than ever before. I used to tell my freshman students, 'You know, you're probably as smart as the professors, so

don't be taken in about just accepting everything that a professor says." He smiles broadly.

He and his wife had four children, two of whom live nearby. "I have 15 grandchildren and 15 or 16 great-grandchildren. The number of great-grandchildren keeps changing." He laughs.

"My eldest son, Linus Pauling, Jr., is a physician in Honolulu and a member of this institute's board of trustees. I see him and his wife every few months when they come and stay at the ranch.

"My second son Peter is retired after a career of teaching chemistry in the University of London and is living in Wales. He comes to California about once a year and stays with me. My daughter Linda Kamb worked as a chemist, married, and raised four children. She and her husband live in Pasadena. She's coming up this weekend and taking me to Berkeley. And Crellin is the youngest. He's head of biology at San Francisco State University. I see him often."

Photos of the family fill his office. He proudly points to one of "the clan," as he calls it, gathered for his eighty-fifth birthday party. On his ninetieth birthday, he recalls attending six parties, including a banquet at Cal Tech for 300 people.

What age do you feel in your heart? I ask.

He thinks for a moment. "Well, what is it they say? That a fat person has a thin person inside him struggling to get out. I suppose I feel like a boy inside the frame of an old man." He smiles winsomely.

His frame is lean, due to great care he's taken of his body. He's never smoked. He's been on a low-protein diet since 1941, when he was diagnosed with chronic glomerulonephritis, a kidney disease.

"My doctor Thomas Addis put me on a minimum protein diet, a very carefully selected diet that I followed for 14 years. He also had me take vitamins and minerals, just the ordinary amounts. I'm sure that did a lot of good. Bed rest was part of it, too. And I didn't spend my time worrying about dying. I just kept on working."

Dr. Pauling still favors that diet. "I take 40 grams of protein a day," he explains. "You see, a glass of milk is eight grams, a serving of beef can be 60 or 70 grams. So for 14 years, I ate practically no meat. Now I eat meat, but rather small helpings and not every day. I tend to eat fish rather than beef, although I like beef. I eat a small lamb chop, perhaps, not a large lamb chop. I eat the fat. I need to get food energy, and fat, of course, fat and carbohydrate, are better sources of food energy than protein.

"I don't like vegetables very much," he admits a bit sheepishly. "But I try to eat some fruit and vegetables. Someone says you must have five servings of fruit and five servings of red or green vegetables a day. My goal is to get ONE serving of each. But the vitamin supplements pretty much take care of it all."

He also admits to avoiding exercise. "My daughter especially keeps pestering me to exercise more," he says glumly. "My wife and I used to go regularly for walks, but I find it hard to force myself. There's always something else I'd prefer to do." He looks at me cheerfully. After his broken leg healed, he made an effort to walk and improve the muscle tone. "I try to exercise every day, especially at the ranch. I walk around, back and forth." His dress is shirt, sweater, and "old pants," he says.

A doctor friend tested his hearing and gave him a hearing aid. "But I forget, I just never use it. I prefer just asking people to speak up."

He has a magnifier to help read. "Vitamin C is supposed to protect against cataracts and I don't think it protects completely," he says. "I still drive. My driver's license is for two years more. I don't drive at night and I don't drive myself on long trips. My children got after me and said, 'Why don't you rest on a long trip?' So I get driven back and forth to my home."

He points to a photo. "That's my home, right by the Pacific Ocean. The ranch is 45 miles south of Point Sur, 20 miles north of San Simeon. The road, Highway 1, goes through my ranch. It's 160 acres and I raise polled, white-faced Herefords. They're meat cattle, they're very good mountain cattle. Polled means they don't have horns, they're a genetic mutation. I've had the ranch 37 years. A ranch hand takes care of the cattle. Sometimes my son comes from Honolulu and helps with the branding and castration."

The ranch is a refuge, a memory of his wife. He misses her sorely. "She and I liked solitude, liked to be off by ourselves and not with other people all the time. At the ranch, I was able to do serious thinking and writing. On the 1st of August, 1970,

I sat down and started writing longhand, and on the 31st of August, I'd finished this manuscript *Vitamin C and The Common Cold*. It was published in November of the same year.

"We didn't have a telephone. In fact, one day my wife said, 'Here we've been married for I don't know how many years, and this is the first time that we've ever been alone together, you and I, for a week, without having seen another person.'

"The telephone interrupts me occasionally at the ranch now. I've refused to have a fax machine installed." He laughs with satisfaction. "Usually I can sit down there and often work for eight hours steadily, with the flow of thought not being interrupted. So I get my work done at the ranch.

"I'm writing several books at the same time," he says. "One is *How to Control Cancer With Vitamins*, with Abram Hoffer. My book with Ewan Cameron, *Cancer and Vitamin C*—just the day before yesterday, I wrote half of the preface to the revised edition. The day after tomorrow, I expect to write the other half.

"I do almost everything in longhand," he continues. "Once in a while, I dictate something. My first book *General Chemistry*, a college freshman book, I wrote out longhand. Then the publisher wanted a somewhat shorter version and I dictated the whole volume *College Chemistry*. But I had the first text available, so I could dictate in such a way that there was practically no correction necessary."

Do you use a computer? I ask.

"No," he replies.

"Do you type?

"Yes, I learned to type when I was 18," he says. "The stenographer in my chemistry department taught me touch-typing."

When he's at the ranch, he sticks to a self-imposed rule. "I stop work at 4 o'clock. Sometimes I find it hard to stop, I'll want to keep working. But overnight I can think about what I'm doing and next day I can go on.

"At 4 o'clock, I'll get out the vodka. I don't drink, but in recent years, I've been drinking a couple of slugs of vodka every day. Sometimes I miss the vodka and don't take it, but I don't have to have it. I just add ice, have it on the rocks.

"Alcohol, I think, is an orthomolecular substance, in that it's a natural tranquilizer and human beings in history, I'm sure, were drinking fermented liquors. I don't know when beer came into use. Of course, beer and wine saved a lot of lives." He chuckles. "People drank it instead of drinking water, which would have given them typhoid or cholera.

"I quote a paper where the investigators found that hypertension was the least at a given age in people who had a couple of drinks, a couple of jiggers of vodka a day, or perhaps even three or four. But then you have to worry about becoming an alcoholic and developing a liver problem." He laughs, then frowns.

He watches *The People's Court* on television and after dinner, he reads scientific literature for several hours. "Part of that is science fiction," he says, almost apologetically. "I like science fiction."

Did you ever think of writing any? I ask.

"Yes," he replies. "But I didn't ever get around to doing it. There were other things that I preferred doing. I didn't think that I could compete with the great master Isaac Asimov.

"I wrote to him," he goes on, "because I read that he'd had a heart attack, and I said, 'You must do something.' I think he got my letter before his death, but I didn't get an answer from him. I'd corresponded with him earlier about things, but not about his health." Dr. Pauling sounds concerned.

He also watches news on TV. "I can get three stations, three networks," he says. "One of them I get clear. The other two, I have trouble with, too far away, or mountains in between. So I watch the one, I think it's CBS, with Dan Rather.

"In a sense, I HAVE to keep up with current events, because every day or two, I'm asked to sign an appeal." He laughs heartily. "I've been involved in so many things that nearly anyone who writes an appeal thinks that it would be good to get my signature.

"For a long time, I subscribed to *The New York Times*, but I decided to give it up six or seven years ago. When I'm in town, I buy *The San Francisco Chronicle* and read it, especially the comic strips. The comic strips were developed before I was born and were an important part of life when I was a boy: the *Katzenjammer Kids*, *Old Doc Yak*, he was a yak, he had horns, but he lived in the U.S., and he had an automobile with license number 348. So Old Doc Yak and 348 were important!" He jabs an index finger in the air.

"I like the comic strip *Doonesbury*," he goes on enthusiastically. "When I'm at the ranch, I don't get the paper and I miss that more than anything. There's a recent comic strip, I forget its name, about a woman who has a family, she's a housewife, a couple of kids," he thinks, sighs, and suddenly remembers. *"Calvin and Hobbes!"*

Do you giggle when you read them? I ask.

"Yes," he says, smiling.

Do you have a sense of humor?

"Oh, yes," he says quickly. "Let me see if I can think of a story that I could tell. The jokes that I like have the characteristic that the analysts of humor say is the important characteristic of humor. They end with some connection between ideas that one hadn't thought of before." He pauses a moment, takes a breath, and begins.

"There was a fellow who went to the psychiatrist and said, 'I'm worried. I think perhaps my mental functions have gone wrong, so I've come to you for help,' The guy said, 'All right, I'll give you some tests. What is it that, when you go across your front lawn at night in the dark, you step in it and say, "Damn, that dog!"' And the man said, 'A hole that he has dug.'

"The psychiatrist said, 'What is it that a man does standing up, a woman does sitting down, and the dog does on three legs?' The man said, 'Shake hands.'

"So the psychiatrist said, 'Well, you don't need to worry, there's nothing, absolutely nothing wrong with you. You're quite all right, you can go away feeling happy. Don't worry anymore. But do you know, some people give the damnedest answers to those questions!'"

Dr. Pauling grins.

He rises and shakes my hand. I thank him and impulsively give him a big hug. He returns it easily. He asks if I have all the papers and books that he's given me, and I say yes. I pack up my equipment and leave.

A few minutes later I discover I've left something and return to his office. He's bent over his manual typewriter, deeply immersed in touch-typing, and doesn't hear me. I find my things and take one last photo of him—working.

Jewel Plummer Cobb

Born: January 17, 1924,
  Chicago, IL
Profession: Biologist, educator,
  retired college president and
  dean, social activist
Home: Los Angeles, CA

I administer a pre-college math and science program for middle-school youngsters in an East L.A. Hispanic community. We've got some good results. It's inspiring to get youngsters to like math and science. I retired as president of California State University at Fullerton when I was 65, the mandatory retirement age, but I'm as busy as ever. I go to work four days a week at Cal State, Los Angeles, where I'm a trustee professor. I'm on the board of California Institute of Technology and Claremont Graduate University, and I'm a trustee at the California Science Museum in L.A. When I was retiring I was panicky. "What should I do?" I said. I realize that was a natural feeling, a fear that you'll just sit around and nobody will ever see or talk to you. It hasn't happened. One thing I have to work on is being less busy. I really do.

As a black woman, I have things against which to strive and problems to solve and issues to confront. My situation INNERvates me, gives me drive every day. It starts me off. I can't sit back and say I'm one of the privileged people, I don't have to worry. I have so many things to do! I have more ambitious plans than I can get done.

I'm writing an autobiography *Musings*. It's about my family, including my great Aunt Nelly, a slave in Annapolis, Maryland. She wrote a book *Triumph of the Cross: The Sin of Slavery* and it's going to be a part of mine. Her twin was my grandfather.

I'm very anxious to return to tennis and walking. I have a stress fracture of my ankle, which is slowly mending. I've always been very physically active.

My friends, long-time friends, are very important to me. I'd like to see them more than I do. Most of them live on the East Coast. The older you get, the more mutual experiences you share.

My greatest joy is my son. He is a very special person, a fine young man, a neuroradiologist. I enjoy being with him and his wife and daughter. They live on the East Coast and I see them two or three times a year, and in the summer. They're very vibrant people. I enjoy being around young people very much. There's a certain vibrancy being on a college campus that gives me a special refreshment.

I tell young people to enjoy every moment. Savor the good things that they're talented at doing. Make sure they're in a position to express their maximum talents. Don't live in a situation that keeps them from doing what they want to do. Get as much education as possible. It's an irreversible acquisition of wealth. You can lose all your money, but if you have knowledge, that can't be taken away from you.

Being young and feeling young and staying young is an internal spirit. It has nothing to do with an audience seeing you as "being young." It's inside yourself.

"Getting old is just not a concept in my thinking.
Every day is so full, sometimes I wish the days were
longer so I could get more done. Time doesn't drag."

RUTH STAFFORD PEALE

Born: September 10, 1906,
  Fonda, IA
Profession: Chair, *Guideposts
  Magazine*, co-founder, Peale
  Center for Christian Living
Home: Pawling, NY

Ruth Peale, 92, is so sure she'll live to be 100 that she's planning her birthday party.

"I'll go down to Marble Collegiate Church in New York, where Norman was pastor for 52 years, and we'll have an anniversary service," she says, smiling serenely, referring to her late husband, the Reverend Norman Vincent Peale. "We had one for his 100th birthday. I spoke at that time, but I doubt I'll speak at mine. I don't know as I could suggest that," she says diplomatically. "We'll just wait and see.

"I'll plan a family reunion to follow the service," she goes on enthusiastically. "We always have a reunion every year. We've been on an African safari and we've traveled to the Holy Land. Once we went to Tanglewood in Massachusetts, where the Boston Symphony plays in the summer. This May, we're having a reunion in Cincinnati, to honor Norman's 100th birthday. It's near the little town where he was born. The house where he was born is still standing.

"I have three children, eight grandchildren, and six great-grandchildren, so with their spouses, there will be 20 of us. That's quite a reunion."

Why do you want to live to be 100? I ask.

"Oh, just so I'd be able to say I was!"

A petite woman with a silver bubble of hair and a warm smile, she sits at the large desk of her late husband in the Peale Center for Christian Living. Next door is her office, somewhat smaller. This room is neat and modestly furnished, filled with photographs and awards, including the Presidential Medal of Freedom, which Dr. Peale received from President Reagan in 1984. In one corner stands a large American flag.

Mrs. Peale is at her desk every morning at 8 o'clock, and she is the keystone of the center.

"We are not standing still," she says spiritedly, touching a mound of magazines at her side. "New things are happening here all the time. They're very important and very exciting." Her turquoise eyes flash.

"We are now up to five magazines. The most recent is *Angels on Earth*. The American Magazine Association says it's the fastest-growing, subscription magazine ever published in the United States. So, you see, we've been guided. Angels are very high right now."

She smiles brightly, a colorful figure in Chanel-style suit, red lipstick, and traditional jewelry: pearls and an American eagle brooch. "I've always done that," she explains. "I felt that as a pastor's wife of a Fifth Avenue Church, Marble Collegiate, the way I dressed was very important." Now living in the country, three hours north of New York, she's traded her heels for sturdy black walking shoes.

Recently recovered from hip-replacement surgery, she walks every day for two miles on her 217-acre farm. She leads an active social life with family members, old friends, and fellow worshipers at the local Quaker Hill Church. Most important to her, she carries on the work of her late husband, with whom she founded the Peale Center.

A division of *Guideposts Magazine*, the Peale Center distributes inspirational literature to more than one million people worldwide. It hosts leadership conferences for CEOs, provides a national prayer hotline manned by hundreds of volunteers, and maintains a museum of art from all the great religions.

As chair of *Guideposts*, Mrs. Peale edits copy for all five magazines. "*Guideposts* is unique," she says with a touch of pride. "There's never been a spiritual magazine in the U.S. that even approaches it. It's entirely made up of true, first-person stories of people using their faith in everyday life."

She also reviews religious books that are sent by publishers, in hopes that *Guideposts* will reprint them. "I read every book before we offer it to our list," she says. "I make sure it has approval of what we stand for. We're publishing close to 50 books this year. We do a continuity series. We do what we call one-shots.

And we do novels and essays. It's a very prestigious book department. We distribute over one million books every year."

She adheres to a rigorous schedule. Every weekday morning, she drives her 1984 blue Cadillac down Quaker Hill to the office. Often she's at her desk before her secretary arrives. Mrs. Peale brings handwritten replies to letters that she receives from people around the world.

"I get hundreds of letters every day," she says. "I have a wonderful staff and I don't get all the letters that are directed to me, but I do get a sampling they give me, to let me know what's coming in. If there's anything personal in the letters, they always come to my desk. I work on letters in the afternoon at home and bring them in for my secretary to type next morning."

Who writes to you? I ask.

"Generally people who've had a spiritual experience they want to share with me," she replies. "Many times they've just finished one of Norman's books, like *The Power of Positive Thinking* or some of the Peale Center material."

She also receives letters praising her book *Secrets of Staying in Love.* "It's for anyone who's having trouble in a relationship or wants to make one better," she explains, handing me a copy. "People's letters tell me I've helped them, because I use down-to-earth illustrations of relationships, how you can have a discussion with your spouse without it becoming a fight, and how to parent children."

She feels that some parents are too permissive. "They don't give children a sense of ambition or a sense of vision of the future, or a spiritual background that will be the basis of their joy in life," she says. "But I think the majority of parents are practicing good, old-fashioned values at home. The letters I receive indicate that is true."

Every Monday, she attends the center's weekly prayer fellowship. Sometimes she brings a sandwich and eats lunch with colleagues. More often, she drives back up Quaker Hill, prepares lunch at home, and works on correspondence. Then she changes into jogging clothes and takes the first of two walks.

She and her husband used to walk together and she recalls those days with pleasure. "Many times, I'm sure you're aware that in editorial and writing, you sometimes come to an impasse and the flow stops. If that happened with either of us, we'd say, 'Let's go for a walk.' It's amazing how that refreshes not only your body, but clears your mind."

Later she walks a second mile and watches the sunset. "I walk specifically to keep in shape and because I like it. I swing my arms back and forth, to keep the muscles in tune." She speaks like a teacher giving instructions. "I FORCE myself. I'll go out for a walk whenever I think, 'Well, I'd rather read this book.' Sometimes I'll time myself. If I have a tight schedule, I'll be careful about that."

At dinner, she listens to the news on the radio, then delves into her pile of books. "I used to be content with seven or eight hours sleep," she says. "But now I like eight to ten hours. I always take a book to bed with me and read for an hour or so before falling asleep. I do a lot of reading at night."

Her eyes are still good. She's had one cataract removed and is monitoring the other. She takes no medicine. "Not one single bit of medication, not even aspirin, I should say not!" she exclaims.

She admits to having a bit of arthritis in her hands. "But I'm a great believer in vitamins," she adds quickly. "I take a handful every day." She doesn't have the patience to list them all for me.

She's more interested in describing her diet. "I've always believed in a very simple diet, with plenty of fruits and vegetables. I eat fish quite frequently. We have a wonderful fish market here in Pawling. I eat very little meat. And always 2 percent milk. I have that with my cereal in the morning.

"I've just grown up this way," she says. "Even though I'm a little bit older, I still am careful about my diet. I feel my diet is very helpful to my good health. And I'm in good health largely because I've always been active and kept my mind working." She shops and cooks for herself. A caretaker and his wife keep the property and house in working order. They've lived on the farm for 50 years.

"I prefer living alone," says Mrs. Peale. "I'm hoping I'll never have to do anything but that." After her husband died in 1993, she chose to stay in the home they'd owned since 1934. "One of the great problems is loneliness," she admits. "But I did not want a companion living with me. I wanted my own home and I had my work here in Peale Center. Between my work and responsibility at the center and the correspondence that I answer and the books I read, I'm very busy.

"I often work on Saturday and Sunday. It doesn't matter what day it is. The thing that matters is what task is before you. If something isn't done, why then, you go and finish it. If you get an inspiration for a new idea for the book, you go and do it.

"Of course, I go to church every Sunday and join in the social hour after church." Her church is interdenominational, as is Marble Collegiate.

Once a month, she travels to New York City to make speeches or attend board meetings of various religious groups. She used to travel regularly to speak and receive awards around the country. But she's reduced that to four trips a year.

She also flew often to Hong Kong to visit kindergartens set up by the Peale Center. Her last visit was in 1992. "We have a wonderful person in charge," she says. "We've now put a kindergarten in mainland China. We're debating about whether we'll go to see that one."

Your life is regular and disciplined, I observe.

"Oh, definitely," she replies contentedly. "When you say 'discipline,' it's a little hard to picture. I don't feel as though I'm restricted. I can do exactly as I want. But if you're going to accomplish anything—your reading program, your exercise program, your letter-writing program, then you have to have some discipline. It's so much a part of me, I don't think of it as discipline."

She's never known depression, but to anyone who has it, she recommends diving into an activity. "Be CREATIVE," she says. "Everybody has to admit that their life isn't over yet. They might as well enjoy it like they've always enjoyed life. Find what brings them that enjoyment.

"For some, it's reading books," she goes on eagerly. "That's part of it for me. Other people may enjoy bridge parties or tea parties or going to all the affairs a church will plan. Try to be creative and keep busy. Really WORK at it. The best way is to volunteer because you can do it in all kinds of areas, the hospital, a community center, a nursing home.

"I feel everybody needs to have a purpose in life, all their life," she goes on earnestly. "That's what makes it a joy. I try

to be an example of what they can do. I have people write me
and say I've inspired them. Especially if I go out and make a
speech and then they find out how old I am! They're just amazed.
So they write me and are very kind."

She stays in close touch with her three married children.
Elizabeth, vice president of Peale Center, lives nearby with her
family. Mrs. Peale spent last Thanksgiving and Christmas with
them. "They did all the cooking," she laughs. "That's one of
the perks of age. You don't have to cook the holiday meals.
Isn't that nice?" Her eyes twinkle.

A second daughter Margaret "Maggie" Peale Everett and her
family live in Pittsburgh, where she organizes community *Guideposts* groups. Mrs. Peale's son Dr. John Stafford Peale teaches
philosophy at Longwood College in Farmville, Virginia. He and
his wife recently returned from a year at Beijing University. He's
writing a book *The Emerging Christian Church in China*.

Family reunions are important to Mrs. Peale. "They're one
way to keep your grandchildren knowing one another," she jokes.
"Because I have one granddaughter in San Francisco and one
grandson in Wyoming. Most of them are in the Boston area."

She enjoys young people tremendously, especially her own.
"They give back enthusiasm, a questioning of what's happening in the world, and their ideas of what's wrong and what's
right. It creates a very interesting discussion.

"Not always is the discussion in great depth," she goes on
with a laugh. "For instance, one of our granddaughters is in the
development and fund-raising department of the American Museum of Natural History, and she loves to cook. She's
become one of these chefs who prepares a dish by saying, 'Well,
Grandma, I use a little of this and a little of that.' So I know
she's going to be a gourmet cook.

"Another granddaughter is fascinated with design and marketing. She has a job in a big department store in Boston. So I
can always go to her and say, 'Jennifer, are the skirts going up
or down? What are the best colors for the coming season?'
Young people keep me in the midst of the present world."

She's disturbed by the number of broken homes in America
and its effect on children. "My concern is how much young
people have MISSED, because they've not had a stable family

situation. Some haven't been in education or in school to have the proper training.

"I'm concerned, more so today than any other time. There seem to be more distractions, more temptations, and more acceptance of the things that are really not true value. The pressures on these young people are terrific." She frowns and shakes her head. "Unless they can have a home atmosphere or a group atmosphere where they can discuss values, they're pretty much at sea."

Giving to others is the most important thing in her life. "Our whole lives, both Norman's and mine, have been based on giving," she says quietly. "It's amazing: as you give, you get. Because you get the love, the appreciation, the ideas, the stories of people who've taken your advice and done remarkable things."

She's not afraid of death. "I don't think about it," she says lightly. "I don't expect to die for a long time. I'm very busy. Death is simply a transition from mortal life to immortal life."

She has three secrets of staying young, and she reels them off quickly. "Never think about your age. Always have something interesting to do. And read every single book you can get your hands on! Beyond that, love people and be glad to have the chance of being with them."

She suddenly stops talking, signaling the end of the interview. I thank her and gather up my things. She gives me a hug, hands me a bagful of *Guideposts* publications, and thanks me for my time.

Then she strides into her secretary's office and starts talking business.

MAURICE
ABRAVANEL

Born: January 6, 1903
  Salonika, Greece
Profession: Musician, teacher,
  retired conductor, Utah
  Symphony
Home: Salt Lake City, UT

I have an incredible love of music. This is one thing that keeps me alive. I still study music, all the scores that I didn't have time to study because I was busy conducting. I love discovering something new. I get up in the morning because I have something new to learn!

I've had heart operations, I've had bypasses, I had the balloon, and I have a pacemaker, which I highly recommend. They're recommended in the Bible. "Blessed be the pacemakers."

I was 82 when Lucy, my wife of 38 years, died. I had health problems. They gave me six months to live. But I decided to go all over the world and to Tanglewood Music Center in Massachusetts. Against all logic, I found Carolyn, a very beautiful woman, 35 years younger than I, perfectly sane except for loving me and wanting to marry me! She keeps me alive. Also, I can still be useful. They ask me to do workshops for young conductors, which I do all over America.

Of course, people treat me differently, now that I'm older. At 80, you become an octogenarian. Sounds good! At 79, you still get arguments from people. At 80, you are a fountain of wisdom. It just pours out. Any damned thing that I say normally and nobody pays attention to, at 85—ah! It is very profound. I think that's very funny.

I usually feel much more at ease with young people than with people my age, and young people feel at ease with me. That's why Tanglewood is so good. I'm very popular because the kids love me. I do very little for them. I teach and do a couple of seminars. But I have one gift. I can go to the center of a question and I can say the three words that will change the whole attitude.

Find something that you love more than yourself. Even today, I don't think I was that much gifted that I could have the kind of career I've had. But I loved music, above myself. Find something outside of yourself. If it's a woman, fine, or a man, good, or same sex, I don't mind. But find something more than yourself. Then you start living.

Hank Spalding with his cat Maruska

"Since my heart surgery, the day doesn't pass when
I wake up and think, 'Wow, I made it again.
Another day to enjoy a bowl of chicken soup!'"

HANK SPALDING

> Born: February 2, 1915,
>   New York, NY
> Profession: Author, journalist,
>   gardener
> Home: Northridge, CA

Hank Spalding is young at heart because he's optimistic and believes passionately in adventure, the wonder of things, and love.

He's also very funny.

I read his book *The Encyclopedia of Jewish Humor* (1969) and believed he'd be a good candidate for this book. When I called to ask for an interview, he was genuinely surprised, modest, and only casually interested. "Sure, come on over and we'll talk," he said.

Hank was working in his organic vegetable garden when I arrived at his house, a small, one-story bungalow north of Los Angeles. "It's nice to meet you," he said, wiping his hands on his work pants and shaking my hand firmly. "Let's go in the kitchen. Would you like some wine? I'm having some."

We sit at the kitchen table and talk, finding that we have many common interests: a love of music, writing, gardening, and spirituality. I stay all day, meet his wife, their neighbors, and passers-by who admire his roses. We walk in his gardens, have a bite to eat, and find some of his books stored in the garage. He gives them to me, and autographs every one, including *Joys of Irish Humor* and *Joys of Italian Humor & Folklore*. He shows me a copy of his latest work, a bibliography of books on plants. Later he promises to send me a copy of *The Ninth Note*, a work in progress, and ask my opinion.

"Oh, yeah, I wrote eight or ten books about humor," he says, leaning back in his chair and taking a drag on a long, brown cigarette. "The one on Jewish humor enabled me to pay for all four of my kids' college educations." He laughs shortly. "Pretty good for a guy without a high school education." He flicks a cigarette ash into a folded napkin. A nicotine patch on his arm shows an effort to stop smoking.

Hank grew up on the Lower East Side in New York and quit school at age 12 to help support his family after his father went blind and was fired from his teaching job. "My mother was Russian Jewish, my father was American Anglican."

Hank worked as a shoeshine boy, newspaper hawker, leather presser, and ditch digger at the Bronx Botanical Gardens. He also played harmonica. At 15, he joined Borah Minevitch and His Harmonica Rascals. "Borah was a graduate of the Moscow Academy of Music. I was one of the rascals. We played the Palace Theater in New York City five times."

He also devoured books on creative writing and sold his first short story to *Collier's* magazine when he was 17.

All the time, he was listening to voices of the immigrants around him, Italians, Irish, and Jews. "Ever since I was a small boy, surrounded by pushcarts, I'd hear stories from the old-timers, people who could have been my father and grandfather," he says. "I'd write them down, these little tales, accents and all, with no idea except that I enjoyed them. I just wanted to remember." His voice is deep and gravelly, with a New York accent.

"My research was composed of three-by-five cards and pieces of paper, scraps in shoe boxes. I had a whole garage full of shoe boxes. Jokes I heard on the street, jokes from my own family. About 20 percent were jokes I wrote. One day, I started classifying them, to see what these were all about. By then I said, 'I think I'll publish these, as they were told to me.'"

The Encyclopedia of Jewish Humor (1969) was his first book. Others followed, a total of 18, including collections of Black humor that he researched when he lived in Harlem, and a book of American folk humor.

Hank still remembers the jokes and tells me some, with a Yiddish accent. We both laugh. "I shouldn't laugh at my own jokes, should I?" he asks dryly. "But I have a good, strong sense of humor, and it's not just repeating jokes. I make them up. Sometimes I have a dream and wake myself up laughing. I keep a notebook on my night table and jot them down."

Can you laugh at yourself? I ask.

"Oh, sure," he says expansively. "That's who I laugh at mainly, because you can never offend anyone else when you deflect the joke to yourself."

He gets up, stretches, and excuses himself to check on his wife Bert, who is bedridden in the next room. Then he lets a gray, long-haired cat inside and fills her dish with food. "This is Maruska," he introduces us. "She comes and goes. She loves the garden, sits with me when I'm working on the roses. She's my sweetheart."

After Maruska finishes her meal, she walks over and begins to lick my toes. "That's all right," Hank assures me. "She nibbles when she likes somebody. She won't bite, never bites. She's not usually this affectionate with strangers. She's very timid. When anyone comes in the house, she's out of here!"

Hank moved to California 20 years ago in hopes of writing for one of the motion picture studios. That dream didn't materialize. "I took an instant dislike to Hollywood," he says with a short laugh. "Writers don't get no respect!" He wrote several screenplays, hundreds of magazine articles, and then books.

"My sense of humor has really kept me alive, even through disappointments and tragedies," he says. "You know, if you see your own problems in context with the problems of the world, they're pretty trivial. They aren't all that important.

"I have a standard expression. I ask myself, 'How important will this be next year at this time? Will I remember it next year, or ten years from now? How important will this be even tomorrow?'

"I don't take life too seriously, because NOBODY gets out alive." He arches his eyebrows and nods. "We're born red and we die bald, so in between, why not enjoy ourselves a little?" He grins and pours us another glass of wine.

"Probably my sense of humor prevents me from acting the sage," he goes on. "My sense of the ridiculous is enough to see and know myself as only I could see and know."

Along with humor, he loves and appreciates women. With age, it's become more intense. "A man my age enjoys female friends more than he did during his younger years," he explains. "Because now he can concentrate and discover them for who they really are, without the secret agenda of back-of-the-mind thoughts and plots of luring them into intimate affairs." He tilts his head and smiles.

"My female friends give me new and broader insights into their personalities. I really did not know women until after midlife. I genuinely like them now for what they are and can be, if they seize the opportunities pioneered by other, earlier women."

He enjoys looking at *Playboy* magazine, but is strictly monogamous. "I've never been with any other women except my wives. I wish it were like that with everybody. They don't know what they're missing. They've told me that I don't know what I'm missing! I say, 'Yes, I do know what I'm missing, and thank God for it.'" He laughs. "Diseases, heartbreak! Going with other women, how many hours a day can you do that? Fifteen minutes, 20 minutes?"

He still feels young. "I feel 35, 40, not physically, I know better than that. In my heart, I'm a child in some ways, because I can identify. I like it that way. I wouldn't have it any other way. I make it a point to win new friends, and if someone says something contrary to what I believe, I just gloss it over, talk about something else. Everybody has something in common. But there are some people I wouldn't allow through my front door: Nazis, racists, people who can't hold a conversation without an obscenity every other sentence.

"I see wonders around me all the time, new wonders. I'm amazed sometimes at things and say, 'How did I ever miss this?' Like Maruska, our cat. That's Mary in Russian. And her mama, I had her 18 years. She's a wonder, Maruska." He calls her over. She walks daintily to his chair and rubs against his ankle.

"She hears. Sometimes the little tip of her tail will twitch to let me know that she hears me. She's a good friend. She goes out to the garden with me. Sometimes I have to chase her home when I'm going up to the store on the corner for something. I look around and there she is, right at my heel. I don't want her to get run over or lost, though I doubt she'd get lost around here, she's been everywhere there is. I let her run free, she goes out through her special cat door in the kitchen." He motions to a corner near the refrigerator.

Hank lives freely, ready for the next adventure. That means taking risks and chances, something he's done all his life.

"Every time I saw a door, whether it was closed or not, I tried the knob. I've held a few jobs, got along, sent four kids through college, with no education, because I had to stop school early. So I had to take chances."

He holds a deep spiritual belief. It centers on love and kindness. "The spiritual person reacts to an unkind act with understanding and compassion. He recognizes that the act may be due to causes unknown to the victim or others, or, if known, then with reasonable sympathy, and, if possible, help.

"He understands that it's not enough to live and let live, but to live and HELP live. His or her love for all life extends from the least of the life chain up to humankind.

"The love that two people have for each other and who are committed to that love for life, is God's blessing. Or call it Nature's. It's anything but a biochemical reaction. And when that blessing is consummated with the intimacy of physical expression, that blessing is raised to a benediction." He gazes into space.

"Anybody can say, 'I love you,' before sex. It's when you say it after sex, you understand? I don't limit that to sex. There's an afterglow to music, too. You listen to music and you just feel it for hours later.

"Yes, Virginia," he goes on, "those two elderly people, probably married for half a century, sitting at a restaurant table and barely exchanging a word during their meal, have no need for verbal expression. They communicate with a kind of mental telepathy. They are aware of each other's thoughts. They are content. They love each other."

Hank admits he's old-fashioned. He doesn't like the practice of men and women living together, outside marriage. "There's no commitment on the part of the man. He has the best of everything and the woman hasn't anything. In marriage, there's a family unit.

"A family unit is a wonderful thing to contemplate. It's a little world. If a family unit is peaceful and full of love, you'll usually have a peaceful community that's full of love. That gives you a peaceful state. A peaceful state gives you a peaceful nation. It all starts right here in the house.

"If a man loves a woman, he marries her. I've been married to Bert, that's short for Alberta, for 20 years. My first wife Mildred passed away ten years before that. She had diabetes. We were also married 20 years. Both marriages were gorgeous times.

"I believe there are no obstacles that can't be overcome to a happy, loving relationship. Marriage is the greatest gift that God gave to man and woman. I loved Mildred until the day she died, and I'll love Bert until the day she dies.

"I had four children from my first marriage. I could've had 50, but it didn't take every time." He chuckles. "I have four grandchildren. My first son was a Baptist minister, a fundamentalist in Virginia who preached hellfire and brimstone, with a nice Jewish wife from the Bronx.

"He was sending me pamphlets. I said, 'I wish you wouldn't talk about your Father in heaven. I'm right here, the only father you need.' He passed away seven years ago. It broke my heart. He was my first, and, you know, it's tough to outlive a son. You expect them to outlive you. My other three kids are out here and doing well."

Maruska jumps up on his lap and settles down, purring. He strokes her fur and talks quietly to her.

Do you believe in God? I ask.

He pauses. "I'm conscious of an enveloping power that keeps our planet in an orderly fashion, a power of unsurpassed beauty that has its dwelling place somewhere in our mind or heart, if you prefer. That spark of beauty may be called our conscience, soul, spirit, or whatever. That spirit is everywhere and suffuses everything that is good, decent, and beautiful in life. But we can see or feel it only if we seek it out. In the old days, that was called 'Pantheism.'

"God is everywhere," he goes on. "In the rocks, in the rivers, trees, grass, and sky. I feel the presence of God all around me. I walk in the aura of God. I'm not talking about a man with a long, white beard. I explain it in my latest book *The Ninth Note*."

He also believes in reincarnation. He's hypnotized himself many times and done past-life regressions. "All of my lives were adventures," he smiles gently. "All wonderful adventures."

He had a drama in March 1991 during quadruple bypass surgery. At one point, he was half-dead, according to his doctor. "I went through the whole tunnel bit, the light at the end of the tunnel, the people calling me, 'Come forward,' and I wanted to. I heard this gorgeous music that was in ME.

"But I heard other voices calling me, and they sounded somehow familiar and I said, 'I think I'll check these out first before I go forward to that light.' Beautiful it is and I wanted to go, but the other voices were doctors and nurses, screaming at the top of their lungs. I heard so faintly. They were slapping my face, 'Wake up, wake up! Open your eyes.' I said, 'Okay, you don't need to beat me to death.'" He laughs.

"I heard a giggle from someplace. One of the nurses giggled and I said, 'You don't have to punch me in the jaw to wake me up.' I did die and they brought me back. Well, you know, when your heart is on one table and your lungs are on another table, if they didn't put me back together again...." He floats off.

"I think my adventure on earth wasn't over yet," he says slowly and forcefully. "I wasn't ready to go. I wasn't ready to give up. I want to live, I LIKE this life. Because I believe in reincarnation, I know I'm going to be back and then some. So how could I fear something like that?" He stretches his legs and strokes Maruska.

Hank has some good years ahead. "My doctor just gave me another nine-year lease on life and that's nice to know. So I enjoy being here, and I'll enjoy it as long as I'm mentally there.

"I want to live as long as I'm mentally able to enjoy it. Because this is just an adventure to me. This is my current adventure and I'm going to have another adventure, and another, and another." He has a satisfied, Sylvester-the-cat grin.

That adventurous spirit makes him an optimist. "For example," he says, "during surgery, I lost the vision in my left eye. I can see day and night, and I can see a blur, but that's all. When they put the new veins in, you know, from my leg, it brought a rush of circulation to my body. The blood hadn't been circulating, that's why I couldn't breathe, that's why I had the heart attack. So at the back of my eyeball, one of the veins burst.

"It's silly, you can't see it because it's in the back of the eye. The doctor said it may clear up. The only thing I regret is that it's my attractive eye." He laughs at his own joke. "I'm really not bothered that I can't see to the left of me. I'm not even interested in what's on that side. If I am, I'll turn my head and take a look."

He stops abruptly. "People my age are too prone to talk about their operations. I have to check myself that I don't talk about my bypasses too much."

If he had to move to an old-age home, he'd do it. "I'll find friends there and things to do," he says stoutly. "This is part of my adventure."

We talk about the California lottery, which is at a record high this week. He throws out his arms and smiles. "Of course, I'd LOVE to win the lottery. I'd buy a big home across the street in Sherwood Forest, a gated community, where the houses are two or three million dollars. I'd have a four-room kitchen and wall-to-wall carpets in my garage. And then, I'd be on my next adventure." He winks. "I have plenty of time, all eternity."

A good part of Hank's time is spent talking with people. When he's pruning his prize roses in the front yard, students at nearby California State University at Northridge greet him like an old friend. "It's a continuous parade," he laughs. "They're my buddies," he says. "I'll fix a nice bouquet of roses for the girls, and when I do that, I never see the end of them. They're always back, which is fine with me.

"The girls tell me about some nasty one in their class, and I say, 'Well, you stop picking on her. It'll probably turn out to be your best friend or the president of the U.S.'

"And the fellas, I get the latest ball scores from the colleges they're playing, who's on the team. We talk about soil preparation and the planet and environmental conditions. I've been an environmentalist since I can remember.

"All the kids, I ask them about school, family life, their boyfriends and girlfriends, what sports they're into. If they're not majoring in anything, I get after them. They ask me a lot about the old days, and boxing. I was in boxing. It was my favorite sport, it still is.

"I remember one student told me, 'Gee, it must have been terrible walking around when there were no electric lights when you were young.' I told her, 'Well, believe it or not, there were a few, but not too many. We had gas lamps on the corners and octagon or hexagon lights, glass cases over the bulbs. Sometimes the bulbs were yellow.'

"She said, 'Wasn't that kind of scary?' I said, 'It was the warmest, nicest glow you'd have in the street and people didn't walk in mortal fear of their lives in those days. We were closer.'

"There was only one thing we lacked," he says. "Novocaine! I remember having a tooth yanked out when I was six or seven years old, and the pain!" He grimaces. "So, if there's any God to thank, I thank Him for novocaine." A big laugh.

"One guy Bob, he's a professor from the college, still comes by to say hello. I met him when he was a student and now he teaches English. He has kids in their teens.

"There's another guy, an agriculture instructor from the college. He came by to ask me why I didn't have any yellow roses, he said he had yellow roses in the botanical section up there. I told him they were suffering from chlorosis, a deficiency in iron, and I told him what to do. He did it and he's been coming by ever since. He's about 35, I guess. That's not young, but it certainly isn't old.

"Yeah, I like young people," he goes on. "They keep me young. I like to listen to people because I don't want to lose touch. I can think 'teenage.' I know what they're thinking because I was a teenager. I may not approve of everything they do. I don't even approve of everything they think. But I know they're going to go beyond that.

"My father once told me, 'When a young man or young lady is deep into socialism or is an avowed communist, it means really that they're soft-hearted. But if they're still the same way when they're 40, they're soft-headed!'" He laughs. "So it's a progression, and you think in the age group that you're with."

Young people inspire him. "They make me remember that youth is not a passing phase of one generation. It's a phase passing by, as though it were on parade—ALL younger generations. I particularly like the early generations of this country, the young ones.

"I'm reminded of the similarities between the kids of the early nineteenth century and early twentieth century, and the kids now. There's very little difference, except their jobs are different, their goals may be a little different, sometimes a lot. But they're all seeking peace and contentment, which is what I finally attained. Within myself."

Hank encourages his student friends to get all the education they can. "Stay in school! Because sooner or later, they'll find a hand hold, they'll grab onto something, and they won't be lost. Staying in college is important. I spent a lifetime learning what I could have learned in four years of college, although I do not downgrade 'mother wit,' native, inborn intelligence." He takes a sip of wine and shifts in his chair.

"Education is the cement that bonds our abilities. It serves as a launching pad to the stars and helps protect us from the predators of life. Education in the humanities is equally important to happiness. It opens the door to the best minds and kindest hearts that inspired human spirits throughout recorded history.

"That's why Egyptian hieroglyphics inevitably gave way to phonetic words, character by character, to spell out abstract thoughts such as a god, spirit, or other mystic concept which could not be transmitted by 'written' symbols." He doodles on his napkin.

"An education cannot be absorbed by rote," he warns. "The educated person drinks in the THOUGHT behind the teacher's explanation, or the author's or educator's instructions."

When Hank was young, he couldn't get a job because he had no education beyond the eighth grade. "It was the same thing with George Burns," he says. "He feels the way I do and sometimes he gets bitter. I get bitter, too.

"But I also realize the correctness of the system. You have to have that. It took me all my life to learn what I could've learned in school," he repeats. "The School of Hard Knocks teaches you another kind of education. In my case, it taught me love for my brothers and sisters all over the world. It taught me kindness."

He is constantly learning. He's read all the great literary classics. Every day he discovers new things from his neighbors as he takes his doctor-ordered walk in Sherwood Forest. His love of plants and gregarious nature lead to conversations with residents. "First I tell them what a lovely place it is, nice, and I ask, 'What have they got here?' And they'll tell me a variety.

"I say, 'Did you ever stop to think how pretty it would be if you did this or that?' And I end up landscaping their properties. I don't expect them to ask me to do it. Maybe I'd do it anyway. I come over with a few little plants, and everybody is always delighted. I like the atmosphere. It's not a question of money, whether they save 50 cents on a plant. They're all wealthy people."

A passionate gardener, Hank believes that working in the earth keeps him young and healthy. "It's as much of creation as a human being of my generation can do," he explains. "You take a seed, put a little water on it, put it back into mother earth, the breast, and it germinates. It casts off the shell and a little green sprout jumps up. You have to have a magnifying glass to see it at first. You baby it and take care of it, you watch it grow to maturity. You've created it yourself. You didn't create life, you created that incarnation.

"But the seed—life itself is contained in the seed—is every incarnation of the parent, and I can take the seed of THAT. With my sweet peppers and onions, if I like two varieties, I cross-pollinate them. I let them grow in one plant and I've created a different kind of life. That's a fascinating thing to do." He savors the thought.

"Here, let me show you." He jumps up from his chair and invites me to his gardens. Maruska follows, sniffing the plants. He lifts up a pot of cross-bred onions, still small plants. "These onions grow to be giant-sized and are so mild, you can eat them like an apple." He kisses the air. His onion seedlings sell out quickly at the annual fair of the San Fernando Valley Garden Club, which Hank founded in 1976.

That year he began writing a garden column for *The Los Angeles Daily News*. He won an award from the American Association of Nurserymen's Garden Communicators in 1988. He's no longer a columnist, but still writes the club's newsletter. "Sometimes I get outrageously funny and forget all about writing gardening," he confesses.

Nearby are neat rows of corn, asparagus, okra, and garlic. "We could eat our way through it, my tropical soup garden." We laugh.

"Okra is a Southern delicacy that's gradually made an invasion of the North. There's a very unlovely name applied to it —slimy—but it's a soup thickener and can be rolled in flour or cornmeal and fried or steamed. It tastes good. I like it.

"I was introduced to okra because I married a Southern girl who said, 'Why don't you raise okra?' I said, 'What the hell is that?' She told me, so I said, 'Let me get some seeds.' When she first fixed it, I said, 'Honey, I want a divorce!'" He laughs. "'You don't expect me to eat that, do you?'" Times changed and Hank got the knack of cooking it just right.

"Oh, remind me to give you some garlic before you go," he says. He points out nine fruit trees, including pear, apple, peach, nectarine, banana, lemon, and orange. "See that orange tree? There's one right here in the next yard, exactly the same distance, and up and down the block, as far as the eye can see, orange trees, all in a perfectly straight line. That's what's left of the orange grove that used to cover this place, before my time.

"Across the street was a walnut grove," he says, walking to the front yard. "The fella who lives there, Jim, he's head pediatrician at Children's Hospital. He has walnut trees. We exchange. I give him fruits and vegetables and I get walnuts, 20 or 30 pounds of walnuts every year. He and his wife are very sweet people."

Hank's front garden contains 152 rose bushes, All-American selections in pink, red, orange, and white. Some look like small trees. Petals litter the lawn. He can't pick them fast enough. Everything's organic in Hank's gardens. "I was organic before it was chic," he quips. "I've been an environmentalist since I can remember.

"I started a ditch in the back, where the garden is, about four feet deep, and all the garbage went in there. I'd cover it up with a foot of soil and then some more, until it was about a foot from the top, so the animals wouldn't get at it. Then I'd start another ditch, and I always have my own topsoil. I don't like to spoil this beautiful blue planet of ours."

Most of the time Hank is smiling or laughing. Why? I ask.

"Because life has been fun for me. Two beautiful marriages, love, four children, my writing. I was SO lucky in life," he says emotionally. "And I intend to keep going."

What about old people who don't have your optimism?
I ask.

"I'd tell them to go to the park or a garden, any place, and
take a close look at a blade of grass. That little blade of grass,
only four or five inches high, has got bugs on it, it's keeping the
soil fertile. That one little blade of grass is doing a lot of important work in this world. Someday it'll go into the soil and
become compost and become part of earth. And we're all part
of the earth. Enjoy it!

"'This is your adventure,'" I'd say. "'You're on an adventure now. You're almost reaching your goal. And that's not the
finish line, that's a goal.'

"I like George Burns' explanation very much: you accept
age philosophically. Sure, you got aches and pains," he warms
to his story. "Look at an old tree. It's a couple of hundred years
old. All the branches are gnarled and arthritis is setting in. You
can see the twisted limbs in the wintertime. Every spring they
come out with new clothes on. They don't own the birds living
there, but the birds flock to the trees and they're nurtured by the
trees. The trees give them shade and berries and food, they
give them shelter. It's symbiosis. All life is symbiosis.

"My greatest joy is a sense of oneness with the smallest of
violets to the tallest of sequoias, from the field mouse to the
elephant, and from the minnow to the great white shark. We're
all part of Earth's family, held together by a universal need for
each other," he says.

We return to the house and sit in the living room, where he
can monitor Bert. Her caregiver has gone home for the day.

"Lead a symbiotic life, be part of it," he continues fervently.
"DO something. Join a senior citizens' club. Get involved with
people your own age who have exchanged other peoples' problems for their own. You're not as bad off as you now think.
Other people need you, even if for as little as a warm smile or a
cheerful hello.

"Seek out those who were in the same profession or trade
that you had when younger. Tell them about your problems.
Chances are they shared them and will be happy to tell you how
they overcame their misgivings about old age.

"Get MAD at somebody or some institution. Mad enough to do something about it. Search out others who feel as you do and join forces with them for a combined effort to change things. Have a hobby, make your hobby or your own job, if nobody will hire you because of your age. That's their loss, not yours."

He shakes his head. "I had a fella come here with tears in his eyes. He was really sobbing. He said, 'Nobody wants me.' I said, 'I want you.' I remember five minutes before that, I was out in the front yard, cutting my roses and pruning them back. I said, 'Haven't you got any children?' He said, 'They don't want me.' I said, 'They don't want you to live with 'em, huh?' He said, 'Yeah.'

"'Well,' I said, 'why should you live with 'em? You're a nice guy, you've got an apartment?' He said, 'Yeah, I have a little apartment here.' I said, 'Well, you're out of the rain, out of the bad weather, you're out of the cold, you're out of the heat. If it's too hot in there and you haven't got air conditioning, you can buy yourself a fan. And be happy! The world wants you, people want you, God wants you, if you believe in that.'

"You see, his kids had their own lives to live."

After a life of admitted excess—excess smoking, drinking, and eating—Hank is happy just to be alive. "I never did anything in moderation, nothing," he says gruffly. "Whatever it was, I had to do it. I don't know, maybe, to prove something to myself. I ate everything I felt like, drank a lot, smoked. I attribute my old age to drinking, smoking, good sex, and staying up late." He laughs. "I did it all and made it, until the day I didn't make it." He grows serious.

"I'm not sure how I got through the bypass surgery. It might be good genes. My doctor said I had the constitution of a horse. When I woke up and knew I was alive again, I said, 'Thank you, I'm still here. By golly, I made it.'"

The doctor put him on a diet and exercise regime. Hank already had given up beer and white bread after he married Bert. He was in fairly good shape from walking and dancing the tango all his adult life. But he had to get fitter. He's started walking in earnest.

"I'm supposed to walk at least five miles a day, but I can't," he says. "It's too much for me. I do two or three miles. I get exercise working in the garden. I eat chicken mostly, almost no red meat. I keep a balanced diet, so I don't think I need vitamins. I use that artificial salt, it's potassium.

"The doctor says a little wine won't hurt me a bit, so I have a glass once in a while. I used to drink all I wanted. I just don't drink anymore, I don't have the taste for it. Oh, sometimes, I like something a little extra, like apricot brandy." He steals a quick glance at me and grins.

He resumed gardening and compiled the plant bibliography. He "came out of retirement" and wrote his ninteenth book.

"I wanted to write *The Ninth Note* since I was twelve," he says with affection. "It's about my first experience with classical music. It transcended anything I've ever felt. It's about the eight notes of a musical scale, then the ninth note that lingers after the music is over. It's something MORE, for those people who can feel it. It's love, a resonation of everything, the perfection of things. A lot of people don't hear it.

"When I was a boy, I went to an outdoor concert by the Goldman Band in Central Park. When they started to play, I never DREAMED that anything like that existed. I even remember the names of the songs, the compositions—all classical pieces. The Goldman Band was a big band, 25, 30 pieces.

"At the end of the concert, I was absolutely transfixed. I couldn't utter my feelings and thought that everybody felt the way I did. But when I looked around and saw their expressions and heard their polite applause, I knew they didn't.

"I said, 'That's funny, there are only eight notes. Everybody heard the same eight notes that I did.' I looked around again and saw a few people whose faces expressed the rapture I was feeling. I said, 'Now I know. There aren't eight notes. There's a ninth note someplace. Only a few people can hear it, and it transcends the music. The ninth note was inside the person listening.' It's also God talking to you.

"I wanted to tell that story, but it had to be poetry. I said, 'I've got to go to school and learn how to write and keep moving. I can't stay in the eighth grade.' That was the same year I left school.

"So I went to the library and asked the librarian what books I should read. I educated myself to a degree. I read just about every book there was on creative writing. Some of it sank in, because when I was 16 or 17, I sold my first short story to *Collier's* magazine. I've been working on *The Ninth Note* ever since.

"It's a short book, for everyone from children to adults. Writing that book was my only reason for learning to write, back when I was a kid. Besides, retirement is a bore," he booms. "And I've got a lot more to say."

Hank gets up from the sofa and goes into the bedroom to check on Bert. "She's okay, she's watching one of her TV programs," he reports. "Bert is my greatest joy. She had a music publishing company when we met. Every day I tell her that I love her. Every day! I kiss my wife goodnight and good morning, kiss her good afternoon.

"She's had a catheter and a kidney disorder for the past five years. It hasn't been easy, but that's all right. I have her and I want her to stay as long as possible. We have another two years, I guess. Maybe more. She's a tough old bird." He laughs affectionately.

"Love has always been important to me," he says softly. "Love is a constant, the constant fulfilling of your better nature. When I say love, I'm talking about loving and being loved in return. It makes you a nice, rounded person.

"I'm in there with Bert all the time. I run in and out. If I hear a funny joke or I'm thinking of something funny, I'll go in and tell her. She has her TV programs, so she'll shoo me out and say, 'Tell me after the show.' I say, 'Fine, okay.' And we kiss. We have a nice relationship, very loving. We're affectionate with each other, we tell each other so. I think that's one of the most precious gifts in the world: love and the ability to communicate it.

"I bring her flowers from the garden all the time. I made some bouquets for her on Mother's Day. I kiss her cheek and ask, 'Anything special you'd like?' I cook on Saturday and Sunday, when the nursing aide girls are off. I sort of spoil her and bring her out here in the living room to eat.

"I make things as easy for her and as pleasant for her as possible, and she's happy. She knows she'll never have to go to an institution. I'd rather go myself," he says brusquely. "Never! I wouldn't do that to her. You don't do that to people you love."

Love is the key to Hank's life. "I stay young at heart because I still believe that first love will last forever," he says. "I stay young because I believe in miracles. Because each spring, a whole new world has greened just for me, and winter is years away.

"I stay young because I know that the fear of old age is just as irrational as the fears my youngster friends have about striking out on their own. I stay young at heart because I love the better nature of human beings and they love mine.

"I am young! Seventy-seven years young."

Marjorie Van Ouwerkerk Miley

Born: June 11, 1898,
  Lima, WI
Profession: Artist, writer,
  gardener, homemaker
Home: Sheboygan Falls, WI

I went back to college and when I was 81, I got my A.A. in art from the University of Wisconsin. I felt it was unfinished business. I should've finished college, but I went for only one year and got married. I love learning. I just love it! My one regret is that I didn't go to Oxford University in England to study literature at summer school. I was too busy.

I wrote an article for the university newspaper called "Banish All Mirrors!" That says it all! If I stay away from mirrors, it's fine. I'm not that white-haired person. You're as old as you feel and I feel pretty young. I've been fortunate that I'm as well and strong. It's all in the genes.

If I'm sane and alive, I'd like to live to 2005!

I have an aneurysm or something in my neck that could explode any minute. But I just don't think about it. I don't pay any attention to it. I've had it now for 10, 15 years.

I love gardening. When I'm in the garden and my hands are in the soil, everything slips off. The troubles slip away. When I have a hoe in my hands, I'm in charge. I get rid of frustrations. It's the same thing when I make bread. I throw the dough down on a stool. I'm brutal. I throw it down 15, 16 times with all the strength I have.

I had an art show called "8 to 80" when I was 88, at the John Michael Kohler Arts Center in Sheboygan. I found pictures I'd made as a child and added some of my oils, pastels, watercolors, and woodcuts.

I live with my daughter. We older people are the "gainers" when we live with young people.

Mary Morgan and Benjamin Spock

"You must stay involved.
Most old people seem too cautious, conservative, dull."

BENJAMIN SPOCK

> Born: May 2, 1903,
>   New Haven, CT
> Profession: Child-development
>   pediatrician, author, social
>   activist
> Home: Camden, ME

Dr. Spock, the baby doctor, settles his huge, lanky frame into an overstuffed chair in the breakfast room of The Lord Camden Inn. Dressed in a pink shirt, purple sweater, beige corduroy pants, and beige lace-up shoes, he strikes a handsome figure, with blue eyes, white hair, and stubbly beard. "I have a cold," he says in a deep rumble. "And my wife Mary will be back in an hour, so I must hold this down to reasonably brief answers."

Then he smiles and says, "So I'm now impatient."

During our hour together, he relaxes, speaks thoughtfully, and laughs every few minutes, usually at himself. He sneezes and coughs, but keeps talking. At 91, he still cares deeply about society's ills. That's his focus today, not himself.

He deplores what he sees as a decline of world society, due to parents who teach children the wrong values. "We've got to raise our children differently, not to compete and not to get ahead in life, although I've got nothing against getting ahead," he states emphatically. "It's entirely wrong to put 'getting ahead' the highest priority by far." He speaks with a New England accent that omits the "r" in words.

"We should raise children with the idea of service. This is my standard speech for the last several years. Children LOVE to be grown-up in any way. They love to serve and to feel important and they feel EXHILARATED. We ought to give them the idea of service right from the beginning, certainly from the age of two." He blows his nose.

"Begin at two years with setting the table," he goes on strongly. "As teenagers, they ought to be serving the community in some way, like helping out in an institution or tutoring younger children who are having trouble in school. Anything that's helpful."

He presents his ideas in a new book *A Better World for Our Children* (1994). Dr. Spock believes that Americans should rededicate themselves to honesty, love of family, respect for others, and a sense of idealism.

Children have always been a passionate interest: his classic manual *Baby and Child Care* (1946) educated parents around the world. He recently updated it, and now it's in a seventh printing. It's sold 40 million copies, second only to the Bible.

What keeps you going? I ask.

"My terrific conscience!" he thunders, throwing up his arms and looking at me with piercing eyes. "I and all the Spocks of my generation had a terrific conscience, the result of having a very moralistic, disapproving mother. We all felt guilty until proved innocent. There were six of us and we all got into school teaching or psychology.

"When I was 14, I remember my mother telling me, 'You ought to be ashamed of yourself, worrying about what people think of you. Don't you know that it doesn't make the slightest difference? All you have to know is that you're right!'

"Today my main interest is politics. That has nothing to do with details of who's going to win this election, but with the question, are the United States and the world going to keep slipping further and further into deeper and deeper trouble? Are people going to get hold of their lives and their governments? All the statistics show that we're getting worse in every way: riots, anti-Semitism, racism, materialism, competitiveness."

He pauses a moment, shifts in his chair, and looks pained.

"I think excessive competitiveness is one of the great mistakes in the United States," he goes on. "That idea of rugged individualism is the most poisonous of all. The greatest evils are overcompetition and excessive materialism. America is naturally materialistic. People all want to have a good income and if they're not getting a good income, they want to blame somebody. The so-called ethnics want to blame the blacks.

"Americans should be participating in politics much more than they're doing at the present time." He draws out each word dramatically. "Half of Americans don't even bother to vote! This, to me, is the most shocking thing in the world. It wouldn't be so bad if everything in America and the world were going smoothly. But, my God! The world and America are going down the drain from my point of view," he sputters.

Dr. Spock delivers this message wherever he goes to promote his book. He's always taken his crusades on the road. Audiences love him. He travels less frequently than he did in the 1960s and 1970s, when he spoke at 800 universities in an eight-year period. He was protesting American involvement in the Vietnam War and working for the National Committee for a Sane Nuclear Policy. In 1972, he ran for president on the National People's Party ticket.

His life is quieter now. He has a new wife Mary Morgan, 40 years his junior. "Mary is much more particular about whom she lets me speak to," he says. "I used to accept all invitations, but Mary wants to be sure that there's good pay, travel, and a fee. She coordinates my business and professional life."

He coughs and clears his throat. This cold hit him hard, he says. He hasn't had a single cold since he went on a macrobiotic diet about a year ago. But this one sneaked in.

The diet was the idea of a friend, "an auntie, a traditional person," he explains. "She said to Mary and me, 'So-and-so is coming to town, he's in the macrobiotic business, and I'd like you to see him.'

"Mary wrote it down in her book, the months rolled by, and it was time for this man to arrive. I said to Mary, 'What is it going to be?' She said, 'I don't know,' I said, 'It's probably massage,' because Mary is always getting herself involved in massage. She's a pushover for massage." He speaks affectionately.

"Well, anyway, we found out it was a diet! Mary's an enthusiast, she jumps right in, and I went along in a more reserved way. First thing I knew, I was eating brown rice. I was NOT allowed to eat cream on my cereal, not allowed to have cream of any kind, not allowed to have cheese. Oh, that was a terrible deprivation," he groans.

"Mary's been a vegetarian for years, so I hadn't had much meat, except when we went out to a restaurant. So we slipped into this without knowing what we were doing.

"I lost 37 pounds in six weeks without trying. That was impressive to me. I read some of the literature, including a book by a doctor, a Philadelphia doctor, who cured himself of advanced cancer with a macrobiotic diet. That doctor is a back-slider. He gave up on it and died of the cancer which recurred, a sequence you ought to know. At least," he laughs heartily, "you need to know if you begin to backslide too fast, too much. It can pounce on you!

"Sure, I miss the cheese and cream and everything, because after all, the vegetables I'm eating are Chinese vegetables or Japanese vegetables. You're supposed to eat leafy greens three times a day and you can have fish once or twice a week. But no meat. I've gotten so that I don't mind it," he says mildly. "It makes a lot of difference who's cooking and whether they're artistic or not.

"I can't have any wine," he says with disappointment. "It's forbidden on the macrobiotic diet. Before that, for a year or two, wine was forbidden, because I do have some serious conditions that are all under control. I have atrial fibrillation. I have a pacemaker, I've had it for a number of years, and that keeps my heart working fairly regularly. I bitterly accuse my cardiologist in Boston of having no sense of humor. I say, 'Steve, can't I even have a sip of red wine?' 'No!' he says." He shrugs his shoulders and looks dismayed.

"First it was the heart condition and that gave me a stroke three and one half years ago. Miraculously, it was a 15-minute stroke. I just talked gibberish for 15 minutes. And then it came back. Stroke is obviously the thing that kills off Spocks in the end. That's what killed my mother at the age of 92.

"I'm on Coumadin, a blood thinner. It keeps you from getting another stroke. It works, but it's a poison, it's a rat poison. That's what the commonest rat poison is," he assures me. "The dosage has to be just right. And you have to check it first every week, then every month.

"Anyway, Mary doesn't like me to emphasize that, because, after all, she has determined that...." He looks into space and smiles. "The figure I have in mind is Mary holding me by the ankles while I'm slipping into the grave! She's the one who gets determinedly into this diet, never gives me any leeway.

"I believe in using a sense of proportion in things like this and occasionally enjoying yourself. All I want, for instance, is a half-ounce to an ounce of red wine occasionally. I just LOVE the taste of it.

"But it's INCONCEIVABLE to Mary to drink even a half-ounce of red wine when you've been told that it might give you another stroke." He looks at me with resignation and smiles ruefully.

Years ago, he smoked, but stopped after being told he was endangering his life. "A doctor in Cleveland scared the hell out of me about smoking, so I haven't smoked for 20-some years. I think it was a good thing I stopped. I was coughing a lot."

Every morning he and Mary get up between 5 and 6 o'clock. She gives him a body massage, then joins him in Transcendental Meditation for 20 minutes and yoga stretches for 30 minutes. He has leg problems: diminished strength and less coordination, so she pulls and stretches his legs. He does leg lifts, followed by neck, shoulder, arm, and chest exercises.

After breakfast, they go to the local YMCA and swim for 30 minutes. "In the six months of winter, we swim religiously in the Virgin Islands where the water is about 80 degrees," he says, smiling at the thought. "In Maine, I wear a wet suit in the pool. With my weight loss, I get colder faster."

After lunch and dinner, they walk for 15 minutes, and in the evening, they do another 20 minutes of Transcendental Meditation. Bedtime is about 9 o'clock. "When I was writing *Baby and Child Care*, I used to be able to survive on six hours of sleep. But now, I don't HAVE to get up," he looks conspiratorial. "Certainly I sleep eight or nine hours."

Reading is a great joy. "I waste a lot of time reading *The New York Times*," he admits. "As you know, it takes hours and hours to read a copy of *The Times*. I read *The Nation* magazine pretty much cover to cover. I used to read *The New Republic*, but it's come on evil days." He frowns.

He doesn't watch television news or listen to radio. He says he never got into the habit, but if he had, he'd be watching public TV.

Young people have played a big role in his life: patients, students, children, and grandchildren. "They've all helped keep me young," he acknowledges. "I married Mary Morgan 16 years ago. I divorced my first wife of 49 years, who was scolding me more and more. I'd been scolded enough by my mother." He speaks tersely.

"Mary is 40 years younger than I, and she has a daughter Ginger, who was eleven years old when we got married in 1976. So Ginger brought home teenaged friends." Mary was a program coordinator for continuing education in the Department of Psychiatry at University of Arkansas. They met and fell in love when she invited him to lead a workshop.

"Mary is a very youthful, late 40-ish," he says admiringly. "She can make friends with anybody, as Ginger can. Mary is young, even for a 48-year-old, and it definitely keeps me young. I find young women very attractive still, and enough young women act as if they think I'm attractive." His voice becomes hushed, and he smiles. "Secret passions! Maybe that's one of mine.

"They do find me attractive and I can tell," he goes on. "They pat me on top of the head, they pat me on the shoulder. Well, they don't have to!" he exclaims, looking at me defensively.

"People are much more apt to show affection today than before. When I was growing up in New Haven, nobody showed affection, even in their own family. You knew you were loved and took it for granted. You didn't have to talk about it, you didn't have to show it." His voice has a trace of sadness.

Is love important to you? I ask. If you were alone today, would it be tough?

"Yes, it would," he replies quickly. "Marital love—I'm not talking so much about sexual love; I'm talking about somebody to really be a companion, a tight, close companion—that's important. Love and friendship are important always.

"But I don't show a great dependence," he adds. "I don't have to look people up when I go to a town, for instance. Mary always plans ahead of time to look up friends. It never occurs to me to look people up. But then I'll miss seeing people whom I know and people who admire me. I still need to be admired," he says candidly. "I need to see that visibly. In a sense, 40 million copies of *Baby and Child Care* is proof. I don't have to see the people beaming at me.

"And, too, people treat me more respectfully, simply because of my age," he acknowledges. "I presume that being a public figure has helped me age gracefully more easily. There's more approval, less criticism."

Dr. Spock stays in touch with his two sons Mike and John and their children. "But we're not a close family in the sense of needing to get together," he explains. Mike, who lives in Chicago, has three children, two of them living. "Dan is in Boston, he's gone into museum work like his father. Susannah is in college in Minneapolis. She's one of the independent young people.

"When I was in college, we used to think it was very BOLD to go to France for the summer. Susannah went to Nepal for one year and supported herself by teaching English. I never would've had that kind of boldness, at that time. She's finally settling down and going to college."

His son John has four-year old twins. They live in California and he doesn't see them often.

Until last year, he and Mary divided their time between the British Virgin Islands, living on their boat, and Camden, Maine, living in a house. "I was always MAD about sailing," he explains. "I was absolutely obsessed with boats, and the Virgin Islands was great sailing country. That was long before Mary came along.

"Well, it was a year ago, on a miserable, rainy, foggy, cold day and I had a bad cold. I was lying coughing, coughing, coughing all day. And I said to Mary, 'Why can't we have a cozy place to go to, at a time like this, the way other people do?'

"And she said, 'Good idea.'

"So we began looking for a house up here in Maine and we're still hung up, trying to collect the money to actually get started. It's just incredible the number of blockages there can be starting to build a house, all the loans and applications. Well, it's being built now. And it's a fundamental change of life."

Getting used to old age is also a change. "The worst part about being 89 are the infirmities and indignities," he snarls. "Incontinence! Being even more absent-minded than I was at an earlier stage! I dread the day when I simply can't give a speech." He laughs at the thought. "I'm up there in front of the audience and can't remember what I wanted to say! I still bring three-by-five cards with me. All through my political phase, beginning in the early 1960s, I carried these cards with the main points. So if I run out of gas on one point, I can jump to the next."

He sits up suddenly in his chair and beams. "The BEST part of being 89 is that you summarize your philosophy of life from different age periods. You see things in perspective and you see why you deviated in this direction. I can see why I was so interested in clothes and the man-of-the-world appearance. It was because my mother wasn't the least bit interested in those things.

"I think there is wisdom that comes if you're not ossifying at the same time. I hope I'm not, but who knows?" He looks hard at me. "I don't think anybody thinks he's ossifying." He breaks into a grin.

Do you have any regrets? I ask.

"There are certain things I'm ashamed of, that I wouldn't confess to you or to anybody else, that BURN inside me. If I allow them," he says quietly. "If I wake up too early in the morning or in the middle of the night, I might say, 'Why did I do that? Why did I say that?' But I don't regret anything." He relaxes into the chair.

Are you flexible? I ask.

A pause and a smile. Then, in a low voice, "My wives don't tell me that."

Do YOU think you're flexible?

"I think I am, yes," he booms. "I mean, it's my wives who are inflexible!" He laughs. "Trouble is, I grew up with a mother who was so dominating. And my first wife, she's dead now, and my second wife. They both were scolds and both very opinionated. They wouldn't take my opinion. I wanted them just to accept my opinion, because it's me." He looks a bit hurt.

Even your present wife? I ask.

"Yes," he replies. "And she's even more determined."

But she's charming, I say.

"Yes, she is," he assents.

So it's easier, right?

"Right," he says.

Do you have a sense of humor? I ask.

"I think a sense of humor is important," he says. "I don't laugh hysterically a lot of the time, but I think that I see my foibles and other people's foibles."

He's unafraid of death, but does fear senility. "I'd like to live to be 100, if I'm not senile. I have a HORROR...." His face becomes contorted. "I once saw the architect Frank Lloyd Wright in an elevator in the Plaza Hotel in New York City. He was dressed very dashingly, but his jacket was all covered with spots, food spots." He shakes his head. "That's just a miserable representation of what can happen in old age.

"I still care very much what people looking at me think of me," he explains. "In general, when I go speaking in the eastern United States, I still wear a three-piece suit with a gold watch chain across my vest. I wouldn't have any conviction in my talk if I were dressed in a more hippie style. So it's a sort of a relic."

Do you have a spiritual belief? I ask.

"Yes, I'm spiritual, I believe man is spiritual," he replies slowly. "I explain it in terms of emotional development, using Freud's more positive concepts. I think idealism comes from children's over-estimation of their parents when they're three or four years of age. They're meant, like all species, to keep a sharp eye on their parents at that stage and learn everything they can from their parents.

"This is obviously true of other mammals, but it's incredibly more complicated and strong in the human species. I think the idealization of sexuality, the spiritualization of sexuality, are very powerful forces being played out in the negative at the present time in the United States." He looks somber.

Do you believe in life after death? I ask.

"Not really," he says. "I think it's very important what you DO in your life. Everything you do that's to the good in life, will live AFTER you. It's most important in your family. As for being a conscious person after death, watching your family grow up and things like that, no, I don't believe that.

"I'm very optimistic," he continues vigorously. "I say if people will bring up their children differently, if people will use the democratic political process, we could have a wonderful country and the beginnings of a wonderful world."

The hour is over and he rises slowly from his chair. "We ought to go downstairs and see if Mary's waiting." We find her, resplendent in white cotton blouse and full skirt, with a lacy white parasol for sun shade.

He realizes he's left his Panama hat upstairs. I go back to fetch it. It's a wide-brimmed, cream-colored straw hat with a black ribbon around the brim.

I hand it to him and he thanks me. "You're very thought-ful," he says. Mary is wearing the same kind of hat. I ask to take a photo and we walk outside. It's a sunny summer day. They pose smiling at the back porch railing.

I thank him for the interview and we say goodbye. They link arms and stroll down the walk to Camden, bending their heads together and talking animatedly.

DOROTHY DAVIS BOHANNON

Born: January 15, 1910,
  Lebanon MO
Profession: Retired office
  worker, homemaker
Home: Lebanon, MO

I never much thought about getting old until recently. I was always active, I got around fast, I felt good. To me, getting old was way off in the distance. I expect in some cases I'm still full of orneryness and mischief. When you're like that and just mean it for fun, it's good for you and those around you. Just something funny, to make everybody laugh. Jolly, poppin' off, joking.

I loved work, and I worked until I was 67. I worked pretty hard and enjoyed meeting so many nice people. I was very organized with everything. I had a routine that I followed and it worked well. I didn't get nearly as lonely then as sometimes I do now. My husband died in 1970 and I still wear my wedding ring.

My greatest joy is my son Jim. He's a very special thing in my life. I was so lucky to have him come along. I'm so very interested in what he does. Otherwise I wouldn't get up so early every morning. I listen to his radio program "America in the Morning" at 4:07 a.m. on a San Antonio station. Then I hear the whole show again when it comes on our local station.

I wouldn't want to get so old that I'd be a burden or couldn't do things for myself. I do hate to think about having to leave my house, but if it comes to that, I'd pick a nursing home over a member of the family. When you go into a person's home, it tears things up a little. It's hard on the family.

I'm surprised I got so wrinkled. I lost about 60 pounds this past year and I guess that makes the wrinkles show more. This summer they took my picture at church and told me they could take out those wrinkles. I asked how much it would cost. They told me and I said, "I believe I'll leave it as is and let them remember me as I really am!"

I used to be a little frightened of death, but it's a natural thing that comes to everybody. We all go through that sometime. If we don't, it's going to be something rare, isn't it?

"I pray. That goes back to my childhood.
I came up in a family that prayed.
I sincerely believe that prayer helps.
I say thanks too. That's a very important part of it."

BILLY TAYLOR

> Born: July 24, 1921,
>   Greenville, NC
> Profession: Pianist, composer,
>   teacher
> Home: Bronx, NY

At 78, he's deluged with work.

"These last three months are the busiest I've ever been," he says, long, slender fingers ruffling through a date book. "I've had a day off here and there. But I love doing what I'm doing. It took me a long time to get it like this."

He plays piano with the Billy Taylor Trio in concert halls around the country. He teaches music at several colleges. He directs the Kennedy Center Jazz Program in Washington, D.C. and does a National Public Radio series, *Billy Taylor's Jazz at the Kennedy Center*. He's a long-time arts correspondent for CBS-TV, for which he's won an Emmy. And he delivers speeches to lovers of the arts.

Most of the time he's on the road. At home, he's busy in his workroom, composing at a state-of-the-art piano, experimenting with new ideas, answering calls. Young musicians ask advice, old friends report in, reporters want interviews.

"Come in," he says, as I arrive at his apartment. His voice is smooth and rich as molasses. He has a huge smile, dazzling ivory teeth, and a warm handshake.

Billy's a tall, powerfully built man, with huge arms and hands. He sports a dark, dense Afro and big, black, rectangular-framed glasses that look like aviator goggles. When he ushers me into the living room, I see a shiny Steinway grand piano at one end. I make a mental note to ask him to please play for me.

We sit at a glass table where he's placed his calendar. "You see my schedule," he says, pointing to a page crowded with notations and cross-outs. His voice is a soft bass that goes up and down the scale.

"I started out in January with a keynote speech to the Texas Arts Alliance. I came back and was involved in the International

Association of Jazz Educators Conference. That was four days here in New York City, the biggest conference we ever had. More than 7500 people attended." He is flush with enthusiasm.

"The next day I was in Washington and I had Roy Hargrove, a young trumpeter, as my guest at the Kennedy Center series with my trio. Then my wife Teddi and I traveled to Atlanta, Georgia, to rehearse and perform a work of mine, 'Peaceful Warrior.' It was commissioned by the Atlanta Symphony, and it's dedicated to the memory of Dr. Martin Luther King Jr.

"On the 19th," he continues, "I had a phone interview. Then I had to call one of my producers at CBS and reschedule an interview with some people from my alma mater, Virginia State. They want to involve me in a project. I had a meeting about a Cuban concert. Then I had to lay down a track for National Public Radio." He takes a breath and, eyebrows raised, flashes a "What can I do?" look at me.

"I went down to Washington again for another concert and a programming meeting. I go about two weeks out of every month. The Kennedy Center season runs about five or six months, and we're in our fourth year at the Terrace Theater." He grins with pride.

"Then I went up to the University of Massachusetts, where I got my doctorate, and taught a class, 'The Lively Arts.' I do that twice a semester. The teacher brings in interesting co-teachers who are experts in some area. I have a Wilma D. Barrett appointment there."

He continues rapidly. "Then I boarded a plane for Seattle, and the trio played in Bellingham, Washington. The next night we played in Everett. We were there about five days, and then we went to Escondido.

"That says 'day off.'" He points to one day on the calendar. "But that's a lie, because we had to travel to Chico, California. Oh, I misspoke," he says quickly. "That WAS a day off, the only day off that we had. So we played Chico and Riverside, California. Then we went to Greenville, South Carolina, and played there. We play mostly colleges and universities, sometimes elementary schools.

"Then the trio came home and I went onto Houston. Actually it was Lubbock, Texas, where I played with Ramsey Lewis.

Two pianos, that was on Valentine's Day." He pauses for a breath. "Then I came home, and the next day we had house guests. The next day I left and went to West Palm Beach, where Ramsey Lewis and I did another concert.

"We went to Williamsburg and played at William and Mary College. That was very nice. And Richmond the next night. This is a full schedule and I knew it was going to happen because February is Black History Month," he explains.

After that marathon, he decided to cut back, say no to offers. "It's the travel that's tiring," he says. "The airlines are very inconsiderate and really don't make it pleasant for you to travel. It tells on you. I need at least a day off between these things. I am so frustrated with travel problems that I don't want to travel and then do something immediately when I get there." Not wasting a minute, he brings records and books, and works on projects in hotel rooms.

Ninety percent of his time is spent playing with the trio, usually outside New York. "The trio guys are KIDS, they don't mind the travel. Not kids, but younger than I am," he adds quickly. "They're going through what I went through many years ago." Lean and hungry. In his heart, he feels at least as young as they. "I feel somewhere between five and ten years old." He laughs.

The telephone rings and he picks it up, walking into the next room. After a couple of minutes, he returns. "Excuse me, that was one of my students. He's a very fine professional piano player and he's calling about a record that he just did and sent to me. It's his first record, self-produced.

"I'm just suggesting to him that he might want to consider what the first track is, because many programmers don't bother to listen to the whole record. They assume you put your best thing first. My student's concept was to take an original piece and put it first track, then put it at the end: two different versions of the same piece. That's a very nice programmatic idea, but if he wants to get it played on the radio, he might want to rethink it."

Billy makes a point of giving back to young people, the same way jazz greats Art Tatum, Papa Jo Jones, and Teddy Wilson did to him. "Many of the young people whom I work with, especially at UMass and other schools where I'm teaching, are terrific in terms of their focus, their dedication, and the things they're trying to prepare themselves for. Which makes me all the more concerned about the way we try to educate them."

He grows quiet. "We don't challenge some of them enough," he says. "We don't give them the kind of support that would help them meet the challenges we give them. Much of the fault in young artists I work with comes from the older generation." He accentuates each word. "We have not done our job. We've left their instruction to television and movies and people in the street."

Are parents to blame? I ask.

"Yes," he replies decisively. "Parents have not done the job. They have passed off the education to schools and churches and other societal organizations."

It began in the 1950s, he believes, when parents allowed their children more freedom than ever before. It continued in the 1960s when "parents wanted to be buddies with their children. We didn't want to discipline them or do things that are necessary to help people develop in the way we'd like to see them develop."

Teaching is one way to counter that, and it's another way in which Billy gives back. "Music is one of the best ways to get to kids," he says, enthusiastic again. "Because music transcends language.

"I often say to my students, 'One of the reasons I play the piano is that, although I consider myself an articulate person, there are things I can't say as well with words as I feel I say with music. I can convey certain feelings of joy and sadness and melancholy better in music than to say that I don't feel good today or I don't want to be bothered. My head is somewhere else."

Billy serves on the faculty of the UMass and has been a visiting professor at Berkelee School of Music in Boston and Yale University in New Haven. This spring, he'll do a residency at the International University of Florida in Miami.

"I teach the historical basis of the music we play, not the long, detailed account of what the history was," he says. He has a doctorate and loves to be called "Doctor." He exclaims, "I worked HARD for that degree!

"Teaching young people rejuvenates me, because you get all kinds of questions. The young people today are much better focused than ten, even five years ago. Back then, I'd get questions like, 'How can I get everything you have and not work for it?' Yeah, that blatant!

"They'd say, 'I don't really want to practice, I don't really want to go through it. But I really do want to have a Mercedes and be a big star. I want to be on television, I want to be on the radio, I want people to know who I am.' And they were serious!" He laughs deeply.

"I didn't tell them so gently," he goes on with asperity. "I told them, 'There's NO way. In the first place, you're not going to make it, if that's your attitude. You might be lucky, but believe me, that's a million-to-one chance. Look at your competition! You say you want to be a star and you don't want to learn how to play a C scale? Lots of luck! What you want to do, a whole lot of guys who can play you into the corner, want to do, too.'" He looks disgusted.

"Today there are more reality checks," he continues. "People have looked around and seen an older brother or friend who was in school and floundering, say, 'Well, hey, I'm going to New York and be a star,' and he'd come back very unhappy. If you're not prepared, you can't take advantage of whatever happens."

Billy had good teachers. The best, he says was Dr. Undine Smith Moore at Virginia State. "Dr. Moore is one of the great black composers and a wonderful pianist, a wonderful lady. After I started playing professionally in New York and became relatively famous, I had a special thrill.

"I was invited down to Roanoke, Virginia, to speak to the local chapter of the Music Educators National Conference. I remember being a musician and having to go in the back door of that particular hotel, I remember how badly we were treated back in the 1940s.

"Well, I went into the same hotel and I was the principal speaker. They said, 'Is there anyone you'd like to invite?' I said, 'I'd like to invite my music teacher.' We invited Dr. Moore and I explained to that audience that this was the kind of teacher I hoped they were. That gave me a lot of pleasure."

When he's not playing music, he composes. "I've written seven or eight larger works," he says. "The first was 'Suite to Jazz' for the piano and orchestra, commissioned by Maurice Abravanel, conductor of the Utah Symphony in Salt Lake City.

"'Peaceful Warrior' is for orchestra, mixed chorus, and jazz trio. This last time we played it, we were proud that Mrs. King was in the audience. I'd worked with Dr. King in the 1960s, doing fund-raising for the Southern Christian Leadership."

At home in New York, Billy works in a neat, but crowded music room lit by the morning sun. He shows me a Trinity Music Work Station, a double keyboard connected with a computer that prints out what he plays. He wears headphones to hear every note and improvise to his heart's content.

Suddenly he turns apologetic. "This room is a mess. Teddi wouldn't want you to take photos in here." He steers me gently back to the living room. "This is all hers, her artistic work." He throws out giant hands that encompass black velour armchairs with plump pillows in red, pink, and olive green. African and Native American art cover the walls and tables. Two huge vases display feathery forsythia and brilliant orange sunflowers.

Would you please play something on the piano? I ask.

He graciously responds, "What would you like to hear?"

Something that you wrote, I say.

He sits down, positions his hands over the keys, pauses a moment, and begins. The melody is soft, fluid, and beautiful. He is totally focused on the music. His fingers ripple up and down the keyboard, making unusual harmonies. He finishes on a quiet note.

"That was 'For Art Tatum,'" he says. "He was my main mentor. I played one of two movements. I rarely play the fast movement, even though I like it. I like the ballad aspect of this slower movement. It speaks volumes about the harmonic invention and continuity of ideas that Tatum had. He was one of the GREAT jazz pianists."

Billy practices every day, "but not always at the piano because I practice in my head," he explains. "So many things happen to me that sometimes I can't get to a piano. So I'll think about musical things and I'll go over a certain piece or song or composition, a certain concept in my head. When I do get to a piano, I'll say, 'Well, this was what I was thinking. Does that really work?' I try it out. Sometimes it does, sometimes it doesn't.

"When I go to UMass, I carry a keyboard with me, because I have a lot of work to do and it just saves time. You can carry a keyboard onto a plane. I always travel first-class because of my advanced years, so I have a little more room." He smiles indulgently.

Are you in good health? I ask.

"Yes," he replies. "I feel better than I've felt in many years. I don't take vitamins, oh, maybe every now and then, but not on a regular basis. I've had the usual things that go along with age. And some years ago, I had phlebitis. That scared me to death.

"After that, I started flying first-class, so I could stretch my legs, mainly my right leg. I did take medicine at that time, Coumadin, and it seemingly cleared up by itself. I probably still have a residue of it, because every now and then I have some problems. They're a reminder that I should either not be doing what I'm doing, or I should do more of what I haven't been doing." He laughs heartily.

Teddi keeps him on the straight and narrow. "Having a wife who cooks very well, who prevents me from eating many of the things I love to eat and shouldn't, keeps me in good health. I don't have any allergies. I can eat anything, but I just shouldn't eat so much of it!

"We work together. We eat a lot of fruits, vegetables, not much red meat, a drink now and then, but never when I'm working. I learned that long ago." He sees a doctor regularly for check-ups, and wears those big glasses that have become a trademark.

Why are they so big? I ask.

"Anything smaller, I keep seeing the edge of the glass. That bothers me," he says.

His only exercise is walking. He does it briskly, "like I'm GOING somewhere," he says, eyes dancing. "Usually I walk alone, because a lot of times I'm not at home, I'm on the road." He reads and listens to music in his hotel room when he returns from performing, and falls asleep around 2 a.m.

Occasionally Teddi travels with him. "There's nothing for her to do, unless it's a place that she's interested in and people she knows," he says sympathetically. "She's been to most of the places I've been, to China, to South America. She was supposed to go to India when I went on the Mideastern tour, but she chickened out at the last moment.

"She took all the shots and when she realized WHY she was taking all the shots, she said, 'I don't know whether I really want to do that!'" He smiles. "She decided not to go and she regrets it. But I'm really glad she didn't, because that was a very difficult trip, physically, and I was sick, eating all kinds of stuff."

He's devoted to his wife. "This apartment is all messed up because Teddi isn't home," he apologizes again. "If she were here, that music room would be neatly arranged. She's very neat and she wants things in place. Organized! She does that, she keeps me like that. She's a big influence in my life.

"She's my best friend and my most severe critic. She's not going to tell me something that's not so. She's going to tell me something I don't see. If I think I'm doing something and it is not coming off the way I think, she tells me."

They met when she was a model. She stopped modeling and became a wife and mother. "She's very good at both," he says with admiration. "I believe love is very important. Love means the other person will do something for you that's beyond expectation. It's just something they're going to do because that's what they want to do. If you're as fortunate as I am to get someone who cares enough about you, you're very lucky."

He invites me into the den to view a wall of family photos: Teddi, their two children Kim and Duane, Teddi's sisters, a favorite nephew, Billy's mother with President and Mrs. Nixon, his father, and Billy with all the presidents.

"I've played the White House on many occasions," he says easily. Awards and plaques abound: a 1975 Emmy for a CBS-TV story on jazz musician Quincy Jones, a Peabody for *Jazz Alive* on NPR in 1980, and Billy's Doctorate of Education in 1975. "There are 20 more honorary doctorates somewhere in storage," he says nonchalantly.

Do you ever take a vacation? I ask.

"Yeah, I did that not long ago," he answers with alacrity. "I always try to take off the month of August. "I have four or five cameras and I really do like to take pictures. It's the closest thing I have to a hobby. When we go away on vacation, I'm torn, because it's usually to rest, so many of my pictures are scenic pictures. But I like to take pictures of people and I have a lot of people pictures. One of these days, I'll put them all together.

"I also try to take off the month of December. That's because my wife's birthday is December 31st. For much of our early life together, I was always working on New Year's Eve, because that's a big night for jazz musicians.

"As soon as I was able to afford it, I decided to take time off and we'd enjoy her birthday together. So now we do that, every year. I used to get the whole month off, but they keep creeping up on me now." He grits his teeth and raises his eyebrows in mock fear.

In the next breath, he vows to cut back on work. "I can't serve on the board, I'm too busy," he says to one caller. "I don't want to travel AT ALL in my later years," he tells me. "I'm going to be like the old sages I read about. I'm going to have everybody come to me. Really!

"Teddi and I are looking for a place with a little more room, where we can have folks come and be comfortable. This apartment is just too crowded." He gestures toward a wall of shelves crowded with books, records, CDs, and tapes. "I've already given the Library of Congress something like 88 boxes of records, music, and books. They're sorting it out. It'll be a Billy Taylor Collection.

"I also gave a lot of stuff to the Schomburg Center in Harlem. That's part of the New York City Public Library, where I did a lot of my research for music and things I've written. So I thought I'd give them something."

He wants to keep helping young jazz musicians, as his mentors did. "I hope I can put things in place that will really be as helpful to other people as things were for me. I was the first African-American musical director on television. I was music director for David Frost back in the early days of TV. I also had a big band on *The Tony Brown Show* broadcast on public TV.

"My experience made it possible for a lot of other guys to come along and say, 'I'd like to do that,' to go out and do it better. A lot of the things I've done on radio have made other musicians go into radio. I've talked to several of them.

"There's a young man over at WBGL who's a drummer. He told me that he used to come home from school and turn on the radio and hear me and say, 'I want to do that.' So now he's doing it very well and he's one of the better young drummers around."

Billy breaks into a big smile. "I can't give it back to Jo Jones or Art Tatum or Teddy Wilson or any of those guys. They're gone. So the best thing I can do is to do whatever I can for someone else who is YOUNGER."

The phone rings and I hear him talking in the other room. He's giving advice again.

MOLLY YARD

Born: July 6, 1912,
  China
Profession: Social activist,
  retired president NOW
  (National Organization for
  Women)
Home: Washington, DC

I'm recovering from a stroke. It's hard work, let me tell you. It's really the pits. I have no use of my left arm. But my brain is still functioning, thank goodness. The exercises are very painful, which is really surprising to me. I'm highly disciplined about my exercises, when my husband is around. I have no choice. He wants me to do my exercises two and three times a day. I do them for an hour every night.

I try to walk every day, at least half a mile. I go to my office every day and to the hospital for physical therapy four times a week.

NOW is very important to my recovery. I can't tell you the letters I got from NOW members, so supportive you couldn't help but get well, because you felt they were expecting you to be there for them. I used to wonder if it made sense to write letters to people when they were sick. Now I know it makes a lot of sense. It's very helpful.

I think a family is very important. My husband and I spend at least a month together with our three children and their children in the summer. I can't believe my kids are as old as they are. That's always a total shock—to think of them as 50. That seems old to me! How can I have a child who's 50? Impossible!

One of the things that always struck me as you grow older is that you really have to work at keeping your friends. Otherwise, they tend to forget you.

At this age, I find myself realizing there are a lot of things in life that are pretty boring, like housework, and to go through them over and over is not that enticing. You might be just as well off rid of them.

I've been an activist all my life. I believe people should do something that makes a difference in the world. I don't care what it is, but do something. Don't just sit there and read a book and watch television and listen to music. There's so much more to life than that, as enjoyable as it might be. Get yourself involved. Life is much more exciting if you're on the edge of change.

Helen and Lucky, her toy poodle

"I believe you make your own environment. You're in control
of your own life. You take responsibility for what you do."

HELEN
VER STANDIG

Born: July 11, 1920,
  Washington, DC
Profession: Businesswoman,
  philanthropist
Residence: Washington, DC

She beats me at Scrabble.
  But she never gloats. "How many points did we make TOGETHER?" she asks. "We're getting better. We should go on the road! Come, let's have a glass of wine."

And we adjourn for drinks and dinner.

Helen loves to have a good time. But she's also a serious businesswoman who founded and ran several businesses, guest-lectured at the Wharton School of Finance for 20 years, and served on boards of an AIDS clinic and charter schools. She works closely with a charity that delivers food to the poor.

At 83, she still goes to work every day.

"I've worked since I was 12 years old and I'm totally accustomed to getting up and getting out," she says briskly. "I'm very goal-oriented, and win or lose, I've got to get up and have something to do. I've had the privilege of always enjoying what I've worked at." Her voice is strong and throaty.

With her husband Mac, whom she married when she was 20, she began work in newspaper advertising, went on to buy a group of newspapers, then started an advertising agency, which became the largest one south of New York City. Later they built and ran a luxury hotel on Cape Cod. They also founded a simulated-diamond business, first mail order, then retail. At its height, Wellington Jewels had 35 American stores, which she visited regularly, and several overseas stores.

Recently she sold Wellington to QVC, the home-shopping television network. Over the years, she bought real estate and radio stations. Her son John now owns and runs 12 stations in the Mid-Atlantic region.

Every morning Helen gets up at 7 o'clock, reads the paper over coffee, and drives to her office, which she shares with John.

She works until noon, checking her stocks on a laptop computer and overseeing her real estate holdings.

After lunch with friends or business associates, she returns to the office to work, drives home about 4 p.m., and rests until guests arrive for dinner. The phone rings regularly, as her two children, five grandchildren, and friends check in from all parts of the world.

"I'm people-oriented," she says, leaning close to me. "Most nights I have people to dinner. I often hold business meetings here at home. I go to bed at 11, 12, 1. I need very little sleep. Six, seven hours tops." She smiles broadly and takes a sip of white wine.

We sit in her living room, luxurious with brocade furniture, Oriental carpet, a grand piano, and Old Master oil-paintings on the wall. A fire burns in the fireplace, and Lucky, a white toy poodle, whom she rescued from an animal shelter, snuggles in her lap. A housekeeper serves hors d'oeuvres on a silver platter.

Helen is a tiny, silver-haired woman, who wears classic clothes, pearls and diamonds, both real and Wellington, high heels, and bright red lipstick. Her unblinking dark eyes follow me closely.

"I was born July 11, 1920," she says in a strong voice. "Seven-eleven, just like a crap game. Keep that in mind when I play blackjack! I'm excellent; I love blackjack." She admits to enjoying many so-called vices: gambling, drinking, smoking. But soon she returns to the subject of work.

"I'm just like a trained animal," she says, pensively. "That's all I know how to do. I work every day, but I don't go into the office on weekends. We have the radio stations. All my businesses are run under their own management. Each station has its own general manager. It's like a pyramid. My son John has the stations.

"I own real estate. I believe in diversification. It's an economic decision. In fact, I just had a meeting with John about that last week.

"I've never had a mortgage," she continues. "I don't have a mortgage on my radio stations. If I can't pay for it, I don't want it. And that includes anything in business. I think I was right, because look at all the people in debt today.

"I've often said this when I lectured at Wharton, and I had big arguments up there." Her eyes widen. "You see, they taught leverage. Harvard School of Business, Columbia, all of them taught leverage, how to use other people's money.

"John was taught leverage at Wharton. He said, 'Mother, look, we can do this, we can do that, we can re-finance the hotel on the Cape.' The philosophy is that the interest is deductible. But I don't believe in leverage." She shakes her head.

"In business, you always take risk, but it can be a calculated risk, to the best of your ability. I can't throw out a magic ball and say that next year on January the tenth, the recession is over. I think that you constantly review the times. Just like you have to review your life from time to time.

"People don't really plan." She puts one elbow on her knee and leans toward me. "You know, if you have time someday and you want to write a business book, I think it would be fascinating to take some companies and see how they began. Like Sears Roebuck. I think one was a jeweler and one was a printer and they originally went into the mail-order business with a catalogue.

"Marriott came here, he was a professor, and Milton Barlow, who was president of Marriott, they came east from Utah. They were Mormons. At the time nobody had a drive-in restaurant that worked. They started with a root beer stand, and they bought that root beer franchise back. They were clients of ours at the advertising agency.

"When curb service and drive-ins went bad—you know, life changed after the war—they opened up a hotel on a piece of property they had near the airport. That was the first Marriott hotel." She takes another sip of wine.

"Sure, if the Internal Revenue Service hadn't come after us, I'd no more have been in the diamond business than the man in the moon." She cocks an eyebrow and looks at me wryly.

"The IRS says you have to show effort that you're looking for a business. We had to diversify. We had about a million dollars in cash and a million in this hotel. We were looking and we ran ads and all kinds of ding-batty people responded." She laughs and shakes her head in disbelief.

"So I'm sitting in Zurich, in Switzerland, in a bar. God! This is a long time ago, almost 40 years ago. This guy is sitting next to me—can you believe this?" She looks at me and grins. "I love bars, you meet the most interesting people in bars. We shared a drink and we talked. 'What do you do?' 'What do you do?' And he's a physicist. He says to me he's been working on a laser beam and he's developed a process that can make a diamond.

"Well, now, that's music to my ears." She laughs, leaning back in her chair. "He was working with a laser system that could make a man-made diamond. But he didn't have the money to produce it. I tell you, it's luck, the way a lot of businesses start. Most of them are accidents.

"So this flake is sitting there, and we're drinking, and in those years I used to LOVE Gibsons, I can't do that anymore. And he's giving me this pitch and finally he says, 'Oh, if I only had $10,000.' So I call my husband up and he says, 'Listen, honey, you get that flake and give him the ten grand.'

"Mac called our tax attorney and got the paperwork done. I NEVER in my life expected we'd hear from him. I knew he wasn't a thief, but I figured, 'Who in the hell is going to make diamonds?'

"About four months later, a box comes in the mail, like a little jewelry box, and in this box are little jewel papers. Mac and I open them and he says, 'They look like diamonds!'" She laughs uncontrollably.

"We didn't know a thing about the jewelry business, but damn! They looked like diamonds. HE MADE DIAMONDS. He really made the Wellington diamonds. His name was Walters, he's dead now. Anyway, Mac says, 'Don't worry about it, it'll never work anyway.' But we had to show effort.

"We closed the Cape for the winter, came down to Washington, and created a brochure. We got a focus group, a group of people together, to find a name and we came up with Wellington. We had about 20 or 30 of these stupid stones." Her voice is animated.

"In those days, 1964, 1965, a full-page ad in *The Wall Street Journal* cost maybe $10,000. So we took a full-page ad. And the ad said, 'We loaded ourselves with counterfeit diamonds which set the world on fire!' We said to ourselves, 'Don't worry, the ad won't pull. And we've shown our effort.'

"We had a pretty nice yacht down here in Washington, we're really bums at heart," she smiles. "And we took off. When we got to Nassau, our secretary Nancy calls and says, 'I've got 37,000 pieces of mail.' I said to her, 'You've got to be out of your.... mind!' And that started it. Can you believe this?" She laughs and shakes her head.

"Unfortunately, Mac died in 1967. So I'm diddling with this diamond business and wondering, 'Where do I go from here?' We started it mail order. We were downtown in the Bender Building at 1120 Connecticut Avenue, NW, over Paul Young's Restaurant. I used to go there for lunch every day.

"So I'm down there, drinking my Gibsons, and I get a call." Her voice drops to a dramatic whisper and her eyes widen. "'Call from London.' Now, you know how odd the name Ver Standig is. This name's haunted me for a lifetime. Ver Standig was my husband's name, but it was also my maiden name. We weren't related in any way. It's a Dutch name.

"A guy gets on the phone and says his name is William Ver Standig and he heads a cartel. Now I KNOW he's not a relative," she laughs. "No QUESTION. But he was very nice and very embarrassed. He says he's one of the largest diamond dealers in the world.

"It's very embarrassing because *The Wall Street Journal* made me put Helen Ver Standig as president of Wellington, and he was getting my mail. He said, 'Oh, when I come stateside, can we have lunch? We'll eat at the Plaza Hotel.' NICE guy, they have offices in New York. And he did.

"He must have handed me 300 or 400 letters from people accusing him of being involved in these counterfeit diamonds, and he's telling me he's the largest diamond dealer." She laughs and shakes her head.

"So I said, 'Look, I'm really caught with these,' because my product was so suspect. The newspapers wanted somebody responsible. They needed a name. So I called up Al Hirschfeld, the artist.

"We knew of him—he was not a close friend—and he always needed money. He did a caricature of me, and it looked just like a madame. I said, 'Gee, this is great! We'll make the business Madame Wellington!'

"And that got me off the hook. You know, the stupid *Wall Street Journal* thought I got married, I suppose, to LORD Wellington!" She erupts in laughter.

Hirschfeld drew three caricatures of Helen, crowned with a tiara, dripping with jewels, and dangling a lighted cigarette. She used them in her newspaper advertisements and brochure, and they became her trademark.

"A sense of humor," she muses. "You need it. If I can leave my kids anything, I leave them a sense of humor. They both have one. My children fascinate me.

"I have two very nice children, John and Joan, whom I'm very close to and who are very close to me, probably because we don't see each other that much and we all live in Washington. And I work with my son, so, you know, working with your mother is no deal." She laughs. "No, I'm kidding. We get along great. We don't have problems, because we're so diversified.

"My children are religious and I believe that's fine. My children don't drink or smoke. Can you believe it? I said to them one day, 'Thank God, your father's not alive to see this. He'd be so upset!' Because Mac and I used to drink and smoke together.

"They all go in for exercise. They're going to live forever!" Another laugh. "They're more spiritual than I am. They're involved in temple activities and their children are. And I believe in that. If that gives them comfort, great. But I don't get all my jollies going into temple and having somebody sit on an altar and spread the word."

Do you believe in God? I ask.

She chooses her words carefully. "I believe the only goodness that exists is within yourself and how you express it. I don't believe that God makes me good or bad, or that there is a God who does this. I believe if God is goodness or if there is such a thing, it's within a human being.

"I was raised in Judaism, but I stopped going to synagogue as soon as I could get the hell out—when I became an adult. Now I donate to all churches, including my synagogue, because I believe that people need it. Just because I don't BELIEVE, doesn't make me RIGHT. If this is what makes people happy, I'm willing to support it."

Helen is vivacious. We've been friends for ten years and only once or twice have I seen her tired. "I do have a lot of energy," she admits. "I always did. I must have good genes. And I was very fortunate, I had very happy parents. My mother was a housewife, my father was a tailor and had a dress store. I used to work for him. They were wonderful people and good human beings. They gave me as good a background as any parents could do.

"I used to smoke three packs of cigarettes a day, minimum, and never had trouble breathing. You know why I stopped smoking? Because you can't smoke in restaurants anymore. It was just too much trouble. I really don't miss it and I didn't have trouble stopping. I didn't gain weight.

"I eat whatever I want," she goes on. "I'll eat ANYTHING you feed me. Meat, vegetables. I don't eat breakfast, but I do eat lunch and dinner. Last night I went out and had crab cakes and baked potatoes with oodles of butter.

"I'm not really a health bug. I don't take vitamins and I don't exercise. I don't have a muscle in this body. No way!" She laughs heartily. "Certainly I don't walk if I can ride. And I don't go to doctors. I go to the dentist. You see, my teeth are in good shape. But I'd never go to the doctor."

She drinks, although not as much as she used to, and never when she drives. "I drink Scotch and wine, but not every night," she says. "If I have a meeting or something, obviously I'm not going to go there loaded. But if I have some fun and some company at home, I do whatever I want."

Twice she's broken bones below her hip and had metal plates installed. Each time she recovered quickly. She also beat a major bacterial infection that put her in a coma. "A mystery to mankind. And I survived," she says dramatically, then breaks into a grin. "I was quite ill for several months, but it went away. Naturally. I'm here," she says brightly. "They gave me different antibiotics."

Helen has no intention of starting to exercise now. "I'm not going to the gym, I'm not going to swim laps," she says resolutely. "I think all these people with all this regime of staying alive is ridiculous. Because I'm not so sure that, subconsciously, they think they're going to live forever, and that has to worry them to death!" She explodes in laughter.

Are you afraid of death? I ask.

"I have absolutely no fear of dying," she replies quickly. "It doesn't bother me one bit. I wasn't afraid of dying when I was young. I don't think anyone wants to suffer. It's important to me how I live and have a good time before I'm finished. I'm not going to extend my life one day by not eating a piece of meat or being a vegetarian or running around loose and breathing pure air and all this crap!"

What do you think death is? I ask.

"Well, certainly the end of the way I live. And perhaps there's some kind of extension that I don't understand. It may be a natural progression. If you assume that there is a cycle to whatever is living, whether a leaf falls from a tree and regenerates itself into the soil—I know that's becoming very philosophical.

"But I don't believe in the end that my spirit's going to float around and come down and haunt my kids. Although," she looks mischievous, "it wouldn't be a bad idea. I keep telling my kids I'm coming back. They'll never forget ME." She grins.

Helen doesn't worry. She's been through enough tough times to know they'll turn around. "Nothing lasts," she says. "Good times don't last and bad times don't last. Life goes trotting along, don't you think?" She looks hard at me. "You have to keep going. What options do you have? Why dwell on it? My husband used to say, 'Life is a roller coaster.' I agree. Peaks and valleys.

"If I lost all of my money tomorrow morning, all I have to do is change my way of life. If I lived in a tent, what the hell is the difference? I can still have a bottle of wine. So it'll be Blue Ripple instead of what we're drinking."

Do you truly believe that? I ask.

"Yes, because I've done it," she says forcefully. "And it doesn't matter. When my husband was alive, we used to live on due bills. Do you know what a due bill is? A due bill is when you run an ad, know some money is coming in, and can use that as credit.

"Today, if something happens, I can change. It doesn't matter if I live in this house or have to move tomorrow. What matters is people. I'm a people-oriented person. I would hate to think that you wouldn't come to see me if I didn't live here." She pauses, waiting for an answer, and I reassure her.

She continues earnestly. "I believe people become insecure because they value their possessions. When I was a kid and first married, we worked on a little newspaper in Cranston, Rhode Island. For three bucks, you could take the Fall River boat to New York City. Now this was a long time ago, 60-some years ago. It was a gorgeous ride, a great boat trip.

"Anyway, there was a hobo on this boat. Do you know what a hobo is? A hobo is not a beggar. A hobo has no possessions. He earns his money wherever he is. He will earn a day's pay. He might give a lecture, he might work and paint your door.

"Anyway, the King of the Hobos was on this boat. God! He was good-looking. And he gave a lecture for ten cents. You know how something in life stays with you? I'll never forget as long as I live what that man said. Let me get it straight." She stops for a moment.

"He said, 'Always remember everything you own will finally own you. If you buy a car, you'll work the rest of your life to put gas in it. If you buy a house, you'll work the rest of your life to keep that house. But always remember, if you really want to be free, you don't need it.'

"And he is so right," says Helen. "That made me more secure than anything I have ever learned in my life. We all accumulate baggage we don't need." I look around the room at dozens of *objets d'art* on tables and in cabinets.

"Yes," she nods. "I'm surrounded by it. Everybody's bringing me stuff. I give a lot of it away, as quick as it comes in. Anybody who wants anything, and I know they like it, they can have it. I have no reason to get rid of anything. But if I couldn't afford it, I'd get rid of it. You'd better believe it." She looks at me and nods defiantly.

The doorbell rings and Lucky jumps up, barking furiously. "That's George," she says. George is a long-time friend who comes for dinner most nights and spends Sundays with Helen.

He maintains his own home, and works six days a week in his real estate business. George is 85.

"Hello, George," she calls. "Come, let's have dinner." We all troop appreciatively into the dining room for a meal of chicken and mashed potatoes.

It is delicious and we hear all about George's day.

EPILOGUE

STEVE ALLEN

Steve died in October 2000 of cardiac complications, following a minor traffic accident. He was 78. His son Bill says the night before, Steve performed to a sell-out crowd in the Master Artist Series at Victor Valley College in Victorville, California.

I remember Steve telling me in our interview that he'd be lucky if he had another ten years left. "How many people live to be 80?" he said animatedly. "Damned few, statistically. I always appreciated life. The fact that I'm a poet would be consistent with that statement."

Steve's son Bill now runs the family business Meadowlane Enterprises, keeping his father's legacy alive through the licensing of Steve's music, books, and television programs throughout the world.

Steve left a prodigious legacy of creative work. He wrote 54 (published) books and 9,000 songs, the most of any composer, according to the *Guinness Book of Records*.

He also helped raise the level of TV decency. In 1998, he became honorary chair and spokesman for the Parents Television Council, a national group that challenges TV sponsors to pull their ads from TV shows that contain sex, vulgarity, and violence, and to redirect them to family-safe programs. Steve worked tirelessly to spread that message. On the day he died, he had just completed the manuscript for his book *Vulgarians at The Gate: Raising the Standards of Popular Culture*, released in 2001. It became a bestseller.

LINA BERLE

Lina died at home in June 1996. She was 102. The cause of death was congestive heart failure, complicated by pneumonia. "Her mind remained very, very sharp to the end," says her niece Mary Clay Berry. Toward the end, her other niece Beatrice Berle Meyerson heard Lina murmur, 'This is the process of dying.'

Says Beatrice, "What an entirely lucid lady this was. Such an entirely rational woman!" She and Mary took alternate four-hour shifts with Lina.

Lina was cremated and, at her request, her ashes scattered in the place close to her heart. "Lina's family had a summer

house in Boscawen, New Hampshire, just north of Concord,"
says Mary. "She had this idea that she wanted to be in a river
that flowed to the sea. My husband and I went up that August,
along with Lina's nephew Peter A.A. Berle and her grand-
nephew Frederick Meyerson. We stood on an old bridge over
the Merrimack River and threw her ashes into the water. It was
a perfect New Hampshire summer day with a crystal blue sky
and sunlight so bright that the ashes glittered in the water as
they started on their way to the Atlantic Ocean."

Lina would have loved that.

SAMMY CAHN

Sammy died of congestive heart failure in January 1993.
He was 79. His dream of establishing a Songwriters Hall of Fame
Museum in New York is still alive. Museum supporters give
regular fund-raisers and have created a Sammy Cahn Lifetime
Achievement Award.

He did not appear in a Woody Allen movie. Sammy's wife
Tita says, "Every time we'd see Woody at Le Cirque Restaurant,
he'd say, 'Next one!' Sammy would say, 'You'd better hurry!'"

Sammy is buried at Westwood Memorial Cemetery in Los
Angeles. His marker reads, "Sleep With A Smile." Tita says he
used to sign his letters, "Sleep with a smile. You are loved."

ELIZABETH CAMPBELL

Mrs. Campbell died peacefully in January 2004 at the age
of 102. Her son Ben was at her side. Until recently, she had
gone to work every day. Her assistant Juliet Spall says, "Mrs.
Campbell remained intensely interested in all workings of
WETA." She is buried in the Home Moravian Church Cemetery
in Old Winston-Salem, North Carolina.

GEORGIE CLARK

Georgie died at home in Las Vegas, in May 1992. She was
81. Her disease was ovarian cancer, for which she refused medical treatment, except for drainage of fluid that built up in her
body. Her office manager came by every day to care for her.

Georgie is buried in Henderson, Nevada.

On the Colorado river trip she told me that she wasn't afraid of death. "It's all right with me," she said, smiling. "I'm calm. I don't get nervous about death. When you're calm, you're not seeking it, but neither do you care. I just figure it's the way it's supposed to be, whenever it comes, whatever it is.

"I am a COMPLETE fatalist," she went on. "I've been a fatalist from the ground up, from a kid. My mother said, 'Everything's gotta be up, you're on the bottom.'"

When she was diagnosed in the winter of 1991, Georgie sold her business to another river-running company. She had all her pets put to sleep. "She didn't want them to be a burden on anyone else," says long-time friend Ron Hancock. "They were her animals and hers alone. If Georgie went to heaven, she wanted her animals to be there first."

Marjory Stoneman Douglas

Marjory died quietly at home in May 1998. She was 108. Long-time friend and neighbor Helen Muir, a fellow writer, recalls fondly, "Marjory kept a little *joie de vivre* going," even at her advanced age. Her cottage, which she designed and had built in the 1920s, is owned by the state of Florida and managed by the Land Trust of Dade County, Inc. The trust is working to make the house a museum.

"Marjory envisioned her home as a workshop for environmentalists to gather," says friend Joe Podgor, former executive director of the Friends of the Everglades. "She created the great main room for that purpose."

Marjory was cremated and a memorial service held in her beloved Everglades National Park. Afterwards, the park superintendent scattered her ashes in a section named after her, an area of saw grass and slow-flowing water.

Her book on W.H. Hudson is being prepared for publication by her friend and collaborator Sharyn Richardson.

Edmund deTreville Ellis

Colonel Ellis died in January 1995 at the age of 105. The last three months, he lived in a nursing home.

His grandson Tracy explains, "It was necessary to give him the care we didn't think we could give him." Just a month earlier, West Point had declared him the oldest graduate in its history, and presented him a plaque at a ceremony in the nursing home.

At Christmas, the colonel wrote his usual cards and notes to friends. He continued to handle his checkbook and exercise, grasping handrails in the corridors and propelling himself and his wheelchair up and down the halls. It was his goal to return home as soon as possible.

One day, while trying to get up and walk, he fell. "At that time, he must have concluded that he wasn't likely to go back home," says Tracy gently. Colonel Ellis died two days later in his sleep. He is buried in Arlington National Cemetery.

I remember the colonel as a man of grace, discipline, and dignity. He was articulate and well-read. He treated people with kindness and respect. "He is a man of endurance," reported his 1915 West Point yearbook *Howitzer*. "A man who puts duty before pleasure, who can keep giving without frequent rests and who is without vices."

The colonel once told me he considered himself a son of the South. Indeed, he was a Southern gentleman, in the best sense of the word.

DALE EVANS AND ROY ROGERS

Roy died in July 1998. He was 86. I spoke to daughter Cheryl, who recently came to work at the museum. She said Dale missed Roy very much. "You know, he was pretty ill for the last four years, and the last year he was in and out of the hospital all the time.

"Congestive heart failure takes you so slowly," said Cheryl. "He just hated it. At the end, he was with hospice at home. But Mom still wasn't ready for him to go. They were partners since 1943 and married since 1947. He always wanted to make that 50th anniversary—and he did."

In 1996, Dale had a stroke that affected her left side. Cheryl moved to Apple Valley to direct her mother's health care, and Dale improved, with the help of good doctors, twice-weekly physical therapy, home caregivers, and acupuncture treatments for arthritis and back pain. She wrote a book *Rainbow on a Hard Trail*, describing her recovery and how she coped with the loss of Roy. Her book total rose to 26 and the number of great-grandchildren reached 36.

She resumed speaking engagements once a month, traveling with a family member to cities around the country. She continued to host her cable tv talk show. At 87, she used a wheelchair, a walker, and a strong arm of a friend, reported Cheryl. Dale often talked about Roy and visited his gravesite at Sunset Hills Memorial Park in nearby Apple Valley. The park has manmade waterfalls and is surrounded by mountains, the Sycamore Rocks. "We tried to keep her busy without overwhelming her," said Cheryl. "Her mind was as clear as ever."

Dale died of congestive heart failure at home in February 2001. She was 88. Her children and many of her grandchildren were at her bedside. She is buried next to Roy at Sunset Hills. "Dale had a strong spirit up until the last couple of months of life," says the family.

The board of directors, half of which are family members, voted to move the Roy Rogers-Dale Evans Museum to Branson, Missouri, in order to remain economically viable. Son Roy, Jr., nicknamed "Dusty," explains, "Sometimes you have to make changes in order to preserve what's important to you. In our case, it's the traditions and ideals that Mom and Dad dedicated their lives to. We owe it to our parents to continue their legacy. I'm not going to ride a pony down until there are no legs on it."

Branson, the new Country Music Capital of the World, attracts over eight million visitors a year. Dusty plans to be on hand to welcome fans to his parents' museum and play twice a day in the new theatre with his band, The High Riders & I. Along with other visiting family members, they perform songs that Dale, Roy, and the Sons of the Pioneers made famous for more than 50 years.

J. WILLIAM FULBRIGHT

At a birthday celebration in 1993, Senator Fulbright received the Presidential Medal of Freedom from a fellow Arkansan and former office intern, President Bill Clinton. Mr.

Clinton, visibly moved, introduced his mentor. "The American political system produced this remarkable man, and my state did, and I'm real proud of it."

Fulbright died in February 1995, at the age of 89. His wife Harriet says, "He had a massive stroke that put him into something of a coma, and he stopped eating and drinking. I brought him home because the hospital said they could do nothing to improve his situation, and I thought he would much prefer to depart this world at home." He was cremated and his ashes are buried in the Fayetteville Cemetery with other family members.

Harriet gives speeches about his legacy and high ideals. "I deeply admired his thoughtful, independent approach to the issues of the day," she says. "Not willing to follow anyone's advice without examination, he would read the history of events or developments before forming his own opinion."

She also hopes that people remember his human side. "Bill had the most wonderful sense of humor," she says. "He also had a fierce loyalty to family. I loved his criteria for friendship and his choice of friends. They came from all backgrounds and education levels, and they were, by and large, people without pretensions."

Harriet continues to travel around the world as ambassador for the Fulbright Scholarship Program. In New Zealand, she spoke at Parliament House in Wellington. She also gave speeches at the universities in Perth and Adelaide, Australia. In Sydney, she was honored at a luncheon given by Premier Bob Carr of New South Wales.

For four years, she served as executive director of the President's Committee on Arts and Humanities in Washington, an appointment of Mr. Clinton. She resigned to wage a full-time fight against Waldenstrom's Macroglobulinemia, a rare blood disease for which she received treatment from Dr. Steve Treon, "an absolutely marvelous doctor," at the Dana-Farber Cancer Institute in Boston.

"There's no cure for this disease," she says. "But I received a special combination of chemotherapy and antigens, and now I have so little cancer left, I go only once every six months for an antigen treatment."

She also saw a nutritionist who specializes in cancer patients and recommended she stop eating calcium, white sugar, dairy products, carbonated beverages, and alcohol. She did. "It's made a vast difference in how I feel," she reports. "At first, the doctors dismissed it, but now they're taking notes!" She laughs. "Dr. Treon has made me 'the poster child.' I've already spoken at two international medical conferences on the disease.

"I'm doing really, really well," she says. "A year and one half ago, I was living on blood transfusions. Last month I spent a month traveling in Australia and New Zealand, and I felt fine. I didn't get sick, even from the recirculated air on the planes!"

PATRICK HAYES

Patrick Hayes died quite suddenly in the hospital in May 1998. He was 89. "It was a particularly virulent staph infection that was hideous," says his wife Evelyn. "When the test results came back, our doctor just blanched and said, 'We don't have much luck with this one.'

"Up to that time, he had been active and alert, keeping a regular schedule of work and concert-going. He had heart problems and he was beginning to look a little elderly. But he was being telephoned from all sides, for all kinds of information, all the time."

Mr. Hayes was cremated and, in a private ceremony, the family scattered his ashes near his beloved Kennedy Center in Washington, D.C.

THEODORE HESBURGH

Father Ted is still President Emeritus of Notre Dame and comes to the office every day. One thing has changed: he doesn't bound up flights of stairs as he used to. He continues to serve on the advisory board of the Kroc Institute for International Peace Studies and works with his four other institutes: human rights, ecology, ecumenism, and third-world development. He guest lectures at his university and does fund-raisers, but doesn't fly commercial airlines anymore, only private planes.

Despite macular degeneration, he continues to read. He's discovered books on tape, which the Library of Congress provides. He still smokes his beloved cigars.

His total of honorary degrees from colleges and universities has now reached 150, the top in the *Guinness Book of Records*.

Father Ted continues to view life philosophically. "As one gets older, it's evident that the old vital forces are fading somewhat. But one goes on doing as much as he can, as long as he can, and hopefully, as well as he can. Finally, the worst that one can do is to COMPLAIN."

HILDEGARDE

Hildegarde has moved to a luxury assisted-living home. "They are very solicitous and treat her like a queen," reports Don Dellair, her long-time friend and manager.

In 2000, she fell and broke a hip. After surgery and rehabilitation at the Howard Rusk Institute in New York, she went to the Mary Manning Walsh Home on the Upper East Side, where she has a private room. Don visits her every day. "Hildegarde will probably stay there, although she keeps her apartment," he says. "She's comfortable and the nurses treat her wonderfully.

"I ask her if she's happy and she says, 'Quite content, quite content, my dear.'

"I helped her move in, brought from her home a lot of posters and photographs, which we hung on the walls. She's recovered from the surgery and is not ill. She takes no medicine, but does have osteoporosis and uses a walker. She calls it 'her pal.' Every day she walks up and down the hall, and I go with her. She uses a wheelchair only to pile her pillows on.

"She knows all the current events because she still has her subscription to *The New York Post*. She reads about all her friends who've died: Arlene Francis, Imogene Coca, Jack Lemmon. She says, 'I suppose I'm next!' I say, 'No, you can't think that way.' She laughs.

"We've been having some very serious talks about death and funerals," says Don. "She says, 'I wonder if I'm going to go through purgatory?' I say, 'No, dear, there's a chair in heaven for you. You are the most honest, honorable, kind person there is.' I've asked her, and she's agreed to give me some signal, after she's gone, so that I know she's okay!

"She still has her sense of humor. I joke with her, 'What would you do without me?' She says, 'Probably a verse and two choruses!' I have to shout because her hearing is atrocious. She refuses to get a hearing aid because she's in denial. She doesn't want a telephone because she can't hear! The doctors speak right into her ear."

Don used to phone her younger sister Germaine and her husband in Texas regularly. Both died in 2002 and that has saddened Hildegarde. But she keeps busy, adheres to a schedule, and enjoys weekly visits from singer Julie Wilson. "She's a lovely girl," she tells Don.

Another singer KT Sullivan recently stopped by to give Hildegarde her latest CD of Richard Rodgers' songs, honoring his centennial. "KT's photo showed cleavage," says Don. "And Hildegarde told her, 'My dear, I can almost see the Great Divide!'"

Hildegarde receives daily letters from Charles Kleibacker, her former secretary, who became a fashion designer and now is a professor at Ohio State University. He visits whenever he's in New York. She's given him many of her evening gowns, which he's donated to Kent State University.

EVELYN BRYAN JOHNSON

Evelyn continues to give flying lessons and FAA flight exams at the Morristown, Tennessee City Airport, which she manages. At 94, she still holds the world record for most flight hours logged by a woman: 57,645, according to the *Guinness Book of Records*. "I know a man who has more hours, but no woman," she says modestly.

GEORGE JONES

Dr. Jones died in March 1998, six months after he turned 100. His daughter Margaret says, "I think he met his goal—100 years. He told me once that his grandparents had lived into their eighties and his parents into their nineties, so that he'd live into his hundreds, and I, of course, would live into my 110s!" The cause of his death was apparently a stroke. Dr. Jones lived for a week afterward, in and out of consciousness, and died in a bed set up in the living room.

"My dad had been terribly frustrated the last six months because his mind was clear enough to know he was declining," she says. "He couldn't even read because he just couldn't concentrate. He sat next to my mother in the living room and told her over and over, 'I love you, I love you.' It was a merciful thing when he passed away.

"I think my parents had 74 years of as close a marriage as anybody I've ever known," says Margaret. "They certainly were devoted."

Dr. Jones was cremated and buried in a family plot nearby in Birmingham, Ohio, where he spent his first years. His wife Mary died in May 2002 at the age of 101. After she was cremated, Margaret unearthed his ashes and put both sets in Oberlin's Westwood Cemetery. "It's fitting," she says. "The Jones family lived in Oberlin 130 years. His memoirs are in the archives at the Oberlin College Library. This is their home."

Long-time colleague Dr. Benzing remembers Dr. Jones as "somebody who taught me all the places to take the students on field trips. I went on many a Sunday walk of his."

Margaret sold her parents' home to an assistant botany professor at Oberlin. She and her husband delight in the grounds and gardens, and have kept some of the Jones' treasures, including the marble kitchen slab that he used for hand-dipping chocolates at Christmas. "It's nice that the house is with a botanist," says Margaret. "It continues as part of Oberlin's history."

A George Jones Memorial Farm was set up on the outskirts of town. The 70 acres is an educational model for sustainable land use and contains a three-acre farm, whose produce is sold locally.

Dr. Jones would have been pleased.

ETHEL KEOHANE

Ethel died of lung disease in October 1995. She was 94. For the last two years of her life, she had full-time help. "A wonderful woman from the Caribbean lived with her and took care of her," says a neighbor.

Ethel was active until the end. She had told me, "When I die, I don't want anyone to be sad. By the time I die, there won't be anyone left! I'm older than God, you know." We both laughed.

I miss Ethel. She was the only interviewee who called to ask how the book was going. "You'd better finish it before I die!" she chided me. "I want to buy a copy."

Her neighbors miss her, too. The new owner of her home says she feels Ethel's presence. "This house has a very special energy," she says. "From what we've heard about her, she's responsible for it."

Ethel is buried in the Newton, Massachusetts Cemetery.

ELISABETH KÜBLER-ROSS

Sometime after we spoke, Elisabeth's farm burned down. In 1995, she moved to Scottsdale, Arizona, where her son Ken lives. Her ex-husband and close friend Dr. Ross died.

Elisabeth had another stroke, from which she is recovering. I call and ask how she is doing. "I'm hanging in barely," she says in a low whisper. "I can hardly hold the phone. I have a healer who is helping me."

I tell her that I've written her chapter of my book. "May I see it?" she asks and gives me her address. I send it to her. A local doctor friend tells me Elisabeth remains indoors most of the time, but can walk and occasionally goes out to make speeches.

I read her latest book *Life Lessons* (2000), written with David Kessler, another expert on death and dying. In the foreword, she writes that she wanted to do one more book, a book about life and living, not death and dying.

The book contains case histories and personal experiences from their lectures, workshops, and discussions with patients and families. It deals with unfinished business and lessons that one must learn. With a certain degree of humility, she comments that she has not yet died because she has more lessons to learn. In October 2002, Ken moved his mother to a group home after she fell two months earlier. "She's 80 percent recovered after being in rehabilitation," he says. "But she's confused and sleeps a lot. Unusually enough, she's more at peace now than ever before."

Perhaps Elisabeth has finally accepted being cared for.

SARAH NEWCOMB McCLENDON

Up until 2002, Sarah continued to write occasionally for her news service and hometown newspaper, but didn't go to the daily White House briefings. She watched them, along with news programs, on all-news cable television channels. Every other Wednesday, she went with an escort to the National Press Club for the McClendon Press Briefing, which she founded. "She really works at keeping busy," reported daughter Sally MacDonald. "Mother still loves dressing up and going places.

"She insisted on coming to the christening of her new great-granddaughter, and she fell," reports Sally. "She recovered at the V.A. hospital and is back home. She's still in a wheelchair, but her spirit is just amazing. Bartholomew House called her V.A. doctor to ask about any change in diet. The doctor replied, 'Mrs. McClendon may have WHATEVER she wishes.'" Sally laughs. "Mother always has a chocolate milkshake every afternoon."

A full-length movie about Sarah is under discussion in Hollywood. Sissie Spacek, a fellow Texan and close friend, wants to play the lead role. "Mother would love that," says Sally.

In January 2003, Sarah died of complications of pneumonia. She was 92. "She lived a terrific life," says Sally. "We had a big memorial service for her at the Press Club and hundreds of people came and told Sarah stories. We had a wonderful time and mother would've loved it. I told the group, 'Now we can truly say that God only knows what mother is up to!'"

Sarah was cremated and her ashes buried in Arlington Memorial Cemetery, outside Washington, D.C.

RUTH SCHICK MONTGOMERY

Ruth died in June 2001 in Naples, Florida. She was one day short of being 89 years old.

LINUS PAULING

Dr. Pauling died at home in Big Sur with his family around him in August 1994. He was 93. His body was cremated and his family plans to scatter some of his ashes at his ranch and bury the rest with his wife's ashes in a cemetery in Portland, Oregon.

Stephen Lawson, chief executive officer of the Linus Pauling Institute, visited him a few months before he died. "I took him a Sunday *San Francisco Chronicle* and he was quite pleased," he says. "He was happy to see me and a colleague who also came. I can't say he was cheerful, but he didn't seem to be desperately unhappy.

"He was resigned to his illness. I don't believe he was in pain. He had a lot of pride. It was hard for him to go through this incapacitation. He retained most of his faculties up to the end.

"One of my fondest memories was watching Professor and Mrs. Pauling walk hand-in-hand," he continues. "She'd visit the institute or come to Christmas parties at a staff member's home. Or they'd invite us to parties at their home in Portola Valley, in the foothills. They were very affectionate with each other. I think he missed her very much after she died."

I recall Dr. Pauling telling me, "Death is just a cessation of the processes of life. I'm not especially eager to experience it." And he laughed.

"Twenty-six years ago," he continued, "in a talk I gave in New York, I said I'd like to live 25 years longer. I ENJOY so much," he said. "I enjoy learning new things about the world, reading in science and nature and other scientific literature about discoveries." He looked at me intently. I could see a fire in his eyes.

His spirit lives on at his institute, which moved to his alma mater Oregon State University in 1996. The institute is becoming an internationally-recognized center for research on micronutrients and phytochemicals and their relationship to optimal health and prevention and treatment of disease. His son Dr. Linus Pauling, Jr. is chairman of the board and Balz Frei, a biochemist and biophysicist, is director.

Dr. Frei writes in the latest newsletter, "Three recent studies by LPI researchers have been featured in the national and international news media...showing that a combination of two naturally occurring compounds, acetyl-L-carnitine and alpha-lipoic acid, improve physical activity and memory performance of old rats...[This] research may have important implications for maintaining human health through old age, thereby extending people's 'health span.'"

Dr. Pauling would be extremely pleased.

RUTH STAFFORD PEALE

Mrs. Peale recently celebrated her 96th birthday with a party for 150 relatives and friends at the Helmsley Park Lane Hotel in New York City. Resplendent in blue silk dress and white orchids, she told the admiring crowd, "I WILL see you at my one hundredth birthday!" Actress Arlene Dahl was mistress-of-ceremony, and actor James Earl Jones read aloud his four favorite pages of *The Power of Positive Thinking*, the classic work of Mrs. Peale's late husband Dr. Norman Vincent Peale.

She is now chairman emeritus of *Guideposts*. She reports to her office "most days," works at home, reads all the books that *Guideposts* considers for republication, and answers correspondence, according to Sybil Light, her secretary of 25 years. Mrs. Peale's latest book *A Lifetime of Positive Thinking* (2002), written with Jo Kadlecek, outlines her beliefs in God, family, and relationships, as told to a younger woman. She's recorded her book and it's available on CD.

Mrs. Peale has eight grandchildren and eleven great-grandchildren. Family reunions are still joyous yearly events, which she plans. The most recent was in Syracuse, New York, where she had met Dr. Peale. The family visited United Methodist Church, where he was minister and they were married in 1930. They also visited Alpha Phi, her old sorority house at Syracuse University, where she recalled how her sorority sisters sat on the steps and quizzed her as she returned from dates with him.

Walking continues to be her favorite form of exercise, and she still walks around the farm twice a day. Her daughter Maggie and husband Paul have moved to within a few miles, so both daughters now live nearby. They celebrate birthdays and holidays together.

HANK SPALDING

In 1996, Hank was hospitalized for pneumonia, emphysema, and congestive heart failure. When he didn't bounce back, he entered a nursing home and his good friend Joyce Riggle brought his wife Bert to be with him. His mind remained clear and he constantly joked with visitors. Bert died in 1998 and he kept a container of her ashes next to his bed.

The night before Hank died, Joyce visited him. "His mind was sharp as a tack," she reports. "He was reminiscing and talking and being Hank! The next day, March 18, 1999, he slipped away, from kidney failure.

"We'd discussed what to do with his ashes. He changed his mind about four times," she laughs. "'Maybe in the mountains?' he'd say. 'Maybe in the ocean?' I said, 'Hank, you HAVE to decide.'"

He never did, so Joyce arranged for his ashes, along with Bert's, to be strewn in the rose garden at Valhalla Cemetery in North Hollywood.

His beloved book *The Ninth Note* will be published soon.

BENJAMIN SPOCK

Dr. Spock died in March 1998, in La Jolla, California, where he and his wife Mary had moved to enjoy a warmer climate and to be closer to his son Dan. Dr. Spock was 94. Mary arranged a New Orleans-style funeral march with a jazz band and led the procession. "Ben would have enjoyed it," she says. He was cremated and is buried in the Sea View Cemetery in Rockport, Maine.

Mary returned to Maine, then went back to California in 2002, and founded DrSpock.com., a media and merchandising company that provides advice from doctors and other experts in parenting and children's health. "I am honored to keep Ben's work alive," she says. "I have found wonderful ways of doing this."

The company also publishes books. "We are revising *Baby and Child Care*, and believe this eighth edition will be the best yet," she says. "Robert Needleman is the co-author and he writes so much like Ben." To date, the classic has sold 50 million copies. DrSpock.com publishes other books in the Spock vein and has produced videos and an eight-part series *Parent Sense* for public television.

"I continue to work in Cuba with Ben's projects in Pediatrics, and I just attended the San Francisco Peace Rally, where Ben's spirit was very much present," reports Mary. "I really do miss him, and I know that his work will live on and history will remember him."

BILLY TAYLOR

Dr. Taylor, 81, continues to play with his trio and head the Jazz Program at the Kennedy Center. He appeared on the PBS special *A Salute to Richard Rodgers*, played some of his music, and praised his genius. "I was pleased they asked me," says Billy. "I didn't know Rodgers, but I was highly influenced by his music. He did things with music, his harmonic ideas, that are applicable to us who play jazz. He knew jazz history."

Billy has cut back on his frenetic schedule. "I've had to," he explains. "I had a stroke early in 2002. It's not as serious as it could've been. I just can't do as many things as I used to and as fast as I used to.

"You know, I never listened when other people said, 'Slow down.'" He chuckles. "So when this happened, it was a blessing in disguise. I feel stronger now, I feel okay." His speech is still the same: fast, strong, and musical.

NIEN CHENG

Nien continues to live alone at home and leads an active social life, welcoming relatives and friends from around the world. She is translating her book *Life and Death in Shanghai* into Chinese. "My book is now on sale in China at government foreign-language bookstores," she says delightedly. "Chinese who read English are buying it. This seems to indicate the book is no longer banned in China."

The book has not yet been made into a movie by the company that she approved. "The film company in Hong Kong has relocated to Shanghai. They have been in touch with me. So far, the Chinese government has not given permission to do a movie. I am glad, as I know they will change the story." Age has not dimmed her realistic look on life.

She had successful cataract surgery. "My eyesight is better now," she reports. "However, I do plan to give up driving next year when I shall be 90." She continues daily Tai Chi exercises and moves better with the help of acupuncture treatments.

Photography Credits

Order Form

QTY.	Title	Price	Can. Price	Total
	Young At Heart Anne Snowden Crosman	$18.95	$24.95	
	Shipping and Handling Add $3.50 for orders in the US			
	Sales tax (IN state residents only, add 6%)			
	Total enclosed			

Telephone Orders:
Call 1-866-828-8935
Have your Visa or
MasterCard ready.

INTL. Telephone Orders:
Toll free 1-877-250-5500
Have your credit card ready.

Fax Order:
1-765-294-5840
Fill out this form and fax.

Postal Orders:
Hara Publishing Group, Inc.
P.O. Box 41
514 N. Sterling Ave.
Veedersburg, IN 47987

E-mail Orders:
info@harapublishing.com

Method of Payment:

☐ Check or Money Order

☐ VISA

☐ MasterCard

Card#

Expiration Date

Signature

Name_____

Address_____

City_____**State**_____**Zip**_____

Phone (   ) _____**Fax**_____

Quantity discounts are available.
Call 1-765-294-5780 for more information.
Thank you for your order.